BROOKINGS PAPERS ON
Economic Activity

William C. Brainard and George L. Perry, Editors

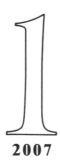

2007

Theodore Papageorgiou, Assistant to the Editors
Laura Salisbury-Rowswell, Research Associate
Michael Treadway, Editorial Associate
Lindsey B. Wilson, Production Associate

BROOKINGS B INSTITUTION

WASHINGTON, D.C.

Copyright © 2007 by
THE BROOKINGS INSTITUTION
1775 Massachusetts Avenue, N.W., Washington, D.C. 20036

ISSN 0007-2303

ISBN-13: 978-0-8157-1355-5
ISBN-10: 0-8157-1355-x

BROOKINGS PAPERS ON

Economic Activity

William C. Brainard and George L. Perry, Editors

2007

Editors' Summary   *ix*

Articles

OLIVIER JEANNE
International Reserves in Emerging Market Countries:
Too Much of a Good Thing?   *1*
Comments by Joshua Aizenman and Lawrence H. Summers   56
General Discussion   71

STEPHEN D. OLINER, DANIEL E. SICHEL,
and KEVIN J. STIROH
Explaining a Productive Decade   *81*
Comments by Martin Neil Baily and N. Gregory Mankiw   138
General Discussion   144

ESWAR S. PRASAD, RAGHURAM G. RAJAN,
and ARVIND SUBRAMANIAN
Foreign Capital and Economic Growth   *153*
Comments by Susan M. Collins and Peter Blair Henry   210
General Discussion   223

MALCOLM BAKER, STEFAN NAGEL, *and* JEFFREY WURGLER
The Effect of Dividends on Consumption   *231*
Comments by James Poterba and Joel Slemrod   277
General Discussion   288

Report

DAVID K. BACKUS *and* JONATHAN H. WRIGHT
Cracking the Conundrum   *293*
Comment by Glenn D. Rudebusch   317
General Discussion   325

Purpose   *Brookings Papers on Economic Activity* contains the articles, reports, and highlights of the discussions from conferences of the Brookings Panel on Economic Activity. The panel was formed to promote professional research and analysis of key developments in U.S. economic activity. Prosperity and price stability are its basic subjects.

The expertise of the panel is concentrated on the "live" issues of economic performance that confront the maker of public policy and the executive in the private sector. Particular attention is devoted to recent and current economic developments that are directly relevant to the contemporary scene or especially challenging because they stretch our understanding of economic theory or previous empirical findings. Such issues are typically quantitative, and the research findings are often statistical. Nevertheless, in all the articles and reports, the reasoning and the conclusions are developed in a form intelligible to the interested, informed nonspecialist as well as useful to the expert in macroeconomics. In short, the papers aim at several objectives: meticulous and incisive professional analysis, timeliness and relevance to current issues, and lucid presentation.

Articles appear in this publication after presentation and discussion at a conference at Brookings. From the spirited discussions at the conference, the authors obtain new insights and helpful comments; they also receive searching criticism about various aspects of the papers. Some of these comments are reflected in the published summaries of discussion, some in the final versions of the papers themselves. But in all cases the papers are finally the product of the authors' thinking and do not imply any agreement by those attending the conference. Nor do the papers or any of the other materials in this issue necessarily represent the views of the staff members, officers, or trustees of the Brookings Institution.

Correspondence   Correspondence regarding papers in this issue should be addressed to the authors. Manuscripts are not accepted for review because this journal is devoted exclusively to invited contributions.

Subscriptions   For information on subscriptions, standing orders, and individual copies, contact Brookings Institution Press, P.O. Box 465, Hanover, PA 17331-0465. Or call 866-698-0010. E-mail brookings@tsp.sheridan.com. Visit Brookings online at http://bookstore.brookings.edu.

Brookings periodicals are available online through both Online Computer Library Center (contact OCLC subscriptions department at 800-848-5878, ext. 6251) and Project Muse (http://muse.jhu.edu).

Editors' Summary

THE BROOKINGS PANEL ON Economic Activity held its eighty-third conference in Washington, D.C., on March 29 and 30, 2007. This issue of the
Brookings Papers includes the papers and discussions presented at the
conference. The five papers in this issue span a range of domestic and
global issues of current importance. The first paper uses risk analysis to
assess the large foreign reserves holdings of emerging market countries.
The second paper models the role of information technology in the rapid
productivity growth of the past decade. The third paper examines the relation between foreign capital inflows and growth among nonindustrialized
economies. The fourth paper estimates the effects of dividends on consumption and the implied effects of the 2003 dividend tax cuts. The final
paper looks for explanations for the failure of long-term rates to respond
as expected to the Federal Reserve's monetary tightening of recent years.

IN 2005 THE INTERNATIONAL reserves of emerging market countries
reached nearly $2 trillion, four times their level of the early 1990s relative
to GDP. Some commentators have argued that such massive reserves are
prudent insurance against the increased volatility of capital flows accompanying financial globalization, but others claim they are excessive and that
these countries could put the funds to better use toward their economic
development. In the first article of this issue, Olivier Jeanne examines
whether the risk of currency crisis or a sudden cutoff in lending justifies the
level of reserves held by these countries.

   Historically, various rules of thumb have been used to make this assessment. Jeanne is much more ambitious. He calibrates a formal model of optimal reserves holdings to country-specific empirical estimates of the
parameters crucial to determining this optimum. He finds that the reserves
held by most Latin American countries can be rationalized with this model,
but the risks of a capital account crisis confronting the Asian emerging

economies in his sample are much too small to justify their current hold-ings. This conclusion has implications both for the need for further accu-mulation and for the management of existing reserves. In the final sections of the paper, Jeanne considers the opportunities for emerging market coun-tries to diversify their investment, the implications of such a change in investment behavior for global financial markets, and possible international arrangements for using this wealth to more efficiently insure against future crises and to promote financial development.

Jeanne begins by documenting the recent buildup in international reserves by thirty-two emerging market countries. In the decade before 1990 these countries held reserves averaging 5 percent of their GDP, a ratio comparable to that in industrial economies. Since then, however, this average has grown by a factor of four, to roughly 22 percent of GDP by 2005. More than half of the dollar growth in these countries' reserves during the period took place in Asia following the 1997–98 crisis in that region. China's ratio of reserves to GDP is similar to that of other emerging Asian countries, but because of its size China now holds the largest stock of international reserves in the world.

Growth in a country's international reserves is necessarily financed by some combination of current account surpluses and capital inflows. Among the Asian emerging market countries, current account surpluses accounted for 63 percent of their reserves accumulation during 2000–05. In contrast, the Latin American economies ran sizable current account deficits, and cap-ital inflows amounted to 137 percent of their reserves accumulation. The experience of the Asian economies dominates the overall picture: for all emerging market countries combined, current account surpluses account for almost 60 percent of reserves accumulation during this period. Jeanne notes that the flow of capital from developing to developed economies was equiv-alent to more than 40 percent of the current account deficit of the United States in the same period. He also documents various salient features of the gross capital flows underlying the net flows to and from countries in his sample. Reserves accumulation constitutes more than 60 percent of the gross foreign asset accumulation of these countries. In contrast, foreign direct investment (FDI) accounts for almost 70 percent of the increase in their gross liabilities. This investment pattern is not new and is evident in the balance sheets of these economies. The share of reserves in gross for-eign assets is almost nine times as large in the emerging market countries as in the industrial countries, whereas the share of FDI in their liabilities is almost twice as large.

How much of the dramatic growth in emerging market countries' reserves can be explained as a prudent response to the increased risks associated with their increased trade and financial integration with the rest of the world? Jeanne reports that the recent buildup is not consistent with any of three conventional reserves adequacy measures: the ratios of reserves to imports, to short-term external debt, and to the M2 measure of the money supply. By any of these yardsticks, reserves ratios have increased enormously since 1990. For example, reserves in the entire sample of emerging market countries in 1990 were roughly in line with the informal rule that a country's reserves should equal or exceed three months of its imports, but reserves today are close to seven months of imports. The Greenspan-Guidotti rule, which states that reserves should equal or exceed short-term debt, was developed to better capture the risks stemming from the capital account after the crises of the 1990s. Reserves in emerging market countries have now risen to five times their short-term debt.

Jeanne notes that reserves also significantly exceed the predictions of regression-based empirical models that do a good job of predicting reserves holdings before the Asian crisis, based on a few key variables that should affect the desired level of precautionary reserves. He observes that such regressions fail to capture the profound effect that the 1997–98 crisis has had on countries' perception of risk. That crisis marked a watershed, after which emerging market countries became painfully aware that even sound macroeconomic policies did not insulate them from contagion and sharp reversals in capital flows. Jeanne points out that capital account instability and large capital account shocks, or "sudden stops," are relatively new phenomena in Asia, where capital outflows and reserves losses in the crisis period were unprecedented.

Neither the informal rules of thumb nor the earlier regression studies that found reserves to be adequate were based on an explicit model of precautionary reserves. Jeanne employs an empirical version of such a model to judge the extent to which reserves in his sample of countries are currently excessive. His analysis builds on a long line of literature on optimal reserves, inspired by a seminal 1996 contribution by Robert Heller, although the traditional models used an objective function only loosely related to domestic welfare. Jeanne specifies a model that is specifically tied to welfare but retains some of the simplicity of the earlier literature.

The model is of a small, open economy vulnerable to crises, where a crisis is defined by the loss of access to external credit and the associated loss of output. Holding reserves involves an opportunity cost but decreases the probability of a crisis and dampens the damaging effect on consumption when a crisis does take place. To capture the intertemporal nature of reserves decisions in the simplest way possible, the model has only three periods. The model economy is populated by a representative consumer who holds a certain amount of foreign assets, or "sovereign wealth," in period 0. This wealth can be invested either in liquid international reserves or in an illiquid asset that has a higher expected return over two periods but is not available for use until the last period. In exchange for lower returns, investing in reserves provides two benefits: it lowers the probability of a crisis occurring in period 1, and it insures consumption in that period against the risk of a crisis, an event that entails a large capital outflow and a loss of current output.

Jeanne captures the first benefit by making the probability of a crisis a decreasing function of the ratio of reserves to short-term debt. When he later calibrates the model, he uses a probit specification, implying that the function is the cumulative distribution of the normal function. The second benefit, that of insuring consumption when a crisis occurs, depends on the amount by which resources available for first-period consumption are reduced in the event of a crisis and on the curvature of the utility function. In a crisis the resources available to support consumption are reduced for two reasons: output is reduced by some fraction of potential output, and the country is unable to roll over the external short-term debt that is due, which reduces imports. This is what the literature calls a "sudden stop" of capital inflows. Subject to this constraint from reduced resources and the inability to borrow, the representative consumer decides what portion of available resources to consume in the first period and what portion to carry into the second period. In the absence of a crisis, the consumer simply decides on current consumption and on the change in debt and reserves, constrained by potential output. Reserves and debt have the same rate of interest between periods 0, 1, and 2, which for two periods is less than that on the illiquid investment. Welfare in period 2 is characterized simply as period-2 wealth, equal to period-2 income plus the balance of assets minus liabilities carried into the period and the interest accrued on that balance. This assumption implies constant marginal utility of consumption in period 2, making solution of the model quite simple.

The qualitative characteristics of optimal reserves holdings are intuitive, increasing in the size of the crisis shock and with the degree of risk aversion, and decreasing with the opportunity cost of reserves. Jeanne shows that if the consumer has constant relative risk aversion and the probability of a crisis is independent of the quantity of reserves, optimal reserves are related to a simple function of the opportunity cost divided by the probability of crisis, and the size of the resource shock. In the event of a crisis all of the reserves are consumed. He observes that the optimal level could be either higher or lower than under the Greenspan-Guidotti rule: higher because of the value of smoothing a fall in output as well as the capital outflow, or lower because of the opportunity costs ignored in that rule. When an increase in reserves reduces the probability of crisis, the optimal level may even exceed the maximum size of the shock that could occur so that some reserves may be saved in the event of a crisis.

Jeanne next turns to calibration of the model, beginning with the role of reserves in crisis prevention. Analysts have distinguished two types of crises, currency crises and sudden stops of foreign capital inflows. Jeanne estimates the effect of reserves on the probability of each type of crisis, which he identifies by four different criteria, covering the broad range of definitions used by various authors. Currency crises are identified by the rate of domestic currency depreciation, or the sum of that rate and the rate of reserves loss, using various thresholds and timings. Sudden stops are identified by a substantial drop in net capital inflows relative to GDP, accompanied or not by declines in output and the current account, again with varying thresholds and timings. Jeanne estimates a univariate probit regression for each definition of crisis for each of five different measures of reserves adequacy.

Since Jeanne uses four different combinations of time and country dummy variables, each measure of reserves adequacy is used in sixteen probit regressions for each type of crisis. Several facts stand out from the results. First, the ratio of reserves to short-term debt is the best predictor of a currency crisis and is both statistically and economically significant in all sixteen probit regressions. In the range of estimated coefficients on this reserves ratio, doubling the Greenspan-Guidotti ratio of 1 reduces the probability of a crisis from roughly 10 percent to 6 percent, assuming a prevention benefit parameter of 0.3. However, there are diminishing returns: increasing the reserves ratio from 5 to 6 lowers the probability by less than 1 percentage point. Two other reserves adequacy measures, the ratio of reserves to imports and that of reserves to GDP, are significant in a majority of the regressions at the 10 percent level or better, but given the superior performance of reserves relative to short-term debt, Jeanne uses the coefficients from those equations to calibrate his later simulations.

None of the measures of reserves adequacy perform well at predicting sudden stop. The ratio of reserves to M2 performs best: it is significant in four of the sixteen equations. Jeanne notes that these results are consistent with the empirical literature, which finds an ambiguous benefit of reserves in reducing the probability of sudden stops. Jeanne also offers an important caveat even to the conclusion that greater reserves decrease the probability of currency crises. Existing studies, including this one, cannot distinguish the prevention of a crisis from its mere postponement. And in some cases trying to maintain a high level of reserves in the face of a loss of confidence in domestic policies may actually hasten a crisis.

Even if reserves have no influence on the probability of a crisis, they have an important role in mitigating the effects of a crisis on output and domestic absorption. Jeanne describes some ways in which international reserves can be used to reduce the loss of output. One way is to intervene in foreign exchange markets to mitigate a rapid depreciation of the currency and its disruptive effects on balance sheets; another is to allow the monetary authorities to provide liquidity to domestic financial markets, the banking sector, and even exporters. He points out that providing such liquidity is especially valuable if there is significant dollarization of bank deposits and other domestic liabilities.

A fall in domestic absorption is an important indicator of the welfare costs of a sudden stop. Domestic absorption, the sum of consumption and domestic investment, is also the sum of domestic output, capital inflows, net income from abroad, and reductions in reserves. Reserves can be used to offset a drop in output or capital inflows, stabilizing absorption. Jeanne examines the behavior of each of these in a five-year window surrounding sudden stops for each country in his sample. Not surprisingly given the criteria he uses to identify sudden stops, net capital inflows drop almost 10 percent relative to GDP in the year of the sudden stop, regaining about 60 percent of that fall in the next two years. Strikingly, a decrease in reserves offsets most of the capital account reversal, with a sudden stop causing domestic absorption to fall by only 3 percent of GDP in the year before the stop. GDP falls only slightly in the year of the shock but grows more slowly than trend in the following two years. It seems likely that the observed fall in output following a sudden stop is less than would have occurred if reserves were not used for stabilization. Since, in his model, a period corresponds to more than a year, Jeanne finds it reasonable to assume in his baseline calibration that the drop in output following a shock is 10 percent of GDP. But he also notes that in some cases the capital flight in sudden stops may itself reflect, rather than cause, a loss of reserves and the associated damage to the economy.

The opportunity cost of reserves—the difference between the return on reserves and that on alternative investments—is of first-order importance in determining optimal reserves, but it is difficult to measure. One approach is to assume that physical capital is the alternative investment. In that case, with an estimated average real rate of return of almost 8 percent a year for seventeen of the countries in Jeanne's sample, and with an average of U.S. real short-term interest rates taken as the return on reserves, the opportunity cost of reserves is 6 percent. But investment in physical capital carries more risk than many other long-term assets, and its return should be adjusted downward to compensate. Using the interest rate on central banks' domestic currency assets (that is, the cost of sterilization) gives a much lower number, and in the case of countries with very low interest rates, such as China recently, the implied opportunity cost would be negative. Jeanne argues that this measure ignores expected depreciation and that although this rate is relevant to central bank profits, it may be a poor measure of the opportunity cost to the country as a whole. A third measure of opportunity cost is the spread between the interest rate on external debt and the return on reserves; by this measure the annual opportunity cost averaged 8.4 percent during 2000–05 for emerging market countries in the aggregate, but it is much higher than the average in Latin America, where it grew rapidly during 2000–02 and then gradually declined. The level and variation of the Latin American spread undoubtedly reflect the risk of default. Jeanne observes that if the default risk premium is a fair reflection of the probability of less than full repayment, it should not be included in the opportunity cost.

Jeanne calculates the forgone earnings on the 2000–05 reserves holdings of emerging market countries using three different estimates of the opportunity cost. Using only the 2 percent term premium, the average annual costs for the Asian countries are 0.45 percent of GDP and a more modest 0.22 percent of GDP for Latin America, where reserves are much lower relative to GDP. Using the return to capital to capture the opportunity cost more than doubles these losses, to 1 percent of GDP in the case of the Asian economies.

How do the reserves actually held by emerging market countries compare with optimal levels? Jeanne begins by calculating the levels implied by his optimizing model, using baseline values suggested by the above discussion: 10 percent of GDP for the size of a sudden stop and the loss of output, and a 3 percent annual opportunity cost of reserves. He considers two alternative measures of the probability of a crisis. The first assigns a fixed probability of 10 percent, consistent with the historical frequency of sudden stops for his sample of countries; in this case optimal reserves depend only on the ratio of the opportunity cost to such an exogenous probability. The second is an endogenous probability that depends on the ratio of reserves to short-term debt as estimated by Jeanne's univariate probit regressions. The only other parameter of the model, the degree of relative risk aversion, is set at 2, a conventional value. The benchmark calibration with a fixed probability of a crisis implies that optimal reserves are 7.7 percent of GDP. This is close to the average ratio of reserves to GDP observed in Jeanne's sample for 1980–2000, but significantly lower than in recent years, especially in Asia. If reserves are credited with a reduction in the probability of a crisis in line with the probit estimates, optimal reserves are much greater, over 20 percent of GDP.

Jeanne shows that the sensitivity of optimal reserves to these parameters is substantial. Doubling the baseline opportunity cost or halving the baseline probability cuts optimal reserves to approximately zero; cutting the opportunity cost to 1½ percent or raising the probability of crisis to 20 percent almost doubles optimal reserves. Similarly, doubling the size of a sudden stop or the output cost of a crisis significantly increases optimal reserves. An implication of these sensitivities is that fixed rules such as the Greenspan-Guidotti rule, although perhaps useful in particular situations, are unlikely to be appropriate for all countries at all times. But it is also clear that the recent levels of reserves in many emerging market countries can only be justified by parameter values that are far from the baseline assumptions.

This conclusion leads Jeanne to examine more closely the differences in countries' vulnerability to sudden stops and currency crises, as evidenced by the experience before the recent buildup of reserves. He runs separate probit regressions for the probability of sudden stops and crises for the period 1980–2000 on the pooled sample of countries, experimenting with a variety of economic indicators as explanatory variables. In his preferred specifications, the deviation of the real exchange rate from trend is significant in both sudden stops and currency crises, with a weak currency lowering the probability. The current account and the public debt, both relative to GDP, and foreign liabilities relative to money are also significant for sudden stops. Consistent with the earlier results, the ratio of reserves to short-term debt is highly significant for currency crises. All these results are robust with respect to the inclusion of fixed country or time effects. Tracking countries, Jeanne finds large differences in the probability of crises over time. The probability of a sudden stop in any given year of the early 1980s reached 14 percent for both the Asian and the Latin American countries. It then declined, more rapidly for the Asian economies, to a common low of about 4 percent around 1990. Since then the experience of the two regions has diverged strongly. Except for an upward blip, the probability of a sudden stop stayed low for the Asian economies in the 1990s, but it rose rapidly in Latin America, with the GDP-weighted average returning to the heights of the early 1980s. The probability of currency crisis followed the same pattern until the 1990s. At the beginning of that decade, the probability rose rapidly in Latin America but then slowly drifted down, paralleling the pattern in Asia but always substantially higher. The estimated probabilities for China are noteworthy: 2.7 percent for a sudden stop, and less than 0.2 percent for a currency crisis in 2000.

The model's estimate of optimal reserves for insurance against sudden stops, using the country-specific probabilities and the baseline values of the other parameters, confirms the view that the aggregate reserves of the emerging market countries in Jeanne's sample are far more than they need for that purpose, and that this is almost entirely a reflection of the large reserves holdings of the Asian economies. According to the model, optimal reserves in 2000 for the Asian countries in the sample totaled $24 billion, whereas actual reserves were $406 billion. The optimal level according to the model is actually zero in China, Korea, and Malaysia, because the probability of a sudden stop for those countries is so low. To rationalize the levels actually held in these countries would require extremely high risk aversion, a low opportunity cost of reserves, or an output loss in the event of a sudden stop in excess of 30 percent. By contrast, the observed level of reserves is actually slightly below the estimate of optimal reserves for the Latin American economies.

Higher reserve levels would be called for if reserves lower the probability of a crisis. Using the estimate of this effect from the probit regressions explaining currency crises, Jeanne calculates the expected benefit, net of costs, for the reserves buildup of 2000–05 assuming a 10 percent output loss in the event of crisis and an opportunity cost of 3 percent. For the Asian emerging market countries as a group, he finds the costs to be more than five times the benefit. The probabilities of a crisis were already so low in 2000 that the further reductions in probability are trivial. But in Latin America, where the probabilities were significant in 2000, the benefit of additional reserves outweighs their cost. Jeanne cites Mexico as an example, where doubling the reserves held in 2000 would have reduced the probability of a crisis that year from 9.6 percent to 5.6 percent.

Given the apparent failure of the precautionary model to explain the accumulation of reserves by the Asian economies, what is likely to be the true explanation? Jeanne's main alternative explanation is that the accumulation is the unintended consequence of a mercantilist policy of pursuing large current account surpluses. Such a policy requires that the central bank accumulate reserves to avoid an appreciation of the currency, together with capital controls and financial repression to avoid inflation. In support of this explanation, he reports cross-country correlations showing that, during 2000–05, reserves accumulation was associated with current account surpluses and unrelated to changes in gross external liabilities. The change in the ratio of reserves to GDP is also correlated with capital account restrictions. These correlations are hard to reconcile with a precautionary explanation, for which the risk of capital outflows is central.

Jeanne notes that a mercantilist strategy involves, at least implicitly, an accumulation of claims against the rest of the world, but also that it need not involve levels of highly liquid international reserves beyond those required for precautionary reasons. He observes that emerging market countries have started to mitigate the cost of holding excess reserves by transferring a portion of their foreign exchange reserves from the central bank to new "sovereign wealth funds," which are not unlike the natural resource–based stabilization funds set up by a number of commodity exporters. He cites the sovereign wealth funds of Korea and China as recent examples, and he reports forecasts that the holdings of such funds, already more than $2 trillion, could exceed $12 trillion by 2015.

Would such a development lead to disruptions in exchange rates and in the relative prices of financial assets in global markets? Jeanne documents the significant difference in size between the portfolios of the official and the nonofficial sectors and considers, as an example, the likely effect of shifting $450 billion of the roughly $2 trillion in foreign assets into a "world" portfolio. His back-of-the-envelope calculations show that although such a shift plays against the dollar, and in particular against fixed-income dollar assets, changes in net demands would be relatively small fractions of outstanding stocks, with moderate effects on prices and exchange rates. But Jeanne also points out that a substantial portion of outstanding U.S. debt is held by the foreign official sector, and that the effect on the interest rate the U.S. government pays may be nonnegligible, depending on the substitutability between U.S. Treasury securities and other forms of dollar debt in the portfolios of global investors. He also cautions that if the pace of diversification is rapid, the effects might be much larger than would be expected in the long run.

Jeanne argues that the abundance of reserves held by emerging market countries reduces the need for collective insurance provided at the global level by the International Monetary Fund (IMF) and various regional insurance arrangements, noting that the increase in reserves in the Asian emerging market counties over 2000–05 was more than four times the IMF's usable assets at the end of 2005 and more than twenty times the bilateral swap agreements to date under the Chiang Mai Initiative launched by a group of Asian countries in 2000. He suggests various other potential uses of the large accumulated stocks, such as collective insurance for risks other than capital account crises; such risks might include severe shocks to countries' terms of trade or output, as well as natural disasters. He also suggests that sovereign wealth could be used to promote the development of regional financial markets, which might in turn serve as a catalyst for private investment in Asian issues and help enable emerging market countries develop investment instruments with long maturities, denominated in domestic currency, which would be safer for borrowers.

Finally, Jeanne observes that even if the recent high rate of reserves accumulation were to abate, the public sectors of many emerging market economies will have to manage stocks of foreign financial assets of unprecedented size for some time to come. Although it may be a challenge to ensure that the diversification of those assets avoids large or abrupt changes in the relative prices of financial assets or exchange rates, the growth in sovereign wealth of these countries provides many new opportunities to benefit the developing world.

THE ACCELERATION OF PRODUCTIVITY GROWTH was an economic hallmark of the second half of the 1990s. After twenty years during which labor productivity growth averaged only around 1.5 percent a year, it rose at an average annual rate of over 2.5 percent between 1995 and 2000. That development had important consequences for the nation's economic performance, not only through the direct effect of raising national income at given levels of employment but also by its effect on the conduct of monetary policy: then–Federal Reserve Chairman Alan Greenspan's early recognition that productivity was speeding up is credited with the continuation of monetary accommodation, which in turn permitted a strong expansion of employment and reduction of unemployment for another five years. Most analysts at the time attributed an important part of the productivity acceleration to the continuing boom in information technology (IT) hardware and software. When IT investment declined sharply after 2000, that diagnosis of the boom period implied that the productivity trend would also slow. It did not. In the second article of this issue, Stephen Oliner, Daniel Sichel, and Kevin Stiroh use the surprising developments of both the pre- and post-2000 periods to refine our understanding of productivity growth, project the likely future path of productivity, and assess the uncertainty surrounding that projection.

As the framework for their analysis, the authors extend the growth accounting model they developed previously to study the role of IT capital in the nonfarm business sector. As in standard growth accounting, growth in aggregate labor productivity in their model can be decomposed into the contribution from the increase in capital per hour worked, the contribution from improved labor quality, and growth in multifactor productivity (MFP), each measured as an aggregate average. The authors extend this standard model in several directions. To focus on the role of IT, they disaggregate total output into five IT-producing sectors and a sixth, non-IT-producing remainder. Data for four of the IT-producing sectors—computer hardware, software, communications equipment, and semiconductors—are taken from the National Income and Product Accounts (NIPAs). Exports of semiconductors are classified as final output in the NIPAs, and the remaining output in this sector is treated as intermediate inputs to the others. The fifth IT sector produces intangible IT capital; since this output is not measured in the NIPAs, the authors introduce their own estimate. This intangible output is treated as investment, whose services are inputs to future production. The authors also take account of cyclical influences on productivity growth (changes in factor utilization) and of the adjustment costs associated with new capital goods; both these factors could have had significant effects on observed productivity movements over the past decade.

Using their six-sector disaggregation, the authors estimate the effect of the business cycle on measured MFP growth, which they take as proportional to the length of the workweek, and of the costs of adjustment, which they take as proportional to investment. Each of these effects drives a wedge between measured MFP growth and the true pace of improvements in technology and similar underlying effects affecting long-run growth. Lengthening the workweek is expected to boost measured MFP growth as firms get more output from their capital and labor, and raising investment is expected to lower MFP growth as firms divert resources from producing market output to installing new capital. Aggregate MFP growth and the aggregate effects of these adjustments are given by the share-weighted sum of the sectoral MFP growth rates, where the weights are shares of each sector's gross output in aggregate value added. Because not all the data required for a thoroughgoing bottom-up estimation of these sectoral relations are available, the authors rely in part on estimates made at the aggregate level and distributed to the sectors, and on estimates of certain parameters from earlier research by themselves and others.

The authors first undertake a growth accounting that does not incorporate the estimates of intangible IT capital. This accounting, using only the familiar standard NIPA data, shows how the effects of the business cycle and adjustment costs on investment influence the accounting for the productivity surge in the late 1990s and after 2000. Average annual growth of labor productivity picked up from about 1.5 percent during 1973–95 to about 2.5 percent in the following five years, and to 2.9 percent during 2000–06. Of the initial 1.0-percentage-point speedup, 0.6 percentage point reflected the quickened growth of IT capital, and another 0.5 percentage point came from the acceleration of MFP in IT-producing sectors, so that IT accounted for slightly more than the entire acceleration in labor productivity. The cyclical and adjustment cost effects were each noticeable. Compared with the pre-1995 long-run average, the strong expansion added 0.16 percentage point to annual MFP growth during 1995–2000, and the adjustment costs associated with high investment reduced MFP growth by 0.15 percentage point in this period. The two effects having opposite signs, their combined effect was negligible.

The accounting for the further acceleration of MFP after 2000 is quite different. The cyclical and adjustment cost effects are again substantial, but of the opposite sign from the previous five years, and again roughly cancel each other out. But compared with 1995–2000, in the post-2000 period IT capital deepening and MFP growth in IT-producing industries are both slower and together contribute 0.7 percentage point a year less to labor productivity growth, whereas in the non-IT sectors capital deepening and MFP growth both contribute substantially more, accounting for more than the entire further acceleration of labor productivity in this period. Averaged over the whole 1995–2006 period, total IT contributions account for roughly two-thirds of the acceleration in labor productivity. However, comparing just the post-2000 period with 1973–95, the total contribution of IT accounts for only about a quarter of the 1.4-percentage-point acceleration.

To better understand these developments and how they may inform projections of future productivity growth, the authors next construct a measure of intangible IT capital and introduce it into their growth accounting. In earlier work, Carol Corrado, Charles Hulten, and Sichel argued that any intangible asset that provides services beyond the current period should be considered as part of the capital stock, with its production counted as investment in current-period output. Using a wide range of data sources, they estimated that such intangible investment, ranging across such categories as research and development, computerized information, and firm-specific organizational capital, totaled roughly $1 trillion a year over 2000–03, or almost as much as business fixed investment.

To obtain up-to-date estimates of the intangible capital that can be associated with IT, the authors turn to a model developed by Susanto Basu and coauthors and based on the idea that intangible capital is a complement of IT capital as measured. That model specifies a function in which tangible and intangible IT capital are treated as complementary factors, with firms optimizing the ratio of the two given their relative costs. Total output then depends on this combined IT input, labor, and non-IT capital. The optimization of tangible and intangible IT capital inputs assumes an elasticity of substitution between them of 1.25, a value that best approximates the trend in the income shares of the two estimated by Basu and coauthors. The estimates are anchored to the values in the original Corrado-Hulten-Sichel data by making the average income share of intangible capital over 1973–2003 equal to the income shares of those intangibles that are IT related in those authors' original estimates. The present authors thus generate a time series for intangible capital and, using a standard perpetual inventory relation, a series for intangible investments associated with it. Although intangible capital investment is linked to IT investment in these constructed series, the price declines in IT capital cause its user cost to trend lower, leading intangible capital to grow less rapidly than IT capital in all periods. This difference is more pronounced after 1995 than before.

Incorporating intangible capital raises both the input and the output sides of the production accounts compared with the standard NIPA treatment. And the augmented framework changes both the pattern of labor productivity over time and the accounting for its growth. In the baseline case, which corresponds to the timing assumptions in the model of Basu and coauthors, labor productivity growth speeds up by 1.4 percentage points in 1995–2000, even more than the 1-percentage-point speedup in the NIPA data, reflecting both the more rapid growth of output when investment in intangible capital is added to the NIPA estimates, and greater capital deepening. Labor productivity then grows by 2.4 percent a year on average in the following period, or 0.4 percentage point less than in the NIPA estimates. Including intangible investment in output has a noticeable effect on MFP growth. Whereas the NIPA data implied speedups in MFP of 0.7 percentage point after 1995 and a further 0.6 percentage point after 2000, the augmented data imply a 0.9-percentage-point speedup after 1995 and only a negligible further change after 2000. The contribution of capital deepening from intangible capital speeds up by 0.1 percentage point after 1995 and then declines by 0.4 percentage point after 2000.

The baseline estimates assume a contemporaneous relation between the growth of IT capital and the growth of intangible capital associated with it. To check the robustness of their results, the authors present three alternative series for intangibles that allow for a smoothing of their relation to IT capital and, alternatively, a one-year lag of intangibles growth behind IT capital growth. The smoothing is accomplished by using a three-year or a five-year centered moving average for the growth rate of IT capital and its user costs in the equations used to generate estimates of intangible capital. In each of these alternatives, after 2000 there are noticeable declines in intangible capital investment and slight declines in the capital services from intangibles. The range of estimates across these four series indicates that the results are quite robust to the variations in timing that are considered. Annual labor productivity growth speeds up by between 1.4 and 1.1 percentage points after 1995 and slows by between 0.5 and 0.1 percentage point after 2000. The contribution of intangible capital deepening speeds up by 0.1 percentage point after 1995 in all alternatives and slows down by between 0.3 and 0.4 percentage point after 2000. And the contribution of aggregate MFP to labor productivity speeds up by between 0.7 and 0.9 percentage point after 1995 and by a further 0.04 to 0.4 percentage point after 2000.

The authors turn next to productivity at the industry level. They rely, alternatively, on annual measures of value added and gross output from the Bureau of Economic Analysis (BEA) and combine each of these with data on hours from the Bureau of Labor Statistics (BLS) to calculate two alternative measures of average labor productivity by industry. The value added-based measures of productivity by industry combine directly to an aggregate measure of labor productivity for all private industry. The gross output–based measures require an allowance for changes in intermediate inputs to be reconciled with that aggregate. The authors also calculate a proxy for capital services, using BEA data on nonresidential capital that is disaggregated by type and industry. The available data permit calculation of average labor productivity growth for sixty industries for the period 1988–2005. The value added–based estimates allow the authors to form a panel of fifteen broad sectors and a private industry aggregate made up of their sixty industries. Labor productivity growth rates for this aggregate differ somewhat from those for the more inclusive BLS data covering the private nonfarm business sector. But the authors capture the pickup in productivity growth after 1995 and the smaller further pickup after 2000 that characterizes the BEA aggregates. Among the fifteen broad sectors, productivity speeded up after 1995 in eight, which together account for 73 percent of value added. After 2000, productivity continued growing faster than it had during 1988–95 in six of these sectors: durable goods; wholesale trade; retail trade; professional and business services; education services, health care, and social assistance; and agriculture. Each of these sectors is a relatively large part of the economy, except agriculture, which is very small. And productivity accelerated sharply in the information industry, leaving its productivity growth over the entire 1995–2005 period well above its previous rate.

To examine the contribution of IT, the authors classify individual industries according to whether they are IT producing, IT using, or neither. IT-producing industries are the four industries classed as such by the BEA, which together produced nearly 5 percent of aggregate value added in 2005: computer and electronics products, publishing including software, information and data processing services, and computer system design and related services. IT-using industries are defined as those whose use of IT exceeds that of the median industry (excluding IT producers). The authors then decompose the changes in labor productivity for their private industry aggregate into the direct contributions of IT-producing industries,

IT-using industries, and other industries, and the contribution coming from reallocations across industries. Using the industry value-added data, they measure the contribution from input reallocations by changes in hours worked across industries. This contribution is positive when hours grow relatively more in high-productivity industries. When the industry gross output data are used, the contribution from reallocations includes, in addition, changes in intermediate inputs across industries. This contribution is positive when gross output is rising faster than purchased material inputs.

Both the gross output–based and the value added–based measures assign a dominant role to IT in the acceleration of labor productivity after 1995. Of the 0.96-percentage-point acceleration in the aggregated industries measure during 1995–2000, the analysis using the gross output data attributes 1.45 percentage points to the direct effect of productivity acceleration in IT-producing and IT-using industries, and a small decline to other industries. The reallocation effects are −0.48 percentage point from intermediate inputs and 0.13 percentage point from hours. The value-added data show direct effects of 1.16 percentage points from IT industries and a small decline in the others, along with a 0.13-percentage-point hours reallocation effect. In both cases the large direct IT contribution comes mainly from IT-using industries. The small further acceleration of 0.32 percentage point in aggregate productivity after 2000 is accounted for very differently in the two data sets. The growth output data attribute −0.94 percentage point to the direct effects of industry productivity growth, with IT-producing, IT-using, and other industries all contributing to the slowdown. The hours reallocation contributes 0.31 percentage point and the intermediate inputs reallocation contributes 0.94 percentage point. The value-added data show no change in direct effects, with a small deceleration in IT producers offsetting a small acceleration in IT users. In both the gross output and the value-added data, over the entire post-1995 period, the direct contribution of IT-using and IT-producing industries accounts for most of the speedup in aggregate labor productivity; the direct contribution of other industries is slightly negative.

The authors perform regressions on their industry-level data to further explore the acceleration of productivity. They construct two alternative measures of IT intensity by industry: one is the share of IT capital services in total capital services, and the other is a dummy variable equal to 1 if an industry's use of IT capital as a share of its total capital is above the median for all industries. Using the gross output data, they find that IT-intensive industries, by either definition, experienced faster productivity growth after 1995, but they find no further significant effect on productivity growth starting in 2000. The value-added data yield less significant results.

Some analysts have speculated that productivity growth after 2000 may have been driven by unusual pressures on firms to restructure so as to cut costs in a more competitive environment. To explore this and related hypotheses, the authors examine the relation between the change in industry profit share from 1997 to 2001 and the growth of hours and labor productivity from 2001 to 2004 across their sixty-industry sample. On average, industries with below-median changes in profitability experienced 2 percentage points slower hours growth and 3 percentage points faster productivity growth than those with above-median changes in profitability. The authors go on to run separate regressions using the change in profits between 1997 and 2001 to explain growth rates in hours, intermediate inputs, labor productivity, and output over 2001–04, the period of extremely rapid productivity growth. The regressions include a number of additional variables to control for demand effects, longer-run trends, and IT intensity. With either the gross output or the value-added data, they find significant negative effects of changes in profits on growth rates of hours and significant positive effects on labor productivity, no effects on intermediate inputs or gross output, and marginally significant effects on value added. These results are consistent with the idea that competitive pressures and restructuring help explain the post-2000 productivity gains. The regressions also reveal no significant effects from IT intensity on productivity or output, which the authors interpret as support for the idea that IT was not an important factor in the post-2000 changes in productivity.

Following their econometric analysis, the authors go on to put recent productivity gains in historical perspective. They show that labor productivity growth in the private sector has averaged 2.2 percent a year since 1909. Dividing that nearly century-long period into several subperiods, they show that annual productivity growth averaged 2.9 percent during 1950–73, the "golden era" of productivity growth, and 2.8 percent during 1995–2006. It averaged around 1.5 percent a year in 1909–28 and 1973–95, the two remaining periods. Thus the recent past is one of unusually rapid growth relative to historical experience.

Looking ahead, the authors report a range of steady-state growth rates that would be consistent with their growth accounting model under various parameter assumptions. The key parameters affecting aggregate labor productivity are the rate of improvement in labor quality and the rate of advance in technology outside the IT-producing sectors. Capital deepening is endogenously determined by the rate of growth of MFP outside IT. Using bounds for these parameter values based on historical experience, they calculate upper and lower bounds for projected steady-state annual productivity growth of 3.1 percent and 1.5 percent, respectively. The center of the range is 2¼ percent. At the lower-bound estimate, capital deepening contributes 0.75 percentage point and MFP growth 0.56 percentage point to productivity growth. At the higher bound, capital deepening contributes 1.39 percentage points and MFP 1.55 percentage points. The authors show that their central projection of 2¼ percent is very near the projections of a number of other studies, and close as well to their own ten-year projections using a Kalman filter model that allows estimation of a stochastic process for productivity growth. But they stress that the uncertainty around their own projections, and presumably around the others as well, is considerable.

ONE PERSISTENT DIFFERENCE BETWEEN the poor and the rich countries of the world is that rich countries have more real capital per worker. All else equal, the marginal return to capital should be lower where capital is more abundant. It follows that investment funds should profitably flow from richer to poorer countries. Since Robert Lucas pointed out in 1990 that it typically does not, analysts have tried to understand the reasons for this seemingly perverse phenomenon. Some invoke financial market inefficiencies that interfere with the productive investment of capital; others point to political or policy instabilities in poor countries that make investments in them exceptionally risky. Recently, Pierre-Olivier Gourinchas and Olivier Jeanne have expanded the Lucas paradox by showing that capital flows to nonindustrialized countries have not been concentrated among those growing relatively fast, even though successful growth would presumably indicate that capital is productive in those countries and that they are relatively creditworthy. Understanding why foreign capital inflows have not been associated with faster growth and, more generally, how international capital flows influence the development process are key issues for developing countries, which must decide whether and how to open their economy to global investors. In the third article of this volume, Eswar Prasad, Raghuram Rajan, and Arvind Subramanian take a further look at these issues.

The authors first lay out several broad trends in international capital flows over the past few decades, focusing on national current accounts, which are the counterpart to the broadest measure of net foreign finance. A current account surplus equals the sum of net outflows of private and official financial capital, net accumulation of reserves, and net errors and omissions. The last of these reconciles direct measures of current account flows, such as exports and imports, with direct measures of capital flows, such as equity and debt purchases, and is generally thought to reflect capital moving through unmeasured channels. Thus a positive number for errors and omissions is customarily treated as a capital outflow, just as a purchase of foreign securities or a deposit in a foreign bank would be. The authors show that, at least since the early 1990s, the sum of current account surpluses in economies with surpluses has risen sharply as a share of world GDP. This might have been expected given the growing globalization of international finance. What is more striking is that, since the early 1980s, the average relative income of the countries with current account surpluses (the capital exporters) has trended down even as the average relative income of countries with current account deficits has trended up. Much of this difference in income trends remains even when the United States and China, two large outliers, are omitted from the calculations.

Going a step beyond the simple association of growth and current accounts, the authors divide their sample of some sixty nonindustrialized economies into four groups depending on whether a country's current account balance, as a ratio to GDP, was above or below the group median and whether its ratio of real investment to GDP was above or below the median. Averaged over 1970–2004, higher investment ratios and larger current account surpluses are both associated with faster growth in GDP per capita. Among countries with high investment ratios, those with less reliance on foreign capital grew faster, by an average of 1 percentage point a year.

To examine these connections more rigorously, the authors turn to regressions using annual data covering 1970–2004 for their sample of nonindustrialized countries. They first present cross-sectional regressions that, following the work of Barry Bosworth and Susan Collins, explain purchasing power–adjusted growth rates in GDP per capita over this period with the ratio of the current account to GDP and a number of control variables: the logarithm of initial GDP per capita, initial-period life expectancy, trade openness, the fiscal balance, a measure of institutional quality, and dummy variables for oil exporters and countries in sub-Saharan Africa. Their baseline regression finds a significant positive association of growth with current account balances, indicating that countries that rely less on foreign finance grow faster. Among the control variables, institutional quality, initial GDP per capita, and life expectancy are all significantly associated with growth. Omitting data for three countries that are outliers has no effect on these results. But when countries receiving aid flows that average more than 10 percent of their GDP are also omitted, the coefficient on the current account balance doubles, and the institutional quality variable becomes highly significant. This indicates that the results are not driven by large aid recipients. When accumulated foreign assets or liabilities are substituted for the current account balance, they are usually not significant, and the regressions do not explain growth quite as well.

It might be thought that slow growth reflects low investment and that current account deficits reveal a lack of domestic resources that constrains investment. However, when the ratio of domestic investment to GDP is added to the regression with the current account, investment is not significant and has little effect on the other variables. The authors take this as evidence that the correlation of the current account balance with growth does not arise because investment is constrained by a lack of domestic resources. By contrast, when the ratio of domestic saving to GDP is added instead of the investment ratio, it is highly significant and the current account balance loses significance. The authors interpret this as evidence that the positive association between current account balances and growth stems largely from a positive relation between domestic saving and growth.

Some further regressions investigate the robustness of these basic results. When estimated over 1985–97, a period when international finance grew rapidly and international financial crises were relatively unimportant, the association of growth with the current account balance is even stronger. When industrialized countries are added to the sample (and distinguished by a dummy variable), the coefficient for the nonindustrialized countries is unaffected, whereas the dummy for industrialized countries has a significant net negative coefficient, indicating that current account balances are negatively related to growth in these countries. The same is true of the countries in transition from socialism when they are added to a regression estimated over 1990–2004. The authors also add the share of the working-age population in total population, an exogenous demographic variable that is expected to be associated positively with saving. Its regression coefficient is significantly positive, and its inclusion reduces the current account balance variable to insignificance. This, the authors reason, supports the idea that the association of growth with the current account balance arises from the relation of domestic saving to growth. Furthering this argument, they average the experience of countries in the years surrounding spurts in their growth rates and show that such growth spurts have led to higher saving, a result consistent with a role for habit formation in consumption.

The authors extend their analysis with panel regressions using five-year averages to capture the changes in a country over time, along with many of the same controls and specifications as in the cross-sectional regressions. In these regressions the estimated effect of the current account balance reaches statistical significance only when countries receiving substantial aid are dropped from the sample, along with the three large outliers. The investment-GDP and saving-GDP ratios are each significant when added separately to the equation, as is the working-age share of the population. For industrial countries the relation between the current account balance and growth is again negative. The panel results thus largely support the cross-sectional results, although with weaker evidence of a positive relation between the current account balance and growth for nonindustrial countries.

The interrelations among the macroeconomic variables being analyzed make it difficult to establish causality. The current account balance, investment, and saving are all endogenous, with shocks to any one potentially affecting the others. Because developments in individual industries have only modest effects on aggregates, estimation with industry-level data is less subject to such endogeneity problems. The authors therefore turn to industry-level data to examine some hypotheses about their aggregate findings. They first examine whether manufacturing industries that are relatively dependent on outside financing for investment, as opposed to financing from internal cash flows, grow faster when foreign capital is more available. Following earlier work by Rajan with Luigi Zingales, they run separate regressions explaining industry growth for each of five measures of foreign capital inflow: the stock of inward foreign direct investment (FDI), the stock of FDI and portfolio investment combined, the net flow counterparts of these two measures, and the current account deficit, each relative to GDP. (Each of these measures is interacted with a measure of the industry's dependence on outside financing.) In separate regressions the above openness measures are also interacted with an indicator of level of financial development. All regressions include the relative size of the industry in the country's manufacturing value added, and all are cross sections run separately for average values of the 1980s and the 1990s. The regressions include country and industry fixed effects, in effect explaining within-country differences in industry growth rates by the industry's dependence on outside financing and the country's use of foreign financing.

The regression results generally support the idea that countries with greater financial development respond differently to external finance. This result is robust for the 1990s, where all five measures of capital inflow interacted with dependence on external finance are significantly negatively related to industry growth for less financially developed countries, and positively related for more financially developed countries. Roughly similar results are obtained for the 1980s. The findings are again the same in panel regressions that include variations across the two decades. The authors discuss in some detail the various ways in which lower financial development might interact with other characteristics of economies to affect growth. Although they can only conjecture about specifics, they reason that improving financial development brings substantial benefits.

The authors recognize that reliance on foreign capital may also affect growth through entirely different channels that change a country's international competitiveness. To explore this possibility, they use regressions to estimate the relations among currency overvaluation, capital flows or stocks, and growth, using a measure of overvaluation developed by Simon Johnson, Jonathan Ostry, and Subramanian that adjusts exchange rates for purchasing power parity. Cross-country regressions using data averaged over 1970–2004 explain overvaluation with the working-age population and various measures of capital stocks and flows. All show a positive association between the presence of foreign capital and overvaluation. The best-fitting regressions are for net FDI flows and net private inflows. And by far the best fits are obtained when industrialized economies are distinguished from non-industrialized economies. In these regressions, capital flows to industrial economies are more or less unrelated to overvaluation, whereas the relation is significantly positive for nonindustrialized economies. Additional regressions show that overvaluation has a significantly negative relation to growth. Finally, regressions using industry data that distinguish industries by their potential for exporting show that the negative effects of overvaluation on an industry's growth depend on that potential.

The authors' conclusions are modest, reflecting the uncertain causality behind the relations they examine and the many factors that influence growth. It is clear that nonindustrial countries that have relied relatively heavily on foreign capital have not grown faster than those that have not. And their results suggest that the less successful developing countries have limited capacity to utilize foreign resources, either because their financial markets are underdeveloped, or because they are prone to overvaluation in the face of rapid capital inflows, or both. Although the authors' results caution against encouraging some forms of capital inflow to reduce the risk of overvaluation, financial openness may be needed to spur development of the domestic financial system. Given this dilemma, the authors reason that policymakers need to take account of country-specific issues when opening the current account and need to be creative and flexible in managing it.

A CENTRAL FEATURE OF the Job Growth and Taxpayer Relief Reconciliation Act of 2003 was a large cut in the tax on dividends, lowering the maximum rate from over 38 percent to 15 percent. A natural prediction is that these lower rates will lead to an increase in dividends over time, both by increasing the distribution of current earnings and by causing a shift from debt to equity financing of corporations. A number of studies have attempted to quantify the effects of the tax cut on dividend payments, but relatively little recent work has been done on how dividends themselves affect consumption. Estimating these effects from aggregate time series is confounded by the multitude of factors correlated with dividends that plausibly influence consumption. In the fourth article of this issue, Malcolm Baker, Stefan Nagel, and Jeffrey Wurgler utilize cross-sectional data on households to infer the effect of dividends on consumption, how those effects differ from the effects of capital gains, and by implication how increases in dividends resulting from tax cuts are likely to affect the saving available for investment.

The authors begin by examining the cross-sectional relationship between dividends and consumption using data from the Consumer Expenditure Survey (CEX) for 1988–2001. Their sample includes interviews of several hundred households per year, each household for five consecutive quarters. The surveys elicit information on households' consumption, income, wealth, and financial returns as well as important demographic characteristics. The authors restrict their attention to households with positive wealth, nonzero holdings of stocks or mutual funds, and unchanged marital

status and household size over the period they were interviewed. Households in this sample had, on average over 1988–2001, after-tax income of
$56,566, total consumption expenditure of $48,076, and nondurables consumption of $15,042, all measured in December 2001 dollars. Their finan-
cial wealth averaged $67,700 and constituted about a third of their average
total wealth. Dividends and interest income averaged $935 and $1,264 a
year, respectively. As expected, the distributions of financial assets and
returns are very unequal, skewed strongly to the right. For example, mean
financial wealth is roughly 1.75 times median wealth, and median dividend
income is zero, even though all of the households in the sample hold some
stock, either directly or through mutual funds.

Variation in household consumption and dividend income in a cross
section of households undoubtedly reflects a variety of households' non-
financial characteristics in addition to income and other financial variables.
The authors are agnostic about what specific model is the most accurate
representation of consumption behavior and instead attempt to isolate the
causal effect of dividends by controlling for a wide variety of demographic
characteristics. In their basic specification explaining the level of either
total or nondurables consumption, the demographic controls include age
of household head, family size, and education. These variables are allowed
to enter linearly, quadratically, and in interactions with each other and the
financial variables. The authors also include a set of year-month fixed
effects to absorb seasonal variation in consumption as well as variation in
macroeconomic factors affecting the consumption of households sampled
at different times. In their words, "In the end the levels specification boils
down to asking whether two consumers in the same financial situation, with
similar income, similar household characteristics, and similar total return
on financial assets, but different *compositions* of total returns across dividends and capital gains, have different consumption."

The authors find that an extra dollar of dividend income has substantial
and statistically significant effects on consumption: the marginal propensity
to consume (MPC) is roughly three-quarters for total consumption and one-
sixth for nondurables consumption. The estimated effects of capital gains
on consumption (given by the coefficient on total returns, since dividends
are entered separately) are near zero and insignificant. In specifications
in which interest is lumped with dividends and included in total returns,
the MPCs are somewhat smaller than those for dividends alone but also
highly significant. The authors include a dummy variable for non-dividend-

receiving households to ensure that their results are not driven by the large
number of zero-dividend observations. They experiment with controlling
for age, noting that dividends are a higher percentage of income for older
households, perhaps because those households are more likely to be in
retirement. The MPC out of dividends for total consumption among those
over 65 is found to be substantially lower than for those younger than 65,
but this result is of borderline statistical significance.

The authors recognize that the correlation of consumption with dividends across households may reflect in part the effect of some unmeasured
differences in households' characteristics that influence both consumption
and dividends, or it may reflect a reversal of causation, with households
with high consumption needs choosing high-yielding stocks. Although the
authors believe the controls they use should do a reasonable job of minimizing this bias, they recognize that it is difficult to fully rule out some
remaining, unobserved differences between households that hold high-
and low-dividend-paying stocks.

Differencing the consumption levels equations reported above would
remove any fixed household effects correlated with the level of dividend
income, providing a check on whether the estimated MPCs in those equations are biased by endogeneity. However, the limited information on the
change in a household's consumption and asset returns in the CEX makes it
impossible to run a true differenced form of the equations. The CEX survey
does provide information for each household on the difference between
quarterly consumption at the second and the fifth interviews, and the difference in dividends in the twelve months preceding each of those interviews. The authors therefore regress the change in consumption between
these two quarters on the change in dividends, the level of total returns,
the age of the household head, and other demographic variables.

In the equations explaining total consumption, the resulting MPC is
0.057. Assuming that the change in annual dividends affects four quarters
of consumption equally, not just consumption in the quarters reported, this
translates to an MPC of 0.228, roughly a third of the MPCs found in the
levels equations. The authors see this reduction as consistent with some
upward bias in the levels equations, but they note that it could also reflect
the noise introduced through the imperfect matching of dividends and consumption measurement periods. If lagged consumption is included in this
equation, the MPC for total consumption is substantially greater, but the
coefficient on lagged consumption is negative, suggesting that more than 60

percent of the increase would be reversed in the following period. Since this is a cross-sectional regression, this negative coefficient could arise if wealthy households with large financial asset holdings and large absolute changes in dividends are relatively less responsive to changes in dividends. The authors add that the lagged level of consumption may be absorbing some of the noise resulting from the imperfect matching of the dividend and consumption measurement periods.

For nondurables consumption the estimated effect of the change in dividends is significant only when the level of lagged consumption is included; the MPC is again about a third of that in the corresponding levels equation and includes a large negative coefficient on lagged consumption. In the log difference equations, which should be free of scale effects, dividend changes are entered simply as a dummy variable, equal to 1 when positive. The estimated effects of dividend increases are large: households with an increase in dividends have a 7- to 8-percentage-point greater increase in total consumption than those without an increase. The corresponding point estimates for growth in nondurables expenditure are also substantial, although not statistically significant.

To supplement these results, the authors turn to a second micro dataset containing portfolio information for a large number of household accounts at a large discount brokerage firm. Although this dataset does not include data on consumption, assets other than those held in the brokerage account, or household demographic characteristics, it provides much more accurate and detailed information about dividends, capital gains, and stock transactions. And although the data do not allow estimation of the effects of dividends on consumption, they do allow investigation of whether the receipt of a dividend leads to a withdrawal from the account, which would be necessary if the dividend were to be used directly for consumption. The brokerage data also have the advantage that they follow individual households over long periods. This provides some information on how households respond over time to dividends and capital gains, whereas in the CEX data this behavior had to be inferred entirely from cross-sectional differences. The authors restrict themselves to households that had an open brokerage account in 1991, and they exclude margin accounts, IRA and Keogh accounts, accounts that are not individual or joint tenancy accounts, and accounts whose value falls below $10,000. They also exclude household-month observations for which they cannot identify the mutual funds or common stock in the portfolio if the unidentifiable assets constitute at least

75 percent of the account's value, and they exclude observations with extreme values of withdrawals. Their final sample includes 92,412 household-months. Because the brokerage data do not explicitly report dividend income, the authors estimate it by matching portfolio holdings with publicly available data on the dividend distributions of specific stocks and mutual funds. Net monthly withdrawals or additions to accounts are then calculated as the difference between the end-of-period account value and the appreciated (end-of-month) value of the assets held at the beginning of the month plus dividends on those assets during the month.

A simple scatterplot of household-month net withdrawals against contemporaneous total dividends, while showing a large dispersion of net withdrawals for a given level of dividends, clearly reveals bimodal behavior: a significant fraction of households at every level of dividends withdraw either exactly that amount or exactly zero. A plot of median or average net withdrawals versus dividends for deciles of total return suggests a very high propensity to withdraw dividends during the month in which they occur; similar plots indicate at most a very small withdrawal propensity from total returns. These graphical results are confirmed by regression. A linear regression of withdrawals on dividends and total returns, with all variables expressed as a percentage of previous-period account value, yields marginal propensities to withdraw dividends and total returns of 0.35 and 0.02, respectively. Both propensities are highly significant statistically. On average, dividends are at reasonable levels, with ordinary monthly dividends averaging 0.12 percent of beginning-of-month wealth. However, the maximum dividends are extremely high, amounting to nearly 30 percent of beginning-of-month wealth in the case of mutual funds and more than 100 percent in the case of special dividends. The estimated 2 percent withdrawal of total returns may seem small, but capital gains, which are much more variable than dividends, may have a nonnegligible effect on withdrawals.

The authors show that the results for total dividends mask an important difference between the propensity to withdraw mutual fund dividends and that for the other two types, ordinary and special dividends. The propensity to withdraw mutual fund dividends, reflecting in part more frequent use of automatic reinvestment options, is only about half that of the other two, and the estimate of the propensity to withdraw ordinary dividends is approximately 0.8 for all but the highest yields, which is considerably larger than the estimates for the aggregate of dividends.

The authors run a second version of these equations that includes a twelve-month lag of dividends. The results provide some clues about the dynamics of withdrawals and the importance of what the authors call "ex ante" effects, that is, the possibility that dividends are endogenous. If unobserved household characteristics, such as retirement, lead some households to choose high-dividend portfolios to support their consumption, causation is reversed, with consumption and withdrawals causing dividends rather than the other way around. The fact that the data include both cross-sectional and intertemporal observations makes it difficult to distinguish the effects of unmeasured household differences from withdrawal dynamics for a given household. The authors report that a one-year lag of ordinary dividends explains 57 percent of current dividends, and together with a three-month lag it explains 81 percent of current dividends. This may reflect the relative permanence of dividends paid on individual stocks, but also unmeasured and relatively permanent household characteristics. The effects of including lags in the mutual fund equation are similar, but smaller. In both cases the coefficient estimates are imprecise. In the case of special and other dividends, which are likely to be unexpected and therefore unlikely to involve reverse causation, the lagged effect has a significant negative coefficient. This may help explain why, in the regressions for total dividends, where the type of dividend is not distinguished, lagged dividends are not significant. The authors conclude that although there is some evidence of reverse causation, it is likely to play a fairly modest role in the case of ordinary and mutual fund dividends, and even less of a role for special dividends. They believe that all of the results are consistent with an important element of causality running from dividends to withdrawals and, based on their analysis of the CEX data, to consumption.

Having concluded that the MPC out of dividends is substantial and much greater than for capital gains, the authors discuss various possible explanations for this behavior. They argue that borrowing constraints, sometimes used to rationalize a high sensitivity of consumption to current income, do not explain the large gap between the MPC from dividends and that from capital gains. While acknowledging that, in principle, transaction costs could explain that gap, they note that the propensities are essentially the same for households that are saving, who could simply save less without incurring additional transaction costs, and that the propensity is the same or higher for households with high portfolio turnover, who also could reinvest dividends with little additional cost.

The authors are skeptical of tax explanations, pointing out that high-tax-rate households withdraw much more than needed to meet the associated tax obligation and that, throughout their sample period, the tax rate was much higher on dividends than on capital gains, suggesting that, if anything, consumption needs should be met by selling stock. They acknowledge there is empirical support for the idea that aggregate consumption responds more to permanent than to transitory changes in asset values, and they recognize that changes in dividends may provide information about the permanent component of stock returns. But they observe that their results are driven largely by cross-sectional, not intertemporal, variations in returns and that the use of time fixed effects in their regressions absorbs aggregate movements in asset values, so that differences in capital gains across household-month observations are relatively permanent. Although the remaining variation in idiosyncratic household stock returns may have a transitory component, they find it difficult to explain the large difference between the consumption of dividends and that of capital gains by its presence.

The authors suggest that mental accounting theories may provide the best explanation of their results. They give as an example a model developed by Hersh Shefrin and Richard Thaler in which households place wealth into one of three mental accounts—current income, current assets, and future wealth—and follow the popular advice to "spend income, not principal." Indeed, Shefrin and Thaler explicitly predict that the propensity to consume wealth categorized as current income, such as dividends, is greater than that from wealth categorized as assets. Not only is this prediction consistent with the authors' main results, and with the fact that their estimate of the MPC of dividends is similar to the MPC of labor income, but mental accounting can also rationalize other features of their results, such as the fact that the MPC for special dividends falls in between that for ordinary dividends and that for capital gains. They recognize that the underlying psychology behind this sort of mental accounting is an important open question, and they suggest that self-control and prospect theory are potential psychological roots.

Many proponents of the Job Growth and Taxpayer Relief Reconciliation Act of 2003 argued that the dramatic tax cut on dividends, by lowering the cost of capital, would stimulate investment and saving. The authors' results suggest that the cuts might indeed have stimulated the economy, but by leading to an increase in consumption rather than in investment and saving.

According to some, the cut would simply raise the price of stocks without necessarily increasing dividend payouts. But even without higher payouts, the reduction in taxes on existing dividends could have significant effects on consumption. The middle range of the estimates of the MPC from before-tax dividends implies an MPC from after-tax dividends above 0.7. Using the IRS figure for individuals' dividend income in 2002 of $103 billion and James Poterba's estimate of the reduction in the average marginal tax rate on dividends resulting from the tax cut, the authors calculate that consumption would increase by about $8.5 billion.

Increases in dividends, induced by the more attractive tax treatment of dividend income, would substantially add to that effect. The authors report that evidence on the importance of the cut tax for dividend payouts is mixed. Survey evidence suggests a relatively minor role, but a study led by Raj Chetty and Emmanuel Saez that compares dividend payouts of firms with different tax incentives credits the tax cuts with virtually all of the increase in dividends from 2002 to 2003. This would imply an additional $5.8 billion in consumption, for a total effect of $14.1 billion. Using the authors' high-end estimate of the MPC would raise that estimate to $23.8 billion. If the cut were credited with the increase in dividends over two years, these effects would be roughly doubled. Although these numbers do not look large relative to total consumption expenditure in 2003 of $7.7 trillion, the authors observe that they are not small relative to the $66 billion standard deviation of consumption increases over the previous five years.

In conclusion, the authors observe that their findings that the composition of financial returns is of first-order importance in explaining consumption has implications for a range of questions in corporate finance, macroeconomics, behavioral economics, and tax policy. They stress that the interesting result is not that the propensity to consume capital gains is low, but that the propensity to consume dividends is so high. And they suggest that this difference may, at least in part, reflect mental accounting processes of the sort summed up in the adage "consume income, not principal."

HISTORICALLY, INCREASES IN short-term interest rates in periods of monetary tightening have been accompanied by increases in longer-term yields. Yet between June 2004 and February 2005, a period in which the Federal Open Market Committee raised the federal funds rate by 150 basis points, the ten-year yield on government bonds *fell* 70 basis points and the ten-year forward rate by more than 100 basis points. Described at the time as a conundrum by then–Federal Reserve Chairman Alan Greenspan in testimony before Congress, this pattern of interest rates perplexed many economists and financial analysts. By June 2005 the ten-year forward rate had fallen a total of 170 basis points, despite further Federal Reserve tightening. Since then the forward rate has rebounded, but by only about 50 basis points. Observers have offered a range of possible reasons for this puzzling behavior, invoking changes in expectations of long-term growth of output or inflation, global increases in saving, declines in macroeconomic and financial uncertainty, better allocation of risk, and developments that change the demand for or the supply of long-term fixed-income securities. In a report that concludes this issue, David Backus and Jonathan Wright discuss the empirical basis for such explanations and the findings of bond pricing models that decompose forward rates into term premiums and expected future short-term rates. Versions of these models that distinguish between the real and the inflation components of interest rates find that declining term premiums, rather than changes in expected real rates or inflation, appear to be the major element in the surprising behavior of long-term rates. This leads the authors to explore the possible influence of various changes in the macroeconomic environment on the term premium itself.

Backus and Wright begin by presenting some basic facts about the conundrum and the behavior of variables often cited as central to the determination of the yield curve. The conundrum is real. They show that during the three preceding episodes of monetary tightening, starting in 1986, 1994, and 1999, the ten-year yield on U.S. Treasurys increased sharply, in stark contrast with the modest decline in long-term yields in the recent episode. Long-term yields are essentially an average of short-term rates and forward rates, and the authors show that the modest decline in long-term yields itself masks a sharp decline in forward rates, offset by the increase in short-term rates. Plotting monthly data on the ten-year Treasury forward rate against the unemployment rate from January 1985 to February 2007, they show that although forward rates in the recent recovery show the same countercyclical behavior as in earlier recoveries, the level is 1½ to 2 percentage points lower than past cyclical patterns would predict.

A change in inflation expectations, suggested by some as the explanation for the drop in long-term rates, should show up in the behavior of nominal, but not real, forward rates. Using the rate on Treasury inflation-protected securities (TIPS) as a measure of real rates, the authors show that the shifts between June 2004 and June 2005 in the nominal and real forward rate curves were similar, although the shift in the nominal curve was greater. At a ten-year horizon, the nominal curve dropped by 172 basis points, whereas the real curve dropped by 96 basis points. In interpreting this difference, the authors note that the TIPS rate includes an inflation risk premium and a TIPS liquidity premium as well as an indication of expected inflation.

Are these shifts consistent with forecasts of inflation, GDP growth, and short-term interest rates in 2004–05? The authors report that the professional forecasts in the Blue Chip surveys for this period show little movement in expected inflation or GDP growth at a five- to ten-year horizon. The long-range forecast of the three-month Treasury bill rate was also flat. They conclude that the recent decline in long-term yields does not come from expected declines in any of these three variables.

Indicators of shifts in investors' perception and pricing of risk are more promising candidates. The authors report that, between 2004 and early 2005, there were sharp declines in the spread between Baa- and Aaa-rated corporate debt and in the implied volatility of one-year interest rate caps, a measure of short-term volatility in the six-month London interbank offer rate. Realized volatility, measured by the standard deviation of daily changes in forward rates and an index tied to the short-term volatility of S&P stock index options, also declined during the period. The authors find this persuasive evidence that financial market risk and risk premiums across a range of assets were substantially lower in 2005 than they had been two or three years earlier.

The source of the decline in asset market volatility is less clear. The authors regard macroeconomic uncertainty, particularly at long horizons, as inherently difficult to measure. Although recent Federal Reserve communications may have given markets more forward-looking guidance, which may have made the path of monetary policy more predictable, the broader impact on asset market volatility is less evident. Taking the view that the dispersion of long-horizon predictions may reflect intrinsic uncertainty, the authors show that the dispersions of predictions of consumer price inflation, real GDP growth, and the three-month Treasury bill rate have all trended noticeably lower. Most of the decline in the dispersion of interest rate and inflation expectations occurred in the early 1990s; both then rose in the last recession before declining again over the conundrum period. The authors note that movements in forward rates for the United States, Germany, and the United Kingdom have been highly correlated in the last few years, and rates have declined in a number of middle-income countries as well. So explanations for the decline in U.S. forward rates should not be confined to U.S. developments and should account for the decline that has occurred more broadly.

Backus and Wright turn from this evidence—that lower risk or term premiums, rather than declines in expected inflation or future short-term real rates, are responsible for the decline in long-term yields and forward rates—to the results of more formal affine bond pricing models, all of which decompose long-term forward rates into expected future short-term rates and a time-varying term premium. Such models all generate yields and forward rates that are linear functions of a vector of state variables, which themselves follow a linear autoregressive process. The models differ in their choice of explanatory variables. The simplest use a small number of "latent" factors characterizing the level and shape of the current yield curve as state variables, but more recent versions add direct information about the dynamics of interest rates or other economic variables.

The authors present results for three such augmented versions. The first uses professional forecasts of Treasury bill rates to identify the expected short-term rate component of the forward rate. This decomposition suggests that nearly the entire decline in ten-year-ahead forward rates from June 2004 to June 2005 comes from a decline in the term premium. Since then the term premium has been roughly constant, with a small rise in the forward rate attributed to a comparable rise in expected future short-term rates. A second version adds the dynamics of inflation to the model, making it possible to price synthetic real bonds and decompose a nominal forward rate into an expected future real short-term rate, expected future inflation, a real term premium, and an inflation risk premium. The third version distinguishes the same four components of forward rates but makes direct use of the information in TIPS yields, which are assumed to equal the sum of yields on a synthetic liquid real bond and a TIPS liquidity premium. This model's estimates of the ten-year forward rate suggest that the real term premium has fallen sharply since June 2004, and the inflation risk premium by a lesser amount. On the other hand, expected future real short-term interest rates have been flat, and expected future inflation has actually risen modestly.

A shortcoming of affine term structure models is the lack of an economic explanation of movements in the latent factors that serve as state variables.

The authors explore the possibility of the role of cyclical movements and inflation uncertainty by regressing the nominal term premiums estimated from the first model just described on unemployment and the dispersion of long-term inflation forecasts. They find that the coefficients in this regression are statistically significant, and the variables explain a substantial fraction of the decline in term premiums since 1990, their rise in 2000–02, and a modest portion of their decline since June 2004.

The authors view the combination of facts about risk spreads and volatilities, survey expectations, and affine model decompositions as persuasive evidence that a decline in term premiums, rather than a decline in future expected rates, is likely to be the principal explanation for the decline in long-horizon forward rates from June 2004 to June 2005. They recognize that the models do not provide conclusive answers. However, they stress that, within this framework, the arithmetic identity that the forward rate is the sum of these two components carries a strong implication. If term premiums did not decline, then the long-run expectation of the federal funds rate must have fallen by about 1.7 percentage points. They note that economic forces—for example, an increase in global saving or a scaling back of expectations about long-run productivity growth amid weak business investment—could have worked to lower the expected real short-term rate. But they doubt that such factors caused the large decline actually observed, given the robust growth during the period and the upward drift in inflation. The same arithmetic implies that if the term premium today equals its 2-percentage-point average over the last twenty years, then the current forward rate of about 5 percent implies an expected federal funds rate ten years hence of close to 3 percent.

What factors could explain the decline in uncertainty about future inflation, interest rates, and growth that Backus and Wright have identified as a partial explanation of the decline in term premiums? Those they identify include more credible and transparent monetary policy, a global trend toward central bank independence, and the greater integration of financial markets, which reduces the potential for short-term gains from adopting a more inflationary policy. As evidence supporting this view, they cite the especially sharp decline in forward rates in the United Kingdom around 1997, when the Bank of England was granted operational independence. But as contrary evidence they note that one would have to explain why it was only in the last few years, long after the disinflation engineered by the Federal Reserve under Chairman Paul Volcker in the early 1980s, that U.S.

investors have suddenly become confident that inflation will remain contained indefinitely. Still, the authors place reduced inflation uncertainty resulting from changes in central bank policy high on the list of plausible explanations.

Backus and Wright cite three other proposed explanations for the decline in term premiums in particular countries, but they note that these have more difficulty explaining the pattern across countries. The decline in real long-term rates in the United Kingdom could reflect the prospect that U.K. corporate pension reform will encourage pension funds to better match the durations of their assets and liabilities, causing a substantial increase in the demand for long-duration securities. But this explanation does not fit the United States, where pension reform has proceeded more slowly. The large purchase of U.S. Treasury securities by Asian central banks might have contributed to the fall in the U.S. forward premium but does not explain the parallel falls in Germany and the United Kingdom, unless the bonds of all three countries are close substitutes. Last, the authors discuss the suggestion that changing demographics may have contributed, as large cohorts nearing retirement shift their savings from risky equities to bonds and other relatively safe assets. Setting aside the question of whether the equity premium has increased coincidently with a decline in the term premium, the authors note that demographics are slow moving and predictable, with no substantial or unexpected shift having occurred in or around June 2004.

The authors conclude that the evidence points to a declining term premium as the primary source of the recent fall in long-term rates, and that such a decline is broadly consistent with observed changes in risk spreads and other measures of uncertainty. But they recognize that the economics profession is far from having a complete understanding of the behavior of bond prices. In their view the next step should be the development of models in which macroeconomic policy and behavior can be tied more directly to the behavior of interest rates. They believe that recent lines of research give hope that eventually economists will better understand the connections between macroeconomic developments and financial market outcomes.

OLIVIER JEANNE
International Monetary Fund

International Reserves in Emerging Market Countries: Too Much of a Good Thing?

WITH INTERNATIONAL reserves four times as large, in terms of their GDP, as in the early 1990s, emerging market countries seem more protected than ever against shocks to their current and capital accounts. Some have argued that this buildup in reserves might be warranted as insurance against the increased volatility of capital flows associated with financial globalization.[1] Others view this development as the unintended consequence of large current account surpluses and suggest that the level of international reserves has become excessive in many of these countries.[2]

I thank Ioannis Tokatlidis for superb research assistance. I also thank my discussants, Joshua Aizenman and Lawrence Summers, as well as Eduardo Borensztein, Stijn Claessens, Fernando Goncalves, Pierre-Olivier Gourinchas, Nancy Marion, Jonathan Ostry, Brad Setser, and Shang-Jin Wei for comments on earlier drafts. This paper benefited from discussions with Romain Rancière (who also generously shared data) and Christian Mulder. The views expressed in this paper are those of the author and should not be attributed to the International Monetary Fund, its Executive Board, or its management.

1. See, for example, Aizenman and Marion (2003) and Stiglitz (2006). According to a survey of central bankers of developing and emerging market countries, the main reason for the recent buildup in reserves was to "secure protection from volatile capital flows" (Pringle and Carver, 2005). In the words of Stiglitz (2006, p. 248) "The East Asian countries that constitute the class of '97—the countries that learned the lessons of instability the hard way in the crises that began in that year: have boosted their reserves in part because they want to make sure that they won't need to borrow from the IMF again. Others, who saw their neighbors suffer, came to the same conclusion—it is imperative to have enough reserves to withstand the worst of the world's economic vicissitudes."

2. See, for example, Summers (2006).

Do emerging market countries hold too much international reserves, and are there better ways to use those funds?

Answering these questions requires a normative benchmark for the optimal level of reserves. I present in this paper a simple welfare-based model of the optimal level of reserves to deal with the risk of capital account crises or of "sudden stops" in capital flows. On the basis of this model, I derive some formulas for the optimal level of reserves and compare them with conventional rules of thumb, such as the Greenspan-Guidotti rule of full coverage of short-term debt. I then calibrate the model for emerging market countries and compare its predictions with the actual data.

One lesson from this exercise is that the optimal level of reserves is subject to considerable uncertainty, because it is sensitive to certain parameters that are difficult to measure. The model nevertheless produces ranges of plausible estimates against which the data can be compared. I find that it is not difficult for the model to explain a reserves-GDP ratio on the order of 10 percent for the typical emerging market country (close to the long-run historical average), and that even higher ratios can be justified if one assumes that reserves have a significant role in crisis prevention. The levels of reserves observed in many countries in the recent period, in particular in Latin America, are within the range of the model's predictions.

Ultimately, however, the insurance model fails to account for the recent pattern of reserves accumulation in emerging market countries. The reason is that most of the reserves accumulation has taken place in Asian emerging market countries, where the risk of a capital account crisis seems much too small to justify such levels of self-insurance. The insurance model can account for the reserves accumulation observed in the Asian emerging market countries only if one assumes that the expected cost of a capital account crisis is unrealistically large (more than 60 percent of GDP for one of the two major types of crisis examined).

The conclusion that most of the current buildup of reserves is not justified by precautionary reasons has some implications for reserves management. There is little reason for countries to invest these funds in the liquid but low-yielding foreign assets in which central banks tend to invest. Rather, reserves should be viewed as a component of domestic external wealth that is managed by the public sector on behalf of the domestic citizenry, taking full advantage of the portfolio diversification opportunities available abroad. Indeed, an increasing number of emerging market countries are transferring a fraction of their reserves to "sovereign wealth funds," mandated to invest in a more diversified way and at a longer horizon than central banks normally do. This is a trend that might take on considerable importance looking forward.

The last part of the paper discusses some policy challenges and opportunities implied by the buildup in emerging market countries' "sovereign wealth." I discuss, first, the impact of sovereign wealth diversification on global financial markets, and second, some ways in which this wealth could be used in collective international arrangements—to insure against future crises or to promote financial development.

The Buildup in International Reserves

The growth in the international reserves of emerging market countries is striking when compared with the contemporaneous trends in reserves in industrial countries (figure 1).[3] Whereas reserves in a group of industrial countries have remained stable below 5 percent of GDP, reserves in the emerging market countries have grown more than fourfold in terms of GDP since 1990. Much of this accumulation—more than half of the dollar amount—has taken place in Asia since the 1997–98 Asian crisis. China now has the largest stock of international reserves in the world, having overtaken Japan at the end of 2005, and it accounts for an important share of the buildup in emerging market reserves. However, China is not very different from the other Asian emerging market countries in terms of its ratio of reserves to GDP.

This development is an important dimension of what Lawrence Summers calls the "capital flows paradox" in the current world financial system,[4] namely, that capital is flowing upstream from developing and emerging market countries toward the industrialized world and principally the United States. The reserves accumulated in my sample of emerging

3. My sample of emerging market countries is based on JP Morgan's Emerging Markets Bond Index Global (EMBIG); my sample of industrial countries includes all countries that were members of the Organization for Economic Cooperation and Development in 1990. Appendix table A-1 lists the countries in both samples. Neither sample includes three large reserves holders in Asia: Hong Kong, Singapore, and Taiwan.

4. Summers (2006).

Figure 1. International Reserves in Emerging Market and Industrial Countries, 1980–2005ᵃ

Trillions of current dollars

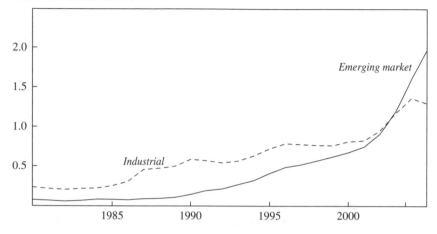

Percent of GDPᵇ

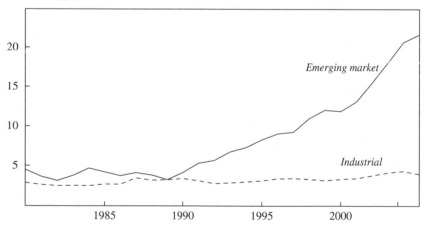

Sources: IMF, International Financial Statistics; World Bank, World Development Indicators.
a. Total reserves minus gold. Countries included in each group are listed in appendix table A-1.
b. Unweighted averages of reserves as a percent of GDP in the countries in each group.

Table 1. Reserves Accumulation and the Financial Account in Emerging Market Countries, 2000–05[a]

Percent

Item	All emerging market countries	Asia	Latin America
Net capital inflows as share of change in reserves	40.6	36.6	137.0
Composition of the increase in gross foreign assets			
Direct investment	8.8	5.6	20.9
Portfolio investment	8.7	8.7	13.0
Other investment	22.3	11.7	36.0
Reserve assets	60.2	73.9	30.0
Composition of the increase in gross foreign liabilities			
Direct investment	67.9	63.3	104.0
Portfolio investment	20.9	28.2	6.8
Other investment	11.2	8.5	−10.8

Source: IMF, Balance of Payments Statistics.

a. The data come from the standard presentation of the Balance of Payments Statistics. Net capital inflows are computed as the sum of the financial account over the period 2000–05. Reserve assets include foreign exchange reserves, monetary gold, special drawing rights, and the reserve position in the International Monetary Fund.

market countries between 2000 and 2005 are equal to a significant fraction (about 40 percent) of the U.S. current account deficit in the same period and may thus have contributed to keeping global interest rates low.

Table 1 provides some insights on whether the reserves buildup has tended to be financed by current account surpluses or through capital inflows. The first line of the table reports cumulative net capital inflows as a percent of the increase in reserves over 2000–05 for the sample of emerging market countries, with a breakdown for Asia and Latin America. About 40 percent of the reserves buildup has been financed by capital inflows on average. Whereas Asia has relied more than the average on net exports to accumulate reserves, Latin America has run current account deficits, so that its (relatively smaller) increase in reserves has had to be financed more than one for one by capital inflows.

Another way to look at reserves is in the broader context of the country's external balance sheet. The bottom two panels of table 1 show the composition of the increase in both external assets and external liabilities that were traded in the financial accounts of emerging market countries between 2000 and 2005. More than 60 percent of their foreign asset accumulation consisted of reserves (more than 70 percent in Asia). By contrast,

Figure 2. Composition of the Stock of Foreign Assets and Liabilities in Emerging Market and Industrial Countries, 2000–05 Averages

Percent of total

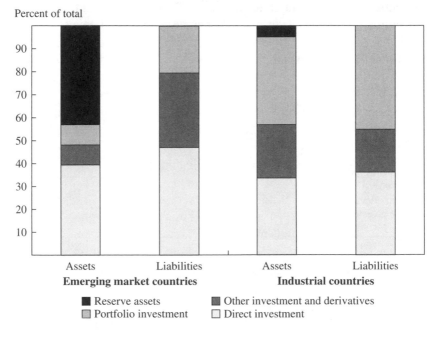

Sources: IMF, Balance of Payments Statistics.

foreign direct investment (FDI) accounted for almost 70 percent of the new liabilities accumulated by these countries.

That emerging market countries tend to have external assets that are more liquid than their external liabilities is confirmed by looking at stocks rather than flows. Figure 2 compares the external balance sheets of emerging market and industrial countries (taking the average over 2000–05), using the International Monetary Fund (IMF) data on international investment positions. The share of reserves in gross foreign assets is almost nine times as large in the emerging market countries as in the industrial countries, whereas the share of FDI in their liabilities is almost twice as large.

The level of reserves in emerging market countries has thus increased since the early 1990s, but so has their trade and financial integration—and with it the associated risks. How much of the increase in reserves can be explained as self-insurance in response to an increase in the hazards of globalization?

As numerous studies have pointed out, the recent accumulation of reserves by emerging market countries seems difficult to explain using the conventional rules of thumb for reserves adequacy. Figure 3 tracks three conventional reserves adequacy ratios in emerging market countries since 1980: the ratios of reserves to imports, to short-term external debt, and to broad money (M2).[5] Although imports and M2 have increased over time in these countries, international reserves have increased by much more. All three reserves adequacy ratios have increased markedly and are now much higher than any of the conventional rules of thumb would prescribe. In 2005 reserves in emerging market countries were close to seven months of imports and five times the level of short-term debt. That reserves deviate even more from the Greenspan-Guidotti rule than from the three-months-of-imports rule is surprising, since the former was developed to better capture the risks stemming from the capital account after the crises of the 1990s.

The reserves buildup is also difficult to explain using regression-based empirical models for precautionary reserves. A large empirical litera-ture explains the cross-country and time variation in reserves by a few key variables: economic size of the country, current and capital account vul-nerability, and exchange rate flexibility. Recent studies find that although such regressions do a good job of predicting reserve holdings over a long period, they significantly underpredict the reserves accumulation of emerg-ing market countries after the Asian crisis, especially in Asia.[6]

It could be, however, that such regressions fail to capture the impact that the severe capital account crises of the 1990s had on how these coun-tries perceived the risks associated with their international financial inte-gration. It has been argued that the Asian crisis marked a watershed, in that emerging market countries became painfully aware that even sound macroeconomic policies did not insulate them from contagion and sharp reversals in capital flows. The buildup in reserves could be a rational adaptation to this new, more volatile world.

---

5. The ratio of reserves to imports should equal 0.25 according to the three-months-of-imports rule. The ratio of reserves to short-term external debt should equal 1 according to the Greenspan-Guidotti rule, the idea being that reserves should allow a country to live without foreign borrowing for up to one year. A conventional range for the ratio of reserves to broad money is 5 to 20 percent. The rationale for this ratio is that broad money reflects a country's exposure to the withdrawal of assets (Calvo, 1996; De Beaufort-Wijnholds, Onno, and Kapteyn, 2001).

6. See IMF (2003), Aizenman and Marion (2003), and Aizenman, Lee, and Rhee (2004).

Figure 3. Reserves Adequacy Ratios in Emerging Market Countries, 1980–2005

Reserves to imports

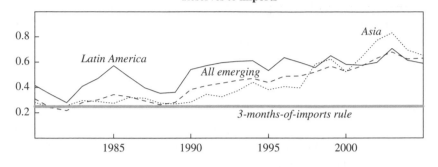

Reserves to short-term debt

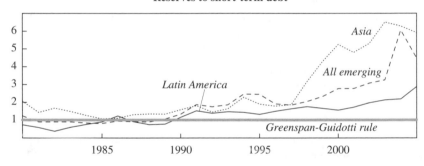

Reserves to M2[a]

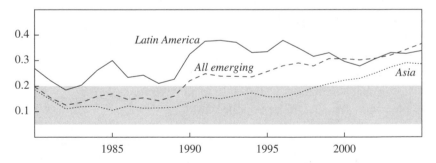

Sources: IMF, International Financial Statistics; World Bank, Global Development Finance.

Figure 4. Sudden Stops in Emerging Market Countries, 1980–2000ª

No. of episodes

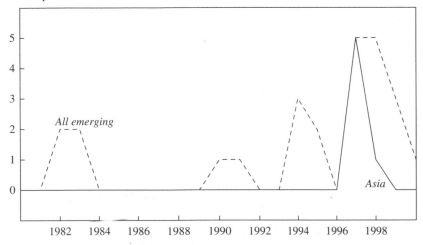

Sources: Frankel and Cavallo (2004); IMF, International Financial Statistics; World Bank, World Development Indicators.
a. Using the SS2 definition of a sudden stop. (See table A-2 in appendix A for crisis definitions.)

The concept that came to epitomize the capital account instability of the 1990s is that of a "sudden stop" in capital inflows. Figure 4 shows that although sudden stops were not a total novelty for emerging market countries as a whole, they were a relatively new phenomenon in Asia. For the five Asian countries most affected by the 1997–98 crisis, furthermore, the size of the shock to the capital account and the loss of reserves were unprecedented, in recent decades at least, as figure 5 shows. It may not be a coincidence, from this point of view, that most of the recent buildup in international reserves has taken place in Asia.

In sum, the recent buildup in emerging market countries' international reserves cannot be explained by conventional adequacy ratios or by simple linear regressions. But it may be that neither approach fully captures how the instability of the 1990s changed the perception of risks and the desire for insurance on the part of the countries most affected. For this reason, looking at the implications of a cost-benefit analysis of the optimal level of reserves might be more informative than historical regressions. This is the approach that I take in the rest of the paper.

Figure 5. Yearly Changes in Reserves Ratio in Five Asian Countries, 1980–2005[a]

Percent of GDP

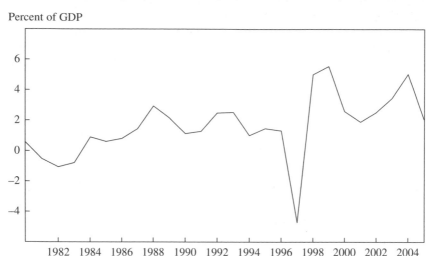

Sources: IMF, International Financial Statistics; World Bank, World Development Indicators.
a. Indonesia, Korea, Malaysia, Philippines, and Thailand. Data include crisis loans received from the IMF.

An Insurance Model of Optimal Reserves

I present in this section a simple framework for a cost-benefit analysis of the optimal level of reserves to deal with capital account crises. The model features a small, open economy that is subject to being hit by a capital account crisis. Reserves are useful both in terms of *crisis prevention* (reducing the probability of a crisis) and in terms of *crisis mitigation* (reducing the welfare cost of a crisis, once it has occurred). I start with a brief review of the literature on cost-benefit analyses of international reserves, before presenting the model.

Cost-Benefit Analyses of the Optimal Level of Reserves

The idea of a cost-benefit approach to the optimal level of reserves has inspired a long line of literature that goes back to a seminal contribution published by Robert Heller in 1966.[7] In Heller's analysis the optimal level

7. Heller (1966). The dynamic aspect of the authorities' optimization problem was treated more rigorously in the buffer stock models of international reserves of Hamada and Ueda (1977) and Frenkel and Jovanovic (1981).

of reserves was determined in the context of a trade-off between their opportunity cost and the risk of an external disequilibrium leading to a costly adjustment—a contraction in domestic absorption. Heller simply posited that the optimal level of reserves should minimize the sum of the expected cost of adjustment plus the opportunity cost of reserves.

One problem with traditional models of optimal reserves is that the objective function maximized by the authorities is only loosely related to domestic welfare. This leaves room for ambiguity in the definition and in the measurement of key variables of the model. First, it is not very clear how the cost of an external disequilibrium should be measured.[8] Second, the lack of a rigorous welfare criterion also leads to some ambiguity in the definition of the opportunity cost of reserves, as I will show later.

I will therefore rely on a model of the optimal level of reserves that is welfare-based but preserves some of the simplicity of the earlier literature. This section concludes with a brief summary of the main features of my analytical framework. After reading this summary, those primarily interested in my predictions on the optimal level of reserves can skip the remainder of this section, which presents the model in more detail, and proceed directly to the discussion of the numerical findings.

The model features a small, open economy that is vulnerable to crisis, defined as a loss of access to external credit associated with a fall in output. The economy is populated by a representative consumer who holds a certain amount of foreign assets.[9] This wealth can be invested in liquid international reserves or an illiquid asset. Reserves yield benefits in terms of crisis prevention and crisis mitigation but entail an opportunity cost relative to the more profitable illiquid investment. The optimal level of reserves will depend on the following parameters of the model:

L and ΔY, the size of the capital flight and of output loss in a crisis, respectively, expressed in terms of potential output;

---

8. Whereas Heller (1966) interpreted the adjustment cost as a transitory fall in domestic absorption, Ben Bassat and Gottlieb (1992) and Garcia and Soto (2004) define it as a fall in domestic output. The two are not equivalent for domestic welfare.

9. The representative-consumer assumption implies that one must look at the optimal level of reserves from the point of view of the country as a whole, without distinguishing between the private sector and the public sector. See, for example, Caballero and Krishnamurthy (2004) for a model of international reserves that includes a meaningful distinction between the private sector and the government.

δ, the opportunity cost of accumulating reserves;

σ, the relative risk aversion of the domestic consumer; and

π, the probability of a crisis (which is endogenous to the level of reserves if they have a role in crisis prevention).

Assumptions

The model assumes a small open economy and three periods of time $t = 0, 1, 2$. The last period (period 2) represents the long term. The intermediate period (period 1) is the time during which a crisis could occur. During the initial period (period 0) the country adjusts its reserves to the risk of a crisis in period 1. This simple time structure makes it possible to preserve the simplicity of Heller's original approach but does not preclude a more dynamic interpretation of the model, as I will show shortly.[10]

At the end of period 0, a representative consumer in the small open economy structures his or her external assets and liabilities to deal with the risk of a crisis in period 1. To keep the problem simple, I assume that the consumer allocates wealth net of foreign liabilities, W_0, between two assets: liquid bonds (or reserves, R_0) and an illiquid asset I. This asset can be defined as a negative variable, in which case the consumer issues a long-term external liability $D = -I$. The welfare of the representative consumer is given by

$$(1) \qquad\qquad U_t = E_t \left[u(C_1) + \frac{W_2}{1+r} \right],$$

where $u(\cdot)$ is an increasing and concave function of consumption, and W_2 is the consumer's net foreign wealth at the beginning of period 2. Foreign wealth can be traded between periods at interest rate r. The consumer thus desires a level of consumption C^* in period 1 that satisfies the first-order condition,

$$(2) \qquad\qquad u'(C^*) = 1.$$

10. Aizenman and Marion (2003) and Miller and Zhang (2006) present two-period precautionary savings models of reserves. Caballero and Panageas (2005) and Durdu, Mendoza, and Terrones (2007) present more dynamic precautionary savings models of international reserves. These models do not yield closed-form solutions for the optimal level of reserves but can be solved numerically.

The reserves are more liquid than the asset in the sense that they are the only form of wealth that can be sold in period 1. The illiquid asset cannot be sold in period 1 but brings a higher return in the long run (period 2). The difference between the return on the illiquid asset and the return on reserves is the opportunity cost of reserves, the price that the consumer must pay in order to keep wealth in liquid form.

The sequence of events and actions is as follows:

Period 0. The consumer allocates wealth net of foreign liabilities between reserves and the illiquid asset,

(3) $$W_0 = R_0 + I.$$

Period 1. An external liability L comes due. The consumer repays L and consumes C_1 under the budget constraint,

(4) $$Y_1 + L' + R = C_1 + L + R'.$$

where Y_1 is domestic output, L' is new debt issued in period 1, $R = (1 + r)R_0$ is the stock of reserves at the beginning of the period, and R' is the stock of reserves at the end of the period.

Period 2. The consumer's net foreign wealth is equal to output in period 2 plus the net return on net foreign assets,

(5) $$W_2 = Y_2 + (1 + r)^2 (1 + \delta)I + (1 + r)(R' - L'),$$

where r is the interest rate on reserves and external liabilities between periods, and δ is the excess return on the illiquid asset (or "illiquidity premium").

In period 1 the economy can be in either of two states that differ by the level of output and the consumer's access to external credit:
  —*the no-crisis state:* output is at its potential, $Y_1 = Y$, and the representative consumer has complete access to external credit (there is no restriction on L'), or
  —*the crisis state:* output is below potential, $Y_1 = Y - \Delta Y$, and the representative consumer has no access to external credit in period 1 (L' is equal to zero).

The crisis state thus consists of both an output drop and a sudden stop in capital flows. As equation 4 shows, the negative impact of the fall in output and capital inflows on domestic consumption can be mitigated by running down reserves ($R' = 0$).[11] I shall assume, as a matter of normalization, that $Y = 1$, so that the output cost of a crisis ΔY and the size of the sudden stop L are expressed in terms of potential output. I also assume that the desired level of consumption is equal to potential output ($C^* = Y$) so that there is no predictable trade deficit in period 1.

The ex ante probability of a crisis is denoted by π. To capture the idea that reserves might provide a benefit in terms of prevention, I assume that the probability of crisis is a decreasing function of the ratio of reserves to short-term debt,

$$(6) \qquad\qquad \pi(R) = F\left(v - a\frac{R}{L}\right),$$

where $F(\cdot)$ is an increasing function, and v is a measure of vulnerability to a crisis, summarizing the fundamentals other than reserves. I will at times refer to the coefficient a as the prevention benefit parameter. In calibrating the model I will use a probit specification, implying that $F(\cdot)$ is the cumulative distribution of a normal function.

The interesting question is how the optimal level of reserves R depends on the relevant determinants: the country's vulnerability to a crisis, measured by v; the magnitude of the crisis, measured by the size of the shock to the capital account L and of the output loss ΔY, and the opportunity cost of reserves, δ.

The Optimal Level of Reserves

As shown in appendix B, the optimal level of reserves minimizes a loss function that equals the opportunity cost of reserves plus the expected welfare cost of a crisis:

$$(7) \qquad\qquad \text{Loss} = \delta R + \pi(R)f(R),$$

11. Note that the consumer always repays the short-term debt that is not rolled over; that is, default is ruled out by assumption as a way of smoothing domestic consumption.

Figure 6. Total Loss and the Optimal Level of Reserves

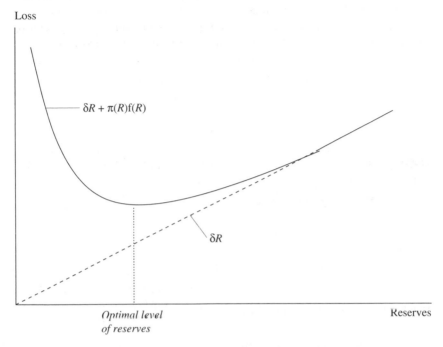

where $f(R)$, the welfare cost of a crisis, is increasing with the size of the crisis (L and ΔY) and decreasing with the level of reserves R.

Equation 7 is reminiscent of the loss function postulated in some earlier cost-benefit analyses of optimal reserves.[12] It captures in a simple way the trade-off between the opportunity cost of reserves δR and their benefits in terms of crisis prevention $\pi(R)$ and crisis mitigation $f(R)$. It can be interpreted, in a more dynamic context, as the average intertemporal loss of a country maintaining a constant level of reserves R. The consumer bears the opportunity cost δR in every period but pays the welfare cost of a crisis with a frequency $\pi(R)$. Equation 7 thus sums up the average cost of crises and the average cost of insuring against those crises. As shown in figure 6, for low levels of reserves the gains from increasing reserves, in

---

12. See, for example, Heller (1966), Ben Bassat and Gottlieb (1992), and Garcia and Soto (2004).

terms of crisis prevention and crisis mitigation, dominate the opportunity cost, whereas the opposite holds for high levels of reserves.

Closed-form expressions for the optimal level of reserves can be obtained if one assumes that reserves have no benefits in terms of prevention— that is, if π is exogenous. The first-order condition for the minimization of the loss function in equation 7 can then be written as

$$(8) \qquad u'\left[C^{*} - \left(\bar{R} - R\right)\right] = 1 + \frac{\delta}{\pi},$$

where $\bar{R} = L + \Delta Y$ is the "full insurance" level of reserves, that is, the minimum level sufficient to maintain consumption at the desired level in a crisis. This condition implies that the optimal level of reserves is increasing with the probability of a crisis and decreasing with the opportunity cost of holding reserves—as one would expect.

If the consumer has constant relative risk aversion σ, then the optimal level of reserves is given by the formula

$$(9) \qquad R = L + \Delta Y - \left[1 - \left(1 + \frac{\delta}{\pi}\right)^{-1/\sigma}\right].$$

In words, the optimal level of reserves is equal to short-term external debt plus the output cost of a crisis minus a term reflecting the opportunity cost of holding reserves.

Note that in this model the optimal level of reserves could be higher than under the Greenspan-Guidotti rule ($R = L$), because reserves smooth the impact on consumption of the fall in output, and not only the impact of the debt rollover crisis. The optimal level of reserves could also be lower than short-term debt because of the opportunity cost of holding reserves, which the Greenspan-Guidotti rule ignores.

The optimal level of reserves does not have a closed-form expression in the general case where the probability of a crisis is endogenous to the level of reserves. Then the optimal level of reserves minimizes

$$(10) \qquad \text{Loss} = \delta R + F\left(v - a\frac{R}{L}\right)f(R).$$

Taking into account the benefits of crisis prevention leads to an increase in the optimal level of reserves, other things equal. In fact—and this is an important difference from the case where the probability of a crisis is exogenous—the optimal level of reserves may now exceed the "full insurance" level $\bar{R} = L + \Delta Y$. Crisis prevention could make it optimal for a country to hold more reserves than it is willing to spend in a crisis.

The Benefits of International Reserves

I now turn to the calibration of the model, starting with the benefits of reserves. In my model reserves yield benefits in terms of crisis prevention $\pi(R)$ and crisis mitigation $f(R)$. To calibrate the model I thus try to identify each type of benefit in the data.[13]

Crisis Prevention

The international financial crises of the 1990s triggered a search for reserves adequacy ratios that would capture the vulnerability of emerging market countries' balance sheets and capital accounts in a world with highly mobile capital flows. The staff of the International Monetary Fund concluded that the ratio of reserves to short term external debt was the "single most important indicator of reserves adequacy in countries with significant but uncertain access to capital markets,"[14] although this ratio should be taken as only a starting point for an analysis that should also look at other reserves adequacy ratios in light of each country's specific conditions.[15]

This view was supported by a vast body of empirical research showing that the ratio of reserves to short-term external debt tended to perform well as an early indicator of *currency crises*. By contrast, the (relatively

13. In line with the model, my discussion will focus on crisis management and will not deal with some benefits that reserves may have in noncrisis times, such as limiting exchange rate volatility (Hviding, Nowak, and Ricci, 2004) or providing liquidity to the foreign exchange market. Reserves can also yield benefits if the government is able to invest them more wisely than the average citizen, or if they promote capital market integration and domestic financial development.

14. IMF (2000, p. 6).

15. Those conclusions were presented in two documents: "Debt- and Reserve-Related Indicators of External Vulnerability" (IMF, 2000) and "Issues in Reserves Adequacy and Management" (IMF, 2001). One study that contributed to crystallizing the official sector's conventional wisdom about the importance of this ratio was Bussière and Mulder (1999). See also Mulder (2000).

smaller) empirical literature on *sudden stops* in capital flows has been less conclusive, generally failing to detect a significant preventive role for reserves.[16]

In order to take a broad view of the preventive role of reserves with respect to both currency crises and sudden stops, I ran a number of univariate probit regressions using various crisis definitions and reserves adequacy ratios. The regression results are based on four different definitions of a currency crisis (denoted by CC1 to CC4) and four different definitions of a sudden stop (denoted by SS1 to SS4). Appendix table A-2 gives these definitions, and table A-3 lists the years when each type of crisis occurred in each country. For the first of the currency crisis definitions (CC1), I use Frankel and Rose's criterion of a nominal depreciation of the currency of at least 25 percent relative to the previous year that is also at least a 10-percentage-point increase in the rate of depreciation.[17] The other three definitions (CC2 to CC4) are based on a crisis pressure index that adds the percentage nominal depreciation of the currency to the percentage loss in foreign reserves.[18]

I first identify sudden stops as those years in which net capital inflows fell by more than 5 percent of GDP (SS1). This simple criterion has been criticized for various reasons, in particular because it captures some episodes in which capital net inflows slowed down but remained positive (such as Malaysia in 1994, following the imposition of controls on capital inflows). For robustness, I also consider three sudden stop measures that are more stringent (SS2 to SS4).[19]

---

16. The literature on early warning signals and the empirical determinants of crisis in probit/logit regressions is too large to be reviewed here—the reader is referred to the reviews by Kaminsky, Lizondo, and Reinhart (1998), Berg, Borensztein, and Pattillo (2005), and Frankel and Wei (2005). Another way in which reserves might stabilize the domestic economy is by lowering the interest rate on foreign debt (Levy Yeyati, 2006). Evidence that larger reserves decrease the sovereign spread is provided in Hauner (2005), Duffie, Pedersen, and Singleton (2003), and Eichengreen and Mody (2000). By contrast with currency crises, Calvo, Izquierdo, and Mejía (2004) and Frankel and Cavallo (2004) did not find that reserves had a statistically significant effect of reducing the probability of sudden stops.

17. Frankel and Rose (1996).

18. Frankel and Wei (2005).

19. The precise definitions are given in table A-2 in appendix A. The crisis dates for SS2 to SS4 are taken from Frankel and Cavallo (2004), who apply the criteria of Calvo, Izquierdo, and Mejía (2004) to a larger sample of countries and a longer time period.

Table 2. Regressions of Crisis Variables on Alternative Measures of Reserves, 1980–2000

No. of regressions achieving statistical significance[a]

Measure of reserves adequacy	Dependent variable (type of crisis)	
	Currency crisis	*Sudden stop*
Ratio of reserves to imports	9	1
Ratio of reserves to short-term debt (World Bank measure)	16	0
Ratio of reserves to short-term debt (BIS measure)	4	1
Ratio of reserves to M2	0	4
Ratio of reserves to GDP	12	1

Source: Author's calculations.

a. For each pair of reserves adequacy measure and type of crisis, regressions were performed combining each of four crisis definitions with one of four fixed-effects specifications (no fixed effects, country fixed effects only, time fixed effects only, and both country and time fixed effects), for a total of sixteen regressions. Each cell of the table reports the number of regressions out of the sixteen in which the coefficient on the indicated reserves adequacy ratio was negative and significant at the 10 percent level or better.

Table 2 summarizes the results of 160 univariate regressions using various reserves adequacy ratios, crisis definitions, and probit specifications. For each crisis definition and reserves adequacy ratio, I ran four probit regressions of the crisis dummy variable on the lagged reserves ratio and a constant: without fixed effects, with country fixed effects, with time fixed effects, and with both country and time fixed effects. Since currency crises and sudden stops each have four different definitions, each cell in the table is based on sixteen probit regressions. The table reports the number of regressions in which the coefficient on reserves was both negative and significant at the 10 percent level or better.

Several facts stand out. First, the denominator of the reserves adequacy ratio that "works" best to predict a currency crisis is short-term debt.[20] The benefit of increasing reserves in terms of crisis prevention, furthermore, is economically significant. To illustrate, figure 7 shows how the probability of a crisis varies with the Greenspan-Guidotti ratio

20. More precisely, the measure of short-term debt that works best is that from the World Bank Global Development Finance database rather than that in the Bank for International Settlements (BIS) data. This result is surprising because the BIS data should be a better measure of the denominator in the Greenspan-Guidotti ratio (the BIS reports debt maturing in the following year, whereas the World Bank data are based on maturity at issuance). However, the BIS debt measure might be less significant because it is available for fewer of the countries in the regressions.

Figure 7. Reserves and Crisis Prevention[a]

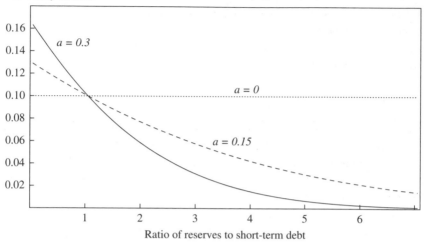

Sources: Author's calculations.
a. The variable *a* is the prevention benefit parameter, the coefficient on the Greenspan-Guidotti ratio in the crisis probability function (equation 6 in the text). It is assumed that the probability of crisis is 10 percent for $R = L$.

R/L for values of a in the range of estimation of the probit. As the figure shows, if $a = 0.3$, doubling the ratio of reserves to short-term debt from 1 to 2 reduces the probability of a crisis by almost 4 percentage points. However, there are diminishing returns to further increasing reserves: increasing R/L from 5 to 6 reduces the probability of crisis by less than 1 percent.

Second, the reserves adequacy ratios do not perform as well at predicting sudden stops as they do at predicting currency crises. The ratio that works best is that based on M2, but even this ratio is significant in only one-fourth of the regressions. This result also seems consistent with the empirical literature, which is ambiguous with regard to the benefits of reserves in preventing sudden stops rather than currency crises.

One important caveat is necessary before one accepts the conclusion that reserves help to prevent crises. The existing empirical studies do not really distinguish between two possibilities: whether high levels of reserves allow countries to *prevent* crises, or whether spending the reserves merely *postpones* the crises.[21] This identification problem does not affect the rationale for using reserves as an early warning indicator of crisis, but it may lead to an exaggeration of the benefits of reserves in terms of crisis prevention. In many cases, countries might actually have *hastened* the crisis, and not reduced its probability, by trying to maintain a high level of reserves in the face of a loss of confidence in domestic policies.

Crisis Mitigation

There are two ways in which reserves can help to mitigate the impact of a balance of payments crisis on domestic welfare. First, the reserves can be used to mitigate the fall in domestic output. Second, the reserves can be used to buffer the impact of the balance of payments shock on domestic absorption.

The authorities can reduce the output cost of a crisis by using international reserves through various channels. Foreign exchange interventions can mitigate the depreciation of the domestic currency, and thus the disruption induced by currency mismatches in balance sheets. Reserves help the monetary authorities in providing liquidity to the domestic financial markets, the banking sector, and even exporters; this is especially valuable if there is significant dollarization of bank deposits and other domestic liabilities.[22]

As for the second benefit, I present a simple accounting exercise that shows the extent to which international reserves help smooth domestic absorption in the face of balance of payments shocks. In a small, open

---

21. This ambiguity is certainly present in the theoretical literature on crises and reserves. In some models, a large volume of reserves effectively reduces the probability of crisis by making the economy more resilient to adverse shocks (Chang and Velasco, 2000; Aizenman and Lee, 2005) or to self-fulfilling changes in market sentiment (Morris and Shin, 1998). By contrast, in the Krugman-Flood-Garber framework, a speculative attack made unavoidable by excessive money growth is merely delayed by a larger stock of reserves (Krugman, 1979; Flood and Garber, 1984). In addition, countries often shorten the maturity of their debt before a crisis, further reducing the Greenspan-Guidotti ratio (Detragiache and Spilimbergo, 2001).

22. Jeanne and Wyplosz (2003) and Calvo (2006) emphasize that lending the reserves to domestic agents is a more effective tool than foreign exchange intervention in preventing and mitigating crises. Calvo (2006) points to an interesting example of a nonstandard way of disposing of international reserves: in August 2002 the central bank of Brazil employed some of its international reserves to make loans to the export sector through commercial banks.

economy, domestic absorption can be written as the sum of domestic output, capital inflows, and reserves decumulation (net income from abroad
is omitted because it typically varies little in a crisis):[23]

(11) $A_t = Y_t + KA_t - \Delta R_t.$

There is an exact correspondence between this decomposition and equation 4 of the model, which can be written

$$C_1 = Y_1 + \underbrace{(L' - L)}_{KA} - \underbrace{(R' - R)}_{\Delta R}.$$

Thus information about the behavior of the components of equation 11
can help in calibrating the model. I now look at how the components of
equation 11 behave in observed sudden stop episodes. Sudden stops will be
identified, in my sample of emerging market countries, as a year in which
net capital inflows fall by more than 5 percent of GDP (definition SS1).

Figure 8 shows the average behavior of domestic absorption and the
contribution of the various components on the right-hand side of equation
11 in a five-year event window centered around a sudden stop. Real output
is normalized to 100 in the year before the sudden stop. All the variables
are converted from current dollars into constant local currency units so that
the changes in output and domestic absorption can be tracked in volume
terms.[24]

A large fall in net capital inflows is observed in the year of the sudden
stop, amounting to almost 10 percent of the previous year's output on average. This is not surprising, since a large fall in those inflows is the criterion
used to identify sudden stops. More interestingly, most of the negative
impact of the capital account reversal on domestic absorption is offset

23. See Jeanne and Rancière (2006). This decomposition of domestic absorption results
from two national accounting identities. First, domestic absorption (the sum of domestic private and public consumption and investment) is the difference between real output and the
trade balance, $A_t = Y_t - TB_t$. Second, the balance of payments equation $CA_t = KA_t + \Delta R_t$, where
$CA_t = TB_t + IT_t$ is the current account balance (the sum of the trade balance and income and
transfer from abroad), can be used to substitute out the trade balance from the first identity.

24. The dollar value of output and domestic absorption falls by a larger amount than
indicated in figure 8 because of the real depreciation of the domestic currency. The variables are converted from current dollars to constant local currency units using the nominal
dollar exchange rate and the local GDP deflator. IMF loans are counted as a loss of reserves
rather than as capital inflows.

Figure 8. Domestic Absorption, Output, Net Capital Inflows, and Reserves in Sudden Stops[a]

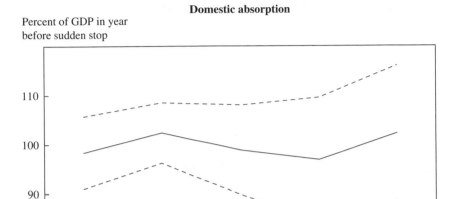

Domestic absorption

Percent of GDP in year
before sudden stop

Years before or after sudden stop

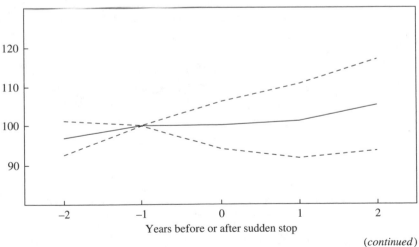

Domestic output

Years before or after sudden stop

(continued)

Figure 8. Domestic Absorption, Output, Net Capital Inflows, and Reserves in Sudden Stops[a] (*Continued*)

Net capital inflows

Percent of GDP in year
before sudden stop

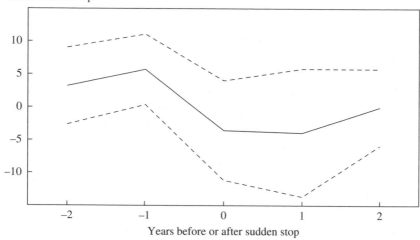

Years before or after sudden stop

Decrease in reserves

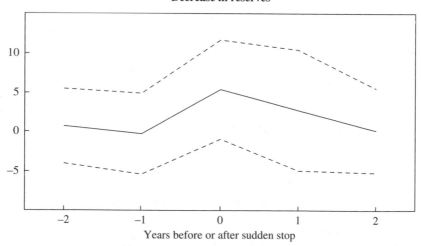

Years before or after sudden stop

Sources: Author's calculations using data from the IMF, International Financial Statistics, and the World Bank, World Development Indicators.

a. A sudden stop is defined as a fall in the financial account of more than 5 percent of GDP (SS1). Events that occurred before 1980 or within the five-year window of a previous sudden stop are excluded from the calculation. The solid line is the sample mean; dotted lines indicate the mean plus and minus one standard deviation.

by a fall in reserves accumulation. Thus domestic absorption falls by only 3 percent of GDP on average in the year of the sudden stop—much less than the capital inflows. Figure 8 also shows that the contribution of output to the decline in domestic absorption is relatively small: real growth merely falls to zero at the time of the sudden stop.

This evidence is consistent with the view that emerging market countries accumulate reserves in good times so as to be able to decumulate them, thereby smoothing domestic absorption, in response to sudden stops. This smoothing effect is potentially large. To illustrate, if reserves accumulation were equal to zero in the year of the sudden stop, domestic absorption would fall by 9 percent of output on average instead of 3 percent, other things equal. This counterfactual experiment should be interpreted with caution, because the magnitude of capital flight could in part be endogenous to the fall in reserves. It does suggest, however, that foreign exchange reserves may well make a sizable contribution to the smoothing of domestic absorption in response to sudden stops.

The case of Uruguay in 2002 provides a striking illustration of the role of reserves in a very severe sudden stop episode. Following the Argentine crisis, net capital inflows to Uruguay fell by 26 percentage points of precrisis GDP. The Uruguayan government used a large amount of foreign exchange reserves (a significant part of which was made available in the context of an IMF arrangement) to cover the withdrawal of dollar-denominated deposits from the domestic banking system. As a result, the decline in domestic absorption, although quite substantial (14 percent of GDP), was much smaller than the shock to the capital account.

The Costs of International Reserves

The cost of holding reserves is measured in the literature—as in the model—as the difference between the return on the reserves and the return on more profitable alternative investment opportunities.[25] One term of the

25. My discussion focuses on the opportunity cost of carrying the reserves and does not deal with the challenges to monetary and financial stability posed by large-scale sterilization (see Mohanty and Turner, 2006, and European Central Bank, 2006, for a discussion of those costs). Another cost that I do not discuss is the false sense of confidence that reserves may instill in foreign investors, allowing the domestic authorities to postpone necessary adjustments. Finally, large-scale purchases and sales of reserves could induce exchange rate changes that cause valuation losses on the reserves.

comparison, the return on the reserves, is generally proxied as the return on short-term foreign currency assets. The appropriate definition of alternative investment opportunities, on the other hand, raises several thorny questions.

One approach is to consider higher-yielding investment opportunities in the domestic business sector or in the building of public infrastructure. However, the marginal product of capital is difficult to measure in a way that is comparable across a large number of countries. Caselli and Feyrer's recent estimates can be used to compute an average annual real return to capital of 7.8 percent in seventeen emerging market countries in my sample.[26] This, together with an estimate for the short-term real interest rate of 2 percent a year—roughly the average U.S. real short-term rate over 1980–2005—would lead to an opportunity cost of around 6 percent a year.

Given the difficulties involved in measuring the returns to physical investment, most measures in the literature assume that the alternative to holding international reserves is to invest in other financial assets or to repay existing financial liabilities. One approach defines the opportunity cost of reserves as the quasi-fiscal cost of sterilization by the central bank, that is, the difference between the return on the central bank's domestic currency assets and the return on international reserves.[27] This differential is generally positive, but in countries where domestic interest rates are very low—such as China recently—this approach leads to a negative opportunity cost of reserves.

There are two serious issues with measuring the opportunity cost of reserves in this way. First, this measure is not adjusted for the expected appreciation or depreciation of the domestic currency. For example, the fiscal cost of reserves could be found to be negative because the domestic currency is expected to appreciate relative to the dollar—and interest rate parity applies—but this measure fails to take into account the expected valuation loss on the reserves. Second, the central bank's profit is not a measure of domestic welfare. Selling high-yielding domestic bonds for reserves may reduce the central bank's flow of profit but increases the income of the domestic investors who purchase the bonds. The opportu-

26. Caselli (2007) computes the return to capital using production functions calibrated as in the development accounting literature. They find that the return to capital is not higher in developing countries than in industrial countries once one adjusts for non-reproducible capital (land).

27. See, for example, Frenkel and Jovanovic (1981), Flood and Marion (2002), and Mohanty and Turner (2006).

Figure 9. Alternative Measures of the Opportunity Cost of Reserves, 2000–05[a]

Percent a year

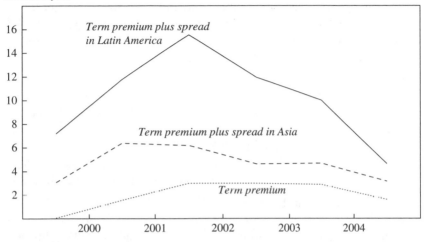

Sources: Author's calculations using data from Bloomberg and IMF, International Financial Statistics.

a. The term premium is the difference between the return on long-term dollar assets and liquid dollar assets. The spread is the difference between the interest rate on external debt and the return on reserves.

nity cost of reserves should therefore be measured by looking at the budget of the country as a whole rather than that of the central bank. This might be a reason to measure the opportunity cost of reserves by reference to *external*—rather than domestic—assets and liabilities.

Reserves can be accumulated by issuing—or can be used to repay— external debt. Given this observation, some authors measure the opportunity cost as the spread between the interest rate on external debt and the return on reserves.[28] By this measure the opportunity cost of reserves was 8.4 percent a year in emerging market countries on average in 2000–05, but this figure masks important disparities between Asia, where the spreads were low, and Latin America, where they were much higher (figure 9).

One might argue that these spreads overstate the true opportunity cost of holding reserves, because they include the default risk premium on foreign debt. As shown more formally in appendix B, the welfare-based

28. This measure was initially proposed by Edwards (1985). It is used by Garcia and Soto (2004) and Rodrik (2006).

Table 3. Average Annual Cost of Holding Reserves, 2000–05[a]
Percent of GDP

Assumption	All emerging markets	Asia	Latin America
Opportunity cost of reserves is 6 percent a year	0.93	1.29	0.65
Opportunity cost of reserves is the term premium (2 percent a year)	0.32	0.45	0.22
Opportunity cost of reserves is the term premium plus the spread on external debt	1.06	0.99	1.00

Source: Author's calculations using data from Bloomberg; World Bank, World Development Indicators; and International Monetary Fund, International Financial Statistics.

a. The sample includes all the emerging market countries listed in appendix table A-1, except Korea and India. Data are unweighted averages for the countries in each group. The term premium is the difference between the return on long-term dollar assets and liquid dollar assets. The spread is the difference between the interest rate on external debt and the return on reserves.

approach suggests that the default risk premium should not be included, because it is, on average, a fair reflection of the probability of less than full repayment. Pushed to its logical extreme, this approach suggests that the true opportunity cost of reserves is the U.S. term premium, that is, the opportunity cost of financing a stock of liquid dollar assets with default-free long-term dollar debt. This would lead to a much lower measure of the opportunity cost of reserves of at most 2.5 percent.[29]

Table 3 presents some measures of the average opportunity cost of reserves in terms of domestic GDP in my sample of emerging market countries over the period 2000–05. The measures are based on a uniform opportunity cost of 6 percent as well as the term premium, with and without a spread. With an opportunity cost of 6 percent a year, the average cost of reserves amounts to 1 percent of GDP.[30] The estimated cost of reserves is significantly lower if one considers the term premium, but larger if one includes the emerging market spread. On average, the total cost of holding reserves was substantially lower in Latin America than in Asia if one uses the same opportunity cost per unit of reserves for both regions, but it was relatively similar in the two regions when one uses the term premium plus the spread. This is explained by the fact that, whereas on average the

29. The differential between ten-year U.S. Treasury bonds and three-month U.S. Treasury bills was almost 2.5 percentage points on average over 2000–05. Expectation-adjusted measures lead to even lower estimates of less than 1 percentage point (Rudebusch, Sack, and Swanson, 2007).

30. This is consistent with the estimates obtained by Rodrik (2006) and Bird and Rajan (2003).

Table 4. Benchmark Calibration Parameters

Parameter	Baseline	Range
Size of sudden stop	$L = 0.1$	[0, 0.3]
Probability of sudden stop	$\pi = 0.1$	[0, 0.25]
Output loss	$\Delta Y = 0.1$	[0, 0.2]
Opportunity cost	$\delta = 0.03$	[0.01, 0.06]
Risk aversion	$\sigma = 2$	[1, 10]
Prevention benefit parameter	$a = 0$	[0, 0.3]

reserves-GDP ratio is more than twice as high for Asian countries as for Latin American countries, the sovereign spread is substantially higher in Latin America than in Asia.

Model Predictions

The model presented above is used here to predict the optimal level of reserves in emerging market countries. This is done in two steps. First, I calibrate the model by reference to an average emerging market country, as a way of getting a broad sense of the quantitative implications of the model and their sensitivity to the parameters chosen. Second, I calibrate the model by reference to country-specific data, to study how far the model can go in explaining the reserves buildup in emerging market countries.

Benchmark Calibration and Sensitivity Analysis

The benchmark calibration is based on the parameter values given in table 4. I assume that reserves provide no benefits in terms of prevention, so that the formula in equation 9 applies. The probability of crisis was set to the unconditional frequency of sudden stops (SS1) in my sample of emerging market countries, which is close to 10 percent a year. The value for the opportunity cost of reserves, $\delta = 3$ percent, is close to the middle of the range of estimates discussed earlier. The chosen values for risk aversion and its range of variation are standard in the growth and real business cycle literature.

Capital flight (L) and the output loss (ΔY) are both set to 10 percent of GDP. These figures are in line with the behavior of capital flows and of output during the sudden stops documented in figure 8.[31] The output cost figure was obtained by cumulating the average output gap in the year of a sudden stop and the following year, under the assumption that output would have grown at the same rate as before the crisis in the absence of a sudden stop. An output loss of 10 percent of GDP is in the ballpark of the estimates reported in the literature on currency crises and sudden stops.[32]

The benchmark calibration implies an optimal level of reserves of 7.7 percent of GDP, or 77 percent of short-term external debt. This is close to the ratio of reserves to GDP observed in the data on average over 1980–2000, but significantly below the level observed in the most recent period, especially in Asia. It would be interesting to know what changes in the parameters are required to increase the optimal level of reserves to something approaching the recently observed level.

Figure 10 shows the sensitivity of the optimal level of reserves to the probability of crisis, the opportunity cost of reserves, the degree of risk aversion, and the elasticity of the crisis probability to the level of reserves. In each case the level of reserves computed using the sudden stop model is contrasted with that implied by the Greenspan-Guidotti rule. Several interesting results emerge.

The optimal level of reserves is quite sensitive to the probability of crisis, the opportunity cost of reserves, and the risk aversion parameter. This offers an interesting contrast with the Greenspan-Guidotti rule, which does not depend at all on these parameters. The optimal level of reserves is zero if the probability of crisis falls below 5 percent, but it almost doubles, from 7.7 percent to 13.3 percent of GDP, if the probability of crisis increases from 10 percent to 20 percent. Risk aversion also has a first-order impact on the optimal level of reserves. A shift in the risk aversion

31. Using instead the ratio of short-term external debt to GDP would give similar values for *L*. For my sample this ratio is 8.2 percent on average over the period 1980–2000 according to the World Bank's Global Development Finance (GDF) data set, and 11.7 percent according to the BIS database.

32. Hutchison and Noy (2006) find that the cumulative output loss of a sudden stop is around 13 to 15 percent of GDP over a three-year period. Becker and Mauro (2006) find an expected output cost of 10.2 percent of GDP for currency crises and 16.5 percent of GDP for sudden stops. On one hand, the estimated output cost of a crisis can be significantly larger if the output gap is cumulated until output has returned to potential, which typically takes longer than two or three years. On the other hand, using the precrisis growth rate to estimate postcrisis potential output may exaggerate the size of the output gap if the crisis was preceded by an unsustainable economic boom.

Figure 10. Sensitivity of the Optimal Level of Reserves to Changes in Model Parameters[a]

Probability of a sudden stop

Reserves (percent of GDP)

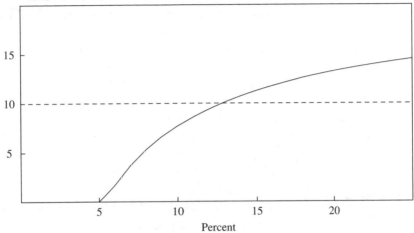

Percent

Opportunity cost of holding reserves

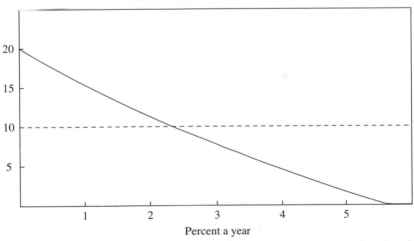

Percent a year

(continued)

Figure 10. Sensitivity of the Optimal Level of Reserves to Changes in Model Parameters[a] (*Continued*)

Risk aversion

Reserves (percent of GDP)

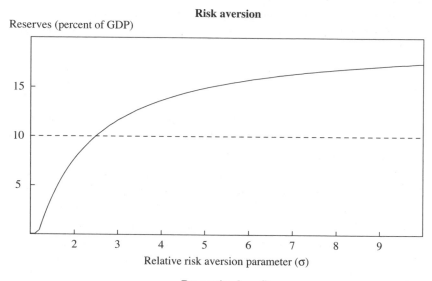

Relative risk aversion parameter (σ)

Prevention benefit

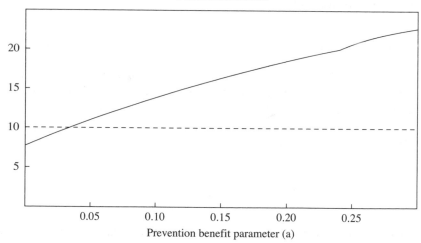

Prevention benefit parameter (a)

Sources: Author's calculations.

a. Dashed line indicates the optimal level of reserves using the Greenspan-Guidotti rule, assuming that short-term debt is 10 percent of GDP.

parameter from 2 to 8 increases the optimal level of reserves from 7.7 percent to 16.8 percent of GDP.

Figure 10 also shows that the optimal level of reserves can be significantly larger if one assumes that reserves have benefits in terms of crisis prevention (parameter a). If, in line with my univariate probit results for currency crises, a is set between 0.2 and 0.3, then the optimal level of reserves can reach 23 percent of GDP, about three times the optimal level if reserves have no effectiveness at crisis prevention.

To summarize, there are two ways in which the model can potentially explain a level of reserves of the order of magnitude currently observed in Asia. The first is to assume very large numbers for capital flight or for the output cost of a crisis. To illustrate, if the size of the sudden stop or the output cost amounted to 40 percent of GDP, instead of 10 percent in the benchmark calibration, the model would predict an optimal level of reserves in excess of 35 percent of GDP. Such an assumption, however, seems out of line with the historical record on currency crises and sudden stops. The second and perhaps more plausible way in which the model can predict a higher level of reserves is if reserves offer substantial benefits in terms of crisis prevention.

Country Estimates

I now bring the model closer to the data by estimating the optimal level of reserves for each emerging market country in my sample in 2000. For each country I estimate the level of reserves that minimizes the loss function in equation 10, that is, the sum of the opportunity cost of reserves and of the expected welfare cost of a crisis,

$$\text{Loss}_i = \delta R_i + F\left(v_i - a\frac{R_i}{L_i}\right) f(R_i),$$

where i is the country index. This loss function is calibrated based on a probit estimation of the crisis probability for each country. The model indicates excess or insufficient reserves, depending on how the optimal level of reserves, R_i^*, compares with the observed level, R_i.

The first step is to estimate the probability of a crisis for each country. This is done by running a probit regression of the probability of crisis on the countries' economic fundamentals in my sample of emerging market

Table 5. Probit Regressions of the Probability of Crisis on Macroeconomic Fundamentals, 1980–2000[a]

Type of crisis and independent variable	Regression specification			
	None	Country effects only	Year effects only	Country and year effects
Crisis is sudden stop SS1[b]				
Real exchange rate deviation from	−1.240***	−1.295**	−1.102**	−1.192**
Hodrick-Prescott trend[c]	(0.438)	(0.521)	(0.442)	(0.519)
GDP growth[c]	−2.047***	−2.028**	−2.511***	−2.856***
	(0.749)	(0.830)	(0.884)	(1.038)
Ratio of foreign liabilities to money[d]	0.025***	0.031**	0.028***	0.037***
	(0.008)	(0.014)	(0.008)	(0.014)
Ratio of current account to GDP[d]	−0.045**	−0.053***	−0.044**	−0.056***
	(0.019)	(0.019)	(0.021)	(0.021)
Ratio of total public debt to GDP[d]	0.544**	0.333	0.578**	0.324
	(0.220)	(0.415)	(0.234)	(0.464)
Constant	−1.712***	−1.834***	−2.276***	−1.724***
	(0.168)	(0.495)	(0.629)	(0.575)
No. of observations	511	394	511	394
Pseudo-R^2	0.12	0.16	0.14	0.19
Crisis is currency crisis CC1[b]				
Ratio of reserves to short-term debt[d]	−0.162**	−0.261**	−0.130**	−0.201*
	(0.065)	(0.104)	(0.064)	(0.108)
Real exchange rate deviation from	−1.441***	−1.332***	−1.598***	−1.547***
Hodrick-Prescott trend[c]	(0.463)	(0.496)	(0.504)	(0.528)
Consumer price inflation[d]	0.331**	0.134	0.392***	0.161
	(0.134)	(0.210)	(0.141)	(0.231)
Constant	−1.148***	−0.571*	−2.109***	−1.019*
	(0.111)	(0.324)	(0.404)	(0.585)
No. of observations	560	483	560	483
Pseudo-R^2	0.07	0.12	0.13	0.18

Source: Author's regressions.
a. Numbers in parentheses are robust standard errors. Asterisks indicate statistical significance at the ***1 percent, **5 percent, and *10 percent level.
b. Sudden stops and currency crises are defined in appendix table A-2.
c. Average of one-year and two-year lags.
d. One-year lag.

countries over 1980–2000. The preferred specifications are reported in the top panel of table 5 for sudden stops (defined as SS1) and in the bottom panel for currency crises (CC1). The explanatory variables have been selected using a general-to-specific approach, starting from a set of eighteen potential regressors, which are listed in table A-4 in appendix A. All explanatory variables are lagged at least one year and are thus predetermined with respect to the crisis. The results are robust to the inclusion of time and country fixed effects.

I find that the main explanatory variable is the real exchange rate (or, more precisely, its deviation from a trend), which appears with the expected sign in both sets of probit regressions. Consistent with the univariate evidence presented earlier, the ratio of reserves to short-term debt is significant for currency crises but not for sudden stops. The GDP growth rate, the ratio of foreign liabilities to money (a measure of dollarization in the banking sector), the current account, and total public debt are also significant in the regressions for sudden stops. Finally, the probit estimation for currency crises finds a role for inflation.

Figure 11 tracks the estimated probability of crisis over time in my sample of emerging market countries (the averages are GDP-weighted and based on the regressions without fixed effects). The probability of crisis is significantly lower in Asia than in the other emerging market countries, especially at the end of the 1990s because of the weak real exchange rates, large current account surpluses, and strong economic growth that prevailed in that region. To illustrate, the probability of a sudden stop is estimated at 2.7 percent in China in 2000, and that of a currency crisis is less than 0.2 percent.

In the second step, I compute the optimal level of reserves R_i^* for each country in 2000. Parameter v_i, which captures the country's intrinsic vulnerability to a crisis, is calibrated using the probit regression for sudden stops reported in table 5. Capital flight, the output cost of the crisis, and the values for the opportunity cost of reserves and for the risk aversion parameter remain the same as in the benchmark calibration (table 4).

The results of this exercise are reported in table 6. At $234 billion, the total predicted level of reserves for all countries in the sample is significantly below the actual level observed in 2000 (just over $650 billion). However, the discrepancy comes mainly from the Asian countries, where the predicted level of reserves is extremely low. The estimated optimal level of reserves is zero in several important Asian countries (China, Korea, and Malaysia), because the probability of a sudden stop was below the 5 percent threshold (see figure 10). By contrast, the model works well for Latin America, where the observed level of reserves is actually slightly below the model prediction.

The last two columns of table 6 give the "implied" values for the risk aversion parameter σ and the expected output loss in a crisis ΔY, that is,

Figure 11. Probabilities of Currency Crises and Sudden Stops, 1980–2000[a]

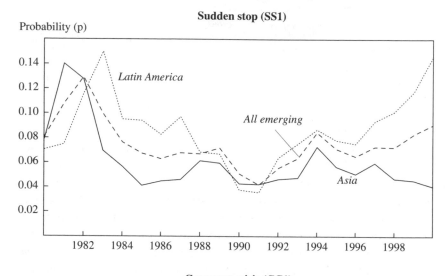

Sudden stop (SS1)

Probability (p)

Latin America

All emerging

Asia

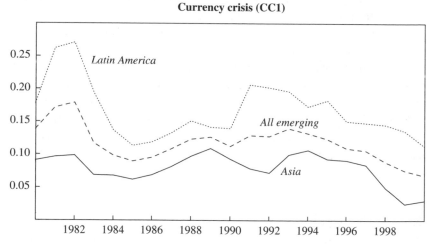

Currency crisis (CC1)

Latin America

All emerging

Asia

Sources: Author's calculations based on model described in text.
a. Results are GDP-weighted country averages. Excludes Russia and Ukraine.

Table 6. Actual and Model-Predicted Levels of Reserves

Country group	Actual, 2000 (billions of dollars)	Predicted benchmark[a] (billions of dollars)	Implied risk aversion (σ)	Implied output cost of a crisis (ΔY, percent of GDP)
All emerging market countries	651	234	5.2	20.8
Asia	406	24	11.7	30.6
Latin America	145	153	1.9	9.6

Source: Author's calculations.
a. Level that minimizes the loss function in equation 10, calibrated using the probit estimation for sudden stops (SS1) reported in table 5. Excludes Russia and Ukraine.

the values that one must assign to these parameters for the model to explain the observed level of reserves. In Latin America the implied values are very close to those in the benchmark calibration (reflecting the fact that the model fits the observations well in that region). By contrast, in Asia the implied values are implausibly high—almost 12 for risk aversion and more than 30 percent of GDP for the output cost of a crisis.

The results in table 6 assume that reserves have no benefits in terms of crisis prevention. As mentioned before, the optimal level of reserves may be significantly higher if reserves have preventive benefits. Might this explain the reserves buildup in Asia? I look into this question by estimating the benefits of the reserves accumulation between 2000 and 2005 in terms of crisis prevention. For simplicity, I assume that the welfare cost of a crisis is equal to the output cost. Then increasing the level of reserves from R to R' is optimal if

$$\left[\pi(R') - \pi(R)\right]\Delta Y \geq \delta(R' - R),$$

that is, if the decrease in the expected output cost of a crisis exceeds the opportunity cost of increasing reserves. To calibrate this condition, I compute for each country in my sample the decrease in the crisis probability induced by the reserves accumulation observed between 2000 and 2005, $\Delta\pi = \pi_{i2000} - \pi_{i2005}$. The probabilities are estimated using the probit regression for currency crises reported in the bottom panel of table 5. The benefits and costs of the observed reserve accumulation are computed under the assumption that a crisis costs 10 percent of potential output and that the opportunity cost of reserves is 3 percent.

Table 7. Benefit and Cost of Reserves Accumulation, 2000–05[a]

Item	All emerging markets	Asia	Latin America
Change in ratio of reserves to GDP (percentage points)	8.7	13.8	2.8
Reduction in crisis probability (percentage points)[b]	2.2	1.7	2.6
Benefit of reserves accumulation (percent of 2000 GDP)[c]	0.22	0.17	0.26
Cost of reserves accumulation (percent of 2000 GDP)[d]	0.63	1.04	0.14
Implied expected output cost of crisis (percent of GDP)[e]	28.5	62.7	5.5

Source: Author's calculations using IFS and WDI data.

a. The sample is composed of the emerging market countries listed in appendix table A-1 minus Morocco, Russia, and Ukraine. All results are country averages weighted by 2000 GDP.

b. Estimated from the probit regression for currency crises (CC1) reported in table 5.

c. Equals the reduction in crisis probability times the output cost of a crisis (10 percent of 2000 GDP).

d. Equals the increase in reserves times the opportunity cost of reserves (3 percent).

e. Output cost that equalizes the benefit of reserves accumulation and the cost of reserves accumulation.

Table 7 reports the results of this exercise for emerging market countries as a whole as well as for Asia and Latin America separately (country averages weighted by GDP). It appears that, on average, the cost of reserves accumulation exceeded the benefits in terms of crisis prevention by a factor of about 3. But again the average masks an important difference between Asia, where the cost was more than five times larger than the benefit, and Latin America, where the benefit of reserves accumulation in terms of crisis prevention actually exceeded the cost.

The reason for this difference is that the probability of a currency crisis was much lower in Asia than in Latin America in 2000 (see figure 11), implying that the marginal returns to reserves accumulation in terms of crisis prevention were much higher in Latin America than in Asia. To illustrate, in 2000 Mexico could have reduced its estimated crisis probability from 9.6 percent to 5.6 percent by doubling its reserves. By contrast, in China the estimated probability of crisis was 0.2 percent in 2000 and so could not have been reduced much further. It is nevertheless in emerging market Asia that most of the recent reserves accumulation has taken place.

Finally, the last line of table 7 reports the "implied" output loss for each country, that is, the minimum output cost that one must assume for the observed accumulation of reserves between 2000 and 2005 to be worth the cost. To rationalize the reserves buildup in Asian emerging market countries, one needs to assume that the output cost of a crisis amounts to more than 60 percent of GDP; the implied output cost is less than one-tenth that size in Latin America.

The conclusion is that the model cannot reasonably account for the increase in reserves in Asian emerging market countries as self-insurance against capital account crises. It can only do so by assuming that a capital account crisis costs more than 60 percent of one year's output, which is out of line with the historical experience.[33]

Discussion

To summarize, one justification for emerging market countries holding liquid international reserves is as a means of dealing with capital flow volatility and the risk of capital account crisis, but the evidence suggests that most countries (especially in Asia) hold more international reserves than can be justified by this objective. This raises several questions. Why have Asian emerging market countries accumulated such large reserves? How should those reserves be managed? And looking forward, what are the implications of this buildup in emerging market countries' foreign assets for the international financial system?

Trade Surpluses and Sovereign Wealth

Having rejected the view that the recent reserves accumulation can be justified on a precautionary basis, one has to consider as the main alternative explanation that these reserves are the unintended consequence of large current account surpluses.[34] The "mercantilist" variant of this view holds that the central banks of these countries are accumulating reserves in order to resist the appreciation of the domestic currency.[35] For this effort not to be defeated by domestic inflation, it must be augmented by

33. However, this may not be an implausible order of magnitude for the cost of a severe banking crisis.

34. Another alternative is the view that the high-growth developing countries are exporting their savings abroad because of a shortage of domestic assets for their residents to invest in (Caballero, 2006). These capital outflows must take the form of reserves accumulation if residents' holdings of foreign assets are restricted by capital controls.

35. The nonmercantilist variant would hold that these countries' competitiveness results from natural factors (for example, that wages are kept low in the export sector by a reserve army of labor migrating from the traditional sectors) rather than policy-induced distortions. Mercantilism is at the core of the "Bretton Woods II" view (Dooley, Folkerts-Landau, and Garber, 2004) of the international financial system. Although many commentators find this view quite plausible, it is not obvious how to confirm or reject it empirically. For example, Aizenman and Lee (2005) find that variables associated with the mercantilist motive (lagged export growth and deviations from predicted purchasing power parity) explain very little of the cross-country difference in reserves accumulation.

policies that repress domestic demand—for example, capital controls or domestic financial repression.

Table 8 shows, for the same sample of emerging market countries, the cross-country correlations between the increase in the reserves-GDP ratio between 2000 and 2005 and some key macroeconomic variables. It appears that reserves accumulation is strongly correlated with the current account surplus and not correlated at all with the change in gross external liabilities. This suggests that, to a first approximation, the accumulation of reserves reflects net export flows rather than balance sheet operations.

The change in the reserves-GDP ratio is also positively correlated with capital account restrictions and with the real GDP growth rate.[36] The correlation with capital account restrictions is the opposite of what one would expect based on the precautionary view of reserves accumulation, which predicts that countries with a more open capital account should hold more precautionary reserves because they are more vulnerable to the volatility of capital flows. The positive correlation with the growth rate is also puzzling if one thinks that high-growth developing countries should be importing foreign capital to finance their development, but it is consistent with the mercantilist view, if one thinks that undervaluation of the domestic currency stimulates growth.[37]

One could develop a cost-benefit welfare analysis of a mercantilist development strategy in the same way as I have done for the precautionary view, but the trade-offs involved would be very different. On the cost side, one would have to count the various distortions that are necessary to repress domestic demand, as well as the valuation loss on the foreign assets accumulated by the authorities when the inevitable real appreciation eventually takes place. The benefit side would include the gains in terms of productivity and growth from stimulating the export sector.

It is important to understand that what such a cost-benefit analysis would endogenize is not the level of reserves R, but rather the level of total publicly held foreign assets, which was denoted by W_0 and taken as exogenous in my model of reserves. Endogenizing W_0 would not affect my con-

36. The correlation is less significant for capital account restrictions than for the current account balance or the growth rate, and it seems less robust—it is no longer significant if one uses Edwards' (2001) measure of capital mobility rather than Chinn and Ito's (2005).

37. As Gourinchas and Jeanne (2006) have shown, high-growth developing countries tend to export capital, a puzzle that is explained in part by reserves accumulation. See also Prasad, Rajan, and Subramanian in this volume.

Table 8. Correlations between the Change in the Reserves-GDP Ratio and Selected Macroeconomic Variables, 2000–05[a]

Correlation coefficients

	Change in reserves-GDP ratio, 2000–05	Average current account–GDP ratio, 2001–05	Change in gross external liabilities–GDP ratio, 2000–05	Capital account restrictions index,[b] 2000–04	Average real GDP growth rate, 2000–05
Change in reserves-GDP ratio, 2000–05	1.00				
Average current account–GDP ratio, 2001–05	0.585***	1.00			
Change in gross external liabilities–GDP ratio, 2000–05	0.072	0.014	1.00		
Capital account restrictions index,[b] 2000–04	0.337*	0.184	−0.281	1.00	
Average real GDP growth rate, 2000–05	0.460***	0.223	0.422**	0.288	1.00

Sources: IMF, Balance of Payments Statistics; World Bank, World Development Indicators; Chinn and Ito (2005).
a. Simple cross-country correlations for the emerging market countries reported in appendix table A-1.
b. One minus the average Chinn-Ito measure of capital account openness.

clusion that most emerging market countries in Asia have excess reserves from the point of view of crisis insurance. Those excess reserves are costly, first in terms of forgone returns and portfolio diversification, and second because they generate difficulties for domestic monetary control that can be mitigated only by introducing or maintaining costly distortions in the domestic banking and financial system.

The governments of emerging market countries have started to mitigate these costs by transferring a fraction of foreign exchange reserves from the central bank to "sovereign wealth funds."[38] These funds are mandated to invest in a more diversified portfolio and at a longer horizon than central banks—not unlike the natural resource–based stabilization funds set up by a number of commodity exporters. For example, since July 2005 a fraction of Korea's reserves have been managed by an independent entity, the Korean Investment Corporation, with the aim of seeking higher yields. China recently established the State Foreign Exchange Investment Corporation to manage reserves outside of the central bank.

According to some estimates, the holdings of sovereign wealth funds already amount to more than $2 trillion, mostly consisting of funds derived from oil and gas exports, but their size could increase to $12 trillion by 2015, surpassing official reserves within five years.[39] If those estimates are correct, sovereign wealth funds are set to become a major force in the international financial system.

Portfolio Diversification

Although, as just described, central banks in emerging market countries have recently been diversifying their allocation of reserves, this trend has been slow, and central banks continue to allocate their portfolios in a significantly different manner than private investors do.[40] To illustrate, figure 12 compares the allocation of U.S. assets held by the foreign official sector with that of foreign private investors. The foreign official sector invests much more in U.S. government debt and much less in equity or

38. See Rozanov (2005) and Johnson-Calari and Rietveld (2007). Another approach would be to give the private sector more direct control over the allocation of the country's foreign assets, as in Prasad and Rajan's (2005) proposal to set up closed-end mutual funds that purchase reserves from the central bank and invest the proceeds abroad.
39. See Jen (2007).
40. On recent trends in reserves diversification see Knight (2006), Woolridge (2006), and Truman and Wong (2006).

Figure 12. Composition of Foreign Official and Nonofficial Holdings of U.S. Assets, 2005

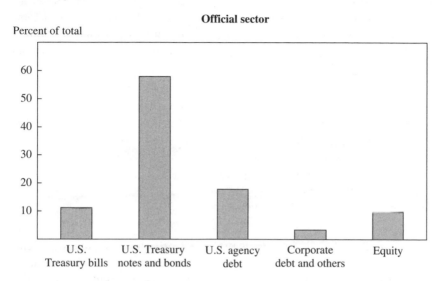

Official sector

Percent of total

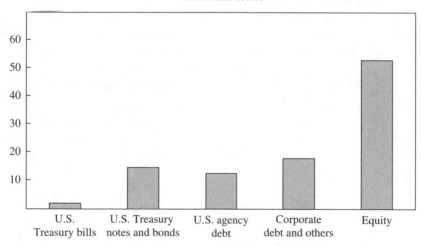

Nonofficial sector

Sources: U.S. Treasury, Treasury International Capital database.

Table 9. Impact of Emerging Market Reserves Diversification on Financial Market Capitalization[a]

Item	United States	Euro area	Japan	United Kingdom
Equity				
Current stock (billions of dollars)	16,800	6,000	4,200	3,000
Expected change in demand[a] (percent)	(+0.40)	(+0.66)	(+0.66)	(+0.66)
Bonds				
Current stock (billions of dollars)	19,800	8,400	8,700	1,000
Expected change in demand (percent)	(−1.39)	(+0.66)	(+0.66)	(+0.66)
Of which: U.S. Treasury marketable debt				
Current stock (billions of dollars)	4,000			
Expected change in demand (percent)	(−7.1)			

Source: Beck, Demirgüç-Kunt, and Levine (2005) and author's calculations.

a. Under the assumption that emerging market countries reallocate $450 billion of reserves from the official sector's portfolio given in figure 12 to the global financial portfolio given in the table in 2005.

corporate debt than do private investors. Clearly there remains significant scope for diversification, a trend that should be facilitated by the transfer of emerging market countries' reserves to sovereign wealth funds.

Some have expressed concern that the diversification of emerging market countries' reserves could lead to disruptions in exchange rates and the relative prices of financial assets. To shed light on this question, consider, for the sake of argument, the following experiment. The total stock of foreign exchange reserves in my sample of emerging market countries amounted to approximately $2 trillion dollars in 2005. Assume that $1.2 trillion of this (60 percent of the total) was invested in dollar assets, of which $900 billion was invested in the asset classes represented in figure 12.[41] Assume further that the emerging market countries in my sample reinvest half of the assets currently invested in the official sector's portfolio shown in figure 12 ($450 billion) in the global financial portfolio. What would be the impact on the net supply of financial assets for the rest of the global investor community?

Table 9 details the current structure of the global portfolio of financial assets. The table was constructed by aggregating World Bank cross-

41. Figure 12, which is based on data from the Treasury International Capital (TIC) database, does not report foreign official investment in onshore or offshore dollar deposits and repurchase agreements, which amount to about one-fourth of the total (Knight, 2006, table 2).

country data on stock and bond market capitalizations in the industrial countries. The table also shows, for each asset class, the net demand from emerging market countries that would be induced by the assumed portfolio reallocation, as a percentage of the outstanding stock. For example, the demand for U.S. bonds would decrease by 1.39 percent of the outstanding stock, while the demand for Japanese equity would increase by 0.66 percent of the outstanding stock.

As one would expect, the selling pressure would play against the dollar, especially fixed-income dollar assets (net demand for U.S. equity would actually increase with the diversification). Net demand for U.S. assets would decrease by 0.5 percent of the outstanding stock, while that for non-U.S. assets would increase by 0.66 percent.

Overall, this back-of-the-envelope calculation shows that the changes in net demand would amount to relatively small fractions of the outstanding stocks. This suggests that moderate price and exchange rate changes would suffice to restore equilibrium. This conclusion, however, comes with several caveats. First, the net supply exceeds 7 percent of the outstanding stock if one restricts one's attention to marketable U.S. Treasury debt. This results from the fact that the foreign official sector holds a significant fraction—about one-third—of outstanding U.S. government debt.[42] The impact on the interest rate that the U.S. government pays on its debt might thus be nonnegligible, depending on its substitutability with other forms of dollar debt in the portfolios of global investors.[43]

Second, the short-run price effects of portfolio diversification will depend on the pace of the diversification and on the reaction of private investors. Whereas the literature on sterilized foreign exchange intervention suggests that such interventions have moderate and transitory effects on exchange rates, the microstructure literature shows that their impact might be large (at least in the short run), especially in markets that lack depth and in which information is fragmented. Furthermore, private speculation may not be stabilizing—private investors might want to get out in front of any government moves rather than offset them as they occur. So, although it is

---

42. See Parisi-Capone and Setser (2006).

43. Warnock and Warnock (2006) find that foreign demand for Treasury securities has a significant impact on Treasury yields. A study by the European Central Bank (2006) finds that the interventions conducted by Asian central banks cannot be shown to be responsible for the low yields in the United States, although they have certainly played a role.

unlikely that large price and exchange rate adjustments must result, in the long run, from increased diversification of emerging market countries' foreign assets, there certainly is a need for the international community to assess and monitor the risks in the transition.

Collective Arrangements

The abundance of reserves held by emerging market countries reduces the need for collective insurance—such as that provided by the IMF at the global level, or by the Chiang Mai Initiative or the Latin American Reserve Fund at the regional level. Indeed, the resources of collective insurance arrangements have become relatively small compared with the reserves that emerging market countries have recently accumulated. For example, the increase in reserves in the Asian emerging market countries over 2000–05 amounts to more than four times the IMF's usable resources at the end of 2005, and more than twenty times the bilateral swap agreements under the Chiang Mai Initiative signed over 2001–05. The buildup in reserves explains in part the recent decline in IMF credit outstanding, which is likely to persist for some time.[44]

Looking forward, one question is whether the large accumulated stocks of sovereign wealth could be used to collectively insure risks other than capital account crises. Emerging market countries face other risks that are now largely uninsured, such as natural disasters, epidemics, terms of trade shocks, and severe output drops.[45] Although some of these risks may be uninsurable because of the potential for moral hazard, there might be scope for expanding insurance through appropriate collective intervention at the regional or the global level.

Finally, sovereign wealth can be used to induce the development of regional financial markets. An example of this is the Asian Bond Fund, created in 2003 to diversify the investment of Asian central banks' reserves away from U.S. and European securities into Asian bonds. Since 2005 the Asian Bond Fund has also invested in domestic currency bonds issued by

---

44. Using various models of the demand for IMF loans, Ghosh and others (2007) project that IMF credit outstanding will decline from an average of SDR 50 billion over 2000–05 to SDR 8 billion over 2006–10, in part because of the increase in the reserves-to-short-term-debt ratio in emerging market countries.

45. See Becker and others (2007).

regional sovereign issuers, as a catalyst for private investment in Asian issues.[46] Such initiatives might enable emerging market countries to develop debt instruments (with long maturities and domestic currency denomination) that are safer for their borrowers.

Summary and Conclusions

This paper has argued that reserves accumulation in Asian emerging market countries is difficult to justify—at least since 2000—in terms of self-insurance against capital flow volatility and capital account crises. The main piece of evidence behind this claim is the failure of a simple cost-benefit model of optimal reserves to account for the reserves buildup in these countries since 2000: their vulnerability to a capital account crisis was too low in that year to justify the cost of the accumulated reserves. That reserves were excessive from the point of view of crisis insurance is also suggested by recent moves to reallocate reserves from central banks to sovereign wealth funds investing in less liquid, higher-yielding assets.

Even if the rate of accumulation of reserves were to abate—and notwithstanding the good reasons that it should—the public sectors of a number of emerging market countries, especially in Asia, will have to manage stocks of foreign financial assets of unprecedented size for some time to come. This generates both policy challenges and opportunities for the international community. One challenge is to ensure that the diversification of those assets is conducted in an orderly manner, to avoid large or abrupt changes in the relative prices of financial assets or in exchange rates. An opportunity lies in the fact that this increase in sovereign wealth could provide the basis for cross-country insurance arrangements against risks other than capital account crises, or could catalyze regional financial development.

---

46. Eichengreen (2006) recommends that the Latin American Reserve Fund follow a similar course of action.

APPENDIX A

Data and Definitions

Table A-1. Countries in the Sample

Emerging market countries[a]		Industrial countries[b]	
Argentina	Mexico	Australia	Norway
Brazil	Morocco	Austria	Portugal
Bulgaria	Nigeria	Belgium	Spain
Chile	Pakistan	Canada	Sweden
China	Panama	Denmark	Switzerland
Colombia	Peru	Finland	United Kingdom
Côte d'Ivoire	Philippines	France	United States
Dominican Republic	Poland	Germany	
Ecuador	Russia	Greece	
Egypt	South Africa	Iceland	
El Salvador	Thailand	Ireland	
Hungary	Tunisia	Italy	
India	Turkey	Japan	
Indonesia	Ukraine	Luxembourg	
Korea	Uruguay	Netherlands	
Malaysia	Venezuela	New Zealand	

a. All countries in the JP Morgan Emerging Market Bond Index Global (EMBIG) as of August 31, 2005, excluding Serbia and Montenegro and Lebanon because of data availability, and adding India and Korea.

b. Countries that were members of the Organization for Economic Cooperation and Development in 1990 and are not in the list of emerging market countries.

Table A-2. Crisis Definitions

Crisis type	Source	Definition
Currency crises		
CC1	Frankel and Rose (1996)	A nominal depreciation of the currency of at least 25 percent relative to the previous year that is also at least a 10 percent acceleration, year over year, in the rate of depreciation.
CC2	Frankel and Wei (2005)	A year is identified as a crisis year if, in at least one month, the sum of the monthly percentage nominal depreciation and the percentage loss in foreign reserves exceeds 15. The sum of the percentage nominal depreciation and the percentage loss in reserves must also be 10 percentage points greater than in the previous month. In cases where successive years may satisfy the crisis criterion, only the first year of crisis is counted within any three-year window.
CC3	Frankel and Wei (2005)	Same as CC2 except that the sum of the percentage nominal depreciation and the percentage loss of foreign reserves must exceed 25.
CC4	Frankel and Wei (2005)	Same as CC2 except that the sum of the percentage nominal depreciation and the percentage loss of foreign reserves must exceed 35.
Sudden stops		
SS1	Jeanne and Rancière (2006)	The ratio of net capital inflows[a] to GDP falls by more than 5 percent relative to the previous year.
SS2	Frankel and Cavallo (2004), "sudden stop 1"	A reduction in the financial account from a surplus position with respect to the previous year that is 2 standard deviations above the mean standard deviation (the average of standard deviations of the financial account over the entire sample). A fall in GDP per capita and in the current account deficit must accompany the financial account reduction, during either the same year or the next year.
SS3	Frankel and Cavallo (2004), "sudden stop 2"	Same as SS2 except that the mean standard deviation of the financial account is that over the corresponding decade only.
SS4	Frankel and Cavallo (2004), "sudden stop 3"	Same as SS2 except that the mean standard deviation is computed for the year-to-year change in the financial account rather than the level.

a. Net capital inflows are measured as the sum of the capital and financial account plus net errors and omissions minus reserve assets and use of Fund credit (from IMF, Balance of Payments Statistics).

Table A-3. Currency Crises and Sudden Stops in Emerging Market Countries, 1980–2000

	Currency crises			
Country	CC1	CC2	CC3	CC4
Argentina	1981 1984 1987	1981 1984 1987 1990 1995	1981 1984 1987 1990 1995	1981 1984 1987 1990
Brazil	1981 1983 1987 1992 1999	1982 1985 1988 1991 1995 1998	1982 1985 1988 1991 1998	1982 1987 1990 1998
Bulgaria	1990 1993 1996			
Chile	1982 1985	1982 1985	1985	1985
China	1984 1994	1980 1989 1992	1980 1992	1992
Colombia	1985 1997	1984 1995	1985	
Côte d'Ivoire	1994	1982 1985 1988 1991 1994 1998	1980 1983 1986 1989 1992 1996 2000	1980 1983 1986 1989 1992
Dominican Rep.	1985 1987 1990	1981 1984 1987 1990 1994 1998	1980 1983 1986 1989 1994	1982 1985 1988 1994
Ecuador	1982 1985 1988 1995 1998	1982 1985 1988 1991 1998	1982 1986 1990 1998	1982 1986 1990 1999
Egypt	1989	1981 1984 1989	1981 1986 1990	1990
El Salvador	1986 1990	1982 1985 1988 1991 1995	1981 1985 1990	1980 1986 1990
Hungary				
India	1991	1988 1991	1991	1991
Indonesia	1983 1986 1997 2000	1982 1986 1997	1983 1986 1997	1983 1986 1998
Korea	1997	1980 1983 1986 1997	1997	1997
Malaysia	1997	1992 1997		
Mexico	1982 1985 1994	1981 1985 1988 1993 1998	1981 1985 1988 1994	1982 1985 1990 1994
Morocco		1981 1984 1987	1982 1985 1988	1980 1983 1986 1989
Nigeria	1986 1989 1992 1999	1981 1984 1987 1992 1995 1999	1982 1986 1992 1995 1999	1982 1986 1992 1999
Pakistan	1982	1980 1984 1987 1990 1993 1996 1999	1985 1988 1991 1995 1998	1988 1991 1996
Panama		1981 1984 1987 1991 1997	1982 1985 1988 1992 1997	1980 1983 1986 1997
Peru	1982 1987 1990	1982 1987 1990	1987 1990	1987 1990
Philippines	1983 1997	1982 1985 1988 1991 1997	1982 1985 1988 1997	1982 1985 1990
Poland	1982 1986 1989 1992			
Russia	1998			
South Africa	1984	1982 1985 1988 1991 1994 1998	1982 1985 1988 1992 1995 1998	1981 1984 1994
Thailand	1997	1997	1997	
Tunisia		1980 1984 1987 1991 1994 2000	1984 1987 1991	1986 1991
Turkey	1988 1991 1994 1996 1999	1982 1985 1988 1991 1994 1998	1980 1983 1989 1994	1980 1983 1994
Ukraine	1998			
Uruguay	1982 1984 1989	1981 1984 1991	1982 1985 1991	1982 1985
Venezuela	1984 1986 1989 1994	1980 1984 1989 1994	1984 1989 1994	1984 1989 1994
Frequency (%)[a]	10.3	20.1	15.7	12.2

	Sudden stops			
Country	*SS1*	*SS2*	*SS3*	*SS4*
Argentina	1989	1989		1989
Brazil	1983		1983	
Bulgaria	1990 1994 1996 1998			
Chile	1982 1983 1985 1981 1995 1998	1982 1983 1998	1998	1998
China	1984 1994	1980 1989 1992	1980 1992	1992
Colombia		1998 1999		
Cte d'Ivoire	1983 1984 1996		1984	
Dominican Rep.	1981 1993			
Ecuador	1983 1986 1988 1992 1999 2000	1983 1999	1983	1983
Egypt	1990 1993	1990	1990	1990
El Salvador				
Hungary	1994 1996			
India				
Indonesia	1997 1998	1997	1997	
Korea	1986 1997	1997	1997	1997
Malaysia	1984 1987 1994 1999	1997		
Mexico	1982 1995	1982 1994 1995	1982	1982 1995
Morocco	1995	1995	1995	1995
Nigeria	1984 1985 1987 1992 1996 1999	1999		
Pakistan				
Panama	1982 1983 1985 1987 1988 2000	2000	2000	2000
Peru	1983 1984 1998	1998	1998	1998
Philippines	1983 1997	1997 1998	1983	1983
Poland	1988 1990			
Russia	1998 1999			
South Africa	1985			
Thailand	1982 1997 1998	1997	1997	1997
Tunisia				
Turkey	1994	1991 1994 1993		1988
Ukraine	1998			
Uruguay	1982		1983	1983
Venezuela	1980 1989 1990 1994	1994		
Frequency (%)[a]	11.2	4.5	2.7	2.5

Sources: Author's calculations; Frankel and Cavallo (2004); Frankel and Wei (2005).
a. Percent of all available observations for the sample period.

Table A-4. Variables Considered in the Probit Analysis

Variable[a]	Source[b]
Annual growth in GDP	WDI
Current account balance	IFS
Reserves	IFS
M2	IFS
Debt	
Ratio of lagged real public debt to real GDP	GDF, WDI
Ratio of lagged short-term debt to real GDP	GDF, WDI
Exchange rate	
Second lag of exchange rate regime dummies	Reinhart and Rogoff (2004)
Lagged real effective exchange rate deviation from Hodrick-Prescott trend	IFS
Trade	
Ratio of lagged sum of exports and imports to GDP	WDI
Lagged growth in terms of trade (percent)	IFS
Index of current account openness	Quinn (2000)
U.S. interest rates	
Interest rate on Treasury bills (percent a year)	IFS
Change in the interest rate on Treasury bills (basis points)	IFS
Business cycle indicators	
Average of first and second lags of real GDP growth	WDI
Financial account openness	
Ratio of lagged absolute gross inflows to GDP	IFS
Ratio of lagged sum of absolute gross inflows and absolute gross outflows to GDP	IFS
Stocks of foreign assets and foreign liabilities	
Ratio of lagged net foreign assets to GDP	Lane and Milesi-Ferretti (2006)
Ratio of lagged stock of foreign liabilities to GDP	Lane and Milesi-Ferretti (2006)
Ratio of stock of debt liabilities to stock of total liabilities	Lane and Milesi-Ferretti (2006)
Ratio of lagged stock of FDI to stock of total liabilities	Lane and Milesi-Ferretti (2006)
Other	
Ratio of foreign liabilities to money in the financial sector	IFS
Consumer price inflation (percent a year)	IFS

a. Lags are one-year lags except where stated otherwise.
b. Definitions: GDF, Global Development Finance (World Bank); IFS, International Financial Statistics (IMF); WDI, World Development Indicators (World Bank).

APPENDIX B

Solving for the Optimal Level of Reserves

RESERVES MANAGEMENT IN A CRISIS. How does the country in the model use its reserves in period 1? If there is no crisis, the consumer achieves the desired level of consumption C^* and saves any residual wealth (which could be positive or negative) as net reserves. But if there is a crisis, the consumer may be unable to consume C^*. Then, using equation 4 in the text, $Y_1 = Y - \Delta Y$, and $L' = 0$, period-1 consumption is given by

$$C_1 = Y - \Delta Y - L + R - R'.$$

The question is whether the consumer can achieve the desired level of consumption $C_1 = C^*$ by running down reserves ($R' = 0$). This is the case if reserves R exceed the following threshold:

$$\bar{R} = L + \Delta Y + (C^* - Y).$$

$\bar{R}$ is the "full insurance" level of reserves, that is, the amount that allows the consumer to maintain consumption as if there were no crisis. It is also the maximum amount of reserves that the consumer is ready to spend in a crisis. The "full insurance" level of reserves is equal to the sum of the capital outflow and output fall in a crisis, plus the period-1 trade deficit. The last term is equal to zero because of the assumption that $C^* = Y$.

THE LOSS FUNCTION (EQUATION 7). Period-0 welfare is given by

$$U_0 = (1 - \pi)U_1^n + \pi U_1^c = U_1^n - \pi f(R),$$

where U_1^n is the welfare level conditional on no crisis, and U_1^c is that conditional on a crisis, and $f(R) = U_1^n - U_1^c$ is the welfare cost of a crisis. Using equations 3 and 4 to substitute out I and $R' - L'$ from equation 5, we can write period-1 welfare as

$$U_1 = u(C_1) + \frac{W_2}{1 + r}$$
$$= u(C_1) + Y_1 + (1 + r)(1 + \delta)W_0 - L - C_1 - \delta R.$$

(I set $Y_2 = 0$ to reduce the amount of algebra.) If there is no crisis, $C_1 = Y_1 = C^* = Y$, so that welfare is given by

$$U_1^n = u(C^*) + (1 + r)(1 + \delta)W_0 - L - \delta R$$
$$= \bar{U} - \delta R$$

where $\bar{U}$ is the consumer's ex ante welfare if there is no crisis risk and W_0 is invested in the illiquid asset. By contrast, if there is a crisis, $Y_1 = Y - \Delta Y$ and $R' = 0$ (assuming $R \leq \bar{R}$), so that $C_1 = Y - \Delta Y - L + R = C^* - (\bar{R} - R)$, implying a welfare level of

$$U_1^c = u[C^* - (\bar{R} - R)] + (1 + r)(1 + \delta)W_0 - L - \Delta Y + (\bar{R} - R) - \delta R.$$

Taking the difference, one obtains $U_1^n - U_1^c = f(R)$, with

$$f(R) = \underbrace{\Delta Y}_{\text{output cost}} + \underbrace{u(C^*) - u[C^* - (\bar{R} - R)] - (\bar{R} - R)}_{\text{consumption smoothing cost}}$$

(if $R \leq \bar{R}$). The welfare cost of a crisis is the sum of two components: the output cost of the crisis and the cost of distorting the path of domestic consumption away from the unconstrained equilibrium. The second component, which is decreasing with R and equal to zero if $R \geq \bar{R}$, captures the benefit of reserves in terms of crisis mitigation in my model. Finally, period-0 welfare can be written

$$U_0 = \bar{U} - [\delta R + \pi f(R)].$$

An Extension with Debt and Default

Assume that reserves are financed by long-term debt $D = -I$, and assume $W_0 = 0$, so that $R = D$. There is no need to assume that debt is illiquid in the same sense as the physical investment—the debt could be traded in a liquid market. What is important for my results is that I cannot be decreased (or, equivalently, D cannot be increased) in a crisis. For debt this is an implication of the credit constraint to which the consumer is subject during a crisis.

Let us assume that the consumer fails to repay long-term debt D with probability μ and therefore pays a risk premium $[1/(1 - \mu)] - 1$. Then the expression for final wealth (equation 5) is

$$W_2 = Y_2 - \eta \frac{(1 + r)^2 (1 + \delta)}{1 - \mu} D + (1 + r)(R' - L'),$$

where η takes the value of 1 if the consumer repays the debt and 0 if not. The expression for the expected wealth $E_1(W_2)$, and thus the expressions for U_1^n and U_1^c, are the same as before. Hence the default probability μ has no impact on the optimal level of reserves; only δ should be counted in the opportunity cost of reserves.

However, the risk of default could be relevant if there are default costs. Assume that Y_2 is stochastic and default occurs only if the debt repayment exceeds the cost of default γY_2. Then, given $D = R$, the probability of default μ is endogenous and is solved by

$$\mu = \Pr\left[\gamma Y_2 < \frac{(1 + r)^2 (1 + \delta)}{1 - \mu} R\right].$$

This equation implicitly defines a default threshold $\bar{Y}(R)$ that is increasing with R. The ex ante loss becomes

$$\text{Loss} = \delta R + \gamma \int_0^{\bar{Y}(R)} Y_2 g(Y_2) dY_2 + \pi(R) f(R).$$

The opportunity cost of reserves includes a term for the deadweight cost of default, which is increasing with reserves. This term is not the same as the default risk premium, $[1/(1 - \mu)] - 1$.

Comments and
Discussion

Joshua Aizenman: Since the 1980s, the world economy has witnessed an intriguing development: despite the proliferation of more flexible exchange rate regimes, ratios of international reserves to GDP have increased substantially, and practically all of that increase has taken place in developing countries, mostly in East Asia. This puzzling phenomenon has stirred a lively debate among economists and financial observers, and several interpretations have been offered. These focus on the observation that the deeper financial integration of developing countries into the global economy has increased their exposure to volatile short-term flows of capital (dubbed "hot money"), which are subject to costly and frequent sudden stops and reversals.[1] In these circumstances, hoarding international reserves can be viewed as a precautionary adjustment, reflecting the desire for self-insurance against exposure to future sudden stops, currency crises, and capital flight.[2]

In this paper, Olivier Jeanne appraises the explanatory power of self-insurance models of international reserves. He provides a careful formulation of a utility-based welfare analysis of optimal hoarding of international reserves, and a calibration that allows one to evaluate the degree to which recent hoarding trends are consistent with the model's predictions. The framework is based on an elegant model, providing strong predictions about optimal usable reserves in the context of self-insurance against sudden stops and currency crises. Applying the model to the data produces some intriguing results: for the typical emerging market country, the model

1. See, for example, Calvo (1998) and Edwards (2004).
2. See Flood and Marion (2002) for an overview of the literature explaining international reserves applying the buffer stock approach. See Ben Bassat and Gottlieb (1992), Aizenman and Marion (2003), Lee (2004), Aizenman and Lee (2005), Garcia and Soto (2004), Jeanne and Rancière (2006), and Rodrik (2006) for precautionary and self-insurance models of international reserves hoarding.

can plausibly explain a reserves-GDP ratio on the order of 10 percent, close to the long-run historical average, and it can justify even higher levels if one assumes that reserves have a significant role in terms of crisis prevention. The levels of reserves recently observed in many countries, in particular in Latin America, are within the range of the model's predictions. For emerging market countries in the aggregate, however, the insurance model fails to account for the recent reserves buildup, because the risk of a capital account crisis in the Asian countries where most of the buildup has taken place seems much too small to justify such levels of self-insurance.

Jeanne's paper is an important and timely contribution to the debate about the relative costs and benefits of hoarding reserves. Yet his results raise the question of what factors might account for the sizable gaps between the model's predictions and the actual hoarding of reserves observed during recent years. After briefly summarizing his methodology and key results, I will discuss several alternative interpretations of reserves hoarding during the 2000s that go beyond the self-insurance paradigm, and I will offer several extensions that may improve the explanatory power of Jeanne's model.

THE MODEL AND ITS CALIBRATION. Jeanne's framework explains hoarding of international reserves in the context of a small open economy populated by a representative consumer and exposed to crises triggered by a loss of access to external credit, possibly associated with a fall in output. The model has three periods. The focus of the analysis is on the optimal hoarding of net reserves in period 0, when the representative consumer anticipates the possibility of a sudden stop and a costly foreign currency crisis in period 1. The consumer's welfare is the sum of the expected utility of consumption in period 1 plus discounted expected (terminal) wealth in period 2.

Within this framework, Jeanne provides a carefully worked-out model in which international reserves affect welfare in two distinct ways. The first is through crisis prevention: an increase in reserves may reduce the probability of a crisis and thus directly reduce the expected output cost. The second is through crisis mitigation: reserves may reduce the cost of smoothing consumption during a crisis. In this model optimal international reserves are shown to be determined by minimizing a loss function, where the total loss equals the sum of the opportunity cost of reserves and the expected welfare cost of a crisis.

The model is calibrated in two steps. First, using multivariate probit regressions on data for a group of emerging market countries from 1980 to

2000, Jeanne estimates for each country its vulnerability to a crisis in 2000. Next he computes the optimal level of reserves that minimizes the loss function. He finds that the predicted level of optimal reserves in 2000 across all countries in the sample is about $235 billion, or about 35 percent of the actual level observed (close to $650 billion). The discrepancy comes mainly from the Asian countries, where the predicted level of reserves is extremely low, reflecting a very low estimated probability of a sudden stop. By contrast, the model works well for Latin America, where the observed level of reserves is actually slightly below the model's prediction.

Next Jeanne estimates the benefits of the reserves accumulation between 2000 and 2005 in terms of crisis prevention, assuming that the welfare cost of a crisis is equal to the output cost. The results are striking: on average, the cost of reserves accumulation exceeds the benefits in terms of currency crisis prevention by a factor of three. This average aggregates the differences between Asia, where the cost was more than five times larger than the benefit, and Latin America, where the benefit actually exceeded the cost. These differences reflect the much lower probability of a currency crisis in Asia than in Latin America in 2000, implying that the marginal returns to reserves accumulation in terms of crisis prevention were much higher in Latin America. Applying the model, one can conclude that, to rationalize the reserves buildup in Asian countries, one needs to assume that the expected output cost of a currency crisis in Asia amounts to more than 60 percent of GDP, more than ten times the corresponding cost in Latin America.

Jeanne discusses possible interpretations for this puzzle. The first candidate is mercantilism, in which hoarding of international reserves is aimed at keeping the domestic currency undervalued, as part of an export-led growth strategy.[3] Jeanne points out the theoretical and empirical challenges involved in modeling and testing this hypothesis. He also reports an interesting observation: the change in the reserves-GDP ratio is positively correlated with capital account restrictions. This correlation is the opposite of what one would expect based on the precautionary view of reserves accumulation, which predicts that countries with a more open capital account should hold more precautionary reserves because they are more vulnerable to volatile capital flows. In the next section I will show that this finding is consistent with the outcome of a competitive hoarding game.

---

3. Dooley, Folkerts-Landau, and Garber (2004).

A closer look at the 2000–05 data in Jeanne's sample of countries indicates that reserves accumulation is strongly correlated with the current account surplus and not correlated at all with the change in gross external liabilities. This suggests that, to a first approximation, the accumulation of reserves reflects net export flows rather than balance sheet operations. The change in the reserves-GDP ratio is also positively correlated with the real GDP growth rate. This is puzzling if one thinks that high-growth developing countries should be importing foreign capital to finance their development. Yet this correlation is only one piece of a complex puzzle reported elsewhere by Jeanne himself with Pierre-Olivier Gourinchas: rapidly growing developing countries tend to export capital, an enigma that is explained in part by reserves accumulation.[4]

Jeanne closes the paper with a discussion of several policy implications. The governments of emerging market countries have started to mitigate the opportunity costs of hoarding large reserves by transferring a fraction of their foreign exchange reserves from the central bank to sovereign wealth funds. These funds are mandated to invest in a more diversified portfolio and at a longer horizon than central banks normally do, and they frequently are managed by quasi-independent entities (such as the recently established Korean Investment Corporation and the Chinese State Foreign Exchange Investment Corporation, as well as some older funds including Norway's oil fund). The assets of these sovereign wealth funds amount to about $2 trillion today and are projected to increase rapidly in the future, becoming a major force in the international financial system. Jeanne considers the possible impact of portfolio diversification following attempts by these entities to scale down the dollar share of their international reserves. He finds that the impact of a gradual diversification would be moderate, decreasing net demand for U.S. assets by an estimated 0.5 percent of the outstanding stock, while the net demand for non-U.S. assets would increase by 0.66 percent of the stock.[5]

---

4. Gourinchas and Jeanne (2006). See Aizenman, Pinto, and Radziwill (2007) and Prasad, Rajan, and Subramanian (this volume) for further findings and interpretations of the positive association between economic growth and current account surpluses.

5. The impact would be larger if the substitutability between dollar debt and other currency debt is low, as international reserves diversification by major central banks may imply a net supply exceeding 7 percent of the outstanding stock if one restricts attention to marketable U.S. Treasury debt (reflecting the fact that the foreign official sector holds about one-third of the outstanding U.S. government debt).

ALTERNATIVE INTERPRETATIONS OF RECENT RESERVES HOARDING. I now turn to some possible interpretations of the puzzle that Jeanne has identified. My starting point applies the logic of revealed preferences to argue that the continued large hoarding of international reserves by developing countries must reflect systemic forces supporting this trend. The challenge is to identify those forces and the conditions that may induce changes in the observed patterns. This requires venturing beyond the domain of the representative agent paradigm and entails some conjectures that deserve a more careful evaluation.

Competitive hoarding. The view that ascribes the large increase in hoarding of reserves to self-insurance faces a well-known challenger in a modern incarnation of mercantilism: the view that reserves accumulation is triggered by concerns about export competitiveness. This explanation has been advanced by Michael Dooley, David Folkerts-Landau, and Peter Garber, especially in the context of Asia.[6] They interpret reserves accumulation as a by-product of export promotion, undertaken in Asia's case as a means of absorbing abundant labor migrating from the traditional sectors, especially agriculture. Although intellectually intriguing, this interpretation remains debatable. Some have pointed out that strong export growth in East Asia is nothing new—indeed, it is an important part of the story there since the 1950s. Yet the large increase in reserves has happened mostly since 1997. Jaewoo Lee and I tested the importance of precautionary and mercantilist motives in accounting for the hoarding of international reserves by developing countries during 1980–2000.[7] Although we found that certain variables associated with the mercantilist motive (such as lagged export growth and deviation of exchange rates from purchasing power parity) are statistically significant, their economic importance is small and dwarfed by other variables. Overall, our empirical results were consistent with an explanation based on precautionary demand. The inability of empirical research to validate a robust economic role for mercantilist hoarding through its impact on the real exchange rate, together with the acceleration of large hoardings in East Asia during 2001–07, remains a puzzle.

Arguably, one might reconcile the mercantilist view with the limited support of mercantilism found in cross-country regressions by invoking

6. Dooley, Folkerts-Landau, and Garber (2004).
7. Aizenman and Lee (2005).

the concept of competitive hoarding by countries following an export-oriented growth strategy and competing with each other in the same third markets, such as the United States. Such hoarding might be triggered by more vigorous competition in industries approaching excess capacity. My figure 1 depicts an example of such a competitive hoarding game, one akin to Harry Johnson's classic tariff war model.[8]

The figure illustrates the behavior of two emerging market countries, H and F, exporting similar products to a third market. Increased hoarding of reserves by either country would depreciate its currency, thereby improving its export competitiveness vis-à-vis the other country. Assume that both H and F seek to balance the gain from export promotion against the costs of hoarding reserves (reflecting costly sterilization and other indirect costs). The optimal international reserves level in the absence of competitive hoarding is normalized to 1, given by point O. Curves HH and FF are the reaction functions of H and F in the competitive hoarding game. Curve W_o is H's indifference curve, consisting of configurations of domestic and foreign reserves where H's utility equals the benchmark of no competitive hoarding. H is worse off relative to the no-hoarding equilibrium at points above curve W_o. The Nash equilibrium of the competitive hoarding game is depicted by the intersection of curves HH and FF, at point S. When the two emerging market countries have symmetric costs associated with hoarding reserves (top panel), competitive hoarding tends to dissipate most of the competitiveness gains, leading to self-defeating ("beggar-yourself") outcomes and excessive hoarding. If, however, the countries have asymmetric costs of accumulating reserves (bottom panel), a country with a low enough cost of sterilization may win the hoarding war: its noncooperative outcome, which lies below the curve W_o, is superior to the cooperative one, in a manner akin to the "beggar-thy-neighbor" outcome of asymmetric tariff wars.[9]

Financial repression of the type observed in China may reduce its sterilization costs, thereby increasing the aggressiveness of its sterilization and ultimately increasing its international reserves. Consequently, competitive hoarding in circumstances where financial repression reduces the cost of sterilization is consistent with Jeanne's finding of a negative association between hoarding and financial integration.

8. Johnson (1953).
9. Aizenman and Lee (2006).

Figure 1. Two Cases of Competitive Hoarding in Two Emerging Market Countries

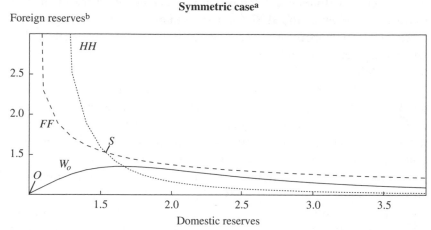

Symmetric case[a]

Foreign reserves[b]

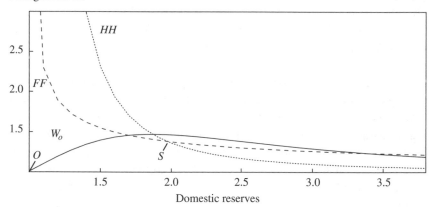

Asymmetric case[c]

Foreign reserves

Source: Aizenman and Lee (2006).
a. The "beggar-yourself" case; the home country (H) and the foreign country (F) have the same sterilization costs.
b. The optimal level of reserves is normalized to one unit.
c. The "beggar-thy-neighbor" case; H has lower sterilization costs than F.

Arguably, the unique role of China in a hoarding game is consistent with recent patterns of sterilization. The accumulation of international reserves accelerated during 2000–05 to more than $100 billion annually on average and has been associated with sizable current account surpluses and inflows of capital of about $60 billion and $50 billion, respectively.[10] Reuven Glick and I also found a significant increase in the coefficient of sterilization following the 1997–98 crisis, a trend that continues today and applies well beyond Asia.[11] These findings suggest that growing financial integration has been associated with extensive hoarding of international reserves. Notwithstanding concerns about sterilization costs, reserves hoarding and sterilization have complemented each other during the last ten years, as developing countries have increased the intensity of both. The costs of sterilization have so far been well below the perceived benefits of monetary stability and the wish to hoard international reserves.

These trends are consistent with aggressive sterilization applied by China, where large inflows of capital and large current account surpluses are associated with sterilization. If China's sterilization costs are lower than those of Korea and other countries competing with China in the U.S. market, China may ultimately win the hoarding game. China's sheer size and low sterilization costs, probably due to financial repression there, may force Korea and Japan to keep hoarding international reserves in order to prevent deeper erosion of their competitiveness.[12]

Such behavior may also explain the inability to find empirical evidence of a robust economic role for the mercantilist approach, as most of the effects tend to dissipate quickly. Competitive hoarding may also reflect coordination failure. If China is the winner by virtue of its low sterilization costs and size, other Asian countries may be made worse off (while, arguably, the welfare impact of the hoarding game on the United States is ambiguous). It also suggests the possibility of gains from regional coordination, possibly in the form of a regional fund, although China may be less eager than other East Asian countries to participate in such a fund. Competitive hoarding is also consistent with the possibility that demand for international reserves is interdependent,

10. These averages mask the remarkable acceleration of China's annual hoardings, from close to zero during 2000, to about $100 billion, $200 billion, and $250 billion during 2003, 2004, and 2006, respectively.

11. Aizenman and Glick (2007). The "coefficient of sterilization" measures the marginal change of domestic credit associated with hoarding international reserves. Specifically, we regress the four-quarter change in net domestic assets on the four-quarter increase in net foreign assets held by the central bank, scaled by reserve money stock, controlling for nominal GDP growth.

12. Arguably, it may also induce Korea and Japan to invest directly in China, in an attempt to minimize their losses in the hoarding game.

as XingWang Qian reported in a study of ten East Asian economies.[13] They found, controlling for conventional variables explaining reserves hoarding, that a one-dollar increase in international reserves by one country was associated with an increase in reserves by the other nine of about 60 cents.

Exposure to latent domestic instability. To put Chinese policies in the perspective of the historical development of East Asia, note that the history of Japan and Korea suggests the near absence of mercantilist hoarding of international reserves during their phase of fast growth, and the prevalence of export promotion by subsidizing heavily the cost of capital in targeted sectors. This has been accomplished with the help of the state banking system and occasionally with the tacit involvement of the central bank. The legacy of subsidized capital has been a rapid increase in M2 and the accumulation of nonperforming loans. Floundering economic growth subsequently led to large hoarding of reserves in both Japan (after 1992) and Korea (after 1997), probably both from mercantilist motives and as self-insurance in view of the growing fragility of their banking systems. These perspectives suggest that the recent massive hoarding of reserves by China may reflect a hybrid of mercantilist and self-insurance motives.[14]

Other explanations of reserves hoarding by China invoke political economy considerations. The Chinese government faces multiple challenges: managing an economic take-off of unprecedented global magnitude, uncertainty regarding the political regime's survival, growing income disparities, a buildup of nonperforming loans, and growing dependency on international trade. An abundance of savings in China provides an opportunity to mitigate the risk of domestic instability by aggressively hoarding international reserves, thereby reducing both the risk of real exchange rate instability and the risk of inflation triggered by domestic crisis.[15] This view is consistent with a 2006 report by Ernst &

13. Qian (2006).
14. See Aizenman and Lee (2006).
15. Arguably, if China were to face a banking crisis of the type experienced by Argentina, a sizable cushion of international reserves would allow the authorities to avoid the collapse of financial intermediation and higher inflation that Argentina suffered. Indeed, one could argue that the sheer size of Chinese international reserves may prevent a run on its banking system in the first place.

Young that China's nonperforming loans almost equaled its international reserves.[16] It also suggests that, for countries averse to real exchange rate volatility and inflation, actually usable international reserves may be limited to what is left over after covering short-term external debt and after any provisions for nonperforming loans in the domestic banking system.

TESTING THE SELF-INSURANCE MODEL IN CHINA AND THE "PESO PROBLEM." Systematic attempts to test the self-insurance model are challenged by a version of the "peso problem," whereby current reserve holdings appear inefficient given current conditions but may be justified by expectations of future conditions. For example, the probability of a deep crisis in China may be low, but the potential damage of such a crisis may be immense. China's take-off remains unique in terms of its sheer size: China's share of global GDP (adjusted for purchasing power parity) tripled within just twenty-five years, from about 5 percent in 1977 to about 15 percent in 2003. This suggests that the experience of other countries is of little help in determining China's optimal level of reserves. The econometric challenges associated with quantifying the self-insurance needs of a country are akin to the challenge of quantifying the optimal design of highways in the San Francisco Bay area. An uninformed tourist visiting San Francisco might conclude that highways there are overbuilt and conjecture that San Franciscans have a strange preference for heavily reinforced roads. Certainly the data of the last fifteen years do nothing to suggest otherwise. Only those who know the city's history, including the great earthquake of 1906, will understand why highways there are designed the way they are, and indeed one may ask why some highways remain underbuilt to this day. Similarly, although China has been reasonably tranquil, economically and politically, during the last twenty years, the region's history during the twentieth century is one of repeated "earthquakes," some triggered domestically and some abroad.

EXTENSIONS OF THE MODEL. I close with several short comments on possible extensions that may provide a better interpretation of the patterns of hoarding in Latin America while also addressing some of the issues involved in dealing with Asia.

16. Jim Peterson, "Balance Sheet: China Offers Fertile Soil for Investor Unhappiness," *International Herald Tribune*, September 11, 2006.

International reserves and sovereign default. The representative agent model used by Jeanne is more appropriate to countries that, although exposed to possible sudden stops and foreign currency crises, view the external default option as too costly to be contemplated. (Korea during the last thirty years is an example.) Understanding the role of international reserves in Latin America, by contrast, requires modeling the implications of sovereign default for international reserves. As a practical matter, international reserves are beyond creditors' reach. This implies that, for countries willing to contemplate it, sovereign default is an alternative, independent instrument for consumption smoothing. Nancy Marion and I have provided a model and some empirical evidence indicating that, in these circumstances, greater political instability and polarization tend to *reduce* reserves hoarding and to *increase* sovereign borrowing.[17] This interpretation may account for Jeanne's observation that, in 2000, Latin America held significantly less reserves than his benchmark model predicted.

Saving and reserves hoarding. With integration of national capital markets still limited, one expects that, all else equal, countries with higher saving rates would opt to hoard more reserves. Hence the same factors that account for the large gap in saving rates between Latin America and East Asia may also explain their different behaviors with respect to international reserves.

International reserves and the real exchange rate. Countries may hoard reserves as a means of stabilizing the real exchange rate in the presence of volatile terms of trade shocks and volatile short-term capital flows.[18] This argument is reinforced by Philippe Aghion and others, who found that real exchange rate volatility reduces growth in countries with relatively weak financial development.[19] Hence factors that mitigate real exchange rate volatility may be associated with superior economic performance. This is of special relevance to commodity-exporting countries and countries with shallow financial systems. Extensions of Jeanne's model that would allow for adverse effects of real exchange rate volatility would imply another rationale for hoarding reserves.

Diversification and agency problems. The lack of deeper diversification of international reserves may be partly due to agency problems. Central

17. Aizenman and Marion (2003).
18. See Aizenman (2006).
19. Aghion and others (2006).

banks may be loss averse, in that the cost of holding too little reserves may be much higher than the opportunity cost of holding too much.[20] If a central bank's loss aversion exceeds that of the representative consumer, a good case can be made for putting some of the international reserves into a "future generation" fund managed by the treasury or some other agency, along the lines of Jeanne's discussion.

In conclusion, Jeanne's paper is a first-rate contribution to the debate over the recent large buildup of international reserves in some countries. The quest for a unified theory and empirical specification of international reserves holdings, although admirable, may not be feasible given the pace of global change. It is constructive to view the observed patterns of international reserves hoarding as the aggregate result of several motives, whose relative importance varies over time. Taking such an eclectic approach, one may conjecture that the hoarding phenomenon has gone through several phases. The first phase, in the immediate aftermath of the East Asian crisis, was dominated by countries seeking self-insurance against exposure to foreign shocks. Countries stunned by the 1997 crisis hedged their growing financial integration by aggressively hoarding international reserves. Yet, as Jeanne convincingly illustrates, the self-insurance interpretation fails to account for the size of the reserves buildup in emerging market countries after 2000. My comments suggest that the levels of reserve holdings observed recently indicate the turn to a second phase, which may be better explained by competitive hoarding, by self-insurance against latent domestic instability, and by exposure to instability associated with a growing weakness of commercial banks' balance sheets.

Lawrence H. Summers: Soon after I arrived at the Treasury as under secretary of international affairs in 1993, I was briefed about the Exchange Stabilization Fund. One of the first questions I asked was why this fund, which holds the foreign currency reserves that the Treasury uses to intervene in foreign exchange markets, was the size that it was. I received two answers. One came from Treasury staff and consisted of a lengthy disquisition on the series of historical events leading from the fund's beginnings to date. The other came from then–Federal Reserve chairman Alan Greenspan, who explained how he and Edwin Truman, when Truman was on the staff of the Federal Open Market Committee, had undertaken a research program to

---

20. Aizenman and Marion (2003).

determine the optimal level of reserves for the United States. Greenspan reported to me somewhat sheepishly their conclusion that, depending upon certain assumptions that were difficult to pin down, the optimal level was somewhere between $20 billion and $2 trillion. So they had abandoned that particular effort.

I am glad to see Olivier Jeanne pick up the torch again and try to analyze the costs and benefits of reserves and arrive at some concept of an optimal level. And I broadly agree with his conclusions. I agree that it is difficult to account for the rise in reserves in East Asia on the basis of a plausible precautionary hypothesis. I agree that those resources should be invested in more imaginative ways, accepting more risk in exchange for a higher return, than they are today. I agree that doing so will not likely cause huge disruptions in the global capital market. And I agree that current patterns of reserves holdings have something to do with mercantilism on the part of the countries holding them. But I am somewhat more skeptical of several aspects of Jeanne's analysis.

Let me first make three points with respect to the cost-benefit analysis of reserves. The first concerns possible nonlinearities. The basic proposition of any cost-benefit analysis that seeks some optimum is that marginal benefit is equal to marginal cost. Unfortunately, in the case of reserves, it is very difficult to establish the shape of either the benefit function or the cost function. With respect to the use of reserves in crisis prevention, that is, reducing the probability of a crisis, it is hard to demonstrate conclusively that there are any statistically significant benefits at all. How those benefits vary for a given change in reserves when reserves are, say, two times short-term debt versus four times short-term debt is even more difficult to estimate. Thus Jeanne's results are heavily driven by his choice of functional form. It would be worth experimenting with alternative, nonlinear specifications, although I suspect it would be difficult to gauge the results with any precision.

Second, Jeanne's analysis requires certain assumptions about the mechanics not only of crisis prevention, but also of crisis mitigation, or how reserves are to be used when a crisis actually happens. These assumptions may not be appropriate. For example, the premise of the analysis using the so-called sudden stop formulation, which looks at changes in the capital account, is that the response to changes in the capital account is a change in the holdings of reserves that maintains domestic absorption approximately constant. Yet this is something that the International Monetary Fund, the institution for which Jeanne works, would never stand for. Rather, IMF conditionality would typically not allow reserves to be used to permit increased absorption but would instead insist that they be used for sterilized intervention—thereby reducing their efficacy in maintaining level output and consumption.

Third, I am not entirely persuaded by the cost side of the analysis. In a perfect capital market, where all assets are perfect substitutes and reserves are financed by issuing domestic debt, holding reserves costs nothing at all. Indeed, to the extent that domestic debt is issued to finance investment in risky international assets to which the country's citizens would not otherwise have access, reserves are plausibly welfare enhancing. (The argument is similar to that made by Peter Diamond and others, that there is a gain to investing a portion of the Social Security trust fund in equities.[1]) The costs of reserves accumulation, I think, lie in rather different areas than those explored here: in the complexity posed for macroeconomic management, and in the moral hazards for policymaking associated with the availability of large amounts of reserves. Perhaps most important, the costs of reserves lie in the consequences, when the assumption of perfect substitutability of assets breaks down, of the (presumably transitory) change in the real exchange rate that results from an intervention that changes the relative supplies of assets.

In short, I find neither the paper's analysis of costs nor its analysis of benefits entirely compelling, and therefore the paper's comparison of optimal with current levels of reserves does not seem to me the most persuasive approach to drawing inferences about the motives of countries that hold large reserves. Perhaps a rather simpler approach is more revealing: Was anyone worried in 2002 about inadequate reserves in the major countries at issue? No. Therefore, if reserves have increased severalfold since then, it does not seem plausible to explain them on the basis of a precautionary motive. To put it another way, does anyone believe that if China, for example, could have maintained the same exchange rate path with half as much reserves accumulation over the last three years, the Chinese authorities would have been unhappy about it? If, as it seems to me, they would not have been, the implication is fairly clear that China's reserves accumulation is an endogenous response to a decision not about the level of reserves but about exchange rate policy. That decision may or may not,

1. Diamond and Geanakoplos (2003).

in a full domestic calculus, have been a wise one. But the simple facts of the case—what China's policymakers said they were doing, and what they actually did—suggest that their accumulation of reserves was primarily a consequence of their exchange rate policy decisions. And the same can probably be said of the other East Asian countries.

If that is so, then the question of how to invest those reserves arises, and here Jeanne and I are in complete agreement. I have argued for some time that any reserves that the authorities do not envision using immediately and proximately in a crisis could surely be invested in a more productive vehicle than U.S. Treasury bills. Just as it would be financial malpractice for a defined-benefit pension fund to invest its reserves only in Treasury bills, so it must be with respect to government reserves that have a very long horizon. There are, as Jeanne recognizes, a variety of institutional issues involved in managing reserves in a more aggressive way. But these issues seem much smaller to me than in the case of investing the Social Security trust fund in equities, because what is envisioned here is the *external* investment of the reserves: to invest them domestically would compromise the macroeconomic objectives associated with reserves management. Since it is domestic investment that raises the most serious political issues, investment of reserves raises fewer concerns. (This assumes that investments are portfolio investments made through asset management intermediaries rather than direct investments, which raise a number of complex issues.)

The final question that this discussion raises is about the international surveillance mechanism. It is only a small exaggeration to say that, under traditional international norms, if a country makes an inappropriate decision about how much money it is going to borrow from its own citizens, that becomes a matter of great and urgent concern for the international community and will be a focal point of IMF surveillance. If, on the other hand, a country chooses to intervene in the foreign exchange market so as to cause its exchange rate and its trade relations to be very different from what they otherwise would have been, that, under current norms, is merely a matter of the country's choice of exchange rate regime and thus lies outside the purview of the IMF. Yet in a world where flows of capital out of many emerging market countries are large, to the extent those flows reflect not private investment decisions but rather conscious government policies directed at moving exchange rates in a particular direction, those decisions are surely an appropriate object of international surveillance and discussion. I hope that the recently debated reforms in IMF surveillance policy will redress this concern.

So, although I appreciate Jeanne's arguments, which are surely correct, that there are many countries that are not accumulating excessive reserves, and that reserves can be appropriately used for collective insurance, it seems to me there is a much larger issue at stake. That is whether something that is presumptively a nonmarket outcome, namely, a public decision to pursue intervention policies to cause exchange rates to differ from what market forces would determine, should be the subject of a more active discussion among the international community, led by the IMF. That it should be seems the most obvious implication of this research for IMF policy. As I said at the outset, it is enormously difficult to construct careful and rigorous models that will yield precise conclusions on these matters, and I have some questions about the particular model presented here. Nonetheless I think this is a very valuable undertaking that will eventually help us understand what I think is a major new feature of the international financial system, and for that we can be very grateful.

General discussion: Richard Cooper reminded the panel that in the 1960s there had been a lively literature on the optimum level of reserve holdings. He reported, however, that he had never met an official who thought in terms of optimal reserves; it should not be surprising, then, that reserves accumulation in many developing economies is not in accord with the normative prescriptions of Olivier Jeanne's model. Cooper suggested that, in order to understand the large international reserves in emerging market countries, one could simply refer to the main lesson that came out of the financial crises of the 1990s: do not run a current account deficit that is financed by private capital inflows. If the officials of such countries have indeed learned this lesson, they will have targeted a balanced current account and should therefore, in the buoyant world economy of recent years, find themselves with a current account surplus and growing reserves. Reserves accumulation, in other words, has been a by-product of other policies. Of course, when reserves fall uncomfortably low, officials will target an increase, but one should not worry too much if reserves exceed their notional target.

Cooper agreed with the paper's conclusion that the reserves of some Asian countries exceed what can be justified on a precautionary basis, but also with the paper's observation that most of these countries are slowly moving funds out of central bank reserves and into so-called sovereign wealth accounts. China, for example, is considering creating a $200 billion overseas investment fund to improve the return on its assets. Most of the official investment funds that already exist are small, Norway's being the largest. Cooper asserted that the consequences of a world financial market in which some of the major investors are official investment funds with assets on the scale of $100 billion or $200 billion, and the rules that will govern the investment of such funds, are important topics for future analysis.

Cooper noted that the extraordinarily rapid aging of some East Asian societies suggests a reason for reserves accumulation that was missing from Jeanne's analysis. These societies are eventually going to have to rely on foreign assets to maintain their consumption. Ideally, the private residents of those countries would be permitted to invest abroad, and they would surely do so if permitted. But except in Hong Kong, institutional and information constraints are strong deterrents. This situation will undoubtedly change eventually, but for the time being Asian central banks are effectively acting as a nonoptimizing intermediary in their citizens' foreign investment.

Replying to Lawrence Summers' point regarding the rationale for the current size of the Treasury's Exchange Stabilization Fund, Cooper noted that the fund is a historical legacy, determined by gold profits and the U.S. revaluation of the price of gold in the 1930s; there was no optimization involved at all.

Raghuram Rajan, echoing Cooper's remarks, agreed that in countries with severe restrictions on private capital flows the central bank's actions substitute for what would otherwise be private outflows. The question is how rapidly to remove the restrictions that today create distortions in saving and investment. He suggested that central banks' perception of the risks that accompany removal of restrictions on private transactions inhibits reform. The People's Bank of China, for example, is worried about the magnitude of private outflows that would result from relaxing its capital controls. In particular, given the poor quality of China's banking system, and given that the ratio of bank credit to GDP is well over 100 percent, one might reasonably expect a tremendous outflow of capital from China in the absence of controls. One mechanism that would allow for measured increases in private capital outflows would be for the central bank to set up a closed-end investment fund that is allowed to invest in foreign assets while maintaining control over the number of shares sold to domestic investors.

Eswar Prasad stressed the potential costs to a developing economy of an undervalued currency. In China, for example, the financial repression that results from undervaluation dictates a ceiling on deposit rates of about 3 percent, which, with inflation at comparable levels, amounts to a zero real rate of return. He suggested that it would be useful to know, in the context of Jeanne's model, how reserves accumulation affects the domestic rate of interest, providing an indication of the potential costs of financial repression implicit in accumulating reserves. He observed that because these costs of repression are largely hidden, spread throughout the financial system, the political system is likely to be biased toward undervaluation, with its more visible benefits for export growth. And he suggested that the costs of repression need to be taken into account when considering a build-up of reserves for other purposes that have been suggested, such as bank recapitalization or the accumulation of foreign assets to cover the needs of an aging society.

In a different vein, Prasad suggested that Jeanne's model overlooked the distributional effects of crises. These effects can have a substantial social cost. Even when a crisis is not large in terms of GDP, the distributional effects can still be enormous. In an economy like China, with a large number of unemployed, both disguised and undisguised, any disturbance could push people over the edge, setting off political and social instability. The Chinese authorities care a lot more about this cost than about the cost to output.

References

Aghion, Philippe, and others. 2006. "Exchange Rate Volatility and Productivity Growth: The Role of Financial Development." Working Paper 12117. Cambridge, Mass.: National Bureau of Economic Research (May).

Aizenman, Joshua. 2006. "International Reserves Management and the Current Account." Working Paper 12734. Cambridge, Mass.: National Bureau of Economic Research (December). Forthcoming in *Current Account and External Financing, Tenth Annual Conference Proceedings, Central Bank of Chile*, edited by Kevin Cowan, Sebastian Edwards, and Rodrigo Valdés. Santiago: Central Bank of Chile.

Aizenman, Joshua, and Reuven Glick. 2007. "Sterilization, Financial Liberalization, and Global Integration." Working paper. University of California, Santa Cruz, and Federal Reserve Bank of San Francisco.

Aizenman, Joshua, and Jaewoo Lee. 2005. "International Reserves: Precautionary vs. Mercantilist Views, Theory and Evidence." Working Paper 05/198. Washington: International Monetary Fund.

————. 2006. "Financial versus Monetary Mercantilism—Long-run View of Large International Reserves Hoarding." Working Paper 12718. Cambridge, Mass.: National Bureau of Economic Research (December).

Aizenman, Joshua, Yeonho Lee, and Yeongseop Rhee. 2004. "International Reserves Management and Capital Mobility in a Volatile World: Policy Considerations and a Case Study of Korea." Working Paper 10534. Cambridge, Mass.: National Bureau of Economic Research (June).

Aizenman, Joshua, and Nancy Marion. 2003. "The High Demand for International Reserves in the Far East: What Is Going On?" *Journal of the Japanese and International Economies* 17, no. 3: 370–400.

Aizenman, Joshua, Brian Pinto, and Artur Radziwill. 2007. "Sources for Financing Domestic Capital—Is Foreign Saving a Viable Option for Developing Countries?" *Journal of International Money and Finance* 26, no. 5: 682–702.

Beck, Thorsten, Asli Demirgüç-Kunt, and Ross E. Levine. 1999. "A New Database on Financial Development and Structure." Policy Research Working Paper 2146. Washington: World Bank (July).

Becker, Torbjörn, and Paolo Mauro. 2006. "Output Drops and the Shocks That Matter." Working Paper 06/172. Washington: International Monetary Fund (July).

Becker, Torbjörn, and others. 2007. "Country Insurance: The Role of Domestic Policies." Occasional Paper 254. Washington: International Monetary Fund.

Ben Bassat, Avraham, and Daniel Gottlieb. 1992. "Optimal International Reserves and Sovereign Risk." *Journal of International Economics* 33 (November): 345–62.

Berg, Andrew, Eduardo Borensztein, and Catherine Pattillo. 2005. "Assessing Early Warning Systems: How Have They Worked in Practice?" International Monetary Fund *Staff Papers* 52, no. 3: 462–502.

Bird, Graham, and Ramkishen Rajan. 2003. "Too Much of a Good Thing? The Adequacy of International Reserves in the Aftermath of Crises." *The World Economy* 26, no. 6: 873–91.

Bussière, Matthieu, and Christian Mulder. 1999. "External Vulnerability in Emerging Market Economies: How High Liquidity Can Offset Weak Fundamentals and the Effects of Contagion." Working Paper 99/88. Washington: International Monetary Fund (July).

Caballero, Ricardo J. 2006. "On the Macroeconomics of Assets Shortages." Working Paper 12753. Cambridge, Mass.: National Bureau of Economic Research (December).

Caballero, Ricardo J., and Arvind Krishnamurthy. 2004. "Smoothing Sudden Stops." *Journal of Economic Theory* 119, no. 1: 104–27.

Caballero, Ricardo J., and Stavros Panageas. 2005. "A Quantitative Model of Sudden Stops and External Liquidity Management." Working Paper 11293. Cambridge, Mass.: National Bureau of Economic Research (May).

Calvo, Guillermo A. 1996. "Capital Flows and Macroeconomic Management: Tequila Lessons." *International Journal of Finance and Economics* 1, no. 3: 207–23.

———. 1998. "Capital Flows and Capital-Market Crises: The Simple Economics of Sudden Stops." *Journal of Applied Economics* 1, no. 1: 35–54.

———. 2006. "Monetary Policy Challenges in Emerging Markets: Sudden Stop, Liability Dollarization, and Lender of Last Resort." Working Paper 12788. Cambridge, Mass.: National Bureau of Economic Research (December).

Calvo, Guillermo A., Alejandro Izquierdo, and Luis F. Mejía. 2004. "On the Empirics of Sudden Stops: The Relevance of Balance-Sheet Effects." Working Paper 10520. Cambridge, Mass.: National Bureau of Economic Research (May).

Caselli, Francesco. 2007. "The Marginal Product of Capital." *Quarterly Journal of Economics* 122, no. 2: 535–68.

Chang, Roberto, and Andres Velasco. 2000. "Liquidity Crises in Emerging Markets: Theory and Policy." In *NBER Macroeconomics Annual 1999,* edited by Ben S. Bernanke and Julio Rotemberg. MIT Press.

Chinn, Menzie D., and Hiro Ito. 2005. "What Matters for Financial Development? Capital Controls, Institutions, and Interactions." Working Paper 11370. Cambridge, Mass.: National Bureau of Economic Research (May).

De Beaufort-Wijnholds, J. Onno, and Arend Kapteyn. 2001. "Reserve Adequacy in Emerging Market Economies." Working Paper 01/143. Washington: International Monetary Fund (September).

Detragiache, Enrica, and Antonio Spilimbergo. 2001. "Crises and Liquidity: Evidence and Interpretation." Working Paper 01/2. Washington: International Monetary Fund (January).

Diamond, Peter, and John Geanakoplos. 2003. "Social Security Investment in Equities." *American Economic Review* 93, no. 4: 1047–74.

Dooley, Michael P., David Folkerts-Landau, and Peter Garber. 2004. "The Revived Bretton Woods System: The Effects of Periphery Intervention and Reserve Management on Interest Rates and Exchange Rates in Center Countries." Working Paper 10332. Cambridge, Mass.: National Bureau of Economic Research (March).

Duffie, Darrell, Lasse Heje Pedersen, and Kenneth J. Singleton. 2003. "Modeling Sovereign Yield Spreads: A Case Study of Russian Debt." *Journal of Finance* 58, no. 1: 119–59.

Durdu, Ceyhun Bora, Enrique G. Mendoza, and Marco E. Terrones. 2007. "Precautionary Demand of Foreign Assets in Sudden Stop Economies: An Assessment of the New Mercantilism." Working Paper 13123. Cambridge, Mass.: National Bureau of Economic Research (May).

Edwards, Sebastian. 1985. "On the Interest-Rate Elasticity of the Demand for International Reserves: Some Evidence from Developing Countries." *Journal of International Money and Finance* 4, no. 2: 287–95.

———. 2001. "Capital Mobility and Economic Performance: Are Emerging Economies Different?" Working Paper 8076. Cambridge, Mass.: National Bureau of Economic Research (January).

———. 2004. "Thirty Years of Current Account Imbalances, Current Account Reversals, and Sudden Stops." International Monetary Fund *Staff Papers* 51 (June): 1–49.

Eichengreen, Barry. 2006. "Insurance Underwriter or Financial Development Fund: What Role for Reserve Pooling in Latin America?" Working Paper 12451. Cambridge, Mass.: National Bureau of Economic Research (August).

Eichengreen, Barry, and Ashoka Mody. 2000. "What Explains Spreads on Emerging Market Debt?" In *Capital Flows and the Emerging Economies: Theory, Evidence and Controversies,* edited by Sebastian Edwards. University of Chicago Press.

European Central Bank. 2006. "The Accumulation of Foreign Reserves." Occasional Paper 43. Frankfurt (February).

Flood, Robert P., and Peter M. Garber. 1984. "Collapsing Exchange-Rate Regimes: Some Linear Examples." *Journal of International Economics* 17 (August): 1–13.

Flood, Robert, and Nancy Marion. 2002. "Holding International Reserves in an Era of High Capital Mobility." In *Brookings Trade Forum 2001*, edited by Susan M. Collins and Dani Rodrik, pp. 1–47. Brookings.

Frankel, Jeffrey A., and Eduardo A. Cavallo. 2004. "Does Openness to Trade Make Countries More Vulnerable to Sudden Stops, or Less? Using Gravity to Establish Causality." Working Paper 10957. Cambridge, Mass.: National Bureau of Economic Research (December).

Frankel, Jeffrey A., and Andrew K. Rose. 1996. "Currency Crashes in Emerging Markets: An Empirical Treatment." *Journal of International Economics* 41 (November): 351–66.

Frankel, Jeffrey A., and Shang-Jin Wei. 2005. "Managing Macroeconomic Crises: Policy Lessons." In *Managing Economic Volatility and Crises: A Practitioner's Guide,* edited by Joshua Aizenman and Brian Pinto. Cambridge University Press.

Frenkel, Jacob A., and Boyan Jovanovic. 1981. "Optimal International Reserves: A Stochastic Framework." *Economic Journal* 91, no. 362: 507–14.

Garcia, Pablo S., and Claudio Soto. 2004. "Large Hoarding of International Reserves: Are They Worth It?" Working Paper 299. Santiago: Central Bank of Chile (December).

Ghosh, Atish, and others. 2007. "Modeling Aggregate Use of Fund Resources— Analytical Approaches and Medium-Term Projections." Working Paper 07/70. Washington: International Monetary Fund (March).

Gourinchas, Pierre-Olivier, and Olivier Jeanne. 2006. "Capital Flows to Developing Countries: The Allocation Puzzle." University of California, Berkeley, Department of Economics.

Hamada, Koichi, and Kazuo Ueda. 1977. "Random Walks and the Theory of Optimal International Reserves." *Economic Journal* 87, no. 848: 722–42.

Hauner, David. 2005. "A Fiscal Price Tag for International Reserves." Working Paper 05/81. Washington: International Monetary Fund (April).

Heller, H. Robert. 1966. "Optimal International Reserves." *Economic Journal* 76, no. 302: 296–311.

Hutchison, Michael M., and Ilan Noy. 2006. "Sudden Stops and the Mexican Wave: Currency Crises, Capital Flow Reversals and Output Loss in Emerging Markets." *Journal of Development Economics* 79, no. 1: 225–48.

Hviding, Ketil, Michael Nowak, and Luca Antonio Ricci. 2004. "Can Higher Reserves Help Reduce Exchange Rate Volatility?" Working Paper 04/189. Washington: International Monetary Fund (October).

International Monetary Fund. 2000. "Debt- and Reserve-Related Indicators of External Vulnerability." IMF Board Paper. Washington (March) (www.imf. org/external/np/pdr/debtres/index.htm).

———. 2001. "Issues in Reserves Adequacy and Management." IMF Board Paper. Washington (October) (www.imf.org/external/np/pdr/resad/2001/reserve. htm).

———. 2003. "Are Foreign Exchange Reserves in Asia Too High?" Chapter 2 in *World Economic Outlook*, pp. 78–92 (September). Washington: International Monetary Fund.

Jeanne, Olivier, and Romain Rancière. 2006. "The Optimal Level of International Reserves for Emerging Market Countries: Formulas and Applications." Working Paper 06/229. Washington: International Monetary Fund (October).

Jeanne, Olivier, and Charles Wyplosz. 2003. "The International Lender of Last Resort: How Large Is Large Enough?" In *Managing Currency Crises in Emerging Markets*, edited by Michael P. Dooley and Jeffrey A. Frankel. University of Chicago Press.

Jen, Stephen. 2007. "Currencies: How Big Could Sovereign Wealth Funds Be by 2015?" New York: Morgan Stanley Research Global (May).

Johnson, Harry G. 1953. "Optimum Tariffs and Retaliation." *Review of Economic Studies* 21, no. 2: 142–53.

Johnson-Calari, Jennifer, and Malan Rietveld, eds. 2007. *Sovereign Wealth Management*. London: Central Banking Publications.

Kaminsky, Graciela, Saul Lizondo, and Carmen M. Reinhart. 1998. "Leading Indicators of Currency Crises." International Monetary Fund *Staff Papers* 45, no. 1: 1–48.

Knight, Malcolm D. 2006. "International Reserve Diversification and Disclosure." Speech at the Swiss National Bank/Institute for International Economics Conference, Zurich, September 8 (www.bis.org/speeches/sp060908.htm).

Krugman, Paul. 1979. "A Model of Balance-of-Payments Crises." *Journal of Money, Credit and Banking* 11, no. 3: 311–25.

Lee, Jaewoo. 2004. "Insurance Value of International Reserves: An Option Pricing Approach." Working Paper 04/175. Washington: International Monetary Fund (September).

Lane, Philip R., and Gian Maria Milesi-Ferretti. 2006. "The External Wealth of Nations Mark II: Revised and Extended Estimates of Foreign Assets and Liabilities, 1970–2004." Discussion Paper 5644. London: Centre for Economic Policy Research (April).

Levy Yeyati, Eduardo. 2006. "The Cost of Reserves." Working Paper 10/2006. Buenos Aires: Centro de Investigación en Finanzas, Universidad Torcuato Di Tella (July).

Miller, Marcus, and Lei Zhang. 2006. "Fear and Market Failure: Global Imbalances and 'Self-Insurance.'" Discussion Paper 6000. London: Centre for Economic Policy Research (December).

Mohanty, M. S., and Philip Turner. 2006. "Foreign Exchange Reserve Accumulation in Emerging Markets: What Are the Domestic Implications?" *BIS Quarterly Review* (September): 39–52.

Morris, Stephen, and Hyun Song Shin. 1998. "Unique Equilibrium in a Model of Self-Fulfilling Currency Attacks." *American Economic Review* 88 no. 3: 587–97.

Mulder, Christian. 2000. "The Adequacy of International Reserve Levels: A New Approach." In *Risk Management for Central Bankers*, edited by Steven F. Frowen, Robert Pringle, and Benedict Weller. London: Central Bank Publications.

Parisi-Capone, Elisa, and Brad Setser. 2006. "Central Banks Active Participants in the Market for Treasuries with a Maturity of up to 10 Years." *RGE Monitor.* New York: Roubini Global Economics (October 17) (www.rgemonitor.com/ redir.php?sid=1&tgid=10000&clid=4042&cid=152505).

Prasad, Eswar S., and Raghuram G. Rajan. 2005. "Controlled Capital Account Liberalization: A Proposal." Policy Discussion Paper 05/7. Washington: International Monetary Fund (October).

Pringle, Robert, and Nick Carver, eds. 2005. *RBS Reserve Management Trends 2005.* London: Central Banking Publications.

Qian, XingWang. 2006. "Hoarding of International Reserves: Mrs Machlup's Wardrobe and the Joneses." University of California, Santa Cruz.

Quinn, Dennis P. 2000. "Democracy and International Financial Liberalization." McDonough School of Business, Georgetown University.

Reinhart, Carmen M., and Kenneth S. Rogoff. 2004. "The Modern History of Exchange Rate Arrangements: A Reinterpretation." *Quarterly Journal of Economics* 119, no. 1: 1–48.

Rodrik, Dani. 2006. "The Social Cost of Foreign Exchange Reserves." *International Economic Journal* 20, no. 3: 253–66.

Rozanov, Andrew. 2005. "Who Holds the Wealth of Nations?" *Central Banking Journal* 15, no. 4: 52–57.

Rudebusch, Glenn D., Brian P. Sack, and Eric T. Swanson. 2007. "Macroeconomic Implications of Changes in the Term Premium." Federal Reserve Bank of St. Louis *Review* 89, no. 4: 241–69.

Stiglitz, Joseph E. 2006. *Making Globalization Work.* W.W. Norton.

Summers, Lawrence H. 2006. "Reflections on Global Account Imbalances and Emerging Markets Reserves Accumulation." L. K. Jha Memorial Lecture, Reserve Bank of India, Mumbai, March 24 (www.president.harvard.edu/ speeches/2006/0324_rbi.html).

Truman, Edwin M., and Anna Wong. 2006. "The Case for an International Reserve Diversification Standard." Working Paper 06-2. Washington: Institute for International Economics (May).

Warnock, Francis E., and Veronica Cacdac Warnock. 2006. "International Capital Flows and U.S. Interest Rates." Working Paper 12560. Cambridge, Mass.: National Bureau of Economic Research (October).

Wooldridge, Philip D. 2006. "The Changing Composition of Official Reserves." *BIS Quarterly Review* (September): 25–38.

STEPHEN D. OLINER
Board of Governors of the Federal Reserve System

DANIEL E. SICHEL
Board of Governors of the Federal Reserve System

KEVIN J. STIROH
Federal Reserve Bank of New York

Explaining a Productive Decade

PRODUCTIVITY GROWTH IN THE United States rose sharply in the mid-1990s, after a quarter century of sluggish gains. That pickup was widely documented, and a relatively broad consensus emerged that the speedup in the second half of the 1990s was importantly driven by information technology (IT).[1] After 2000, however, the economic picture changed dramatically, with a sharp pullback in IT investment, the collapse in the technology sector, the terrorist attacks of September 11, 2001, and the 2001 recession. Given the general belief that IT was a key factor in the growth resurgence in the mid-1990s, many analysts expected that labor productivity growth would slow as IT investment retreated after 2000. Instead labor productivity accelerated further over the next several years. More recently, however, the pace of labor productivity growth has slowed considerably.

We thank Martin Baily, John Fernald, Andrew Figura, Dale Jorgenson, Gregory Mankiw, participants at the Brookings Panel conference, and participants at the March 2007 Productivity Meeting at the National Bureau of Economic Research for useful comments and discussions; we also thank John Roberts for providing code and assistance to implement his Kalman filter model, George Smith and Robert Yuskavage of the Bureau of Economic Analysis for help with the industry data, and David Byrne for assistance with semiconductor data. The views expressed in this paper are those of the authors and do not necessarily reflect the views of the Federal Reserve Bank of New York, the Board of Governors of the Federal Reserve System, or other staff members at either organization.

1. See *Economic Report of the President 2001,* Basu, Fernald, and Shapiro (2001), Brynjolfsson and Hitt (2000, 2003), Jorgenson and Stiroh (2000), Jorgenson, Ho, and Stiroh (2002, 2005), and Oliner and Sichel (2000, 2002). In these papers IT refers to computer hardware, software, and communications equipment. This category often also is referred to as information and communications technology, or ICT. For industry-level evidence supporting the role of IT in the productivity resurgence, see Stiroh (2002b). For an interpretation of the industry evidence that puts less emphasis on IT, see Bosworth and Triplett (2007) and McKinsey Global Institute (2001).

In light of these developments, researchers and other commentators have been intensely interested in the course of productivity growth since 2000. Distinguishing among the possible explanations for the continued strength in productivity growth is challenging, because much of that strength appeared in measured multifactor productivity (MFP), the unexplained residual in the standard growth accounting setup. Nevertheless, potential explanations can be divided into two broad categories: those centered on IT and those unrelated or only loosely related to IT.

The simplest IT-centered story—that rapid technological progress in the production of IT and the induced accumulation of IT capital raised productivity growth—does not work for the period after 2000, because the contributions to growth from both the production and the use of IT declined. A second IT-related story that has received a great deal of attention is that IT investment proxies for complementary investments in intangible capital, and a growing body of research has highlighted the important role played by such intangibles.[2] A third IT-related story identifies IT as a general-purpose technology that spurs further innovation over time in a wide range of industries, ultimately boosting growth in MFP.[3] Because this process takes time, the gains in MFP observed since 2000 could reflect the follow-on innovations from the heavy investment in IT in the second half of the 1990s.

Another broad set of explanations highlights forces not specific to IT. Gains in labor productivity since 2000 could have been driven by fundamental technological progress outside of IT production, as implied by the strong growth in MFP in other sectors.[4] Alternatively, the robust advance in labor productivity could reflect broader macroeconomic factors such as normal cyclical dynamics, a decline in adjustment costs after 2000 as investment spending dropped back, greater-than-usual business caution in hiring and investment, or increased competitive pressures on firms to

2. See Corrado, Hulten, and Sichel (2005, 2006), Brynjolfsson and Hitt (2003), Bresnahan, Brynjolfsson, and Hitt (2002), Basu and others (2004), Black and Lynch (2001, 2004), and Nakamura (1999, 2001, 2003). The National Income and Product Accounts (NIPAs) exclude virtually all intangibles other than software, although the Bureau of Economic Analysis, which produces the NIPA data, recently released a satellite account for scientific research and development; see Okubo and others (2006).
3. Bresnahan and Trajtenberg (1995) were the first to write about IT as a general-purpose technology. See also Organization for Economic Cooperation and Development (2000), Schreyer (2000), van Ark (2000), Basu and others (2004), and Basu and Fernald (2007).
4. Jorgenson, Ho, and Stiroh (2007); Bosworth and Triplett (2007).

restructure, cut costs, raise profits, and boost productivity. The profit-driven cost-cutting hypothesis, in particular, has received considerable attention in the business press.[5]

In this paper we try to sort out these issues using both aggregate and industry-level data.[6] We investigate four specific questions. First, given the latest data and some important extensions to the standard growth accounting framework, is an IT-centered story still the right explanation for the resurgence in productivity growth over 1995–2000, and does IT play a significant role when considering the entire decade since 1995? Second, what accounts for the continued strength in productivity growth after 2000? Third, how has investment in intangible capital influenced productivity developments? Finally, what are the prospects for labor productivity growth in coming years?

Our analysis relies in part on neoclassical growth accounting, a methodology that researchers and policymakers have used for many years to gain insights into the sources of economic growth. Notably, the Council of Economic Advisers, the Congressional Budget Office, and the Federal Reserve Board routinely use growth accounting as part of their analytical apparatus to assess growth trends.[7]

Of course, growth accounting is subject to limitations, and in recent years many analysts have leveled critiques at this methodology. For example, the standard neoclassical framework does not explicitly account for adjustment costs, variable factor utilization, deviations from perfect competition and constant returns to scale, outsourcing and offshoring, management expertise, or the intangibles that are omitted from published data. In addition, researchers have raised a host of measurement issues that could affect

---

5. See Gordon (2003), Baily (2003), Schweitzer (2004), and Stiroh (forthcoming). For references to the business press, see Gordon (2003) and Stiroh (forthcoming).

6. Several other researchers have examined industry data, including Baily and Lawrence (2001), Stiroh (2002b), Nordhaus (2002b), Corrado and others (2007), and Bosworth and Triplett (2007). For references to the literature on industry-level data in Europe, see van Ark and Inklaar (2005).

7. See *Economic Report of the President 2007,* Congressional Budget Office (2007a, 2007b), and the latest available transcripts of the meetings of the Federal Open Market Committee (FOMC). The 2001 FOMC transcripts show that staff presentations on the economic outlook featured growth accounting in the discussion of productivity trends. Private sector analysts also rely on growth accounting; see, for example, Global Insight, *U.S. Executive Summary,* March 2007, and Macroeconomic Advisers, *Macro Focus,* March 22, 2007.

the standard framework.[8] It is well beyond the scope of this paper to deal with all of these critiques, but we augment the standard framework to account for some of the most salient ones. In particular, we take on board time-varying utilization of inputs, adjustment costs for capital, and intangibles. Our intent is to broaden the standard framework to get a fuller view of productivity developments during the past decade.

Briefly, our answers to the four questions we pose are as follows. Both the aggregate and the industry-level results indicate that IT was indeed a key driver of the pickup in labor productivity growth over 1995–2000. IT also is a substantial contributor to labor productivity growth over the full decade since 1995, although its contribution is smaller after 2000. In the aggregate data, this conclusion stands even after accounting for variable factor utilization, adjustment costs, and intangible capital.

Regarding the continued strength in labor productivity growth since 2000 in the published data, our answer has a number of elements. As a matter of growth accounting arithmetic, the smaller—although still sizable— contribution of IT after 2000 was more than offset by several factors, the most important being faster MFP growth outside the IT-producing sector. Just as the aggregate data highlight different sources of productivity growth during 1995–2000 than since 2000, so do the industry data. The industry composition of labor productivity growth across these periods shifted significantly, and we report evidence that IT capital was linked to changes in industry productivity growth in the 1990s but not in the period since 2000.

The industry data also suggest that the rapid post-2000 productivity gains were due, at least in part, to restructuring and cost cutting in some industries as highlighted by Robert Gordon.[9] In particular, those industries that saw the sharpest declines in profits from the late 1990s through 2001 also tended to post the largest gains in labor productivity in the early 2000s. Because these restructuring-induced advances probably were one-

8. Much has been written about the link between management expertise and productivity, including Bloom and Van Reenen (2006), McKinsey Global Institute (2001), and Farrell, Baily, and Remes (2005). Gordon (2003) and Sichel (2003) provide reasons why offshoring and hours mismeasurement may have had a relatively limited effect on labor productivity growth, whereas Houseman (2007) argues that these factors could have had a significant effect in the U.S. manufacturing sector. For a discussion of measurement issues related to the pace of technical progress in the semiconductor industry, see Aizcorbe, Oliner, and Sichel (2006). For further discussion of issues related to critiques of the neoclassical framework, see Congressional Budget Office (2007b).

9. Gordon (2003).

time events (and could be reversed), they are unlikely to be a source of ongoing support to productivity growth.

In addition, the industry evidence indicates that reallocations of both material and labor inputs have been important contributors to labor productivity growth since 2000, a point that Barry Bosworth and Jack Triplett also note.[10] Although it is difficult to pin a precise interpretation on the reallocation results, the importance of these reallocations could be viewed as evidence that the flexibility of the U.S. economy has supported aggregate productivity growth in recent years by facilitating the shifting of resources among industries.

The incorporation of intangibles into the aggregate growth accounting framework takes some of the luster off the performance of labor productivity since 2000 and makes the gains in the 1995–2000 period look better than they looked in the published data. In addition, the step-up after 2000 in MFP growth outside the IT-producing sector is smaller after accounting for intangibles than in the published data. Thus any stories tied to a pickup in MFP growth (such as IT as a general-purpose technology) may apply to the entire decade since 1995 and not simply to recent years. This framework also implies that intangible investment has been quite sluggish since 2000, coinciding with the soft path for IT capital spending. All else equal, this pattern could be a negative for labor productivity growth in the future to the extent that these investments are seed corn for future productivity gains.

Finally, our analysis of the prospects for labor productivity growth highlights the wide range of possible outcomes. We report updated estimates of trend growth in labor productivity from a Kalman filter model developed by John Roberts;[11] these results generate a 2-standard-error confidence band extending from 1¼ percent to 3¼ percent at an annual rate, with a point estimate of 2¼ percent. In addition, we solve for the steady-state growth of labor productivity in a multisector model under a range of conditioning assumptions. This machinery also suggests a wide range of outcomes, extending from about 1½ percent to just above 3 percent, with a midpoint of 2¼ percent. Notwithstanding the wide band of uncertainty, these estimates are consistent with productivity growth remaining significantly above the pace that prevailed in the twenty-five years before 1995, but falling short of the very rapid gains recorded over the past decade.

10. Bosworth and Triplett (2007).
11. Roberts (2001).

The paper is organized as follows. The next section reviews the aggregate growth accounting framework and presents baseline results that account for variable factor utilization and adjustment costs. The section that follows uses the approach of Susanto Basu and coauthors to generate time series for intangible investment and capital services and presents growth accounting results for the augmented framework.[12] This approach complements that in the 2005 and 2006 papers by Carol Corrado, Charles Hulten, and Daniel Sichel, who also developed time series of intangible investment and capital and incorporated those estimates into a standard growth accounting framework. We then turn to the industry data to supplement the insights that can be drawn from the aggregate data. Finally, we discuss the outlook for productivity growth and present some brief conclusions.

Aggregate Growth Accounting: Analytical Framework and Baseline Results

We use an extension of the growth accounting framework developed by Oliner and Sichel to analyze the sources of aggregate productivity growth in the United States.[13] That framework was designed to measure the growth contributions from the production and use of IT capital, key factors that emerged in the second half of the 1990s. The framework has some limitations, however. It excludes intangible capital, which has received much attention in recent research on the sources of productivity gains. It also imposes the strict neoclassical assumption of a frictionless economy and thus abstracts from cyclical influences on productivity growth and from the effects of adjustment costs arising from the installation of new capital goods.

The growth accounting framework in this paper incorporates all of these considerations. We meld the original Oliner-Sichel model with the treatment of adjustment costs and cyclical factor utilization developed by Basu, John Fernald, and Matthew Shapiro.[14] In addition, we take account of intangible capital by drawing on the model of Basu, Fernald, Nicholas Oulton, and Sylaja Srinivasan.[15]

---

12. Basu and others (2004).
13. Oliner and Sichel (2000, 2002).
14. Basu, Fernald, and Shapiro (2001; hereafter BFS)
15. Basu and others (2004; hereafter BFOS).

Analytical Framework

The model that underlies our analytical framework includes six sectors. Four of these produce the final nonfarm business output included in the National Income and Product Accounts (NIPAs): computer hardware, software, communications equipment, and a large non-IT-producing sector. The NIPAs omit production of virtually all intangible capital other than software. Our model accounts for this capital by adding a fifth final-output sector that produces the intangible assets excluded from the NIPAs. In addition to the five final-output sectors, our model includes a sector that produces semiconductors, which are either consumed as an intermediate input by the final-output sectors or exported to foreign firms. To focus on the role of semiconductors in the economy, the model abstracts from all other intermediate inputs.

Following BFS, we allow the length of the workweek, labor effort, and the utilization of capital to vary over time. We also assume that the installation of new capital diverts resources from the production of market output. As in BFS, these adjustment costs depend on the amount of investment relative to existing capital. Boosting the ratio of investment to capital increases the fraction of output that is lost to adjustment costs.[16] To complete the model specification, we assume that the production function in every sector exhibits constant returns to scale and that the economy is perfectly competitive.[17]

Given this model, the appendix in the working paper version of this paper shows that growth in aggregate labor productivity can be expressed as[18]

$$(1) \qquad A\dot{L}P \equiv \dot{V} - \dot{H} = \sum_{j}\left(\alpha_{j}^{\kappa} - \phi_{j}\right)\left(\dot{K}_{j} - \dot{H}\right) + \alpha^{L}\dot{q} + M\dot{F}P,$$

where a dot over a variable signifies the growth rate of that variable, V is aggregate value added in nonfarm business, H is aggregate hours worked, K_{j} is the aggregate amount of type-j capital used in the nonfarm business

---

16. Although BFS also include adjustment costs for labor in their model, they zero out these costs in their empirical work. We simply omit labor adjustment costs from the start. For additional discussion of capital adjustment costs and productivity growth, see Kiley (2001).

17. The results in BFS and in Basu, Fernald, and Kimball (2006) strongly support the assumption of constant returns for the economy as a whole. We invoke perfect competition as a convenience in a model that already has many moving parts.

18. Oliner, Sichel, and Stiroh (2007).

sector, α^L and α_j^K are, respectively, the income shares for labor and each type of capital, ϕ_j is the adjustment cost elasticity of output with respect to type-j capital, q is an index of labor quality, and *MFP* denotes multifactor productivity. The various types of capital include computer hardware, software, communications equipment, other tangible capital, and intangible capital other than software; each type of capital is produced by the corresponding final-output sector in our model. Except for the adjustment cost effect captured by ϕ_j, equation 1 is a standard growth decomposition. It expresses growth in labor productivity as the sum of the contribution from the increase in capital per hour worked (capital deepening), the contribution from the improvement in labor quality, and growth in aggregate MFP.[19]

Aggregate MFP growth, in turn, equals a share-weighted sum of the sectoral MFP growth rates:

$$(2) \qquad\qquad \dot{MFP} = \sum_i \mu_i \dot{MFP_i} + \mu_s \dot{MFP_s},$$

where S denotes the semiconductor sector and i indexes the final-output sectors in our model (listed above). The weight for each sector equals its gross output divided by aggregate value added. These are the usual Domar weights that take account of the input-output relationships among industries.[20] Equation 2 has the same structure as its counterpart in an earlier paper by Oliner and Sichel.[21] The only formal difference is that including intangible capital increases the number of final-output sectors from four to five.[22]

---

19. The weight on $\dot{K_j} - \dot{H}$ represents the output elasticity of type-j capital. In the case without adjustment costs, $\phi_j = 0$, and so the income share α_j^K proxies for this output elasticity. However, in the presence of adjustment costs, the first-order condition for the optimal choice of capital yields the more general result shown in equation 1. In effect, the income share captures both the direct contribution of capital to production and the benefit of having an extra unit of capital to absorb adjustment costs. The weight in equation 1 nets out the portion of the income share that relates to adjustment costs, as this effect is embedded in the MFP term discussed below.

20. Domar (1961).

21. Oliner and Sichel (2002).

22. In contrast to the expression for aggregate MFP growth in BFS, equation 2 contains no terms to account for reallocations of output, labor, or capital across sectors. The particularly clean form of equation 2 arises, in large part, from our assumption of constant returns to scale and the absence of adjustment costs for labor (which implies that competitive forces equate the marginal product of labor in all sectors). In addition, we have assumed that any wedge between the shadow value of capital and its user cost owing to adjustment costs is the same in all sectors. Given this assumption, reallocations of capital across sectors do not affect aggregate output.

Finally, the sectoral MFP growth rates in equation 2 can be expressed as

$$(3) \qquad \dot{MFP_i} = \xi_i \dot{W_i} - \sum_j \phi_{j,i}\left(\dot{I}_{j,i} - \dot{K}_{j,i}\right) + \dot{z}_i$$

for the final-output sectors and

$$(4) \qquad \dot{MFP_s} = \xi_s \dot{W_s} - \sum_j \phi_{j,s}\left(\dot{I}_{j,s} - \dot{K}_{j,s}\right) + \dot{z}_s$$

for semiconductor producers, where the ξ's represent the elasticity of sectoral output with respect to the workweek (W), the I's and K's denote sectoral investment and capital services for each type of capital, the ϕ's represent the sectoral adjustment cost elasticities for each type of capital, and the z's represent the true level of technology. All of the ξ's and ϕ's take positive values.

In the BFS model that we adopt, firms vary the intensity of their factor use along all margins simultaneously, which makes the workweek a sufficient statistic for factor utilization in general. Lengthening the workweek boosts measured MFP growth in equations 3 and 4 as firms obtain more output from their capital and labor. Regarding adjustment costs, faster growth of investment spending relative to that of capital depresses measured MFP growth as firms divert resources from producing market output to installing new plant and equipment. The effects of factor utilization and adjustment costs drive a wedge between measured MFP growth and the true pace of improvement in technology $\dot{z}$.

Data, Calibration, and Measurement Issues

This section provides a brief overview of the data used for our aggregate growth accounting, discusses the calibration of key parameters, and addresses some important measurement issues.[23] The national accounts data that we discuss here exclude virtually all forms of intangible capital except for investment in computer software. We defer the consideration of intangible capital until the next section.

Our dataset represents an up-to-date reading on productivity developments through 2006 based on data available as of the end of March 2007. We rely heavily on the dataset assembled by the Bureau of Labor Statistics (BLS) for its estimates of MFP in the private nonfarm business sector. This

---

23. For details on data sources, see the data appendix to Oliner and Sichel (2002).

dataset extended through 2005 at the time we conducted the analysis for this paper. We extrapolated the series required for our framework through 2006, drawing largely on corresponding series in the NIPAs.

To calculate the income share for each type of capital in our framework, we follow the BLS procedure that distributes total capital income across assets by assuming that each asset earns the same rate of return net of depreciation.[24] This is the same method used by Oliner and Sichel and by Jorgenson, Ho, and Stiroh.[25] Consistent with the standard practice in the productivity literature, we allow these income shares to vary year by year.[26]

These data and procedures generate a series for aggregate MFP growth via equation 1. Given this series as a top-line control, we estimate MFP growth in each sector with the "dual" method employed by various researchers in the past.[27] This method uses data on the prices of output and inputs, rather than their quantities, to calculate sectoral MFP growth. We opt for the dual approach because the sectoral data on prices are available on a more timely basis than the corresponding quantity data. Roughly speaking, the dual method compares the rate of change in a sector's output price with that of its input costs. Sectors in which prices fall quickly compared with their input costs are estimated to have experienced relatively rapid MFP growth.[28]

---

24. The weight on the capital deepening term in equation 1 for type-j capital equals its income share minus its adjustment cost elasticity. As discussed below, empirical estimates of these asset-specific elasticities are not available, which forces us to approximate the theoretically correct weights. Note that the weights on the capital deepening terms in equation 1 sum to one minus the labor share under constant returns to scale. We replace the theoretically correct weights with standard income-share weights that also sum to one minus the labor share. This approximation attaches the correct weight to aggregate capital deepening but may result in some misallocation of the weights across asset types.

25. Oliner and Sichel (2000, 2002); Jorgenson, Ho, and Stiroh (2002, 2007).

26. Year-by-year share weighting embeds the implicit assumption that firms satisfy the static first-order condition that equates the marginal product of capital with its user cost. Strictly speaking, this assumption is not valid in the presence of adjustment costs, as noted by BFS and by Groth, Nuñez, and Srinivasan (2006). Both of those studies replace the year-by-year share weights with the average shares over periods of five years or more, in an effort to approximate a steady-state relationship that might be expected to hold on average over longer periods. We found, however, that our results were little changed by replacing year-by-year shares with period-average shares. Accordingly, we adhere to the usual share weighting practice in the literature.

27. Jorgenson and Stiroh (2000), Jorgenson, Ho, and Stiroh (2002, 2007), Oliner and Sichel (2000, 2002), and Triplett (1996), among others.

28. Oliner and Sichel (2002) give a nontechnical description of the way in which we implement the dual method, and the appendix in the working paper version of this paper (Oliner, Sichel, and Stiroh, 2007) provides the algebraic details.

The expression that links aggregate and sectoral MFP growth (equation 2) involves the Domar weight for each sector, the ratio of the sector's gross output to aggregate value added. For the four NIPA-based final-output sectors, gross output simply equals the value of the sector's final sales, which we estimate using data from the Bureau of Economic Analysis (BEA). For the semiconductor sector we calculate gross output based on data from the Semiconductor Industry Association as well as data constructed by Federal Reserve Board staff to support the Federal Reserve's published data on U.S. industrial production.

The final step is to calculate the influence of adjustment costs and factor utilization on the growth of both aggregate and sectoral MFP. In principle, we could use equations 3 and 4 to calculate the effects at the sectoral level and then aggregate those effects using equation 2. However, as equations 3 and 4 show, this bottom-up approach requires highly disaggregated data on investment and the workweek and equally disaggregated output elasticities with respect to adjustment costs and the workweek (the ϕ's and the ξ's). Unfortunately, estimates of the required sectoral elasticities are not available.

To make use of readily available estimates, we work instead from the top down. That is, we model the effects of adjustment costs and the workweek for the nonfarm business sector as a whole and then distribute the aggregate effects across sectors. Let $\dot{W}$ and ξ denote, respectively, the percentage change in the workweek for aggregate nonfarm business and the elasticity of nonfarm business output with respect to this aggregate workweek. Then the workweek effect for aggregate nonfarm business equals $\xi\dot{W}$. Similarly, we measure the aggregate effect of adjustment costs as $\phi(\dot{I} - \dot{K})$, where $\dot{I}$, $\dot{K}$, and ϕ denote, respectively, growth in aggregate real investment spending, growth in aggregate real capital services, and the aggregate adjustment cost elasticity. To complete the top-down approach, we assume that the adjustment cost and workweek effects are uniform across sectors. Under this assumption, the top-down version of equations 2 through 4 is as follows (starting with the sectoral equations):

$$(5) \qquad \dot{MFP_i} = \frac{1}{\mu}\left[\xi\dot{W} - \phi(\dot{I} - \dot{K})\right] + \dot{z_i}$$

$$(6) \qquad \dot{MFP_s} = \frac{1}{\mu}\left[\xi\dot{W} - \phi(\dot{I} - \dot{K})\right] + \dot{z_s}$$

(7) $M\dot{F}P = \sum_i \mu_i M\dot{F}P_i + \mu_s M\dot{F}P_s = \xi\dot{W} - \phi(\dot{I} - \dot{K}) + \sum_i \mu_i \dot{z}_i + \mu_s \dot{z}_s,$

where $\bar{\mu} \equiv \sum_i \mu_i + \mu_s$. One can easily verify that the second equality holds in equation 7 by substituting for $M\dot{F}P_i$ and $M\dot{F}P_s$ from equations 5 and 6. Equations 5 through 7 serve as our empirical counterpart to equations 2 through 4.

We follow BFS in specifying ξ, $\dot{W}$, and ϕ. Starting with the workweek effect, we specify the aggregate elasticity ξ to be a weighted average of BFS's sectoral estimates of ξ for durable manufacturing, nondurable manufacturing, and nonmanufacturing. Using weights that reflect current-dollar output shares in these sectors, we obtain an aggregate value of ξ equal to 1.24. To measure the workweek itself, we use the BLS series for production or nonsupervisory workers from the monthly survey of establishments. Because the workweek in equations 5 through 7 is intended to measure cyclical variation in factor use, we detrend the log of this monthly series with the Hodrick-Prescott filter (with $\lambda = 10{,}000{,}000$ as in BFS) and use the detrended series to calculate $\dot{W}$ on an annual basis.

With regard to adjustment costs, we set the output elasticity ϕ equal to 0.035.[29] This elasticity is based on estimates of capital adjustment costs by Shapiro.[30] More recent studies provide estimates of adjustment costs on both sides of $\phi = 0.035$. Robert Hall estimates capital adjustment costs in an Euler equation framework similar to Shapiro's but uses more-disaggregated data and a different set of instruments for estimation.[31] Hall cannot reject the hypothesis that $\phi = 0$. In contrast, Charlotta Groth, using industry-level data for the United Kingdom, estimates ϕ to be about 0.055.[32] The divergent results in these studies highlight the uncertainty surrounding estimates of capital adjustment costs but do not suggest the need to move away from a baseline estimate of $\phi = 0.035$. We apply this elasticity to the difference between the growth rates of aggregate real business fixed investment from the NIPAs and the corresponding capital services series $(\dot{I} - \dot{K})$.

To summarize, we use annual data from BEA and BLS through 2006 to implement the aggregate growth accounting framework in equation 1. This

29. BFS used a larger value for ϕ, 0.05, but subsequently corrected some errors that had affected that figure. These corrections caused the value of ϕ to be revised to 0.035.
30. Shapiro (1986).
31. Hall (2004).
32. Groth (2005).

framework yields an annual time series for aggregate MFP growth. We then use the dual method to allocate this aggregate MFP growth across sectors. Finally, we calculate the effects of adjustment costs and changes in factor utilization on both aggregate and sectoral MFP growth, drawing heavily on parameter values reported by BFS.

Results

Table 1 presents our decomposition of labor productivity growth in the nonfarm business sector using the published data described above. These data exclude intangible capital other than business investment in software, which, again, is already treated as an investment good in the NIPAs. The next section fully incorporates intangible capital into our measurement system and presents an augmented set of growth accounting results.

Focusing first on the published data, table 1 shows that average annual growth in labor productivity picked up from about 1.5 percent a year during 1973–95 to about 2.5 percent during the second half of the 1990s and then rose further, to more than 2.8 percent, in the period after 2000. Our results indicate that an important part of the initial acceleration (about 0.6 percentage point of the total speedup of just over 1 percentage point) reflected the greater use of IT capital. In addition, growth of MFP rose notably in the IT-producing sectors, with an especially large increase for producers of semiconductors. The pickup for the semiconductor sector mirrors the unusually rapid decline in semiconductor prices from 1995 to 2000, which the model interprets as a speedup in MFP growth.[33] The last line of the table shows that, all told, IT capital deepening and faster MFP growth for IT producers more than accounted for the total speedup in labor productivity growth during 1995–2000. These results confirm that the IT-centric story for the late 1990s holds up after incorporating the latest vintage of data and extending the framework to account for adjustment costs and utilization effects.

---

33. Jorgenson (2001) argues that the steeper declines in semiconductor prices reflected a shift from three-year to two-year technology cycles starting in the mid-1990s. Aizcorbe, Oliner, and Sichel (2006) report that shorter technology cycles drove semiconductor prices down more rapidly after 1995, but they also estimated that price-cost markups for semiconductor producers narrowed from 1995 to 2001. Accordingly, the faster price declines in the late 1990s—and the associated pickup in MFP growth—partly reflected true improvements in technology and partly changes in markups. These results suggest some caution in interpreting price-based swings in MFP growth as a proxy for corresponding swings in the pace of technological advance.

Table 1. Contributions to Growth in Labor Productivity Based on Published Data[a]

Item	1973–95 (1)	1995–2000 (2)	2000–06 (3)	Change at 1995 (2) – (1)	Change at 2000 (3) – (2)
Growth of labor productivity in the nonfarm business sector (percent a year)[b]	1.47	2.51	2.86	1.04	0.35
Contributions from (percentage points):					
Capital deepening	0.76	1.11	0.85	0.35	–0.26
IT capital	0.46	1.09	0.61	0.63	–0.48
Computer hardware	0.25	0.60	0.28	0.35	–0.32
Software	0.13	0.34	0.20	0.21	–0.14
Communications equipment	0.07	0.15	0.14	0.08	–0.01
Other tangible capital	0.30	0.02	0.24	–0.28	0.22
Improvement in labor quality	0.27	0.26	0.34	–0.01	0.08
Growth of MFP	0.44	1.14	1.67	0.70	0.53
Effect of adjustment costs	0.04	–0.11	0.08	–0.15	0.19
Effect of utilization	–0.03	0.13	–0.09	0.16	–0.22
Growth of MFP excluding above effects	0.42	1.11	1.68	0.69	0.57
IT-producing sectors	0.28	0.75	0.51	0.47	–0.24
Semiconductors	0.09	0.45	0.23	0.36	–0.22
Computer hardware	0.12	0.19	0.10	0.07	–0.09
Software	0.04	0.08	0.13	0.04	0.05
Communications equipment	0.04	0.04	0.05	0.00	0.01
Other nonfarm business	0.15	0.36	1.17	0.21	0.81
Memorandum: total IT contribution[c]	0.74	1.84	1.12	1.10	–0.72

Source: Authors' calculations.
a. Detail may not sum to totals because of rounding.
b. Measured as 100 times the average annual log difference for the indicated years.
c. Sum of capital deepening for IT capital and growth of MFP in IT-producing sectors.

The table also quantifies the influence of adjustment costs and changes in utilization during this period (the two lines under "Growth of MFP"). These two factors, on net, do not explain any of the upward swing in MFP growth from 1973–95 to 1995–2000, which is consistent with the results in BFS. Although the greater utilization of capital and labor had a positive effect on MFP growth during 1995–2000, this influence was offset by the negative effect from the higher adjustment costs induced by the investment boom of that period.

Table 1 tells a sharply different story for the period since 2000. Even though labor productivity accelerated another 0.35 percentage point, the growth contributions from IT capital deepening and MFP advances in IT-producing sectors dropped back substantially. At the same time, MFP growth strengthened in the rest of nonfarm business, adding roughly ¾ percentage point to annual labor productivity growth during 2000–06 from its 1995–2000 average. And, given the minimal growth in hours worked after 2000, even the anemic advance in investment outlays led to a positive swing in the growth contribution from non-IT capital deepening ("Other tangible capital").[34]

All in all, table 1 indicates that IT-related factors retreated from center stage after 2000 and that other factors—most notably, a surge in MFP growth outside the IT-producing sectors—were responsible for the continued rapid advance in labor productivity as reported in the published data.[35] Nonetheless, averaging over the period 1995–2006, the use and production of IT capital are important, accounting for roughly two-thirds of the post-1995 step-up in labor productivity growth. The next section of the paper examines whether the inclusion of intangible capital changes this characterization.

We conclude this discussion with two points. The first concerns the use of the year 2000 as the breakpoint for comparing the boom period of the late 1990s with more recent years. We chose 2000 rather than 2001 to avoid splitting the two periods at a recession year, which would have accentuated the need for cyclical adjustments. However, our main findings are robust to breaking the two periods at 2001. Second, our big-picture results are very similar to those in Jorgenson, Ho, and Stiroh,[36] which contains the latest estimates from the framework pioneered by Dale Jorgenson. Consistent with our findings, their framework emphasizes the role of IT in explaining the step-up in labor productivity growth during 1995–2000. It also shows a reduced contribution from IT after 2000, which was more than offset by other factors. The differences in results are relatively minor and largely stem from the broader sectoral coverage in the Jorgenson, Ho, and Stiroh

34. The combined effect of adjustment costs and factor utilization remained essentially zero after 2000. Although the deceleration in investment spending after 2000 eliminated the negative effect of adjustment costs, the net decline in the workweek pushed the utilization effect into negative territory.

35. Of course, MFP growth is a residual, so this result speaks only to the proximate sources of growth and does not shed light on the more fundamental forces driving MFP growth.

36. Jorgenson, Ho, and Stiroh (2007).

framework. In particular, their framework incorporates the flow of services from owner-occupied housing and consumer durable goods into both output and capital input. The stocks of these assets have grown rapidly since the mid-1990s, and so Jorgenson, Ho, and Stiroh's estimates of non-IT capital deepening are larger than those reported here.

Aggregate Growth Accounting with Intangible Capital

The growth accounting analysis in the previous section relies on published data, which exclude virtually all types of intangible capital except software. As argued by Corrado, Hulten, and Sichel,[37] any intangible asset that generates a service flow beyond the current period should be included in the capital stock, and the production of such assets should be included in current-period output. Applying this standard, in their 2006 paper (henceforth CHS) Corrado, Hulten, and Sichel estimated that the intangible investment excluded from the NIPAs amounted to roughly $1 trillion annually over 2000–03, an amount nearly equal to outlays for business fixed investment included in the national accounts, and they constructed a growth accounting system that includes a broad set of intangibles through 2003.

Of total business investment in intangibles, CHS estimate that scientific and nonscientific R&D each accounted for about 19 percent during 2000–03; computerized information, which consists mostly of the software category already included in the NIPAs, accounted for 14 percent; brand equity accounted for 13 percent; and firm-specific organizational capital accounted for about 35 percent. The last category contains many well-known examples of the successful deployment of intangible capital, including Wal-Mart's supply-chain technology, Dell's build-to-order business model, and Intel's expertise in organizing semiconductor production.[38]

The CHS estimates of intangible investment and capital are a valuable addition to the literature, but the source data for their series are currently available only through 2004 or 2005. Thus their approach cannot be used to develop growth accounting estimates that are as timely as those based on published data. As an alternative, we construct a data system for intangi-

---

37. Corrado, Hulten, and Sichel (2005, 2006).
38. See Brynjolfsson and Hitt (2000), Brynjolfsson, Hitt, and Yang (2002), and McKinsey Global Institute (2002) for interesting case studies regarding the creation of organizational capital.

bles that runs through 2006, based on the framework in BFOS. In the BFOS model, firms use intangible capital as a complement to their IT capital. Because of this connection to IT capital, we can generate estimates of intangible investment and capital from published data on IT capital and related series.

BFOS used their model for a more limited purpose: to specify and estimate regressions to discern whether intangibles could explain the MFP growth patterns in published industry data. They did not formally build intangibles into an integrated growth accounting framework along the lines of CHS. That is precisely what we do here.[39]

Description of the Model

The basic features of the BFOS model are as follows. Firms have a (value-added) production function in which IT capital and intangible capital are complementary inputs:

$$(8) \qquad V_t = F\left[G\left(K_t^{IT}, R_t\right), K_t^{NT}, L_t, z_t\right],$$

where K_t^{IT}, R_t, and K_t^{NT} denote IT capital, intangible capital, and tangible capital other than IT capital, respectively; L_t is labor input; and z_t is the level of technology. For simplicity, BFOS assume that there are no adjustment costs and that factor utilization does not vary. The function G that combines IT capital and intangible capital is assumed to take the constant elasticity of substitution form:

$$(9) \qquad G\left(K_t^{IT}, R_t\right) = \left[a\left(K_t^{IT}\right)^{(\sigma-1)/\sigma} + \left(1-a\right)\left(R_t\right)^{(\sigma-1)/\sigma}\right]^{\sigma/(\sigma-1)}$$

where σ is the elasticity of substitution between K_t^{IT} and R_t, and a governs the income share of each type of capital.

Because K_t^{IT} and R_t are separable from other inputs, firms minimize costs by first choosing the optimal combination of K_t^{IT} and R_t and then selecting

---

39. The BFOS model focuses on intangibles that are related to information technology. This is a narrower purview than in Corrado, Hulten, and Sichel (2005, 2006), who develop estimates for a full range of intangible assets, regardless of their connection to IT. Although we do not provide a comprehensive accounting for intangibles, we highlight the intangible assets that are central to an assessment of the contribution of information technology to economic growth.

other inputs conditional on this choice. For the first-stage optimization, the usual first-order condition sets the ratio of the marginal products of K_t^{IT} and R_t equal to the ratio of their user costs, which implies

$$(10) \qquad\qquad R_t = K_t^{IT} \left(\frac{1-a}{a} \right)^{\sigma} \left(\frac{r_t^{IT}}{r_t^R} \right)^{\sigma},$$

where r_t^{IT} and r_t^R denote the respective user costs. Equation 10 implies the following expression for the growth of intangible capital:

$$(11) \qquad\qquad \dot{R}_t = \dot{K}_t^{IT} + \sigma \left(\dot{r}_t^{IT} - \dot{r}_t^R \right).$$

Importantly, equation 11 enables us to calculate a model-implied series for the growth rate of intangible capital based solely on data for IT capital and user costs and on an assumed value for the elasticity of substitution between intangible capital and IT capital. No direct data on intangible capital are required. We chain together the time series of growth rates from equation 11 to produce an indexed series for the level of real intangible capital, R.

To implement equation 11, we calculate $\dot{K}_t^{IT}$ and $\dot{r}_t^{IT}$ from the same BLS data that we used in the previous section. We also need to specify the user cost for intangible capital (r_t^R) and the elasticity of substitution between IT capital and intangible capital (σ). We use data from CHS to calculate $\dot{r}_t^R$ and σ, as described next.

CHS measure the user cost of intangible capital in accord with the standard Hall and Jorgenson formulation:[40]

$$(12) \qquad\qquad r^R = p^R \left(\rho + \delta^R - \Pi^R \right) T^R,$$

where p^R is the price index for this type of capital, ρ is the nominal rate of return net of depreciation, δ^R is the depreciation rate, Π^R is the expected capital gain over and above that captured in the depreciation rate, and T^R accounts for the tax treatment of intangible assets. Equation 12 is identical to the user cost formula that we employ for all other types of capital in our growth accounting framework. We adopt CHS's specification of each term in the user cost formula.

---

40. Hall and Jorgenson (1967).

To select a value for the elasticity of substitution σ, we examined the CHS series for the income shares of IT capital and intangible capital.[41] If σ were equal to one (the Cobb-Douglas case), the ratio of the IT income share to the intangible income share drawn from data in CHS (which we denote by $\alpha_t^{R,CHS}$) would be constant. In fact, the ratio of the IT income share to the intangible income share trends upward in the CHS data. Given that the user cost of IT capital has fallen relative to that of intangible capital, the upward trend in the share ratio implies more substitution toward IT capital than would occur in the Cobb-Douglas case. We find that setting σ to 1.25 approximates the upward trend in the share ratio.

To complete the system, we need a nominal anchor to convert the indexed series for R_t to dollar values. For the nominal anchor, we require that the average income share of intangible capital in our framework over 1973–2003 (denoted $\overline{\alpha}_t^{R,BFOS}$) equal the average value of the CHS-based share over the same period:[42]

(13) $$\overline{\alpha}^{R,BFOS} = \overline{\alpha}^{R,CHS}.$$

To satisfy equation 13, we scale the indexed levels series for intangible capital, R_t, by ψ. The income share for intangible capital in year t is then

(14) $$\alpha_t^{R,BFOS} = \frac{r_t^R R_t \psi}{p_t V_t + r_t^R R_t \psi},$$

where the denominator equals the sum of published nonfarm business income and the income accruing to intangible capital. We average equation 14 over the period 1973–2003, substitute the average share into the left-hand side of equation 13, and solve for the scaling factor ψ. We then apply this scaling factor to the indexed levels series for R_t and denote the resulting series for real intangible capital by R_t^*. Given R_t^*, the associated

41. Specifically, for the income share of intangible capital, we use the income share series for "New CHS intangibles," that is, those intangibles over and above those included in the NIPAs. We then adjust this series downward to account for the fact that some CHS intangibles are not related to IT and thus do not fit in the BFOS framework. As a crude adjustment, we remove the income share associated with brand equity and one-third of the income share for other components of "New CHS intangibles."

42. We use 2003 as the final year for this calculation because that is the last year of data in CHS.

series for real intangible investment comes from the standard perpetual inventory equation:

$$(15) \qquad N_t^* = R_t^* - \left(1 - \delta^R\right) R_{t-1}^*.$$

We calculate growth in real intangible investment from the series for N_t^*.

We now have all the pieces we need to incorporate intangibles into our growth accounting framework. An important point is that including intangible assets affects both the output and the input sides of the production accounts. On the output side, the growth of production equals a weighted average of growth in real intangible investment N^* and growth in published real nonfarm business output. The weight for each component equals its share in the augmented measure of current-dollar output. On the input side, the total contribution from capital now includes a term for intangible capital, calculated as the income share for intangible capital times the growth rate of this capital in real terms, $\alpha_t^{R,BFOS} \times \dot{R}$. The income shares for all other inputs are scaled down so that the shares (including that for intangible capital) sum to one.[43]

Results

The results from this augmented growth accounting framework, shown in table 2, differ in important respects from the results based on published data. As can be seen by comparing the first two lines, labor productivity growth during 1995–2000 becomes stronger once we include intangibles, but it becomes less robust during 2000–06. Indeed, in the augmented framework, the productivity advance since 2000 is estimated to be well below that posted during 1995–2000, reversing the relative growth rates for the two periods based on published data. This reversal arises from the time profile for real investment in intangibles. As shown in the lower part of the table, real intangible investment is estimated to have surged during 1995–2000, boosting growth in aggregate output, and then retreated during 2000–06.

---

43. See Yang and Brynjolfsson (2001) for an alternative approach to incorporating intangibles into a standard growth accounting framework. Their approach relies on financial market valuations to infer the amount of unmeasured intangible investment and shows that, through 1999, the inclusion of intangibles had potentially sizable effects on the measured growth of MFP.

Table 2. Contributions to Growth in Labor Productivity: Accounting for Intangibles[a]

Item	1973–95 (1)	1995–2000 (2)	2000–06 (3)	Change at 1995 (2) – (1)	Change at 2000 (3) – (2)
Growth of labor productivity in the nonfarm business sector (percent a year)[b]					
Based on published data[c]	1.47	2.51	2.86	1.04	0.35
Accounting for intangibles[d]	1.58	2.95	2.43	1.37	−0.52
Contributions from (percentage points):[e]					
Capital deepening	0.94	1.40	0.75	0.46	−0.65
IT capital	0.44	1.02	0.57	0.58	−0.45
Other tangible capital	0.29	0.02	0.22	−0.27	0.20
New intangible capital	0.22	0.36	−0.04	0.14	−0.40
Improvement in labor quality	0.26	0.25	0.32	−0.01	0.07
Growth of MFP	0.37	1.31	1.36	0.94	0.05
Effect of adjustment costs	0.04	−0.12	0.10	−0.16	0.22
Effect of utilization	−0.03	0.13	−0.09	0.16	−0.22
Growth of MFP excluding above effects	0.36	1.30	1.34	0.94	0.04
IT-producing sectors	0.26	0.72	0.47	0.46	−0.25
Intangible sector	0.01	0.08	0.07	0.07	−0.01
Other nonfarm business	0.09	0.50	0.81	0.41	0.31
Memoranda: Growth rates (percent a year)[b]					
Real intangible investment	5.7	12.0	−4.6	6.3	−16.6
Real intangible capital services	6.8	7.7	−0.7	0.9	−8.4
Real IT capital services	15.6	20.4	8.9	4.8	−11.5
User cost, intangible capital	4.6	1.2	3.6	−3.4	2.4
User cost, IT capital	−2.4	−9.0	−4.1	−6.6	4.9
Nominal shares (percent)					
Expenditure share, intangible investment	4.6	6.2	5.1	1.6	−1.1
Income share, intangible capital	4.7	6.4	6.5	1.7	0.1

Source: Authors' calculations.
a. Detail may not sum to totals because of rounding.
b. Measured as 100 times the average annual log difference for the indicated years.
c. From table 1.
d. Derived using methodology discussed in the text.
e. Contributions to growth of nonfarm business labor productivity with accounting for intangibles.

The growth contribution from intangible capital deepening ("New intangible capital" in table 2) follows the general pattern for IT capital, moving higher during 1995–2000 and then falling back. This similarity reflects the explicit link between intangible capital and IT capital in the BFOS model. The lower part of the table provides full detail on the growth of intangible capital and its determinants from equation 11. Despite the broadly similar growth contour for intangible capital and IT capital across periods, intangible capital increases much less rapidly than IT capital in each period, because of the quality-adjusted declines in IT prices that cause the user cost of IT capital to trend lower. This user cost effect became more pronounced during 1995–2000—when the prices for IT capital goods fell especially rapidly—restraining the growth of intangible capital even though the growth of IT capital jumped.

Taken together, the revisions to the output and the input sides of the growth accounting equation imply a revised path for MFP growth, after controlling for the effects of adjustment costs and factor utilization ("Growth of MFP excluding above effects"). The inclusion of intangibles leaves a somewhat smaller imprint on MFP growth than on the growth of labor productivity, as the revisions to the two sides of the growth accounting equation are partly offsetting. Consistent with the more muted revision from the published data, the path for MFP continues to show the fastest growth after 2000. However, the pickup in MFP growth from 1995–2000 to 2000–06, at 0.04 percentage point, is negligible compared with that indicated by published data (see the equivalent line in table 1).

Robustness Checks

The BFOS model imposes a strictly contemporaneous relationship between the growth of intangible capital and the growth of IT capital. This relationship may be too tight, as the two forms of capital accumulation may be subject to (unmodeled) adjustment costs and differences in project length from the planning stage to final rollout.

To examine the robustness of our results, we consider alternative timing assumptions for the growth of intangible capital. The first two alternatives smooth the growth of intangible capital without introducing leads or lags relative to the growth in IT capital. The idea is that some projects to produce intangible capital may be long-lived and thus may not display the same stops and starts as purchases of IT capital. We implement this timing change by using a three-year or a five-year centered moving average for the growth rate of IT capital and its user cost on the right-hand side of equation 11. The third timing change allows intangible capital growth to lag IT capital growth by a year but does not affect the relative volatility of the series. This timing assumption embeds the often-expressed view that firms take time to accumulate the intangible capital needed to fully leverage their IT investments.

Our reading of the literature suggests that the first two alternatives fit the facts better than the introduction of a systematic lag from IT capital to intangible capital. Case studies published elsewhere portray the installation of IT capital and associated changes in business practices and organization as interwoven rather than strictly sequential.[44] Sinan Aral, Erik Brynjolfsson, and D. J. Wu support this view, noting that "[as] firms successfully implement IT (and complementary intangible investments) and experience greater marginal benefits from IT investments, they react by investing in more IT," a process they characterize as a "virtuous cycle."[45] Nonetheless, we consider the scenario with the lagged accumulation of intangible capital for the sake of completeness.

As the top panel of table 3 shows, these alternative timing assumptions have some effect on the period-by-period growth of real intangible capital but do not change the basic result, namely, that this type of capital essentially has not grown since 2000. The series for intangible investment, shown in the bottom panel of the table, is also reasonably robust to alternative timing assumptions. In each case, real intangible investment is estimated to have declined since 2000. As a further robustness check, the table also displays the CHS series for intangible capital and intangible investment, which we have extended through 2005 based on some of the key source

44. Brynjolfsson and Hitt (2000), Brynjolfsson, Hitt, and Yang (2002), and McKinsey Global Institute (2002).

45. Aral, Brynjolfsson, and Wu (2006, p. 2). Some interpret the econometric results in Brynjolfsson and Hitt (2003) as support for a lag between the installation of IT capital and the accumulation of complementary capital. We believe this interpretation is incorrect. Brynjolfsson and Hitt show that the firm-level effect of computerization on MFP growth is much stronger when evaluated over multiyear periods than when evaluated on a year-by-year basis. Importantly, however, the variables in their regression are all measured contemporaneously, whether over single-year or multiyear periods. Accordingly, their results suggest that the correlation between the growth of IT capital and intangible capital may be low on a year-by-year basis, but that a stronger *contemporaneous* correlation holds over longer periods, boosting the measured effect on MFP growth.

Table 3. Growth of Intangible Capital and Investment Under Alternative Timing Assumptions for Intangible Capital[a]

Percent a year

Timing assumption	Average annual rate		
	1973–95	1995–2000	2000–05
Intangible capital services			
Baseline timing for intangible capital growth	6.8	7.7	−0.9
Three-year centered moving average	6.9	7.1	−0.3
Five-year centered moving average	6.8	6.7	0.4
One-year lag relative to baseline	7.4	7.1	−0.2
Memorandum: Corrado, Hulten, and Sichel series[b]	5.2	7.3	2.8
Intangible investment			
Baseline timing for intangible capital growth	5.7	12.0	−6.2
Three-year centered moving average	6.1	9.1	−5.2
Five-year centered moving average	6.1	8.5	−4.1
One-year lag relative to baseline	6.9	8.8	−8.7
Memorandum: Corrado, Hulten, and Sichel series[b]	5.2	8.3	1.1

Source: Authors' calculations.

a. The alternative timing assumptions pertain to growth of intangible capital. The effect on intangible investment is calculated through the perpetual inventory relationship linking investment and capital.

b. From Corrado, Hulten, and Sichel (2006), series for "New CHS intangibles," with preliminary extension to 2005 estimated by the authors.

data in their framework. (This is a preliminary extension of the CHS series for illustrative purposes only and should not be regarded as official CHS data.) The extended CHS series for intangible investment and capital exhibit patterns across periods that are broadly similar to those in our series. Notably, the CHS series decelerate sharply after 2000, and the growth rates for 2000–05 are the weakest for the three periods shown, confirming an important qualitative feature of our estimates. Because the CHS series are constructed independently from the series in this paper, the qualitative correspondence between them lends credibility to the basic thrust of our results, if not to the precise figures.

Table 4 explores the growth accounting implications of the alternative timing assumptions for intangible capital. For each timing assumption we show three key variables: growth in labor productivity, the growth contribution from intangible capital deepening, and MFP growth (after controlling for the effects of adjustment costs and factor utilization). Most features of the baseline results are robust to the alternative assumptions. In every case,

Table 4. Growth in Labor Productivity and Selected Growth Contributions Under Alternative Timing Assumptions for Intangible Capital[a]

Item	1973–95 (1)	1995–2000 (2)	2000–06 (3)	Change at 1995 (2) – (1)	Change at 2000 (3) – (2)
Baseline[b]					
Labor productivity growth	1.58	2.95	2.43	1.37	−0.52
Contribution from intangible capital	0.22	0.36	−0.04	0.14	−0.40
Contribution from MFP growth[c]	0.36	1.30	1.34	0.94	0.04
Three-year centered moving average					
Labor productivity growth	1.59	2.77	2.56	1.18	−0.21
Contribution from intangible capital	0.22	0.32	0.00	0.10	−0.32
Contribution from MFP growth[c]	0.38	1.13	1.45	0.75	0.32
Five-year centered moving average					
Labor productivity growth	1.59	2.72	2.59	1.13	−0.13
Contribution from intangible capital	0.22	0.29	0.02	0.07	−0.27
Contribution from MFP growth[c]	0.38	1.11	1.46	0.73	0.35
One-year lag relative to baseline					
Labor productivity growth	1.62	2.77	2.51	1.15	−0.26
Contribution from intangible capital	0.23	0.32	0.01	0.09	−0.31
Contribution from MFP growth[c]	0.39	1.13	1.39	0.74	0.26

Source: Authors' calculations.

a. Growth of labor productivity is in percent a year and is measured as 100 times the average annual log difference for the indicated years. Growth contributions are in percentage points.

b. From table 2.

c. After controlling for effects of adjustment costs and utilization.

labor productivity is estimated to have grown more rapidly during 1995–2000 than during 2000–06, reversing the relative growth rates based on published data. In addition, the growth contribution from intangible capital deepening is always largest during 1995–2000 and then drops back to essentially zero during 2000–06. Finally, although the alternative timing assumptions generate a larger step-up in MFP growth after 2000 than in the baseline, they nonetheless temper the increase by 0.2 to 0.3 percentage point relative to the published data.

Industry-Level Productivity

We now turn to the industry origins of U.S. productivity growth during the late 1990s and after 2000. The aggregate data show that the sources of productivity growth changed after 2000, which suggests that the industry-level origins of aggregate productivity growth and the underlying forces may also have changed. To explore this, we construct productivity accounts for sixty industries that span the U.S. private economy from 1988 to 2005. Although measurement error, omitted variables, and endogeneity problems always make it difficult to identify the sources of productivity gains, we make some progress by exploiting cross-sectional variation in industry productivity over time and by examining the link between productivity and observable factors such as IT intensity and changing profit shares.

The industry analysis presented here focuses on labor productivity, reflecting our interest in understanding the industry origins of aggregate labor productivity growth. Moreover, we do not have the detailed data on labor quality, intangible investment, or adjustment costs at the industry level necessary to create comparable estimates of MFP growth. To the extent that intangible capital is correlated with IT investment, however, one can interpret the IT intensity results as broadly indicative of the whole suite of activities that are complementary to IT.

Output Measures, Data, and Summary Statistics

OUTPUT MEASURES. Industry output can be measured using either a gross output or a value-added concept, each with its advantages and disadvantages.[46] Gross output corresponds closely to the conventional idea of output or sales and reflects all inputs including capital, labor, and intermediate energy, materials, and services. Value added, by contrast, is a somewhat artificial concept that strips out the contribution of intermediate inputs and incorporates only capital and labor.

Although both value added and gross output are used for productivity analysis, we favor gross output. Empirical work by, among others, Michael Bruno; J. R. Norsworthy and David Malmquist; Jorgenson, Frank Gollop,

---

46. For background on industry productivity analysis, see Jorgenson, Gollop, and Fraumeni (1987), Basu and Fernald (1995, 1997, 2001, 2007), Nordhaus (2002b), Stiroh (2002a, 2002b), Triplett and Bosworth (2004), and Bosworth and Triplett (2007).

and Barbara Fraumeni rejects the existence of value-added functions on separability grounds.[47] Basu and Fernald show that using value-added data leads to biased estimates and incorrect inferences about production parameters.[48] A later contribution by the same authors argues against the value-added function because failure of the neoclassical assumption about perfect competition implies that some of the contribution of intermediate inputs remains in measured value-added growth.[49] Value added has the advantage, however, that it aggregates directly to GDP.

DATA. We use three pieces of U.S. industry-level data—output, hours, and capital stock—from government sources. The first two create a panel of average labor productivity (ALP) across U.S. industries, and the third is used to develop measures of the intensity of the use of IT. One practical difficulty is the recent conversion of the industry data from the Standard Industrial Classification (SIC) system to the North American Industrial Classification (NAICS) system, which makes it difficult to construct long historical time series or to directly compare the most recent data with earlier results.

BEA publishes annual data on value added and gross output for sixty-five industries that together make up the private U.S. economy.[50] These data, which are based on an integrated set of input-output and industry production accounts, span 1947–2005 for real value added and 1987–2005 for real gross output. Although BEA also publishes various measures of employment by industry, it does not provide industry-level series on hours worked. We obtain hours by industry from the Output and Employment database maintained by the Office of Occupational Statistics and Employment Projections at BLS. Complete data on total hours for all industries begin in 1988.[51] Because these hours data are currently available only to 2004, we use the growth rate of full-time equivalent employees for the disaggregated industries, from BEA data, to proxy for hours growth in 2005.

---

47. Bruno (1978); Norsworthy and Malmquist (1983); Jorgenson, Gollop, and Fraumeni (1987).
48. Basu and Fernald (1995, 1997).
49. Basu and Fernald (2001).
50. Howells, Barefoot, and Lindberg (2006).
51. The underlying sources of these data are the BLS Current Employment Survey (for wage and salary jobs and average weekly hours), the Current Population Survey (for self-employed and unpaid workers, agricultural workers, and within-household employment), and unemployment insurance tax records.

We create two measures of industry ALP—real value added per hour worked and real gross output per hour worked—by combining the BEA output data with the BLS hours data across industries for 1988 to 2005.

The third data source is the Fixed Asset accounts from BEA for nonresidential capital. These data include forty-six different types of nonresidential capital for sixty-three disaggregated NAICS industries since 1987. To estimate capital services we map the asset-specific service prices from Jorgenson, Ho, and Stiroh onto these assets and employ Tornqvist aggregation using the service price and a two-period average of the capital stock for each asset in each industry.[52] The resulting measure of capital services is an approximation, because we miss industry variation in rates of return, asset-specific inflation, and tax code parameters. Nevertheless, it captures the relatively high service prices for short-lived assets such as IT capital, defined as above to include computer hardware, software, and communications equipment.

We combine these three sources of data to form a panel from 1988 to 2005 for a private industry aggregate, fifteen broad sectors, and sixty disaggregated industries. The fifteen-sector breakdown follows BEA's convention, except that manufacturing is broken into durables and nondurables. The number of disaggregated industries is smaller than that available from either BEA or BLS, because of the need to generate consistently defined industries across all data sources. All aggregation is done via Tornqvist indices, except for hours, which are simply summed. Both the broad sectors and the disaggregated industries sum to the private industry aggregates of nominal output from BEA, hours from BLS, and nominal nonresidential capital from BEA. The list of industries and their 2005 value added are reported in appendix table A-1.

SUMMARY STATISTICS. Table 5 reports estimates of labor productivity growth from our industry data and compares them with the latest estimates from BLS. The first two lines of the top panel report average annual growth of ALP for the BLS business and nonfarm business sectors, and the third line reports the private industry aggregate described above. Although our private industry aggregate grows somewhat less rapidly than the BLS aggregates, all three series show similar trends: a pickup of ALP growth of about 1 percentage point after 1995 and a smaller increase after 2000.

---

52. Jorgenson, Ho, and Stiroh (2007).

The second panel of table 5 reports estimates for the fifteen broad NAICS sectors. These sectors range in size from the very large finance, insurance, real estate, rental, and leasing sector, at 23.3 percent of 2005 value added, to the very small agriculture, forestry, fishing, and hunting sector, at only 1.1 percent. In terms of ALP growth, eight of these fifteen sectors, which accounted for 73 percent of value added in 2005, showed faster productivity growth over 1995–2000 than over 1988–95.[53] The further acceleration in aggregate productivity after 2000 occurred in seven sectors, which accounted for only 44 percent of 2005 value added. Although productivity in the large retail trade, wholesale trade, and finance sectors all decelerated after 2000, the two trade sectors continued to post impressive productivity gains through 2005.

The pickup in aggregate productivity growth in the mid-1990s appears to have originated in different sectors than did the subsequent step-up in 2000. Six sectors (agriculture, durable goods, wholesale trade, retail trade, finance, and arts and entertainment) show an acceleration after 1995 but a deceleration after 2000, whereas five sectors (construction, nondurables, utilities, information, and other services) show the opposite pattern. Together these eleven sectors produced 72 percent of value added in 2005. In their analysis of MFP growth, Corrado and others reach a similar conclusion, although Bosworth and Triplett emphasize the continued importance of service industries as a source of aggregate productivity growth.[54]

Table 5 also summarizes, in the third and fourth panels, the disaggregated industry data by reporting the mean, median, and hours-weighted mean productivity growth rates across these industries for gross output and value added, respectively. One interesting observation is the divergence in trends between gross output and value-added measures of productivity: the post-1995 gains are strongest for gross output, whereas the post-2000 gains are strongest for value added. Both series incorporate the same hours data, so that this divergence directly reflects differences between the gross output and value-added output measures.

It is beyond the scope of this paper to investigate this divergence further. For completeness, we report results for both gross output and value added,

---

53. As a comparison, Stiroh (2001, 2002b) reported an acceleration of ALP after 1995 for six of ten broad sectors, which accounted for the majority of output using earlier vintages of SIC data.

54. Corrado and others (2007); Bosworth and Triplett (2007).

Table 5. Estimates of Labor Productivity Growth in the Aggregate and by Sector

Item	Value added, 2005		Average growth rate of labor productivity (percent a year)			Change in productivity growth rate (percentage points)	
	Billions of dollars	Share (percent)	1988–95	1995–2000	2000–05	1988–95 to 1995–2000	1995–2000 to 2000–05
Value added, aggregate measures[a]							
BLS business sector			1.48	2.69	3.07	1.21	0.38
BLS nonfarm business sector			1.46	2.52	3.02	1.06	0.50
Private industry aggregate, this paper	10,892	100.0	1.25	2.24	2.52	0.99	0.28
Value added by broad sector[a]							
Agriculture, forestry, fishing, and hunting	123	1.1	1.95	5.31	5.13	3.36	-0.19
Mining	233	2.1	3.54	0.59	-4.59	-2.95	-5.19
Construction	611	5.6	-0.32	-1.19	-0.98	-0.87	0.22
Durable goods	854	7.8	3.57	7.69	6.04	4.13	-1.65
Nondurable goods	658	6.0	2.26	1.78	4.26	-0.48	2.49
Utilities	248	2.3	5.14	3.43	4.03	-1.70	0.60
Wholesale trade	743	6.8	2.24	5.41	3.64	3.17	-1.77
Retail trade	824	7.6	2.69	4.66	4.00	1.97	-0.66

Transportation and warehousing	345	3.2	3.00	2.48	2.12	-0.52	-0.36
Information	555	5.1	3.70	2.48	8.85	-1.23	6.37
Finance, insurance, real estate, rental, and leasing	2,536	23.3	1.77	1.83	1.73	0.07	-0.11
Professional and business services	1,459	13.4	-0.94	0.16	2.33	1.11	2.16
Education services, health care, social assistance	975	9.0	-2.40	-1.22	0.84	1.18	2.07
Arts, entertainment, recreation, accommodation, and food services	445	4.1	0.65	1.12	0.13	0.46	-0.99
Other services, except government	283	2.6	-0.31	-1.45	-0.32	-1.14	1.13
Gross output by detailed industry[b]							
Mean			1.80	2.95	2.28	1.15	-0.68
Median			1.62	2.19	1.88	0.57	-0.30
Weighted mean[c]			1.59	2.68	2.19	1.09	-0.49
Value added by detailed industry[b]							
Mean			1.78	2.02	2.80	0.24	0.78
Median			1.74	1.16	2.82	-0.58	1.66
Weighted mean[c]			1.33	1.94	2.46	0.62	0.51

Sources: Authors' calculations.

a. Growth of real value added per hour worked, measured as 100 times the average log difference for the indicated years.

b. Calculated across the sixty observations in each period using real gross output or real value added per hour worked.

c. Industries are weighted by hours at the beginning of each period.

although, again, we prefer gross output because it is a more fundamental measure of production and does not require additional assumptions about the nature of the production function.

Finally, we emphasize that there is enormous heterogeneity among the disaggregated industries that lie beneath these summary statistics, both within time periods and across time. For example, thirty-seven of the sixty industries, which accounted for nearly 60 percent of aggregate output, experienced an acceleration of productivity after 1995 but a decline after 2000, or vice versa. This highlights the widespread churning and reallocation of resources among industries, which we show to be an important source of aggregate productivity gains.

Industry Origins of the Aggregate Productivity Gains

We now review how the data for the disaggregated industries can be aggregated to form economy-wide productivity estimates, and we employ this familiar framework to identify the industry origins of the aggregate productivity gains over 1988–2005.

DECOMPOSITION AND REALLOCATIONS. At the industry level, real value added is defined implicitly from a gross output production function as

$$(16) \qquad \dot{Y}_i = \alpha_i^v \dot{V}_i + (1 - \alpha_i^v)\dot{M}_i,$$

where α_i^v is the average share of nominal value added in nominal gross output for industry i, and M_i denotes real intermediate inputs.[55] One attractive property of industry value added is that it aggregates to a simple expression for growth in aggregate value added:

$$(17) \qquad \dot{V} = \sum_i v_i \dot{V}_i,$$

where v_i is the average share of industry i's nominal value added in aggregate nominal value added. Aggregate hours worked, H, is the simple sum of industry hours, H_i,

---

55. BEA uses the "double deflation" method to estimate real value added for all industries as the difference between real gross output and real intermediate inputs (Howells, Barefoot, and Lindberg, 2006). Basu and Fernald (2001) show that this can be approximated, as in equation 16, by defining gross output growth as a weighted average of value added and intermediate input growth.

(18) $$H = \sum_i H_i,$$

and aggregate labor productivity is defined as $ALP^V = V/H$.

Equations 16, 17, and 18 can be combined to yield the following decomposition of ALP growth:[56]

(19) $$\dot{ALP}^V = \left(\sum_i v_i \dot{ALP}_i^Y\right) - \left[\sum_i m_i \left(\dot{M}_i - \dot{Y}_i\right)\right] + \left(\sum_i v_i \dot{H}_i - \dot{H}\right)$$
$$= \left(\sum_i v_i \dot{ALP}_i^Y\right) - R^M + R^H,$$

where ALP^Y is industry labor productivity based on gross output and m_i is the average ratio of nominal industry intermediate inputs to nominal aggregate value added. This equation simplifies to

(20) $$\dot{ALP}^V = \left(\sum_i v_i \dot{ALP}_i^Y\right) + \left(\sum_i v_i \dot{H}_i - \dot{H}\right)$$
$$= \left(\sum_i v_i \dot{ALP}_i^Y\right) + R^H.$$

The first term in equation 19 is a "direct productivity effect" equal to the weighted average of growth in gross output labor productivity in the component industries. The second term, R^M, is a "reallocation of materials," which reflects variation in intermediate input intensity across industries. It enters with a negative sign because when more intermediate inputs are used to raise gross output, $\dot{M} > \dot{Y}$, these must be netted out to reach aggregate productivity. The third term, R^H, is a "reallocation of hours." Aggregate hours growth, $\dot{H}$, approximately weights industries by their (lagged) share of aggregate hours, and so aggregate productivity rises if industries with value-added shares above their hours shares—that is, those industries with relatively high (nominal) productivity levels—experience growth in hours. Equation 20 is a simplification using value-added labor productivity at the industry level.[57]

Table 6 reports estimates of the decomposition framework in equations 16 to 20. The first line in the top panel repeats the productivity estimates that come from the BEA data on aggregate private industry output and the sum of hours worked from BLS. The second line reports the estimates we

---

56. As in Stiroh (2002b).
57. This value-added approach is similar to the decomposition in Nordhaus (2002b).

Table 6. Decompositions of Aggregate Labor Productivity Growth

Item	No. of industries	1988–95 Share of total value added[a] (%)	1988–95 Contribution to ALP growth[b] (% pts)	1995–2000 Share of total value added (%)	1995–2000 Contribution to ALP growth (% pts)	2000–05 Share of total value added (%)	2000–05 Contribution to ALP growth (% pts)	Change in contribution (percentage points) 1988–95 to 1995–2000	Change in contribution (percentage points) 1995–2000 to 2000–05
Aggregates									
Private industry aggregate[c]			1.25		2.24		2.52	0.99	0.28
Aggregated industries[d]	60		1.24		2.20		2.52	0.96	0.32
Decomposition using industry real gross output per hour worked									
Industry contribution	60	100.0	1.79	100.0	3.10	100.0	2.16	1.31	−0.94
IT-producing industries[e]	4	4.0	0.33	5.0	0.50	4.5	0.25	0.17	−0.25
IT-using industries[f]	26	57.3	0.71	58.6	1.99	59.1	1.54	1.28	−0.45
Other industries	30	38.7	0.75	36.4	0.61	36.4	0.37	−0.14	−0.23
Reallocation of materials, $-R^{M\,g}$			−0.20		−0.68		0.26	−0.48	0.94
Reallocation of hours, R^H			−0.34		−0.21		0.10	0.13	0.31
Decomposition using industry real value added per hour worked									
Industry contribution			1.59		2.41		2.41	0.83	0.00
IT-producing industries			0.36		0.70		0.47	0.34	−0.23
IT-using industries			0.48		1.31		1.54	0.82	0.24
Other industries			0.74		0.41		0.40	−0.33	0.00
Reallocation of hours, R^H			−0.34		−0.21		0.10	0.13	0.31

Sources: Authors' calculations.
a. Nominal value added in indicated industries divided by aggregate nominal value added for each period, multiplied by 100.
b. Growth of industry productivity, weighted by nominal value-added shares in each year.
c. Based on BEA and BLS aggregate data from table 5.
d. Weighted aggregate of industry output and hours data.
e. Includes computer and electronics products, publishing including software, information and data processing services, and computer system design and related services, as defined by BEA.
f. Includes all non-IT-producing industries with a 1995 IT capital services share above the 1995 median.
g. Reallocations are defined as in equations 19 and 20.

derive by explicitly aggregating the detailed industries as in equations 17 and 18. There is a small divergence for the middle period, but the two estimates tell the same story of a large productivity acceleration after 1995 and a smaller one after 2000.[58]

The second and third panels of table 6 report the decomposition from equations 19 and 20 using gross output data and value-added data, respectively. Both panels indicate a substantial increase in the direct contribution of industry-level productivity after 1995 (1.31 percentage points for gross output and 0.83 percentage point for value added), followed by a large decline after 2000 for gross output (−0.94 percentage point) and no change for value added.

Both the materials and hours reallocation terms turn positive after 2000, boosting the aggregates and suggesting that an important part of the post-2000 productivity gains stemmed from the shifting of inputs among industries.[59] In fact, we do not observe an increase in productivity growth after 2000 when looking at the direct industry contributions, an insight that is only possible with industry-level data.[60]

The materials reallocation term contributes positively to aggregate productivity growth when gross output is growing faster than materials, which implies that value added is growing faster than gross output (see equation 16). This pattern has held since 2000 and likely reflects some combination of substitution among inputs, biased technical change, and new production opportunities such as outsourcing. Better understanding of these forces is an important area for future work.

---

58. We also aggregated the industry output data using a Fisher (rather than the Tornqvist) index and still found a small difference for the period 1995–2000. We do not have an explanation for this.

59. Jorgenson and others (forthcoming) show an increase in both the intermediate input and hours reallocation terms, although both are slightly negative through 2004. The results in Bosworth and Triplett (2007) are similar to ours in some respects (rising direct contribution of gross output productivity through 2000 followed by a substantial fall, and an intermediate reallocation term that switches from negative to positive after 2000), but their hours reallocation term remains negative through 2005. This divergence reflects differences in the estimation of the hours series. Bosworth and Triplett (2007) use the BEA series on full-time/part-time employees, which they scale by total hours per employee from BLS for 1987 to 2004. They hold hours per full-time/part-time employee constant from 2004 to 2005.

60. This is analogous to the analysis of the sources of productivity growth within the U.S. retail trade sector by Foster, Haltiwanger, and Krizan (2002), who report that the majority of productivity gains reflect entry and exit, with a very small contribution from productivity gains within continuing establishments.

Brookings Papers on Economic Activity, 1:2007

Figure 1. Link between Productivity and Hours Reallocation, 1989–2005

Correlation coefficient   Percentage points

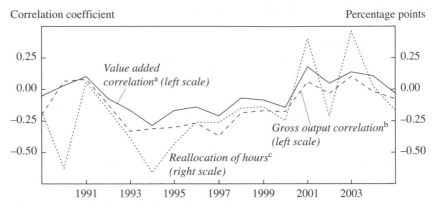

Source: Authors' calculations using BLS and BEA data.
a. Annual cross-sectional correlation between hours growth and the lagged level of productivity for the sixty industries in appendix table A-1, calculated using industry value added.
b. Above correlation calculated using industry gross output.
c. Reallocation of hours to high-productivity industries as defined in equation 19. This is the difference between the aggregate growth rate of hours weighted by industry value added and the aggregate growth rate of hours weighted by hours in each of the sixty industries.

The reallocation of hours is positive when industries with relatively high productivity (in nominal terms) have strong hours growth. Growing reallocations are consistent with the notion that increased competitive pressures, flexible labor markets, and restructuring were part of the productivity story in recent years. Elsewhere Stiroh discusses some evidence of increased flexibility of U.S. labor markets and reports evidence of increased reallocation across industries.[61]

To provide an alternative perspective, we calculate the annual cross-sectional correlation between hours growth and the lagged level of ALP for the sixty disaggregated industries. Figure 1 plots the estimated correlations for both the value-added and gross output measures of labor productivity; the figure also shows the term from equation 19 for the annual reallocation of hours to high-productivity industries. All three series seem to have trended upward, particularly since the early 1990s, which suggests that industries with relatively high productivity have become more likely to show strong hours growth in the following year. There also seems to be a

61. Stiroh (forthcoming).

cyclical component, as the correlations and hours reallocations rise during recessions, consistent with the notion of a cleansing effect of recessions.[62]

This interpretation of the reallocation of hours is suggestive; we have provided neither a deep economic explanation nor sophisticated econometric evidence that might identify the causal factors. Rather we are highlighting what appears to be an increasingly important source of aggregate productivity growth and pointing toward further research.

ROLE OF IT CLASSIFICATIONS. Table 6 also quantifies the direct contributions from IT-producing, IT-using, and other industries. Consistent with the classification scheme used by BEA,[63] we identify four industries as IT-producing: computer and electronic products, publishing including software, information and data processing services, and computer system design and related services. Following Stiroh,[64] we identify industries as IT-using if their IT capital income share (nominal IT capital income as a share of nominal nonresidential capital income) is above the median for all industries, excluding the four IT-producing industries. All remaining industries are labeled "other industries." This leaves four IT-producing industries with nearly 5 percent of aggregate value added in the most recent period, twenty-six IT-using industries with 59 percent, and thirty "other industries" with the remainder.[65]

As shown in table 6, the IT-producing and IT-using industries more than account for the direct contribution from individual industries to the productivity acceleration during 1995–2000. After 2000, however, the impact of IT is much less clear-cut, with the swing in the growth contributions from all three groups of industries concentrated in a fairly narrow range.

For the full decade from 1995 to 2005, the direct contribution from the IT-using industries was far larger than it had been over 1988–1995, despite the decline after 2000 based on gross output data. In contrast, the direct contribution from "other industries" remained smaller throughout

62. Caballero and Hammour (1994).
63. See, for example, Smith and Lum (2005) and Howells, Barefoot, and Lindberg (2006).
64. Stiroh (2002b).
65. Appendix table A-1 shows this classification scheme for the sixty detailed industries based on both 1995 and 2000 IT capital income shares and reports the 2005 share. Baily and Lawrence (2001), Stiroh (2001), and Jorgenson, Ho, and Stiroh (2005) also use relative shares of IT capital in total capital to identify IT-intensive industries in the United States, and Daveri and Mascotto (2002), Inklaar, O'Mahony, and Timmer (2005), O'Mahony and van Ark (2003), and van Ark, Inklaar, and McGuckin (2003) do so in international studies.

1995–2005 than it had been before 1995. This distinction highlights the important role for IT use in driving the faster growth in productivity that has prevailed over the entire period since the mid-1990s.

The contribution from the IT-producing industries moved up during 1995–2000 and back down during 2000–05, with the size of the swing depending on which output measure one uses. That said, both output measures show that the IT-producing industries made relatively large contributions to aggregate productivity growth throughout the sample period. For example, using the value added figures, the four IT-producing industries accounted for 19 percent (0.47 ÷ 2.52) of aggregate productivity growth over 2000–05, far above their 4 percent share of value added.

Potential Explanations for the Industry Variation

We now explore two specific questions about the cross-sectional distribution of productivity growth. First, was the link between IT and productivity growth after 2000 as strong as in the second half of the 1990s? The simple decompositions presented above suggest that it was not, but we examine this more formally here. Second, is there evidence for the idea that competition and restructuring contributed to the strong productivity gains after 2000?

IT AND PRODUCTIVITY GROWTH. This section examines the link between industry-level productivity growth and IT intensity. The intuition is straightforward: if IT plays an important role in productivity growth through either the direct capital deepening effect, a complementary but omitted input, or productivity spillovers, one should expect the most IT-intensive industries to show the largest productivity gains. We estimate cross-sectional regressions that relate the *change* in productivity growth over two periods to IT intensity at the end of the first period as

$$(21) \qquad \Delta A\dot{L}P_i = \alpha + \beta IT_i + \varepsilon_i,$$

where $\Delta A\dot{L}P$ is the change in productivity growth between two periods (from 1988–95 to 1995–2000, from 1988–95 to 1995–2005, or from 1995–2000 to 2000–05).

We use two alternative measures of IT intensity. The first is a qualitative indicator of relative intensity: a dummy variable equal to one if the IT share of total nonresidential capital income exceeds the industry median and zero otherwise.[66] This qualitative approach allows a broad interpretation of IT as a proxy for related investments such as intangible capital and the improved management practices that typically accompany IT. Moreover, this type of indicator variable is robust to the type of measurement error in the capital stock described by Randy Becker and coauthors,[67] but it misses the variation in IT intensity across industries. Our second measure is the actual share of IT capital services in total nonresidential capital services. This quantitative measure better captures differences in IT intensity but is more prone to measurement error. We estimate the IT share regressions with data from all sixty industries and from fifty-six industries after dropping the four IT-producing industries; the latter sample removes some outliers and focuses on the impact of the use of IT.

We define IT intensity as that just before the period of acceleration, for example in 1995 when analyzing the change in productivity growth after 1995, and in 2000 when examining the change after 2000. Although this procedure is not perfect, it helps control for the endogeneity of investment. In the dummy variable specification, β represents the change in productivity growth across periods for IT-intensive industries relative to the change for other industries; in the quantitative specification, β represents the increase in the change of productivity growth associated with a marginal increase in IT intensity.

Table 7 presents the results. The first three columns examine changes in the second half of the 1990s by comparing 1995–2000 with 1988–95. The middle three columns extend the data to 2005 but keep the breakpoint and the measure of IT intensity at 1995. The final three columns focus on the post-2000 gains by comparing the change in productivity from 2000 to 2005 with that from 1995 to 2000. The top panel uses gross output as the output measure, and the bottom panel uses value added. All estimates use ordinary least squares (OLS) with robust standard errors.[68]

66. This specification is identical to a difference-in-difference-style regression with a post-1995 or post-2000 dummy variable, an IT intensity dummy, and the interaction estimated with annual data for the full period.

67. Becker and others (2005).

68. We also estimated (but do not report) weighted least squares estimates, which are appropriate if the somewhat arbitrary nature of the industry classification system makes measurement error more severe in the relatively small industries. See Kahn and Lim (1998) for a more detailed discussion of weights in industry regressions. These weighted estimates are similar to those reported in table 7.

Table 7. Regressions Relating Labor Productivity Growth to IT Capital Intensity[a]

Output measure and independent variable	Regression (Dependent variable: change in labor productivity growth over indicated period)								
	1988–95 to 1995–2000			1988–95 to 1995–2005			1995–2000 to 2000–05		
Gross output									
1995 IT dummy[b]	1.277** (0.585)			1.478*** (0.491)					
1995 IT share[c]		0.038 (0.028)	0.081*** (0.027)		0.037* (0.020)	0.060*** (0.019)			
2000 IT dummy							0.156 (0.931)		
2000 IT share								0.010 (0.044)	−0.031 (0.048)
Constant	0.513 (0.438)	0.543 (0.478)	0.009 (0.478)	0.074 (0.371)	0.216 (0.401)	−0.040 (0.382)	−0.756 (0.480)	−0.865 (0.650)	−0.206 (0.651)
IT-producing industries included in sample?	No	No	Yes	No	No	Yes	No	No	Yes
R^2	0.08	0.06	0.18	0.14	0.07	0.12	0.00	0.00	0.02
Value added									
1995 IT dummy	1.904 (1.173)			1.967** (0.893)					
1995 IT share		0.029 (0.044)	0.066 (0.054)		0.051* (0.026)	0.048 (0.035)			
2000 IT dummy							0.095 (1.448)		
2000 IT share								0.046 (0.066)	−0.041 (0.055)
Constant	−0.709 (0.913)	−0.227 (0.915)	−0.828 (1.009)	−0.352 (0.709)	−0.198 (0.667)	−0.284 (0.725)	0.730 (0.944)	−0.056 (1.149)	1.225 (1.017)
IT-producing industries included in sample?	No	No	Yes	No	No	Yes	No	No	Yes
R^2	0.04	0.01	0.03	0.08	0.05	0.026	0.00	0.02	0.01

Source: Authors' regressions.

a. Data are for the sixty industries listed in appendix table A-1 (fifty-six industries when the four IT-producing industries are dropped). Numbers in parentheses are robust standard errors. Asterisks indicate statistical significance at the ***1 percent, **5 percent, and *10 percent level.

b. Dummy variable equal to 1 for industries with an IT capital share above the median in the indicated year, and zero otherwise.

c. IT capital services as a share of nonresidential capital services in the indicated year.

The estimates through 2000 suggest a link between IT intensity and the change in productivity growth using the gross output data, but the results are weaker using the value-added data. When we extend the data to include the post-2000 period and compare 1995–2005 with 1988–95, both sets of estimates show large and significant IT effects. The final three columns indicate that IT intensity in 2000 is not a useful predictor of the change in productivity growth after 2000.[69]

These results show that the most IT-intensive industries in 1995 experienced larger increases in productivity growth after 1995 and that these gains lasted through 2005. Although the IT intensity variable explains only a relatively small portion of the overall variation across industries, the size of the IT effect is economically large: IT-intensive industries showed an increase in productivity growth that was between 1.5 and 2.0 percentage points greater than in other industries when 1995–2005 is compared with 1988–95. Despite data revisions and the shift to NAICS, the results are similar to those in earlier work, indicating strong support for the view that IT use mattered for the productivity gains after 1995. Of course, to the extent that IT capital is correlated with other factors such as management skills or intangible capital, these gains should be attributed to the whole suite of business activities that accompany IT investment, and not narrowly to changes in physical capital.

By contrast, the post-2000 acceleration in productivity does not appear to be tied to the accumulation of IT assets in the late 1990s. In particular, we find no evidence that industries that sowed lots of IT capital in the late 1990s reaped a particularly large productivity payoff after 2000. Although these results are surely confounded by cyclical dynamics that were especially severe in the high-technology sectors, analysis of an earlier vintage of the industry data by Stiroh shows that the reduced correlation between IT and productivity is not due solely to the high-technology slowdown in 2001.[70]

COMPETITIVE PRESSURES AND PRODUCTIVITY GROWTH. One idea that has received considerable attention is that U.S. firms may have been under increased pressure in the 2000s to cut costs and raise efficiency in order to

---

69. Stiroh and Botsch (2007) report similar results.

70. Stiroh (2006). These results could be consistent with an IT-based explanation if the pervasiveness of IT makes it difficult to identify a link econometrically. That is, if IT is integral for all industries, then measures of IT intensity may not be useful for classification purposes. This view, however, is inherently untestable.

maintain profitability in a more globalized and competitive environment.[71] Robert Gordon, for example, concludes that the "savage cost cutting and layoffs" that followed the profit boom of the late 1990s likely explain the unusual surge of productivity in the early 2000s.[72] Mark Schweitzer notes that managers have stressed the need to realign business processes without hiring additional workers, although he admits that empirical support is limited.[73] Erica Groshen and Simon Potter raise the possibility that new management strategies promoted lean staffing in order to increase efficiency.[74] Firms may have been better able to carry out these strategies in an environment of more flexible and efficient labor markets.[75]

If the cost-cutting hypothesis is true, productivity growth should have been relatively strong and hours growth relatively weak after 2000 in those industries that experienced the biggest decline in profit in earlier years and thus were under the most intense pressure to restructure. To identify those industries, we examine the change in the profit share derived from the BEA industry data, where the profit share is defined as gross operating surplus (consumption of fixed capital; business transfers; other gross operating surplus such as profits before tax; net interest; and miscellaneous payments) as a share of value added. Although one might want to remove the consumption of fixed capital and the normal return to capital, those data are not available at a detailed level. Our profit share measure should be viewed as a broad measure that includes the gross return to capital.

We then compared industry growth from 2001 to 2004—the period of extremely rapid aggregate productivity gains—with changes in industry-level profit shares from the 1997 peak in the aggregate profit share to the 2001 trough. As a first pass, figures 2 and 3 plot the growth of hours and labor productivity from 2001 to 2004 against the change in the profit share from 1997 to 2001 for sixty industries. These scatterplots offer some support for the restructuring hypothesis, as a decline in the profit share is

---

71. Baily (2004) discusses the case study evidence of the impact of competitive intensity on firms' need to innovate and increase productivity and argues that competitive pressure gradually increased during the 1970s and 1980s.

72. Gordon (2003, p. 274). See Nordhaus (2002a) for details on profit trends over this period.

73. Schweitzer (2004).

74. Groshen and Potter (2003).

75. This has been documented by Schreft and Singh (2003) and by Aaronson, Rissman, and Sullivan (2004).

Figure 2. Hours Growth over 2001–04 versus Change in the Profit Share over 1997–2001, by Industry[a]

Hours growth[b] (percent)

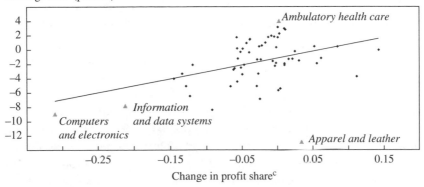

Source: Authors' calculations using BLS and BEA data.
a. Each point is one of sixty industry observations; line plots fitted values from an OLS regression.
b. Average annual rate of growth in hours worked from 2001 to 2004.
c. Change in the ratio of gross operating surplus to value added from 1997 to 2001.

Figure 3. Labor Productivity Growth over 2001–04 versus Change in the Profit Share over 1997–2001, by Industry[a]

Labor productivity growth[b] (percent)

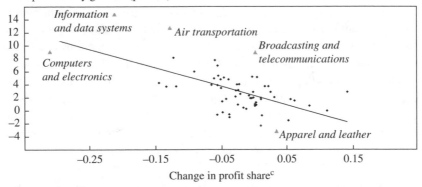

Source: Authors' calculations using BLS and BEA data.
a. Each point is one of sixty industry observations. Line plots fitted values from an OLS regression.
b. Average annual rate of growth of labor productivity from 2001 to 2004 based on gross output.
c. Change in the ratio of gross operating surplus to value added from 1997 to 2001.

associated (significantly) with slower hours growth and faster ALP growth.[76] To gauge the magnitude of this effect, note that industries with below-median changes in the profit share experienced hours growth 2 percentage points slower on average than did other industries and labor productivity growth about 3 percentage points faster.[77]

We also estimate cross-sectional regressions that relate growth in the early 2000s to the lagged change in the profit share as

$$(22) \qquad \dot{X}_i = \alpha + \beta \Delta PR_i + \gamma \mathbf{Z}_i + \varepsilon_i,$$

where $\dot{X}$ is average annual growth of either hours, intermediate inputs, labor productivity, or output from 2001 to 2004, ΔPR is the change in the profit share from 1997 to 2001, and $\mathbf{Z}$ are controls. Equation 22 is obviously a reduced-form regression, and the controls are therefore intended to soak up variation attributable to other factors. $\mathbf{Z}$ includes the contemporaneous change in the profit share from 2001 to 2004, to control for demand effects; lagged growth in the dependent variable from 1997 to 2001, to control for longer-run trends (for example, the possibility that some industries may be in secular decline); and the IT capital service share, to control for IT intensity. Finally, we interacted the IT capital service share with the lagged change in the profit share, to examine whether IT intensity facilitated adjustment to competitive pressures.

Table 8 reports estimates of equation 22 without and with these controls. The top panel uses input growth (either hours or intermediate inputs) as the dependent variable, the middle panel uses labor productivity measures based on gross output or value added, and the bottom panel uses the two output measures. All estimates use OLS with robust standard errors.

The hours growth regressions reveal a strong positive link, as industries with large declines in the profit share over 1997–2001 experienced significantly slower hours growth from 2001 to 2004. There is no similar link with intermediate inputs. Firms might have been expected to economize on all margins, but differences in adjustment costs could explain the different

---

76. The significance of the cross-sectional correlation is robust to dropping the two major outliers—computers and electronics, and information and data systems—on the far left of figures 2 and 3.

77. *t*-tests for differences in the mean growth rates between the two groups of industries reject the hypothesis that the two had equal growth rates for hours and productivity, but fail to reject the hypothesis that the two had equal output growth rates.

Table 8. Regressions Relating Growth in Inputs, Productivity, and Output to Earlier Changes in the Profit Share[a]

Regression (Dependent variable: average annual growth rate of indicated input type)

Independent variable	Hours				Intermediate inputs	
Change in profit share,[b] 1997–2001	19.212***	16.413***	16.170***	−0.069	1.864	1.502
	(4.940)	(5.126)	(5.273)	(10.339)	(10.789)	(11.398)
Change in profit share, 2001–04		−0.115	13.389*		8.244	22.546
		(6.159)	(7.952)		(12.592)	(22.270)
Lagged dependent variable, 1997–2001		0.722***	0.782***		0.255	0.280
		(0.155)	(0.128)		(0.165)	(0.168)
IT service share,[c] 2001		−0.089***	−0.069***		−0.032	−0.009
		(0.027)	(0.025)		(0.064)	(0.067)
Change in profit share, 1997–2001 × IT service share, 2001			−0.444**			−0.474
			(0.173)			(0.522)
Constant	−1.175**	0.239	−0.193	0.533	0.104	−0.459
	(0.459)	(0.478)	(0.463)	(0.733)	(1.076)	(1.499)
R^2	0.17	0.51	0.57	0.00	0.10	0.12

Regression (Dependent variable: average annual growth rate of labor productivity)

Independent variable	Value added			Gross output		
Change in profit share, 1997–2001	−38.487***	−40.655***	−39.835***	−28.456***	−20.929***	−20.851***
	(11.253)	(14.067)	(14.230)	(6.437)	(7.116)	(7.379)
Change in profit share, 2001–04		5.703	0.563		7.013	4.655
		(11.962)	(15.520)		(8.705)	(8.353)
Lagged dependent variable, 1997–2001		−0.055	−0.041		0.169	0.176
		(0.186)	(0.195)		(0.168)	(0.178)

(continued)

Table 8. Regressions Relating Growth in Inputs, Productivity, and Output to Earlier Changes in the Profit Share^a (Continued)

Regression (Dependent variable: average annual growth rate of indicated input type)

Independent variable	Hours			Intermediate inputs		
IT service share, 2001	−0.008 (0.035)	−0.018 (0.041)		0.030 (0.028)	0.025 (0.037)	
Change in profit share, 1997–2001 × IT service share, 2001			0.177 (0.297)			0.077 (0.294)
Constant	3.283*** (0.745)	3.332*** (0.882)	3.540*** (0.871)	2.279*** (0.341)	1.319** (0.522)	1.404** (0.555)
R^2	0.26	0.27	0.28	0.37	0.44	0.44

Regression (Dependent variable: average annual growth rate of output)

Independent variable	Value added			Gross output		
Change in profit share, 1997–2001	−19.274** (9.511)	−19.781* (10.820)	−19.826* (10.794)	−9.243 (6.933)	−0.785 (7.645)	−0.707 (7.729)
Change in profit share, 2001–04		10.770 (11.257)	11.472 (17.752)		10.342 (10.943)	16.689 (16.531)
Lagged dependent variable, 1997–2001		−0.043 (0.150)	−0.044 (0.152)		0.294 (0.211)	0.300 (0.216)
IT service share, 2001		−0.006 (0.028)	−0.005 (0.034)		−0.014 (0.041)	−0.002 (0.040)
Change in profit share, 1997–2001 × IT service share, 2001			−0.023 (0.290)			−0.203 (0.356)
Constant	2.108*** (0.679)	2.058*** (0.680)	2.029** (0.780)	1.105** (0.486)	0.529 (0.552)	0.281 (0.867)
R^2	0.11	0.15	0.15	0.04	0.22	0.23

Source: Authors' regressions.
a. Growth rates of inputs, labor productivity, and output are from 2001 to 2004. Each regression has sixty industry observations. Numbers in parentheses are robust standard errors. Asterisks indicate statistical significance at the ***1 percent, **5 percent, and *10 percent level.
b. Profit share is defined throughout as the ratio of gross operating surplus to value added.
c. Share of IT capital services in nonresidential capital services.

results for hours and intermediate inputs. The results in the middle panel show a strong negative link between the lagged change in the profit share and productivity growth. Finally, the bottom panel reports some evidence that output growth was faster in the industries with a declining profit share, but the link is weaker and far less robust than that between labor productivity and the profit share.[78]

These results support the hypothesis that competitive pressure and restructuring help explain the post-2000 productivity gains. One interpretation is that firms in those industries where profits fell most dramatically through 2001 became cautious, hired fewer workers, and improved productivity and efficiency after 2001. Moreover, the absence of strongly significant effects in the output regressions, together with the robustness of the results to the inclusion of the contemporaneous change in the profit share, suggests that this was not just a demand story, but rather reflects how firms chose to produce a given amount of output. Similarly, the results are robust to including a lagged dependent variable, and so it does not appear that we are merely capturing long-run trends. Finally, these estimates provide additional evidence that IT was not a driving factor in the early 2000s, as both the level of IT intensity and the interaction term are insignificant in all except the hours regressions.

Productivity Trends and Outlook

This section turns to the outlook for productivity growth. After highlighting issues with the recent data, we report long-period averages of labor productivity growth to provide a benchmark for assessing the strength of recent growth. We also present trend estimates from a Kalman filter model and estimates of the steady-state growth implicit in our aggregate growth

78. As a robustness check, we estimated difference-in-difference regressions and found that industries with a below-median change in the profit share from 1997 to 2001 had a bigger decline in the growth of hours and a bigger increase in the growth of gross output labor productivity than did other industries. No significant difference emerged for value-added labor productivity growth. We also ran regressions with more detailed measures of intermediate inputs, including energy, materials, and purchased service inputs, as the dependent variable, but those results were uniformly insignificant and are not reported. As a second robustness check, we compared hours, productivity, and output growth for 1992 with the change in the profit share from 1989 to 1991 and found largely insignificant results, suggesting that the latest cyclical episode was different from the previous one.

Table 9. Effects of Data Revisions and Data for Additional Years on Measured Growth of Labor Productivity[a]

	Period covered by the data				
Vintage of data	*1995–2000*	*2000–03*	*2000–04*	*2000–05*	*2000–06*
March 2004	2.4	3.8			
August 2004	2.5	3.7			
March 2005	2.5	3.7	3.7		
August 2005	2.5	3.4	3.4		
March 2006	2.5	3.4	3.4	3.3	
August 2006	2.5	3.4	3.3	3.1	
March 2007	2.5	3.4	3.3	3.0	2.8

Source: Authors' calculations using BLS data.
a. Measured as 100 times the average log difference over the indicated period, based on annual average data.

accounting model. Finally, we compare these trend estimates with those reported by other analysts.

What Do the Recent Data Say?

Assessing the underlying trend in labor productivity growth since 2000 has been complicated by major data revisions to both output and hours worked and by swings in actual productivity growth. Table 9 displays both dimensions of the recent data. Moving down a column in the table shows the effect of revisions across successive vintages of data, while moving across a line shows the effect of adding additional years to the period covered by the data.[79]

For 2000–03, the average growth of labor productivity was reported initially in March 2004 to have been 3.8 percent. This surprisingly robust gain led many analysts to ask why labor productivity growth had accelerated further despite sluggish investment spending, the 2001 recession, and other adverse shocks. However, subsequent revisions reduced the rate of

79. The figures in table 9 are calculated from BLS's quarterly Productivity and Costs data. The definition of nonfarm business in these data includes government enterprises. In contrast, the definition of nonfarm business in BLS's MFP data, the data we use to calculate the labor productivity growth rates in table 1, excludes government enterprises. This slight difference in sectoral coverage explains why labor productivity growth for 2000–06 differs by 0.1 percentage point across the two tables. The same explanation accounts for the slight difference in the average growth rate for 1973–95 between table 1 and the column for nonfarm business in table 10 below.

Table 10. Growth of Labor Productivity: Long-Period Averages[a]

Period	Private economy or business sector[b]	Nonfarm business sector
1909–1928	1.4	
1928–1950	2.5	
1950–1973	2.9	2.6
1973–1995	1.5	1.4
1995–2006	2.8	2.7
1909–2006	2.2	
1950–2006	2.3	2.1

Source: Authors' calculations using BLS data.

a. Measured as 100 times the average log difference over the indicated period based on annual average data.

b. Data before 1947 pertain to the private economy (defined as gross national product less general government), whereas data for 1947 and later years pertain to the business sector.

advance to 3.4 percent.[80] The initial estimates for 2000–04 and 2000–05 were revised downward in a similar fashion, tempering some of the earlier optimism about the underlying trend. In addition to these revisions, smaller gains in labor productivity over the past few years have brought down the average growth rate, reported in the bottom line of the table. In the current vintage of data (March 2007), growth over 2000–06 averaged 2.8 percent, a full percentage point below the initial reading for the first three years of this period.

Long-Period Averages

Long-period averages of labor productivity growth provide one way to put the recent figures into perspective. The first column of table 10, using data from BLS, shows productivity growth rates over several periods extending back to 1909. These data cover a broader sector of the economy than nonfarm business and so do not line up perfectly with the estimates presented earlier in the paper. That said, labor productivity growth according to these figures has averaged 2.2 percent a year since 1909.[81] The second column shows productivity growth rates over selected periods since 1950 for the nonfarm business sector; here growth averaged 2.7 percent a

80. Jorgenson, Ho, and Stiroh (2007) show that such revisions are not unusual; for example, there was a steady stream of upward revisions to productivity growth in the mid-1990s.

81. There are a number of alternative historical series for labor productivity. Although they yield different results in some periods, the patterns of growth and long-run averages are qualitatively similar to the BLS data presented here. For example, see Gordon (2006).

year during 1995–2006, similar to that during the so-called "golden era" of productivity from 1950 to 1973 and well above the postwar average of 2.1 percent a year. Thus by historical standards the performance of labor productivity since 1995 has been quite strong.

Kalman Filter Estimates

As one approach to obtaining time-varying estimates of the trend in labor productivity, we use a slightly modified version of the Kalman filter model developed by John Roberts.[82] Although alternative implementations could yield answers that differ from the one presented here, the Roberts model has some appealing features.[83] In particular, it allows for shocks to both the level and the growth rate of trend productivity, and it controls for cyclical changes in productivity growth by assuming that hours adjust gradually to output following a cyclical shock. We estimate the model by the maximum likelihood method, using standard BLS data on labor productivity in the nonfarm business sector from the first quarter of 1953 to the fourth quarter of 2006.

For the fourth quarter of 2006, this procedure estimates that the trend in labor productivity growth was 2¼ percent a year, roughly ½ percentage point below the average pace of productivity growth since 2000. Put another way, the model interprets some of the extraordinary growth in the years immediately after the 2001 recession as transitory. The model also delivers a 2-standard-error confidence band around the estimated trend, ranging from 1.3 percent to 3.2 percent. Thus considerable uncertainty surrounds this estimate of trend productivity growth.

Steady-State Analysis of Labor Productivity Growth

As a complement to the Kalman filter estimate of the trend in labor productivity growth, we calculate the growth rate that would prevail in the steady state of our aggregate growth accounting model. For this exercise we use the version of the model that excludes our added intangibles, so

82. In Roberts (2001) the Kalman filter is used to obtain time-varying estimates of trend growth in both potential output and labor productivity. Our implementation first uses a Hodrick-Prescott filter to estimate the trend in hours and then feeds this exogenous trend to the model. Hence we need to estimate a trend only for labor productivity.

83. For other estimates of trend productivity using Kalman filter techniques, see Brainard and Perry (2000) and Gordon (2003).

that our estimates can be compared with those of other researchers. We stress at the outset that we do not regard these steady-state results as forecasts of productivity growth over any period. Rather this exercise yields "structured guesses" for growth in labor productivity consistent with alternative scenarios for certain key features of the economy.

The steady state in our model is characterized by the following conditions. Real output in each sector grows at a constant rate (which can differ across sectors), and real investment in each type of capital grows at the same constant rate as the real stock of that capital. Because $\dot{I} = \dot{K}$ for each type of capital, adjustment costs have no effect on MFP growth (sectoral or aggregate) in the steady state. On the labor side, we require that hours worked grow at the same constant rate in every sector, that the workweek be fixed, and that labor quality improve at a constant rate.

Under these conditions the steady-state growth rate of aggregate labor productivity can be written as follows:[84]

$$(23) \qquad \dot{ALP} = \sum_i \left[\left((\alpha_i^K - \phi_i)/\alpha^L \right)\left(\dot{z}_i + \beta_i^S \dot{z}_s \right) \right] + \dot{q} + \dot{z},$$

where the α's denote income shares, the ϕ's denote the adjustment cost elasticity of output with respect to each type of capital, β_i^S is the share of total costs in final-output sector i represented by purchases of semiconductors, $\dot{q}$ is the rate of increase in labor quality, $\dot{z}_i$ and $\dot{z}_s$ denote the rates of improvement in sectoral technology, and $\dot{z}$ is the Domar share-weighted sum of these sectoral rates of improvement. Recall that the $\dot{z}$ terms (sectoral or aggregate) equal the growth of MFP after controlling for the effects of changes in factor utilization and adjustment costs. No explicit terms for capital deepening appear in equation 23. However, capital deepening is determined endogenously from the improvement in technology, and the terms in brackets account for the growth contribution from this induced capital deepening.[85]

---

84. See the appendix to the working paper version of this paper (Oliner, Sichel, and Stiroh, 2007) for details.

85. Even though adjustment costs have no direct effect on growth in the steady state, the adjustment cost elasticities (ϕ_i) appear in the weights on the capital deepening terms in equation 23, just as they did in the growth accounting equation that applies outside the steady state (equation 1). As in that case, we lack the information to specify these asset-specific elasticities. We proceed as we did before, by replacing the theoretically correct weights with standard income-share weights that sum to the same value (one minus the labor share).

The steady-state equation depends on a large number of parameters (income shares, sectoral output shares, semiconductor cost shares, and so on). We consider a range of parameter values.[86] For the most part, steady-state growth is not very sensitive to these parameters individually. However, the results do depend importantly on two parameters: the rate of improvement in labor quality and the rate of advance in technology outside the IT-producing sectors ("other nonfarm business").[87] Following Jorgenson, Ho, and Stiroh,[88] we assume that labor quality will improve by 0.15 percent a year, well below the historical rate of increase, as the educational attainment of new labor force entrants rises more slowly than in the past and experienced workers reach retirement age. For the value of $\dot{z}$ in other nonfarm business, we consider values ranging from 0.19 to 0.98 percent a year. The lower-bound figure equals the average annual growth of $\dot{z}$ in this sector over 1973–2000, which allows for reversion to the longer-term average prevailing before the recent period of rapid gains. The upper-bound figure equals the average annual increase over 2000–06, minus ¼ percentage point to account for the likelihood that some of the advance during this period was transitory.

Table 11 presents the results from the steady-state exercise using equation 23. The estimated range for steady-state labor productivity growth runs from 1.46 percent at an annual rate to 3.09 percent. The wide range reflects our uncertainty about the values of the parameters that determine steady-state growth. The center of the range is 2¼ percent, about ½ percentage point below the average rate of labor productivity growth since 2000. This step-down from the recent average largely reflects the assumption that improvements in labor quality will slow and that gains in MFP, after controlling for adjustment costs and factor utilization, will not be as robust as the average pace since 2000.

Comparing Results

Table 12 compares the results from our steady-state and Kalman filter analyses with forecasts of labor productivity growth from a variety of sources. All but three of these forecasts have a horizon of ten years. The other three

86. These are listed in the appendix to Oliner, Sichel, and Stiroh (2007).
87. For the IT-producing sectors, the rate of advance in technology is determined endogenously from the assumed rates of change in prices for IT capital and a variety of other parameters.
88. Jorgenson, Ho, and Stiroh (2007).

Table 11. Growth of Labor Productivity: Steady-State Results[a]

Item	Using lower-bound parameters	Using upper-bound parameters
Growth of labor productivity in the nonfarm business sector (percent a year)	1.46	3.09
Contributions from (percentage points):		
Induced capital deepening	0.75	1.39
Improvement in labor quality	0.15	0.15
Growth of MFP	0.56	1.55
Memorandum: MFP growth, other nonfarm business (percent a year)	0.19	0.98

Source: Authors' calculations.
a. Calculated from equation 23 in the text. Values for the parameters that appear in equation 23 are listed in the appendix to Oliner, Sichel, and Stiroh (2007).

Table 12. Alternative Estimates of Future Growth in Labor Productivity
Percent a year

Source	Date of projection	Estimate
This paper: steady-state analysis	March 2007	1.5 to 3.1
This paper: Kalman filter analysis	March 2007	1.3 to 3.2
Robert Gordon	March 2007	2.0
Survey of Professional Forecasters[a]	February 2007	2.2
Global Insight	March 2007	2.2
Macroeconomic Advisers	March 2007	2.2
Congressional Budget Office	January 2007	2.3
Dale Jorgenson, Mun Ho, and Kevin Stiroh[b]	October 2006	2.5
James Kahn and Robert Rich	March 2007	2.5
Council of Economic Advisers	January 2007	2.6

Sources: Gordon (2007, slide 24); Federal Reserve Bank of Philadelphia, *Survey of Professional Forecasters,* February 13, 2007; Global Insight, *U.S. Executive Summary,* March 2007, p. 6; Macroeconomic Advisers, *Macro Focus,* March 22, 2007, p. 11; Congressional Budget Office (2007a, table 2-2); Jorgenson, Ho, and Stiroh (2007, table 3); Kahn and Rich (2006), updated to March 2007 based on the productivity model update posted at www.newyorkfed.org/research/national_economy/richkahn_prodmod.pdf; *Economic Report of the President 2007,* table 1-2.
a. Median of the thirty-eight forecasts in the survey.
b. "Base-case" projection.

have shorter horizons.[89] These forecasts for average annual growth in labor productivity range from 2 percent to 2.6 percent. As noted above, the midpoint of our estimated range for steady-state growth and the estimated trend from the Kalman filter are both 2¼ percent, near the center of the range of these forecasts. Thus there seems to be considerable agreement that labor productivity growth will remain reasonably strong over a medium-term horizon.

89. The horizon in Kahn and Rich (2006) is five years, that in *Economic Report of the President 2007* is six years, and that in the March 2007 Macroeconomic Advisers report is eight years.

That said, one should be humble about this type of exercise, for a number of reasons. First, both the Kalman filter and our steady-state machinery point to a very wide confidence band around the point estimates. Second, the data on labor productivity through 2006 still could be revised significantly. In the future we might be looking at a picture of actual labor productivity growth for recent years that is different from the one we see today. Finally, as a general matter, economists do not have a stellar track record in forecasting trends in labor productivity. Although we think the analysis here moves the debate forward, we are acutely aware of the inherent limitations.

Conclusion

Productivity developments since 1995 have raised many important and interesting questions for productivity analysts and policymakers, four of which we address in this paper. First, given the data now available and the various critiques of neoclassical growth accounting that have arisen in recent years, is IT still a critical part of the story for the observed acceleration in productivity growth over 1995–2000? Second, what is the source of the continued strength in productivity growth since 2000? Third, how has the accumulation of intangible capital influenced recent productivity developments? And, finally, based on our answers to these questions, what is the outlook for productivity growth? We have used a variety of techniques to address these questions, including aggregate growth accounting augmented to incorporate variable utilization, adjustment costs, and intangible asset accumulation; an assessment of industry-level productivity patterns; and Kalman filter and steady-state analysis to gauge trend productivity.

Both the aggregate and the industry-level results confirm the central role of IT in the productivity revival during 1995–2000. IT also plays a significant role after 2000, although its impact appears smaller than it was during 1995–2000. These results stand even after accounting for variable factor utilization, adjustment costs, and intangible capital and so provide strong support for the consensus view that IT was a key source of growth for the U.S. economy over the past decade.

Our results suggest that the sources of the productivity gains since 2000 differ in important ways from those during 1995–2000. Along with the smaller direct role for IT in the latest period, aggregate productivity growth since 2000 appears to have been boosted by industry restructuring in response to profit pressures and by a reallocation of material and labor inputs across industries. We also find considerable churning among industries, with some industries showing accelerating productivity in the second half of the 1990s and different ones accelerating in the most recent period.

Adding intangible capital to our aggregate growth accounting framework changes the time profile for productivity growth since 1995 relative to the published data. The measure of intangible assets used in this paper implies that the fastest gains in labor productivity occurred during 1995–2000, with some step-down after 2000. In addition, the inclusion of intangibles tempers the size of the pickup in MFP growth from 1995–2000 to 2000–06.

Finally, in terms of the productivity outlook, both the Kalman filter and the steady-state analyses deliver broadly similar results and highlight the wide range of uncertainty surrounding estimates of growth in trend labor productivity. In both cases the central tendencies suggest a rate for trend productivity gains of around 2¼ percent a year, a rate that is consistent with productivity growth remaining well above the lackluster pace that prevailed during the twenty-five years before 1995, but somewhat slower than the 1995–2006 average.

APPENDIX A

Industry Data

Table A-1. Value Added, IT Share, and IT Classification of U.S. Industries

Name	Value added, 2005 (millions of dollars)	IT share, 2005[a]	IT_{1995}[b]	IT_{2000}[c]	IT-producing[d]
			\multicolumn{3}{c}{IT classification}		
Agriculture, forestry, fishing, and hunting	123.1	1.4	0	0	0
Oil and gas extraction	159.6	1.8	0	0	0
Mining, except oil and gas	31.5	6.0	0	0	0
Support activities for mining	42.2	8.9	0	0	0
Construction	611.1	19.0	1	1	0
Wood products	39.0	6.4	0	0	0
Nonmetallic mineral products	53.3	9.1	0	0	0
Primary metals	61.1	5.3	0	0	0
Fabricated metal products	130.5	9.3	0	0	0
Machinery	111.1	23.3	1	1	0

(continued)

Table A-1. Value Added, IT Share, and IT Classification of U.S. Industries (*Continued*)

Name	Value added, 2005 (millions of dollars)	IT share, 2005[a]	IT classification		
			IT_{1995}[b]	IT_{2000}[c]	IT-producing[d]
Computer and electronic products	135.3	23.4	1	1	1
Electrical equipment, appliances, and components	47.8	12.8	1	1	0
Motor vehicles, bodies and trailers, and parts	95.4	15.2	1	1	0
Other transportation equipment	71.1	28.4	1	1	0
Furniture and related products	37.1	9.6	0	0	0
Miscellaneous manufacturing	72.6	16.0	1	1	0
Food and beverage and tobacco products	175.7	8.8	0	0	0
Textile mills and textile product mills	23.8	4.0	0	0	0
Apparel and leather and allied products	16.8	7.2	0	0	0
Paper products	54.6	6.5	0	0	0
Printing and related support activities	46.9	12.4	0	1	0
Petroleum and coal products	63.5	9.4	0	0	0
Chemical products	209.2	17.1	1	1	0
Plastics and rubber products	67.7	5.6	0	0	0
Utilities	248.0	5.5	0	0	0
Wholesale trade	743.2	25.4	1	1	0
Retail trade	823.5	14.6	1	0	0
Air transportation	41.0	42.7	1	1	0
Rail transportation	32.3	2.0	0	0	0
Water transportation	9.0	42.3	1	1	0
Truck transportation	114.1	11.5	0	0	0
Transit and ground passenger transportation	17.1	16.8	1	1	0
Pipeline transportation	9.3	27.6	1	1	0
Other transportation and support activities	89.1	15.1	0	1	0
Warehousing and storage	32.7	19.0	0	0	0
Publishing industries (includes software)	150.2	49.8	1	1	1
Motion picture and sound recording industries	40.5	16.5	1	1	0
Broadcasting and telecommunications	304.1	46.5	1	1	0
Information and data processing services	60.4	81.7	1	1	1

(*continued*)

Table A-1. Value Added, IT Share, and IT Classification of U.S. Industries (*Continued*)

Name	Value added, 2005 (millions of dollars)	IT share, 2005[a]	IT classification		
			IT_{1995}[b]	IT_{2000}[c]	IT-producing[d]
Federal Reserve banks, credit intermediation, and related activities	474.7	28.6	1	1	0
Securities, commodity contracts, and investments	167.4	51.8	1	1	0
Insurance carriers and related activities	296.1	38.9	1	1	0
Funds, trusts, and other financial vehicles	19.5	6.6	0	0	0
Real estate	1,472.6	8.7	0	0	0
Rental and leasing services and lessors of intangible assets	105.8	23.1	1	1	0
Legal services	180.9	47.7	1	1	0
Computer systems design and related services	140.8	89.3	1	1	1
Miscellaneous professional, scientific, and technical services	542.5	67.5	1	1	0
Management of companies and enterprises	225.8	45.6	1	1	0
Administrative and support services	336.6	45.5	1	1	0
Waste management and remediation services	32.3	6.2	0	0	0
Educational services	115.8	22.1	0	1	0
Ambulatory health care services	441.9	14.5	1	0	0
Hospitals and nursing and residential care facilities	342.2	13.1	1	0	0
Social assistance	75.4	21.3	1	1	0
Performing arts, spectator sports, museums, and related activities	54.0	10.2	0	0	0
Amusements, gambling, and recreation industries	60.1	4.8	0	0	0
Accommodation	104.6	5.0	0	0	0
Food services and drinking places	225.9	5.8	0	0	0
Other services, except government	282.8	13.8	0	0	0

Source: Authors' calculations based on BEA data.
a. Nominal value of IT capital services divided by nominal value of total nonresidential capital services.
b. Equals 1 if 1995 IT capital service share is greater than 1995 median, and zero otherwise.
c. Equals 1 if 2000 IT capital service share is greater than 2000 median, and zero otherwise.
d. As defined by BEA.

Comments and
Discussion

Martin Neil Baily: The three authors of this paper have made some of the strongest contributions to the productivity literature in recent years, and it is terrific to see them team up to provide an important new analysis of the productivity acceleration that started in the mid-1990s. In particular, I liked the creative way they have adapted the growth accounting framework to take account of intangible capital, and I welcome the new insights provided by their industry-level regression analysis, particularly those highlighting the role for competitive pressure.

Labor productivity accelerated in the United States starting in 1996, after over twenty years of slow growth. That acceleration has been widely attributed to the revolution in information technology, a natural enough inference given that the acceleration coincided with a wave of capital investment in IT hardware and software. Indeed, some fraction of the productivity acceleration can certainly be attributed directly to an acceleration within the IT hardware-producing sector. Around 2000–01, however, the IT bubble burst, and IT investment slumped as the economy went into a mild recession. Yet, surprisingly, productivity growth did not slow down but actually grew even faster over 2002–04. This meant that the simple correlation between IT investment and productivity broke down after 2000.

There are three possible responses to what happened. The first is to conclude that perhaps IT was not as important to the post-1995 productivity acceleration as had been thought. Second, one could argue that IT investment has a lagged effect on productivity, so that the high-technology investment boom in the late 1990s had an impact that spilled over into the post-2000 period. A third hypothesis is that IT investment creates intangible capital that should be counted as part of total output. This last option is the approach taken in the growth accounting section of this paper, and it shifts

138

some of the productivity acceleration from the post-2000 period backward in time to 1995–2000, where it coincides with the surge in IT investment.

Working only with aggregate productivity data, one has very limited information available to identify which (if any) of these three options is correct. Indeed, on the productivity side, there are really only three observations to work with: slow growth until 1995, faster growth after 1995, and even faster growth after 2000. Meanwhile much of the accumulation in intangible capital is very difficult to observe. The paper by Corrado, Hulten, and Sichel discussed by the authors develops measures of intangible capital based on a variety of data sources and includes software investment, company training, consulting, and the labor input of employees in job categories that contribute to organizational capital.[1] The estimates from this work were not available beyond 2003, and so the present authors do a quick update through 2005. They report, in their table 3, that intangible capital accumulation by this measure turned down sharply after 2000.

In this paper the authors do not use the Corrado, Hulten, and Sichel estimates directly but turn instead to the paper by Basu and others to develop their new approach to growth accounting.[2] Basu and others is an interesting and helpful paper, but I am not persuaded that their approach is a real substitute for direct observation of intangibles. The basic assumption is that intangible capital investment is tied very closely to investment in IT hardware, so that the time-series pattern of the former is derived from that of the latter. It is entirely plausible that high investment in IT demands an increase in intangible investment, but whether or not this is the dynamic driving the observed pattern of productivity growth remains unknown. I note also that the Basu and others paper has a mixed record in tracking productivity trends. They do find regression coefficients for the United States that suggest that heavy IT investment can depress measured productivity contemporaneously. But as they themselves note, "For the United Kingdom, the same regression shows little. Almost nothing is statistically significant, and the signs are reversed from what theory suggested."[3]

The growth accounting section of the present paper takes a perfectly sensible approach. The authors observe a puzzle and then construct an analytical framework that explains the puzzle in a manner consistent with

1. Corrado. Hulten, and Sichel (2006).
2. Basu and others (2004).
3. Basu and others (2004, p. 52)

established theory and methods. They then check the consistency of their inferred measure of intangible capital with the Corrado, Hulten, and Sichel approach, which relies more on direct measurement. My own view, however, is that this section of the paper relies too heavily on an IT-related explanation of productivity without addressing the restructuring issue that is supported by the industry section of this paper.

The industry analysis adds an important additional source of information to the story, but this section of the paper is not well integrated with the growth accounting section. There is no effort to measure intangible capital investment by industry or to link such investment directly with the relative productivity performances of the different industries. The authors make the general observation that the role of IT capital is explored in a way that is consistent with the first half of the paper. However, the industry analysis draws inferences from the timing of productivity acceleration that would presumably change quite a bit if the intangible capital approach were used.

An immediate impression from the industry results is that there is a lot of noise in the industry growth rates. The productivity estimates based on value added differ substantially from the estimates based on gross output. The results reported in the second panel of table 5 suggest regression to the mean, as eleven industries show a reversal in sign (an industry with an acceleration of productivity after 1995 slows after 2000, or vice versa). Having worked with both industry and establishment data myself, I sympathize with the authors as they face this problem, but this analysis makes heavy demands on the data by drawing lessons not from productivity levels or growth rates but from accelerations or decelerations. In part the problem may be that price and quantity information in the United States is much better for final goods than for intermediate goods. This problem, which is one that Edward Denison emphasized,[4] has been alleviated by recent improvements in the data, but not eliminated.

A key result the authors are looking for is whether or not the pattern of productivity acceleration by industry is consistent with an important role for IT investment. In earlier work, Kevin Stiroh reported a strong link between industries that had a high share of IT capital input in total capital input in 1995 and the extent to which their productivity accelerated during 1995–2000.[5] This result remains valid here, but the same approach for the

4. See Denison (1989).
5. Stiroh (2002b).

post-2000 period does not work. As the authors note, "By contrast, the post-2000 acceleration in productivity does not appear to be tied to the accumulation of IT assets in the late 1990s."

Thus the breakdown in the correlation between IT capital and productivity growth that I noted earlier for the aggregate time-series data also extends to evidence from the industry-level analysis. The same result is stated even more strongly by Bosworth and Triplett.[6] They report an assertion in a recent survey of the literature that there is a consensus among economists that the U.S. productivity acceleration was the result of innovations in semiconductor manufacturing. Bosworth and Triplett respond, on the basis of their own industry-level research, that "If this is indeed the [economists'] consensus, we contend it is wrong."[7] No one doubts that IT has been an important enabling innovation, but it is not the whole story.

Oliner, Sichel, and Stiroh point to the intense restructuring pressure that occurred after 2000 as a key contributor to growth in productivity, and I agree with this, as I said earlier. We know that in 2001–03 total hours worked in the nonfarm business sector declined quite sharply while output and productivity were both strong. This differs from the traditional pattern of cyclical productivity where employment declines are associated with weak productivity growth. Companies faced intense pressure to improve profits in the wake of the technology bust and the accounting scandals of the period. They reduced employment, kept investment low, and found ways to cut costs. The authors test this hypothesis by showing that the industries that had faced profit pressure before 2000 were the ones that saw the greatest improvement of productivity after 2001. Given the noisiness of the data, there is a case for caution in interpreting these results, but overall I found them interesting.

In 2005 and 2006 labor productivity growth in the nonfarm business sector was 2.1 percent and 1.6 percent, respectively, well below the pace of the recent past and even below the 2.5 percent a year trend of the late 1990s. Is the productivity boom over? The final section of this paper offers a look at the future, and the authors use the John Roberts smoothing model as a basis for estimating the productivity growth trend. They conclude that the trend is now 2¼ percent a year—a more optimistic figure than some, but slower than the 2000–05 rate. I am a little more optimistic (my estimate of the trend is

6. Bosworth and Triplett (2007).
7. Bosworth and Triplett (2007, p. 17).

2½ percent),[8] and I am not comfortable with the Kalman filter approach to figuring it out. The smoothing algorithms became much too optimistic about the trend in 2002–04 and are turning too pessimistic now. U.S. labor productivity has the property that trend growth remains stable for extended periods and then changes abruptly: generally strong growth in 1947–73 was followed by generally weak growth in 1973–95, which was followed in turn by generally strong growth in 1995–2006. It is hard to see why this would be the case, but empirically it is hard to mistake. The trend accelerated after 1995 to 2.5 percent a year, and the corporate restructuring discussed in this paper induced temporarily above-trend growth. It was to be expected that a period of slower-than-trend growth would follow, and that is what we are seeing now. It is certainly possible that the productivity boom has ended. But it is the strong competitive intensity in the U.S. economy, combined with technological opportunities and rapid globalization, that has driven faster productivity growth in the past ten years. Their effects are likely to continue a while longer.

N. Gregory Mankiw: I enjoyed the opportunity to read and reflect on this paper by Stephen Oliner, Daniel Sichel, and Kevin Stiroh. I am an outsider to the vast literature on growth accounting, and this paper does a good job of bringing the reader up to date on the current state of play. I want to begin by reflecting on the broader literature before turning to the results in this paper that I found most intriguing.

   To be honest, in my own life as a practical macroeconomist, I do not spend a lot of time thinking about growth accounting. In fact, I can estimate with a fair degree of precision that I spend fifteen minutes a year on the activity. Those are the fifteen minutes that I teach growth accounting to undergraduate students in my macroeconomics course. I write down a production function, explain how Robert Solow taught us to compute his famous residual, and then show some representative calculations for the U.S. economy. I explain that this residual might be interpreted as a measure of the rate of technological progress, but I then explain how it might reflect other phenomena as well, especially over the short time spans that characterize the business cycle. Having done all this, I then ignore growth

8. Baily and Kirkegaard (2007).

accounting for approximately the next 364 days (365 days in leap years) until it is time to give the same spiel to the next cohort of undergraduates.

While reading this paper I found myself reflecting on my almost complete lack of attention to the growth accounting literature, to which this paper very ably contributes. My guess is that my experience is not all that atypical. There is a small and hardworking band of brothers (and sisters), including Oliner, Sichel, and Stiroh, toiling in the fields of growth accounting. But most macroeconomists, like me, do not spend a lot of time focusing on the results that this literature produces.

One reason is that this literature seems mired in a host of issues that quickly make a reader's eyes glaze over. Some of these issues are technical, such as distinctions between gross output and value added and the index number theory that bridges that gap. Others involve data availability, such as the potentially important role of unmeasured intangible capital. Out of necessity, many of these issues get resolved by imposing assumptions on the production process which, although not outlandish, are neither compelling nor verifiable. This paper, for example, at times makes an assumption about the complementarity between information technology and intangible capital that seems to be just pulled out of a hat.

But I think there is a more fundamental reason why the growth accounting literature fails to have a larger impact. Even if one grits one's teeth to make it through all the technical issues, and even if one has enough credulity to buy into all the necessary assumptions, the exercise does not deliver what we really want. Ultimately, God put macroeconomists on earth for two reasons: forecasting and policy analysis. We want to know how the world is likely to look in the future, and we want to know how alternative policies would change the future course of history. Unfortunately, growth accounting contributes relatively little to either forecasting or policy analysis. Instead it is a deeply data-intensive exercise that often gets so deeply enmeshed in its own internal logic that it never returns to the big questions of macroeconomics.

Long ago, some economist—I believe it was Moses Abramovitz—called multifactor productivity "a measure of our ignorance." That is, we account for changes in capital, labor, labor quality, and the many other determinants of output we can measure, and the changes in output left unexplained are called "multifactor productivity." But that is really just giving a fancy name to something about which we are pretty clueless. When reading this paper I started playing a game where every time I read the authors say something about "multifactor productivity," I imagined putting some version of "a measure of our ignorance" in its place.

Let me give an example. At one point the authors write, "MFP growth strengthened in the rest of nonfarm business, adding roughly ¾ percentage point to annual labor productivity growth during 2000–06 from its 1995–2000 average." I rewrote the sentence as follows: "our ignorance strengthened in the rest of nonfarm business, adding roughly ¾ percentage point to annual labor productivity growth during 2000–06 from its 1995–2000 average." Framed in this alternative way, the statement carries an almost comical hollowness. It also makes it clear why statements about multifactor productivity are of limited use for either forecasting or policy analysis. Measured ignorance is probably better than unmeasured ignorance, but it would be a mistake to confuse it for real knowledge.

The section of this paper I like best is the one that departs most from the standard growth accounting paradigm and instead performs regression analysis on a cross section of industries. The most striking result is illustrated in the paper's figure 3 and confirmed in regressions in table 8. Industries that experienced declining profit from 1997 to 2001 had more rapid productivity growth from 2001 to 2004. This fact is, on its face, consistent with some of the stories popular in the press that increased competitive pressure forced companies to restructure and increase productivity. As a matter of theory, of course, the story is not very complete, as it fails to explain why industries were once content to operate unproductively. But at the very least, the cross-sectional correlation is sufficiently strong and intriguing that it is worthy of further attention in both empirical and theoretical work.

In closing, let me note that the authors have done a vast amount of work here. They have brought to bear a large quantity of data, applying tools that are state-of-the-art within this literature. But when one is working with so much data, it is easy to lose the forest among the trees. This paper presents an impressively large number of trees. What I am less confident about is whether the literature on growth accounting adds up to an equally impressive forest.

General discussion: Robert Gordon agreed with the discussants that the link between investment in information technology and the acceleration of productivity is much weaker after 2000 than in the late 1990s. He compared the paper's analysis of developments after 2000 with that in his own

2003 Brookings Paper, which was based on quarterly data through the middle of that year. Both papers found that the lag of hours behind output was important to understanding the initial postrecession surge in productivity. However, Gordon noted that the quarterly data show a sharp slowdown in productivity in the second half of 2004, which the authors do not explore using their annual data.

Gordon applauded the paper's impressive empirical support for the idea that profit pressures led to unusual cost-cutting efforts after 2000. And he welcomed the attempt to model formally how IT benefits might have had important delayed effects on productivity. However, he questioned the authors' assumption that variations in capacity utilization are proportional to hours worked per employee. The standard counterexample to this assumption is the factory that is operating two assembly lines before the economy goes into recession. The factory chooses to shut down one assembly line, laying off half the workers, so that capacity utilization drops by half, while hours per remaining employee remain unchanged. Stephen Oliner replied that scope for such adjustments exists in only a few industries and that a strong aggregate cyclical relationship can be demonstrated between the work week and output growth.

Richard Cooper pointed out that two of the outliers in the authors' figure 3 are important IT sectors and conjectured that they importantly influence the precision of the regression results. He suggested that using the information available by sector could inform the analysis of the post-2000 productivity increase. For example, it is known that it was not mainly competitive pressure, but rather technological advances, that pushed up labor productivity growth in these two IT sectors. George Perry suggested that the paper's results may be sensitive to the choice of 2000 as the breakpoint. In particular, for the value-added calculations, the behavior of imports of intermediate goods appears very sensitive to that choice. William Brainard remarked that the correlation between industry productivity and profits in the early 2000s could reflect costs of employment adjustment rather than unusual pressures to improve profits. Because such costs lead employers to smooth employment fluctuations, output increases much faster than employment during a recovery, and this produces corresponding changes in productivity and profits.

Benjamin Friedman replied to Gregory Mankiw's comment regarding the usefulness of growth accounting. He noted that, a few years back, productivity in the core European countries had been catching up to that in the

United States, but in more recent years the gap has widened again. Through the work of Dale Jorgenson and others, growth accounting has provided an explanation of this closing and reopening of productivity differentials. Eswar Prasad noted that, according to the authors' appendix table A-1, the retail trade sector's share of IT capital services falls from above the median in 1995 to below the median in 2000. This seems at odds with the stylized fact that large retailers such as Wal-Mart, where technology adoption is very important, are taking over from small mom-and-pop stores, where IT has a much more limited role. This changing composition within retailing should result in a growing rather than declining role for IT in this industry. Kevin Stiroh replied that the IT use indicators are relative, and the data are not inconsistent with the trends Prasad cited. The results do not show that IT became less important in retailing, but only that the rest of the economy was catching up with retailing.

Peter Henry asked the authors for their projection of multifactor productivity. Oliner replied that their forecast of annual labor productivity growth of 2¼ percent is consistent with a growth rate of multifactor productivity of approximately 1 percent, with the rest coming from improvements in labor quality, which are assumed to be small, and capital deepening.

References

Aaronson, Daniel, Ellen R. Rissman, and Daniel G. Sullivan. 2004. "Assessing the Jobless Recovery." Federal Reserve Bank of Chicago *Economic Perspectives* (Second Quarter): 2–20.

Aizcorbe, Ana M., Stephen D. Oliner, and Daniel E. Sichel. 2006. "Shifting Trends in Semiconductor Prices and the Pace of Technological Progress." Finance and Economics Discussion Series Working Paper 2006-44. Washington: Board of Governors of the Federal Reserve System (November).

Aral, Sinan, Erik Brynjolfsson, and D. J. Wu. 2006. "Which Came First, IT or Productivity? The Virtuous Cycle of Investment and Use in Enterprise Systems." Paper presented at the Twenty-Seventh International Conference on Information Systems, Milwaukee, December 10–13.

Baily, Martin Neil. 2003. "Comment." *BPEA,* no. 2: 280–87.

_____. 2004. "Recent Productivity Growth: The Role of Information Technology and Other Innovations." Federal Reserve Bank of San Francisco *Economic Review* (April): 35–42.

Baily, Martin Neil, and Jacob F. Kirkegaard. 2007. "The US Economic Outlook: A Soft Takeoff with Downside Risk." Washington: Peterson Institute for International Economics (www.petersoninstitute.org/publications/papers/baily 0407.pdf).

Baily, Martin Neil, and Robert Z. Lawrence. 2001. "Do We Have a New E-conomy?" *American Economic Review* 91, no. 2: 308–12.

Basu, Susanto, and John G. Fernald. 1995. "Are Apparent Productive Spillovers a Figment of Specification Error?" *Journal of Monetary Economics* 36, no. 1: 165–88.

_____. 1997. "Returns to Scale in U.S. Production: Estimates and Implications." *Journal of Political Economy* 105, no. 2: 249–83.

_____. 2001. "Why is Productivity Procyclical? Why Do We Care?" In *New Developments in Productivity Analysis,* edited by Charles R. Hulten, Edwin R. Dean, and Michael J. Harper. National Bureau of Economic Research Studies in Income and Wealth, vol. 63. University of Chicago Press.

_____. 2007. "Information and Communications Technology as a General-Purpose Technology: Evidence from US Industry Data." *German Economic Review* 8, no. 2: 146–73.

Basu, Susanto, John G. Fernald, and Miles S. Kimball. 2006. "Are Technology Improvements Contractionary?" *American Economic Review* 96, no. 5: 1418–48.

Basu, Susanto, John G. Fernald, Nicholas Oulton, and Sylaja Srinivasan. 2004. "The Case of the Missing Productivity Growth, or Does Information Technology Explain Why Productivity Accelerated in the United States But Not in the United Kingdom?" In *NBER Macroeconomics Annual 2003,* edited by Mark Gertler and Kenneth S. Rogoff. MIT Press.

Basu, Susanto, John G. Fernald, and Matthew D. Shapiro. 2001. "Productivity Growth in the 1990s: Technology, Utilization, or Adjustment?" *Carnegie-Rochester Conference Series on Public Policy* 55: 117–65.

Becker, Randy, and others. 2005. "Micro and Macro Data Integration: The Case of Capital." Center for Economic Studies Working Paper 2005-02. Washington: U.S. Census Bureau (May).

Black, Sandra E., and Lisa M. Lynch. 2001. "How to Compete: The Impact of Workplace Practices and Information Technology on Productivity." *Review of Economics and Statistics* 83, no. 3: 434–45.

_____. 2004. "What's Driving the New Economy? The Benefits of Workplace Innovation." *Economic Journal* 114, no. 493: F97–F116.

Bloom, Nicholas, and John Van Reenen. 2006. "Measuring and Explaining Management Practices across Firms and Countries." Discussion Paper 5581. London: Centre for Economic Policy Research (March).

Bosworth, Barry P., and Jack E. Triplett. 2007. "The Early 21st Century Productivity Expansion Is *Still* in Services." *International Productivity Monitor* 14 (Spring): 3–19.

Brainard, William C., and George L. Perry. 2000. "Making Policy in a Changing World." In *Economic Events, Ideas, and Policies: The 1960s and After,* edited by George L. Perry and James Tobin. Brookings.

Bresnahan, Timothy F., Erik Brynjolfsson, and Lorin M. Hitt. 2002. "Information Technology, Workplace Organization, and the Demand for Skilled Labor: Firm-Level Evidence." *Quarterly Journal of Economics* 117, no. 1: 339–76.

Bresnahan, Timothy F., and Manuel Trajtenberg. 1995. "General Purpose Technologies: Engines of Growth?" *Journal of Econometrics* 65, no. 1: 83–108.

Bruno, Michael. 1978. "Duality, Intermediate Inputs, and Value Added." In *Production Economics: A Dual Approach to Theory and Applications,* vol. 2, edited by Melvyn Fuss and Daniel L. McFadden. Amsterdam: North Holland.

Brynjolfsson, Erik, and Lorin M. Hitt. 2000. "Beyond Computation: Information Technology, Organizational Transformation and Business Performance." *Journal of Economic Perspectives* 14, no. 4: 23–48.

_____. 2003. "Computing Productivity: Firm-Level Evidence." *Review of Economics and Statistics* 85, no. 4: 793–808.

Brynjolfsson, Erik, Lorin M. Hitt, and Shinkyu Yang. 2002. "Intangible Assets: Computers and Organizational Capital." *BPEA,* no. 1: 137–81.

Caballero, Ricardo J., and Mohamad L. Hammour. 1994. "The Cleansing Effect of Recessions." *American Economic Review* 84, no. 5: 1350–68.

Congressional Budget Office. 2007a. *The Budget and Economic Outlook: Fiscal Years 2008 to 2017.* Washington (January).

_____. 2007b. *Labor Productivity: Developments since 1995.* Washington (March).

Corrado, Carol A., Charles R. Hulten, and Daniel E. Sichel. 2005. "Measuring Capital and Technology: An Expanded Framework." In *Measuring Capital in the New Economy,* edited by Carol A. Corrado, John Haltiwanger, and Daniel E. Sichel. Research Studies in Income and Wealth, vol. 65. University of Chicago Press.

——————. 2006. "Intangible Capital and Economic Growth." Working Paper 11948. Cambridge, Mass.: National Bureau of Economic Research (January).

Corrado, Carol A., and others. 2007. "Sectoral Productivity in the United States: Recent Developments and the Role of IT." *German Economic Review* 8, no. 2: 188–210.

Daveri, Francesco, and Andrea Mascotto. 2002. "The I.T. Revolution across the U.S. States." Working Paper 226. Milan: Innocenzo Gasparini Institute for Economic Research (November).

Denison, Edward F. 1989. *Estimates of Productivity Change by Industry: An Evaluation and an Alternative.* Brookings.

Domar, Evsey D. 1961. "On the Measurement of Technological Change." *Economic Journal* 71, no. 284: 709–29.

Farrell, Diana, Martin Neil Baily, and Jaana Remes. 2005. "U.S. Productivity After the Dot Com Bust." Washington: McKinsey Global Institute.

Foster, Lucia, John Haltiwanger, and C. J. Krizan. 2002. "The Link between Aggregate and Micro Productivity Growth: Evidence from Retail Trade." Working Paper 9120. Cambridge, Mass.: National Bureau of Economic Research (August).

Gordon, Robert J. 2003. "Exploding Productivity Growth: Context, Causes, and Implications." *BPEA,* no. 2: 207–79.

——————. 2006. "Future U.S. Productivity Growth: Looking Ahead by Looking Back." Paper presented at the Workshop at the Occasion of Angus Maddison's 80th Birthday, World Economic Performance: Past, Present, and Future, University of Groningen, October 27.

——————. 2007. "Was the Post-1995 Productivity Growth Upsurge a Will-o'-the Wisp?" Paper presented at the National Bureau of Economic Research Productivity Program Meetings, Cambridge, Mass., March 9.

Groshen, Erica L., and Simon Potter. 2003. "Has Structural Change Contributed to a Jobless Recovery?" Current Issues in Economics and Finance 9, no. 8. Federal Reserve Bank of New York (August).

Groth, Charlotta. 2005. "Estimating UK Capital Adjustment Costs." Working Paper 258. London: Bank of England (May).

Groth, Charlotta, Soledad Nuñez, and Sylaja Srinivasan. 2006. "Productivity Growth, Adjustment Costs, and Variable Factor Utilisation: The UK Case." Working Paper 295. London: Bank of England (April).

Hall, Robert E. 2004. "Measuring Factor Adjustment Costs." *Quarterly Journal of Economics* 119, no. 3: 899–927.

Hall, Robert E., and Dale W. Jorgenson. 1967. "Tax Policy and Investment Behavior." *American Economic Review* 57, no. 3: 391–414.

Houseman, Susan. 2007. "Outsourcing, Offshoring, and Productivity Measurement in U.S. Manufacturing." Upjohn Institute Staff Working Paper 06-130. Kalamazoo, Mich.: W. E. Upjohn Institute for Employment Research (April).

Howells, Thomas F., Kevin B. Barefoot, and Brian M. Lindberg. 2006. "Annual Industry Accounts: Revised Estimates for 2003–2005." *Survey of Current Business* 86, no. 12: 45–55.

Inklaar, Robert, Mary O'Mahony, and Marcel Timmer. 2005. "ICT and Europe's Productivity Performance: Industry-level Growth Account Comparisons with the United States." *Review of Income and Wealth* 51, no. 4: 505–36.

Jorgenson, Dale W. 2001. "Information Technology and the U.S. Economy." *American Economic Review* 91, no. 1: 1–32.

Jorgenson, Dale, Frank Gollop, and Barbara Fraumeni. 1987. *Productivity and U.S. Economic Growth.* Harvard Economic Studies, vol. 159. Harvard University Press.

Jorgenson, Dale W., Mun S. Ho, and Kevin J. Stiroh. 2002. "Projecting Productivity Growth: Lessons from the U.S. Growth Resurgence." Federal Reserve Bank of Atlanta *Economic Review* 87, no. 3: 1–14.

_____. 2005. *Productivity,* vol. 3: *Information Technology and the American Growth Resurgence.* MIT Press.

_____. 2007. "A Retrospective Look at the U.S. Productivity Growth Resurgence." Staff Report 277. Federal Reserve Bank of New York (February).

Jorgenson, Dale W., and others. Forthcoming. "The Industry Origins of the American Productivity Resurgence." *Economic Systems Research.*

Jorgenson, Dale W., and Kevin J. Stiroh. 2000. "Raising the Speed Limit: U.S. Economic Growth in the Information Age." *BPEA,* no. 1: 125–211.

Kahn, James A., and Jong-Soo Lim. 1998. "Skilled Labor-Augmenting Technical Progress in U.S. Manufacturing." *Quarterly Journal of Economics* 113, no. 4: 1281–1308.

Kahn, James A., and Robert W. Rich. 2006. "Tracking Productivity in Real Time." Current Issues in Economics and Finance 12, no. 8. Federal Reserve Bank of New York (November).

Kiley, Michael T. 2001. "Computers and Growth with Frictions: Aggregate and Disaggregate Evidence." *Carnegie-Rochester Conference Series on Public Policy* 55: 171–215.

McKinsey Global Institute. 2001. "U.S. Productivity Growth, 1995–2000: Understanding the Contribution of Information Technology Relative to Other Factors." Washington: McKinsey Global Institute (October).

_____. 2002. "How IT Enables Productivity Growth: The US Experience across Three Sectors in the 1990s." Washington: McKinsey Global Institute (November).

Nakamura, Leonard I. 1999. "Intangibles: What Put the *New* in the New Economy?" Federal Reserve Bank of Philadelphia *Business Review* (July/August): 3–16.

_____. 2001. "What Is the U.S. Gross Investment in Intangibles? (At Least) One Trillion Dollars a Year!" Working Paper 01-15. Federal Reserve Bank of Philadelphia (October).

_____. 2003. "The Rise in Gross Private Investment in Intangible Assets Since 1978." Federal Reserve Bank of Philadelphia (June).

Nordhaus, William D. 2002a. "The Recent Recession, the Current Recovery, and Stock Prices." *BPEA*, no. 1: 199–220.

_____. 2002b. "Productivity Growth and the New Economy." *BPEA*, no. 2: 211–44.

Norsworthy, J. R., and David H. Malmquist. 1983. "Input Measurement and Productivity Growth in Japanese and U.S. Manufacturing." *American Economic Review* 73, no. 5: 947–67.

Okubo, Sumiye, and others. 2006. "BEA's 2006 Research and Development Satellite Account: Preliminary Estimates for 1959–2002 and Effect on GDP and Other Measures." *Survey of Current Business* 86, no. 12: 14–27.

Olinert, Stephen D., and Daniel E. Sichel. 2000. "The Resurgence of Growth in the Late 1990s: Is Information Technology the Story?" *Journal of Economic Perspectives* 14, no. 4: 3–22.

_____. 2002. "Information Technology and Productivity: Where Are We Now and Where Are We Going?" Federal Reserve Bank of Atlanta *Economic Review* 87, no. 3: 15–44.

Oliner, Stephen D., Daniel E. Sichel, and Kevin J. Stiroh. 2007 (forthcoming). "Explaining a Productive Decade." Finance and Economics Discussion Series Working Paper. Federal Reserve Board.

O'Mahony, Mary, and Bart van Ark, editors. 2003. *EU Productivity and Competitiveness: An Industry Perspective. Can Europe Resume the Catching-up Process?* Luxembourg: Office for Official Publications of the European Communities.

Organization for Economic Cooperation and Development. 2000. *A New Economy? The Changing Role of Innovation and Information Technology in Growth.* Paris.

_____. 2006. *Economic Policy Reforms—Going for Growth 2006.* Paris.

Roberts, John M. 2001. "Estimates of the Productivity Trend Using Time-Varying Parameter Techniques." *Contributions to Macroeconomics* 1, no. 1, article 3 (www.bepress.com/bejm/contributions/vol1/iss1/art3).

Schreft, Stacey L., and Aarti Singh. 2003. "A Closer Look at Jobless Recoveries." Federal Reserve Bank of Kansas City *Economic Review* (Second Quarter): 45–73.

Schreyer, Paul. 2000. "The Contribution of Information and Communication Technology to Output Growth: A Study of the G7 Countries." OECD Science, Technology, and Industry Working Paper 2000/2. Paris: Organization for Economic Cooperation and Development (March).

Schweitzer, Mark. 2004. "Economic Restructuring and the Slow Recovery of Employment." Federal Reserve Bank of Cleveland (December 31).

Shapiro, Matthew D. 1986. "The Dynamic Demand for Capital and Labor." *Quarterly Journal of Economics* 101, no. 3: 513–42.

Sichel, Daniel E. 2003. "Comment." *BPEA*, no. 2: 287–93.

_____. Forthcoming. "Intangible Capital." In *New Palgrave Dictionary of Economics,* 2nd ed., edited by Steven N. Durlauf and Lawrence Blume. Basingstoke, U.K.: MacMillan.

Smith, George M., and Sherlene K. S. Lum. 2005. "Annual Industry Accounts, Revised Estimates for 2002–2004." *Survey of Current Business* 85, no.12: 18–69.

Stiroh, Kevin J. 2001. "Investing in Information Technology: Productivity Payoffs for U.S. Industries." Current Issues in Economics and Finance 7, no. 6. Federal Reserve Bank of New York (June).

_____. 2002a. "Are ICT Spillovers Driving the New Economy?" *Review of Income and Wealth* 48, no. 1: 33–57.

_____. 2002b. "Information Technology and the U.S. Productivity Revival: What Do the Industry Data Say?" *American Economic Review* 92, no. 5: 1559–76.

_____. Forthcoming. "Volatility Accounting: A Production Perspective on Increased Economic Stability." *Journal of the European Economic Association.*

_____. 2006. "The Industry Origins of the Second Surge of U.S. Productivity Growth." Federal Reserve Bank of New York (July).

Stiroh, Kevin J., and Matthew Botsch. 2007. "Information Technology and Productivity Growth in the 2000s." *German Economic Review* 8, no. 2: 255–80.

Triplett, Jack E. 1996. "High-Tech Industry Productivity and Hedonic Price Indices." In *Industry Productivity: International Comparison and Measurement Issues.* Proceedings of a May 2–3, 1996, OECD Workshop. Paris: Organization for Economic Cooperation and Development.

Triplett, Jack E., and Barry P. Bosworth. 2004. *Productivity in the U.S. Services Sector: New Sources of Economic Growth.* Brookings.

van Ark, Bart. 2000. "Measuring Productivity in the 'New Economy': Towards a European Perspective." *De Economist* (Quarterly Review of the Royal Netherlands Economic Association) 148, no. 1: 87–105.

van Ark, Bart, and Robert Inklaar. 2005. "Catching Up or Getting Stuck? Europe's Troubles to Exploit ICT's Productivity Potential." Research Memorandum GD-79. Groningen Growth and Development Center (September).

van Ark, Bart, Robert Inklaar, and Robert H. McGuckin. 2003. "ICT and Productivity in Europe and the United States: Where Do the Differences Come From?" *CESifo Economic Studies* 49, no. 3: 295–318.

Yang, Shinkyu, and Erik Brynjolfsson. 2001. "Intangible Assets and Growth Accounting: Evidence from Computer Investments." Massachusetts Institute of Technology.

ESWAR S. PRASAD
Cornell University

RAGHURAM G. RAJAN
University of Chicago

ARVIND SUBRAMANIAN
Peterson Institute for International Economics

Foreign Capital and Economic Growth

IN ONE OF HIS most memorable and widely quoted passages, John Maynard Keynes extolled the virtues not only of trade integration but also of financial integration when he wrote, in 1920, of the fabled Englishman who could "adventure his wealth in . . . new enterprises of any quarter of the world, and share, without exertion or even trouble, in their prospective fruits and advantages."[1] Consistency was, of course, not a Keynesian virtue, and in 1933, in one of his less quoted passages, Keynes's musings on globalization turned more melancholy, even skeptical: "I sympathize with those who would minimize, rather than with those who would maximize, economic entanglement among nations. Ideas, knowledge, science, hospitality, travel—these are the things which should of their nature be international. But let goods be homespun whenever it is reasonably and conveniently possible. . . ." He reserved his deepest skepticism for financial globalization, warning, "and, above all, let finance be primarily national."[2]

Which Keynes was right? the Keynes of 1920 or the Keynes of 1933? And why? Or, to put it more mundanely, does foreign capital play a helpful, benign, or malign role in economic growth? The question has fueled passionate debates among economists, policymakers, and members of civil society. It has gained importance in recent years because of the curious, even seemingly perverse, phenomenon of global capital flowing

We are grateful to Menzie Chinn, Josh Felman, Olivier Jeanne, Gian Maria Milesi-Ferretti, Dani Rodrik, Thierry Tressel, and participants at the Federal Reserve Bank of Kansas City meetings at Jackson Hole and the Brookings Panel, especially our discussants Susan Collins and Peter Henry, for helpful comments and discussions. We thank Manzoor Gill, Ioannis Tokatlidis, and Junko Sekine for excellent research assistance.

1. Keynes (1920, p. 11).
2. Keynes (1933).

Figure 1. World Aggregate Current Account Surplus, 1970–2006[a]

Percent of world GDP

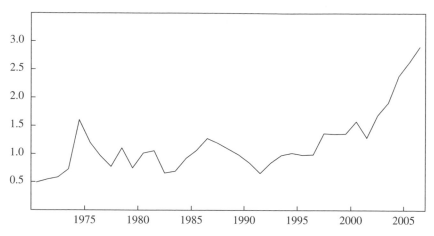

Source: IMF World Economic Outlook (WEO) database and authors' calculations.

a. Each observation is the sum of current account surpluses of countries in the WEO database that had a surplus in that year, as a percent of world GDP as calculated by the IMF.

"uphill" from poorer to richer countries. But it has economic relevance beyond the current conjuncture because it goes to the heart of the process of development and the role of foreign capital in it. It also has enduring policy relevance as developing countries try to decide whether to open themselves up more to financial globalization, and if so, in what form and to what degree.

We undertake an empirical exploration of this question, beginning with some stylized facts that motivate our analysis. The current account balance, which is equivalent to a country's saving less its investment, provides a summary measure of the net amount of capital, including private and official capital, flowing in or out of a country.[3] Figure 1 shows that net

---

3. A current account surplus has to equal the sum of the following: net private and official outflows of financial capital (this includes debt and nongrant aid, but not remittances, which should properly be reflected in the current account itself); net errors and omissions (a positive number could, for instance, represent capital flight through unofficial channels); and net accumulation of international reserves by the government (typically the central bank). Thus the current account surplus summarizes the net amount of capital flowing out of the country in a given period or, equivalently, the excess of domestic saving over domestic investment in that period; correspondingly, a current account deficit summarizes net capital flowing in or, equivalently, the excess of domestic investment over domestic saving.

Figure 2. Relative GDP per Capita of Capital Exporters and Capital Importers, 1970–2005[a]

Percent of highest GDP per capita in indicated year

All countries

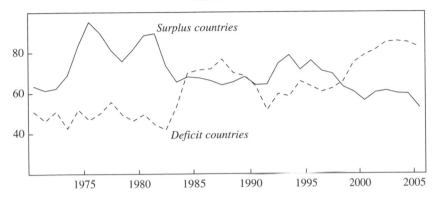

Excluding China and United States

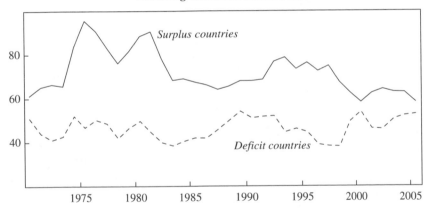

Source: Authors' calculations using data from the WEO database.
a. Each observation is the average GDP per capita (weighted by the country's share of the total current surplus or deficit) of countries in the WEO database with current account surpluses or deficits in the indicated year, expressed as a percentage of GDP per capita in the country with the highest GDP per capita that year. GDP per capita is adjusted for purchasing power parity.

global cross-border financial flows, measured as the sum, relative to world GDP, of national current account surpluses of countries that have surpluses, has been more or less steadily increasing over the last three and a half decades. Although financial globalization was also well advanced in the era leading up to World War I,[4] there appear to be some important

4. See Obstfeld and Taylor (2004) for example.

differences in the current episode: today's globalization involves a greater number of countries; not only are net flows sizable, but there are large flows in each direction as well; and these flows encompass a wider range of more sophisticated financial instruments. But it is the apparent perversity in the direction of flows that is most characteristic, and most puzzling, about the globalization of today.[5]

In the benchmark neoclassical model, capital should flow from rich countries with relatively high capital-labor ratios to poor countries with relatively low ratios. Yet, as the top panel of figure 2 suggests, the average income per capita of countries running current account surpluses (with income measured relative to that of the richest country in that year, and with countries weighted by their surpluses in calculating the average) has been trending downward. Correspondingly, the average relative income per capita of deficit countries, weighted in the analogous way, has trended upward. Indeed, in this century the relative income per capita of the surplus countries has fallen below that of the deficit countries. Not only is capital not flowing from rich to poor countries in the quantities the neoclassical model would predict—the famous paradox pointed out by Robert Lucas[6]—but in the last few years it has been flowing from poor to rich countries. However, this is not a new phenomenon. In the late 1980s as well, the weighted-average relative income per capita of surplus countries was below that of deficit countries.

Nor is the pattern entirely driven by the large U.S. current account deficit and the large Chinese surplus. The bottom panel of figure 2, which excludes these two countries, still shows a narrowing of the difference in weighted-average income between surplus and deficit countries by 2005, not the widening that would be predicted in an increasingly financially integrated world under a strict interpretation of the benchmark neoclassical model.[7]

The Lucas paradox has many potential explanations. The risk-adjusted returns to capital investment may not be as high in poor countries as their

---

5. See, for example, Bernanke (2006).

6. Lucas (1990).

7. Excluding the oil-exporting countries does not alter the basic patterns in figure 2 (not shown). We also constructed similar graphs using initial (1970) relative income, rather than relative income in each period, in order to take out the effects of income convergence. This, too, makes little difference to the shapes of the plots.

low capital-labor ratios suggest, either because they have weak institutions,[8] or because physical capital is costly in poor countries,[9] or because poor-country governments have repeatedly defaulted on their debt finance.[10] But there is a deeper paradox in the data: it seems that foreign capital does not flow even to those poor countries with more rapidly growing economies, where, by extension, the revealed marginal productivity of capital (and probably creditworthiness) is high.[11] Pierre-Olivier Gourinchas and Olivier Jeanne argue that, among developing countries, capital should flow in greater amounts to those that have grown the fastest, that is, those likely to have the best investment opportunities.[12] But does it? Figure 3 divides nonindustrial countries into three equally sized (by aggregate population) groups, plus China and India each handled separately, and computes cumulative current account deficits for each group, in dollars deflated by the U.S. consumer price index. The top panel of figure 3 indicates that, over 1970–2004, as well as over subperiods within that range, net foreign capital flows to relatively rapidly growing developing countries have been smaller than those to the two slower-growing groups. In fact, China, the fastest-growing developing country, runs a surplus in every period. During 2000–04 the pattern is truly perverse: China, India, and the high-growth and medium-growth groups all exported significant amounts of capital, while the low-growth group received a significant amount. Gourinchas and Jeanne have dubbed this failure of capital to follow growth the "allocation puzzle," but it is actually a deeper version of the Lucas puzzle itself.

From a pure financing perspective, a composite measure of net flows of all forms of financial capital is the relevant one for examining the role

8. Alfaro, Kalemli-Ozcan, and Volosovych (2005).
9. Hsieh and Klenow (2003); Caselli and Feyrer (2007).
10. Gertler and Rogoff (1990); Reinhart and Rogoff (2004).
11. Of course, more-rapid growth could imply greater factor employment and even a lower marginal productivity of capital. However, there is a positive cross-sectional correlation between GDP growth and the Bosworth-Collins (2003) measure of total factor productivity growth (based on the updated version of their dataset that goes through 2003) for the nonindustrial countries in our dataset. Caselli and Feyrer (2007) have constructed a measure of the marginal product of physical capital that corrects for the share of natural capital (land) in the total capital stock of each country and for differences in the relative price of capital across countries. For the countries that are common to our dataset and theirs, average GDP growth is strongly positively correlated with the Caselli-Feyrer measure. This suggests that high-growth countries do have more attractive investment opportunities.
12. Gourinchas and Jeanne (2006a); the same authors also provide evidence of a negative correlation between capital inflows and investment rates.

Figure 3. Cumulative Current Account Deficits and FDI Inflows of Nonindustrial Countries, 1970–2004[a]

Billions of 2004 dollars[b]

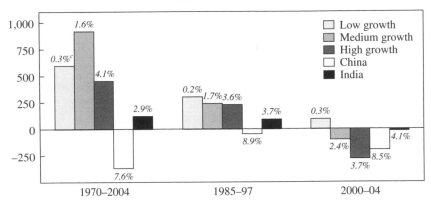

Current account deficits

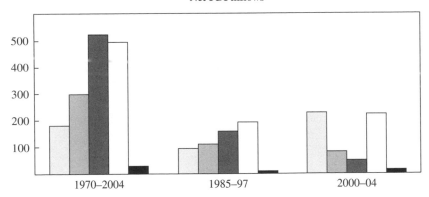

Net FDI inflows

Source: Authors' calculations using data from Penn World Tables (version 6.2) and Lane and Milesi-Ferretti (2006).

a. Our sample of fifty-nine nonindustrial countries, excluding China and India, is divided into three groups of roughly equal total population based on income per capita. Bar heights indicate the sum of each group's cumulative current account deficit or FDI inflows in the indicated period. Negative numbers in the top panel indicate current account surpluses.

b. Deflated using the U.S. consumer price index.

c. Percentages above each bar indicate the period-average median growth rate of real GDP per capita for that group.

of foreign capital in growth. But of course not all types of capital are the same, in terms of either their allocation or their effects on growth. Indeed, the allocation of capital presents a more nuanced picture when net foreign direct investment (FDI) flows are examined (bottom panel of figure 3). During the most recent period (2000–04), net FDI flows do not follow growth, but in the other periods they do (except in the case of India), with the fastest-growing group of nonindustrial countries receiving the most FDI over the period 1970–2004, and China receiving almost as much. This suggests that fast-growing countries do have better investment opportunities, which is why they attract more FDI. Yet they do not utilize more foreign capital overall, and, again, China is a net exporter of capital.

The above figures show that capital does not flow to poor countries, at least not in the quantities suggested by theory. But does a paucity of foreign capital hurt a country's economic growth? Do those poor countries that can fund investment with the greatest quantity of foreign capital grow the most? Of course, growth in steady-state equilibrium will come primarily from increases in total factor productivity, which could stem from the use of foreign capital. But for poor, capital-starved countries that are far from the steady state, and where investment in physical capital is constrained by the low level of domestic saving, growth can also come simply from additions to domestic resources that enable these countries to reach the steady state faster. So does foreign capital help poor countries grow, either by advancing the stock of knowledge and productivity of the economy or by augmenting scarce domestic resources? This question is at the heart of the debate over whether financial integration has direct growth benefits for developing countries.[13]

A small step toward the answers can be taken by looking at the correlation between growth and the current account balance over the period 1970–2004 for roughly the same sample of nonindustrial countries recently analyzed by Barry Bosworth and Susan Collins (figure 4).[14] The correlation is positive, not negative as one might have expected: nonindustrial countries that rely *less* on foreign capital seem to grow faster.[15]

---

13. Henry (2006) argues correctly that the financing provided by foreign capital can have permanent effects on the level of income but only temporary effects on its rate of change. But for the not-so-long horizons examined in this paper, and given how far developing countries are from their steady states, transitional and permanent effects are probably indistinguishable in the data, making the growth effects from additional investment a reasonable focus of inquiry.

14. The sample differs from that of Bosworth and Collins in that it omits Bangladesh, Guyana, and Taiwan; the countries are listed in appendix table A-1.

15. A more negative current account balance indicates larger net inflows of foreign capital. A positive current account balance indicates a net outflow of capital.

Figure 4. Growth in GDP per Capita and Level of Current Account Balances, 1970–2004[a]

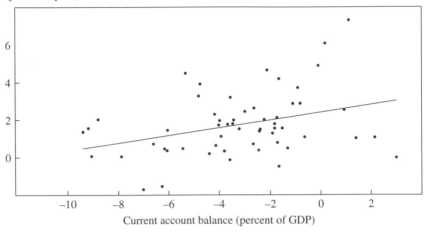

Growth in GDP per capita
(percent a year)

Current account balance (percent of GDP)

Source: Authors' calculations using data from the Penn World Tables and the World Bank, World Development Indicators.
a. Data are for the fifty-six nonindustrial countries in the core sample (the nonindustrial countries listed in appendix table A-1, excluding outliers Mozambique, Nicaragua, and Singapore).

But this might be taking too long run a view. What has happened over specific subperiods in the last three and a half decades? Figure 5 plots the results of nonparametric, Lowess regressions of economic growth on the current account for the entire sample of nonindustrial countries (plus Bangladesh) for four subperiods: the 1970s, the 1990s, 1985–97, and 1999–2004.[16] The 1985–97 period is probably the golden era of financial integration in recent times, and the period 1999–2004 is considered distinctive because of the reserves buildup in some Asian countries in the aftermath of the crises there. The figure shows that the puzzling positive correlation between the current account and growth is absent in the 1970s: the line for that decade slopes downward over most of its range. In every period since then, the slopes are positive over most of their range

---

16. The Lowess procedure estimates a locally weighted regression relationship between the dependent variable and the explanatory variable. It thus allows us to estimate a smoothed, nonparametric relationship between the two.

Figure 5. GDP Growth and the Current Account Balance over Time: Nonparametric Relationship[a]

Growth in GDP per capita
(percent a year)

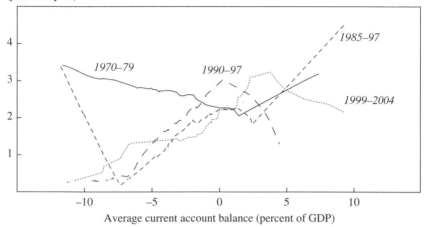

Average current account balance (percent of GDP)

Source: Authors' regressions using data from the Penn World Tables and the World Bank, World Development Indicators.
a. Graph plots predicted growth in GDP per capita growth against the current account balance using estimates from locally weighted regressions for each subperiod. Data are for the entire sample of fifty-nine nonindustrial countries plus Bangladesh.

and almost uniformly positive in the range of current account deficits. There is less uniformity in the range of current account surpluses. It does not appear that our core results are simply an artifact of the long time period that we consider.

Figure 6 offers a clue to the direction this paper will be heading in. The figure splits the sample of nonindustrial countries into four groups depending on whether their ratios of investment to GDP and of the current account balance to GDP are above or below the median. Countries with higher investment are seen to fare better (have faster growth of GDP per capita) than those with lower, which is not surprising. What is noteworthy is that countries that had high investment ratios *and* lower reliance on foreign capital (smaller current account deficits, or larger surpluses) grew faster—on average, by about 1 percent a year—than countries that had high investment but also relied more on foreign capital.

The remainder of the paper starts by placing figure 4 on a firmer footing: we show that, among nonindustrial countries, there is a significantly positive correlation between current account balances (surpluses, not deficits)

Figure 6. Growth in GDP per Capita and Levels of Investment and the Current Account, 1970–2004[a]

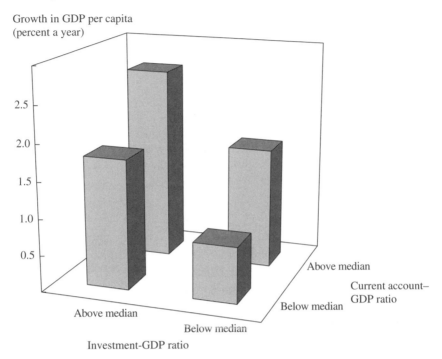

Source: Authors' calculations using data from the World Bank, World Development Indicators.
a. Data are for the fifty-nine nonindustrial countries in the entire sample plus Bangladesh. All data are period averages.

and growth, even after correcting for standard determinants of growth. The correlation is quite robust: it is evident in cross-sectional as well as in panel data, it is not very sensitive to the choice of period or countries sampled, it cannot be attributed just to aid flows, and it survives a number of other robustness tests. Even the most conservative interpretation of our finding—that there is no negative correlation for nonindustrial countries between current account balances and growth, or equivalently, that developing countries that have relied more on foreign finance have not grown faster in the long run, and have typically grown more slowly—runs counter to the predictions of standard theoretical models.

In an interesting contrast, we find that, among industrial countries, those that rely more on foreign finance do appear to grow faster. This difference will need to be taken into account in sifting through possible mechanisms that could explain the correlation for nonindustrial countries.

We explore two, not mutually exclusive, explanations for our main finding. First, it is possible that, when facing improved domestic investment opportunities and associated higher incomes, poor countries do not have corporations or financial systems that can easily use arm's-length foreign capital to ramp investment up substantially. Indeed, we show that countries with underdeveloped financial systems are especially unlikely to be able to use foreign capital to finance growth.

At the same time, poor countries that are growing rapidly are likely to generate substantial domestic saving, because the persistence of household consumption habits is likely to mean that consumption does not respond quickly to higher incomes—a possibility accentuated by the inability of households in these countries to use the financial system to borrow and consume against expected future income. Thus, with both investment and consumption constrained by weaknesses in the domestic financial system, fast-growing poor countries may not be able to utilize foreign capital to finance growth.

A more pessimistic view sees foreign capital as not just ineffective but actually damaging: when it flows in, it leads to real overvaluation of the currency, further reducing the profitability of investment beyond any constraints imposed by an inadequate financial system. Indeed, by stifling the growth of manufacturing exports, which have proved so crucial to facilitating the escape of many countries from underdevelopment, the real overvaluation induced by foreign inflows can be particularly pernicious. We show that foreign capital can indeed cause overvaluation, which in turn has a detrimental effect on manufacturing exports and overall growth.

These two views of foreign capital—that poor countries have little ability to absorb it, especially when provided at arm's length, and that when it does flow in, it could lead to overvaluation, which hurts competitiveness—are not mutually exclusive. Indeed, an underdeveloped financial system is more likely to channel foreign capital not to potentially highly productive but hard-to-finance investment in the tradable manufacturing sector, but rather to easily collateralized nontradeable investments such as real estate. Thus financial underdevelopment, and underdevelopment more generally, could exacerbate foreign capital's contribution to a rise in costs in the nontraded sector, and to overvaluation.

Moreover, consistent with the relationship we have posited between financial development and overvaluation, we do not find evidence of a similar effect of capital inflows on overvaluation in industrial countries. We do find that the ability to avoid overvaluation is helped by favorable demographics, namely, a rapidly growing labor force relative to the population, which provides a relatively elastic supply of labor. Favorable demographics thus plays a key role in generating saving, but also in providing the microeconomic basis for sustaining competitive exchange rates.

The critics of capital account openness point to yet another reason countries may (or ought to) actively avoid foreign capital, namely, the broader risks, including that of inducing greater economic volatility, and especially that of financial or balance of payments crisis. There is little systematic evidence, however, that capital mobility by itself can precipitate crises.[17] Moreover, even though financial openness does seem to induce additional macroeconomic volatility, which in general is not conducive to promoting investment and growth, there is some evidence that volatility resulting from greater financial (or trade) openness by itself is not destructive to long-run growth, compared with volatility induced by other factors.[18] Hence volatility is by itself unlikely to be a major explanation for our results, although this deserves more scrutiny in future work. We do not pursue this further here.

Our paper builds upon the vast and growing literature on financial integration and growth,[19] although this literature has largely focused on measures of financial integration or narrow measures of capital inflows rather than on current account balances. A sizable literature looks separately at the relationship between saving and investment, on the one hand, and growth on the other. Hendrik Houthakker, Franco Modigliani, and Christopher Carroll and David Weil have shown a large positive correlation between saving and growth in a cross section of countries.[20] But this does not necessarily mean a positive correlation between growth and the current account, because investment in high-saving countries could also be higher. Indeed, Philippe Aghion, Diego Comin, and Peter Howitt see high domestic saving as a prerequisite for attracting foreign saving (and

17. See Edwards (2005) and Glick, Guo, and Hutchison (2006).
18. Kose, Prasad, and Terrones (2006).
19. Henry (2006) and Kose and others (2006) provide surveys.
20. Houthakker (1961), Modigliani (1970), and Carroll and Weil (1994).

hence for a current account deficit).[21] Gourinchas and Jeanne conclude that poorer countries are poor because they have lower productivity or more distortions than richer countries, not because capital is scarce in them—the implication being that access to foreign capital by itself would not generate much additional growth in these countries.[22]

In addition to Gourinchas and Jeanne, our paper is related to that of Joshua Aizenman, Brian Pinto, and Artur Radziwill,[23] who construct a "self-financing" ratio for countries in the 1990s and find that countries with higher ratios grew faster than countries with lower ratios. However, the connection of capital flows to growth seems to be more than just the connection through financing. If financing were all that mattered, because it expands the resource envelope, then net foreign liability positions would be positively correlated with growth. As we will later show, the opposite is true: positive net foreign asset positions are positively associated with growth. Moreover, although fast-growing countries do absorb some forms of capital inflows such as FDI, on net they rely little on foreign capital. This suggests that the full explanation for the relationship between growth and foreign capital inflows has to go beyond financing.

Finally, a broad methodological point. Throughout this paper we will employ a variety of data sources, disaggregated in different dimensions, for our empirical analysis. Although our core correlation will be established at the cross-sectional level, we will also exploit time-series variation to confirm the main finding as well as to substantiate the channels through which some of the effects of foreign capital work. The panel data allow us to try and deal with endogeneity issues, albeit in a rather mechanistic fashion. It is still difficult, even using the panel, to disentangle some of these effects—especially the relationship between financial development and capital inflows—in macroeconomic data, and so we complement our analysis by using industry-level data. We do not of course regard the latter as conclusive, since by construction they cannot account for general equilibrium effects. But the industry-level evidence does allow us to make progress in addressing the endogeneity that plagues some of the cross-country regressions, since we can directly control for countrywide shocks and exploit the cross-industry variation within each

21. Aghion, Comin, and Howitt (2006).
22. Gourinchas and Jeanne (2006b).
23. Aizenman, Pinto, and Radziwill (2004).

country. These results suggest a relationship between foreign capital and growth that is far more nuanced and complex than is suggested by traditional theory.

Ultimately, what we offer are a set of strikingly robust correlations that run counter to the immediate predictions of conventional theoretical models, and a set of plausible explanations for these correlations that are buttressed by various types of evidence. Although this evidence may not be conclusive, we hope it will set the stage for progress on the theoretical front that will help get a better handle on these correlations, as well as explanations for the patterns we have detected in the data.

The Relationship between Foreign Capital and Growth

We begin by reviewing the textbook model of how foreign capital inflows should affect economic growth in a country that is open to them. We then proceed to test the model's implications in cross-sectional regressions, check the robustness of the findings, and further confirm the results in regressions using panel data for the same sample of countries.

The Textbook Theory

The textbook model plots domestic saving and investment against the real interest rate (figure 7).[24] When the economy is closed to foreign capital, equilibrium is at point B with the interest rate given by r^{dom}. When the economy is opened and the capital account is liberalized (or frictions impeding the flow of foreign capital are reduced), investment increases to point C, with the increase in investment financed more than fully by foreign saving (the current account deficit). In this world, increases in capital inflows, as impediments come down, result in a steady movement of domestic interest rates toward world interest rates (r^*), and thus in higher investment and faster growth.

Also, given investment, the extent of utilization of foreign saving should have no effect on growth—it really does not matter whether investment is financed by domestic or foreign capital. The question we now turn to is whether these predictions are borne out in the data.

---

24. This discussion draws upon Rodrik (2006).

Figure 7. Saving, Investment, and Economic Growth in an Undistorted Economy

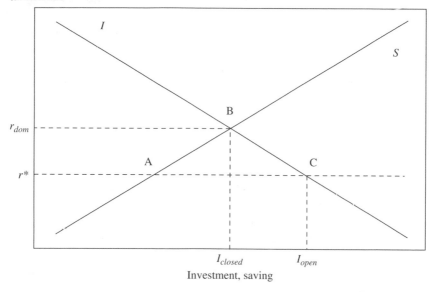

Source: Authors' model described in the text.

Financial Integration and Growth

We begin by testing the relationship between financial integration and growth. Since the traditional textbook model focuses on foreign capital as an aggregate source of financing, we will examine aggregate capital inflows, that is, the current account balance, in what follows.

Of course, different types of flows could well have different consequences. The literature has noted that FDI could be an important source of technology transfer as well as of finance. Also, debt and equity flows could have different implications for a country's macroeconomic volatility. The literature has therefore used a variety of measures of financial integration, including policy or de jure measures but also de facto measures based on actual capital movements in terms of stocks and flows.[25] We will present

25. Kose and others (2006) review these measures and argue that, since de jure ones cannot capture the enforcement and effectiveness of capital controls, they may not be indicative of the true extent of financial integration. Actual capital flows may be more relevant for examining the role of foreign capital in the growth process.

some robustness checks based on these alternatives, but our core measure will be the current account balance, which has the advantage of being related to macroeconomic variables such as saving, investment, and the exchange rate.

Let us start by placing the correlation between the current account balance and growth depicted in figure 4 on firmer ground. Table 1 presents our core regression results, which build on the work of Bosworth and Collins.[26] The dependent variable is the annual average growth rate of purchasing power parity–adjusted GDP per capita over 1970–2004, taken from the Penn World Tables (version 6.2). We include the following controls in the standard specification: log of initial (1970) GDP per capita, initial-period life expectancy, initial-period trade openness (the Sachs-Warner measure),[27] the fiscal balance, a measure of institutional quality, and dummy variables for sub-Saharan African countries and oil exporters.

When we estimate the above equation using data for the full nonindustrial country sample from Bosworth and Collins (regression 1-1), the coefficient on the current account balance is positive and tightly estimated, suggesting that countries that rely less on foreign financing (that is, run smaller current account deficits) grow faster. The coefficient estimate suggests that a 1-percentage-point increase in the current account balance (a smaller deficit or a larger surplus) is associated with approximately a 0.1-percentage-point improvement in the growth rate.

Regression 1-2 drops three outliers from the Bosworth-Collins sample of countries, and regression 1-3 drops, in addition, all countries receiving aid flows that, on average, exceed 10 percent of their GDP. In regression 1-4 the sample is the same as in regression 1-2, but the current account is measured net of aid. In all cases the coefficient is positive and significant. Regressions 1-3 and 1-4 provide reassurance that the results are not driven by poor countries receiving large official aid flows. Since we control for net government saving in all our regressions, our current account coefficient can be interpreted as the marginal effect of private saving on growth, conditional on the level of government saving. In sum, the coefficient estimate is the opposite of that predicted by the standard textbook model postulated earlier.

---

26. Bosworth and Collins (2003). Ourr work is also related to their earlier paper (Bosworth and Collins, 1999).
27. Sachs and Warner (1995).

Table 1. Cross-Sectional OLS Regressions of Economic Growth Rates on the Current Account Balance

Regression (dependent variable is average annual rate of growth of GDP per capita)[a]

Independent variable	1-1	1-2[b]	1-3[c]	1-4[d]	1-5[e]	1-6	1-7	1-8
Current account balance–GDP ratio	0.093	0.107	0.196	0.106			0.107	-0.041
	(0.036)**	(0.056)*	(0.066)***	(0.057)*			(0.053)*	(0.085)
Log of initial GDP per capita	-1.770	-1.722	-1.526	-1.721	-1.695	-1.700	-1.561	-1.520
	(0.242)***	(0.249)***	(0.256)***	(0.250)***	(0.287)***	(0.286)***	(0.266)***	(0.163)***
Initial life expectancy	0.071	0.070	0.070	0.070	0.063	0.046	0.061	0.060
	(0.026)***	(0.026)**	(0.027)**	(0.026)**	(0.030)**	(0.031)	(0.026)**	(0.023)**
Initial trade policy[f]	0.987	1.016	1.702	1.013	1.009	0.897	0.718	0.564
	(0.782)	(0.817)	(0.429)***	(0.819)	(0.811)	(0.836)	(0.777)	(0.814)
Fiscal balance–GDP ratio	0.044	0.048	0.028	0.049	0.049	0.042	0.037	0.040
	(0.041)	(0.043)	(0.046)	(0.043)	(0.044)	(0.045)	(0.044)	(0.041)
Institutional quality[g]	5.759	5.568	4.981	5.589	5.921	6.474	4.469	4.121
	(1.680)***	(1.677)***	(.130)***	(1.686)***	(1.682)***	(1.669)***	(2.111)**	(1.416)***
Net foreign assets–GDP ratio					0.005			
					(0.005)			
Gross assets–GDP ratio						0.013		
						(0.007)*		
Gross liabilities–GDP ratio						-0.007		
						(0.005)		
Investment–GDP ratio							0.074	
							(0.050)	
Domestic saving–GDP ratio								0.108
								(0.040)***
No. of observations	59	56	42	56	55	55	56	56
R^2	0.71	0.69	0.81	0.69	0.65	0.66	0.70	0.73

Source: Authors' regressions using data from the World Bank, World Development Indicators; the Penn World Tables (version 6.2); Lane and Milesi-Ferretti (2006); Rajan and Subramanian (2005); and Bosworth and Collins (2003).

a. Data are period annual averages or initial-period observations for each of the fifty-six nonindustrial countries listed in appendix table A-1, from 1970 to 2004. All regressions include dummy variables equal to 1 for oil exporters and countries in sub-Saharan Africa. Numbers in parentheses are robust standard errors; asterisks indicate statistical significance at the ***1, **5, and *10 percent level. GDP data are adjusted for international differences in purchasing power of the dollar.

b. Sample excludes three outliers: Nicaragua, Mozambique, and Singapore.

c. Sample excludes the above three outliers and all countries receiving foreign aid and averaging more than 10 percent of their GDP

d. Current account balance excludes foreign aid receipts.

e. In this regression and in regression 1-6, data on stock positions are not available for one country (Sierra Leone) in the core sample.

f. Measure of trade openness from Sachs and Warner (1995).

g. Measure of institutional quality from Hall and Jones (1999).

In what follows we focus on the intermediate sample that excludes the three outliers (we will call this our "core sample"), referring to the other samples only when the results are qualitatively different. Given that current account balances, averaged over a long period, should be directly related to the stock of foreign assets, we check the relationship between growth and the stock position.[28] In regression 1-5 we replace the current account with the net foreign asset position and find, consistent with the core result, that it is positively correlated (although not statistically significantly) with growth: countries that have accumulated assets over time have grown faster. Regression 1-6 splits the net asset position into gross assets and gross liabilities positions, and we find that the former is positively and significantly related to growth, whereas the latter is negatively but not significantly related to growth.

If, in fact, the binding constraint for countries in our sample is domestic resources, as in the textbook model, larger current account deficits should foster growth by augmenting investment. But the separate inclusion of domestic investment in the regression equation should greatly diminish the coefficient on the current account: conditional on investment, the split between domestic and foreign saving should not matter. Interestingly, however, as regression 1-7 indicates, the inclusion of the investment-GDP ratio barely changes the coefficient on the current account from that in regression 1-2, even though the coefficient on the investment-GDP ratio has the expected positive sign and is almost statistically significant at conventional levels (thus suggesting that mismeasurement of investment is unlikely to be the explanation).[29] More domestic saving financing a given quantum of investment seems to be positively correlated with growth, a formalization of the result depicted in figure 6. By contrast, when we replace the investment-GDP ratio with the saving-GDP ratio (regression 1-8), the coefficient on the current account loses statistical significance and indeed turns negative. The saving-GDP ratio has the expected significantly positive coefficient. Thus the evidence suggests that the correlation between the current account and growth is positive and stems largely from a relationship between domestic saving and growth, and not negative as in the more

28. These stock measures have been constructed by Lane and Milesi-Ferretti (2006).

29. See Bosworth and Collins (2003), who argue that growth in the capital stock is a better measure than the investment-GDP ratio for the purposes of growth accounting and regressions.

traditional view that foreign capital permits capital-constrained poor countries to expand domestic investment and thereby increase growth.[30]

Robustness

Before turning to explanations, we report in table 2 some important robustness checks. First, we estimated the core specification over a different time period, 1985–97, considered a golden age for financial globalization because it was marked by a surge in flows without any significant increase in crises (the exception being the Mexican crisis of December 1994, which was limited in its fallout). The current account coefficient (regression 2-1) remains positive and significant, and, interestingly, the magnitude is over twice that for the period 1970–2004 (regression 1-2).

Although we have established a general pattern for nonindustrial countries, it is worth asking whether the pattern also is present for more economically advanced countries. We revert to the 1970–2004 time period and add industrial countries to the sample. We allow the coefficients on the current account to differ for industrial countries. It turns out (regression 2-2) that the coefficient on the current account balance for industrial countries is significantly different from that for nonindustrial countries and negative overall ($-0.20 + 0.11 = -0.09$), suggesting that industrial countries that run larger current account deficits experience more growth.

If we restrict ourselves to the period 1990–2004, we can also include economies in transition from socialism and estimate separate coefficients for them. Although the pattern of coefficients for industrial countries is as before (regression 2-3), the transition countries resemble industrial countries in that

---

30. We test in appendix table A-2 whether there is a relationship between financial integration and growth, using the measures of integration that have conventionally been used in the literature. We find, consistent with Kose and others (2006), no relationship, in our sample of countries, either between GDP growth and the level of financial openness, whether measured by stocks or by flows, or between GDP growth and changes in these measures. There is weak evidence that FDI, which is qualitatively different from other flows in bringing in technology, is positively correlated with growth (see Borensztein, De Gregorio, and Lee, 1998). We also tested whether the trade balance (as opposed to the current account balance) is the prime driver (results are available from the authors). It turns out that the trade balance, defined as net exports of goods and nonfactor services, is positively correlated with growth, but not statistically significantly so, and the magnitude of the correlation is smaller than that between the current account balance and growth. Clearly, there are elements in the current account balance (including factor incomes and transfers) that add to its explanatory power. For nonindustrial countries, these items can be quite large.

Table 2. Cross-Sectional OLS Regressions of Growth Rates on the Current Account Balance Using Alternative Samples and Variables

	Regression (dependent variable is average annual rate of growth of GDP per capita)[a]			
Independent variable	2-1	2-2	2-3	2-4
Current account balance–GDP ratio	0.221	0.105	0.203	0.069
	(0.102)**	(0.051)**	(0.121)*	(0.055)
Log of initial GDP per capita	−3.172	−1.795	−1.941	−1.644
	(0.436)***	(0.210)***	(0.657)***	(0.207)***
Initial life expectancy	0.191	0.078	0.175	0.048
	(0.059)***	(0.023)***	(0.060)***	(0.029)*
Initial trade policy[b]	1.391	1.036	0.538	0.679
	(0.800)*	(0.579)*	(0.437)	(0.573)
Fiscal balance–GDP ratio	0.102	0.035	0.122	0.051
	(0.091)	(0.031)	(0.071)*	(0.041)
Institutional quality[c]	7.794	5.144		2.812
	(2.338)***	(1.147)***		(1.348)**
Working-age share of total				0.194
population				(0.072)***
Industrial country dummy × current		−0.202	−0.234	
account balance–GDP ratio		(0.063)***	(0.115)**	
Transition country dummy × current			−0.354	
account balance–GDP ratio			(0.138)**	
Estimation period	1985–97	1970–2004	1990–2004	1970–2004
No. of observations	56	78	99	56
R^2	0.63	0.68	0.34	0.77

Source: Authors' regressions using same source data as for table 1.

a. The sample in regressions 2-1 and 2-4 includes the fifty-six nonindustrial countries listed in appendix table A-1. The sample for regression 2-2 includes, in addition, the twenty-two industrial countries in that table, and regression 2-3 includes as well the twenty-one transition countries. All regressions include dummy variables equal to 1 for oil exporters and countries in sub-Saharan Africa. Numbers in parentheses are robust standard errors; asterisks indicate statistical significance at the ***1, **5, and *10 percent level. GDP data are adjusted for international differences in purchasing power of the dollar.

b. Measure of trade openness from Sachs and Warner (1995).

c. Measure of institutional quality from Hall and Jones (1999).

current account surpluses are negatively correlated with growth; that is, larger inflows of foreign capital boost growth. The phenomenon we have identified thus seems to be largely a nonindustrial, non–transition country phenomenon.[31] The additional value of this result is that it indicates we are not simply picking up some hitherto unnoticed mechanical or accounting relationships in macroeconomic data that link current accounts positively to growth.

31. Abiad, Leigh, and Mody (2007) find that current account balances are negatively correlated with growth among European countries, including a small group of transition countries. Their work is useful in pointing out that the correlation for transition economies is different from that for other nonindustrial economies, a fact we verify above.

Finally, we check whether our results are robust to the inclusion of demographic variables, a key determinant of saving. When we include the ratio of the working-age population to total population in the baseline regression 1-2, the coefficient on the current account is reduced by about 30 percent, while the coefficient on the working-age population ratio is positive and highly statistically significant (regression 2-4). This suggests that something associated with domestic saving is partly responsible for the results we find, a point that was also evident earlier.

There is, however, one key concern. The time horizon we have focused on is the long run, spanning the thirty-five years between 1970 and 2004. Perhaps we are picking up not a cross-sectional result but rather a time-series result: it may be that successful countries started poor and ran large deficits, but eventually became rich enough to run surpluses. Averaged over a long period, successful countries have had rapid growth and low average deficits, while the unsuccessful have grown slowly and still appear to be running deficits. Thus the long-run relationship might be obscuring a pattern over time that is analytically quite different.

One way to get at this is to look at growth over short periods. Figure 8 plots the current account–GDP ratio over time for countries that experienced growth spurts,[32] differentiating their performance before and during the growth spurt. On average, current account balances increase (or, put differently, current account deficits narrow) around the beginning of a growth spurt (top panel). The bottom panel shows saving growing faster than investment in these same countries during the same period. In other words, as they move from slow to sustained faster growth, countries also reduce the foreign financing of domestic investment. It is noteworthy that the turnaround in the current account balance is starker when we exclude, in figure 9, the three industrial countries (Ireland, Portugal, and Spain) from the group of sustained rapid growers. This is also consistent with our findings on the differences in the experiences of the industrial and developing countries.[33]

32. These are growth spurts that occurred after 1970 and were followed by sustained growth, as identified by Hausmann, Pritchett, and Rodrik, (2005).

33. This is not to say that all forms of foreign finance fall during growth spurts. Indeed, the average ratio of FDI to GDP rises from an annual average of 0.2 percent in the five years before the initiation of a growth spurt to 0.7 percent in the five years after. Similarly, using the episodes of growth decelerations identified by Jones and Olken (2005), we find that the average FDI-GDP ratio falls from 1.7 percent in the five years before the deceleration to 1 percent in the five years after. But even these increases and decreases are small compared with the changes in domestic saving following a growth spurt or deceleration.

Figure 8. Current Account Balance, Saving, and Investment before and after Growth Spurts in Eleven Countries[a]

Percent of GDP

Current account balance

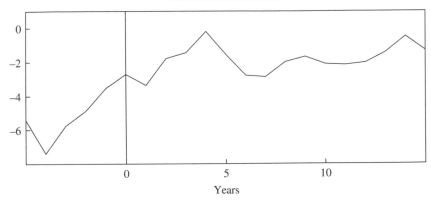

Saving and investment

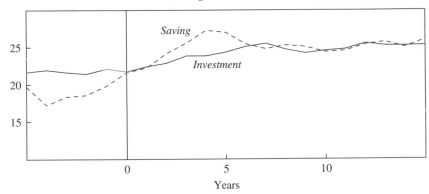

Sources: World Bank, World Development Indicators; the Penn World Tables; Hausmann, Pritchett, and Rodrik (2005); and authors' calculations.

a. Simple averages of current account balance, saving, and investment. Countries and initial year (year 0) of their growth spurts are Chile (1986), China (1978), Egypt (1976), India (1982), Ireland (1985), Korea (1984), Mauritius (1983), Pakistan (1985), Spain (1984), and Sri Lanka (1979).

Figure 9. Current Account Balance, Saving, and Investment before and after Growth Spurts in Eight Nonindustrial Countries[a]

Percent of GDP

Current account balance

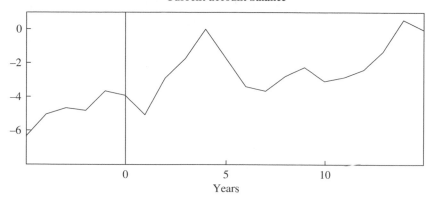

Saving and investment

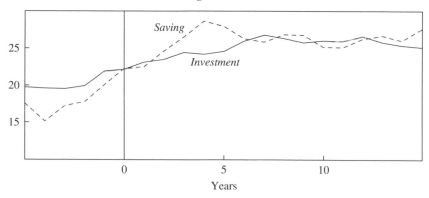

Sources: World Bank, World Development Indicators; the Penn World Tables; Hausmann, Pritchett, and Rodrik (2005); and authors' calculations.

a. Simple averages of current account balance, saving, and investment. Country sample is the same as in figure 8 except that Ireland, Portugal, and Spain are excluded.

Panel Evidence

Another way to confirm that we are not picking up a phenomenon inherent in the life cycle of countries is to turn to panel data and examine growth over shorter periods.[34] This is important for other reasons also. As a matter of robustness, it is always useful to check whether the observed relationship between countries also holds *within* countries. If there were a discrepancy between the panel and the cross-sectional evidence, it would call for caution in interpretation. Another reason for doing panel estimations is that they help address, albeit imperfectly, the problem of omitted variables and endogeneity that afflict pure cross-sectional estimations. The inclusion of country fixed effects in the panel controls for unobservable heterogeneity between countries. We employ the generalized method of moments (GMM) estimation technique in order to take a stab at dealing with the endogeneity issue, although in a rather mechanistic fashion.[35]

Table 3 reports results of panel regressions estimated on five-year averages of the underlying annual data. To maintain consistency with the cross-sectional results, we use the same controls in each regression in table 3 that we use in the corresponding regression (by numbered column)

34. One version of the life cycle model applied to countries has implications for the evolution of current account balances (see the discussion in Chinn and Prasad, 2003). According to this theory, poor countries that open up to foreign capital early in the development process should run current account deficits as they import capital to finance their investment opportunities. Eventually, these countries would become relatively capital rich and begin to run trade surpluses, in part to pay off the obligations built up through their accumulated current account deficits.

35. GMM estimators come in two flavors. There is the difference-GMM estimator of Arellano and Bond (AB; 1991) and the system-GMM estimator of Blundell and Bond (BB; 1998). In both, identification relies on first-differencing and using lagged values of the endogenous variables as instruments. In the AB estimator, lagged levels are used to instrument for the differenced right-hand-side variables, whereas in the BB estimator, the estimated system comprises the difference equation instrumented with lagged levels as in the AB estimator as well as the level equation, which is estimated using lagged differences as instruments. Each estimator has its limitations. The AB estimator often leads to a weak-instruments problem because lagged levels are typically not highly correlated with their differenced counterparts. So, in what follows, we present estimations based on the BB estimator. All specifications include time effects to control for common shocks.

in tables 1 and 2.[36] In regression 3-1 the coefficient on the current account balance is positive and similar in size to that in the cross-sectional regression, although the coefficient is not estimated precisely. In regression 3-2 we drop the three countries that are outliers in the cross section, and the coefficient on the current account increases slightly but remains insignificant. In regression 3-3 we also drop the high-foreign-aid-receiving countries to ensure that our results are not driven by official capital inflows. Now the coefficient increases substantially and is significant at the 5 percent level. Regression 3-4 uses the same sample as in regression 3-2 but nets out aid from the current account balance—the coefficients are similar in the two regressions.

Next, in regression 3-5 we add the domestic investment–GDP ratio as a regressor. The coefficient on this variable is significant, but it does not diminish the estimated coefficient on the current account balance. Regression 3-6 substitutes domestic saving for the investment variable. As in the cross section, this variable is significant and drives the coefficient on the current account balance to zero. Regression 3-7 replaces domestic saving with the share of the working-age population, and regression 3-8 estimates a separate current account coefficient for industrial countries. Although the panel estimates are less precise, the similarity of the coefficient estimates in both the cross-sectional and panel estimations, including when investment and saving are included alternatively as variables, is reassuring for the robustness of the core results. They tend to offer additional support for our finding that foreign capital inflows (current account deficits) and growth are not positively correlated in nonindustrial countries, in contrast to what the standard neoclassical growth model would predict.[37]

---

36. One methodological point bears mentioning. GMM procedures allow a fair amount of freedom, especially in specifying the lag structure for the instruments. There is a trade-off: the greater the lags, the more the information that is used. But greater lags can lead to overfitting and weak instrumentation. Two key diagnostics to use in checking for these problems are the Hansen test for overidentifying restrictions and the Arellano-Bond test for serial correlation. When we used the second lag, our results were stronger than reported in the text, but there were occasional problems of overfitting, reflected in very large p-values for the Hansen test. We therefore report results using the third and fourth lags, which are more reassuring in relation to these two diagnostics.

37. We cannot include data for the transition countries in the panel regressions, as our estimation procedure requires data for at least four time periods for a country to be included in the sample.

Table 3. Panel GMM Regressions of Economic Growth Rates on the Current Account Balance

Independent variable	Regression (dependent variable is average annual rate of growth of GDP per capita)[a]							
	3-1	3-2[b]	3-3[c]	3-4[d]	3-5	3-6	3-7	3-8[e]
Current account balance–GDP ratio	0.100	0.127	0.251	0.130	0.166	-0.001	-0.009	0.086
	(0.095)	(0.112)	(0.122)**	(0.114)	(0.124)	(0.111)	(0.093)	(0.109)
Log of initial GDP per capita	-1.977	-1.540	-2.868	-1.838	-0.766	-0.682	-1.506	-1.246
	(1.387)	(1.264)	(0.981)***	(1.341)	(1.471)	(1.407)	(1.113)	(1.407)
Initial life expectancy	0.057	0.050	0.094	0.072	-0.023	-0.034	-0.028	0.059
	(0.121)	(0.107)	(0.075)	(0.124)	(0.090)	(0.094)	(0.097)	(0.116)
Initial trade policy[f]	2.580	2.108	2.161	2.220	2.132	2.285	1.283	1.350
	(0.762)***	(0.911)**	(0.837)***	(0.941)**	(0.959)**	(0.922)**	(0.867)	(0.797)*
Fiscal balance–GDP ratio	0.167	0.188	0.094	0.182	0.097	0.208	0.126	0.147
	(0.147)	(0.161)	(0.130)	(0.136)	(0.132)	(0.222)	(0.129)	(0.087)*
Institutional quality[g]	16.825	15.182	17.136	14.561	1.562	5.331	8.475	10.462
	(5.616)***	(5.790)***	(5.296)***	(5.912)**	(4.415)	(4.407)	(5.610)	(4.884)**
Investment-GDP ratio					0.288			
					(0.110)***			
Saving-GDP ratio						0.167		
						(0.092)*		
Working-age share of total population							0.296	
							(0.158)*	
Industrial country dummy × current account balance–GDP ratio								-0.292
								(0.126)**
No. of observations	336	320	267	316	311	294	320	462
Hansen test for over-identifying restrictions (p-value)	0.551	0.546	0.485	0.567	0.400	0.466	0.828	0.225
Arellano-Bond AR(2) test (p-value)	0.732	0.676	0.590	0.679	0.514	0.357	0.725	0.630

Source: Authors' regressions using same source data as for table 1.
a. Data are five-year averages or initial-period observations for each of the fifty-nine nonindustrial countries listed in appendix table A-1, from 1970 to 2004. All regressions include dummy variables equal to 1 for oil exporters and countries in sub-Saharan Africa. Numbers in parentheses are robust standard errors; asterisks indicate statistical significance at the ***1, **5, and *10 percent level. GDP data are adjusted for international differences in purchasing power of the dollar. All right-hand-side variables are treated as endogenous, and their third and fourth lags are used for instrumentation.
b. Sample excludes three outliers: Nicaragua, Mozambique, and Singapore.
c. Sample excludes the above three outliers and all countries receiving foreign aid averaging more than 10 percent of their GDP.
d. Current account balance excludes foreign aid receipts.
e. Regression also includes a dummy variable equal to 1 for industrial countries.
f. Measure of trade openness from Sachs and Warner (1995).
g. Measure of institutional quality from Hall and Jones (1999).

What Explains the Observed Relationship between Capital Flows and Growth?

The previous section identified a robust, nonnegative association between current account balances and long-run growth in nonindustrial countries, which is significantly positive across a number of subsamples and estimation procedures. At no point do we find a negative correlation in this group of countries, as the standard theoretical models might suggest, although we do find such a correlation for industrial and transition countries.

From a saving-investment perspective, the evidence seems to challenge the fundamental premise that investment in nonindustrial countries is constrained by the lack of domestic resources. If that were the case, the correlation between the current account and growth should run through domestic investment. It does not. What explains all this? That is what this section attempts to answer.

Some Conjectures

Consider the ingredients we already have for an explanation. First, the positive correlation between current accounts and growth is found primarily in poor countries, suggesting that something to do with the structure of poor economies may be responsible. Second, it appears that the correlation runs through domestic saving and not through domestic investment. In other words, investment does not seem to be highly correlated with net capital inflows, suggesting that it is not constrained by lack of resources.

INSTITUTIONAL UNDERDEVELOPMENT. Let us now venture an explanation, which we will put together with a number of ingredients. We know from figures 8 and 9 that income growth spurts in poor countries lead to greater domestic saving.[38] Theoretical models exist showing that the saving rate could increase even in the face of a persistent increase in income—for example, because of habit persistence in consumption.[39] The link between

38. Bernanke and Gürkaynak (2002) report a positive correlation between productivity growth and saving in a broad sample of countries—they do not break their sample out into different groups of countries based on income.

39. Carroll and Weil (1994), for instance, show that habit persistence may be one way to reconcile the strong positive correlation between saving and growth, a correlation that runs counter to the predictions of the standard life cycle or permanent income hypothesis. Jappelli and Pagano (1994) build a model showing how financial market imperfections that limit the ability to borrow against future income could generate a correlation between saving and growth in a fast-growing economy with a low level of financial development.

income growth and saving in a poor economy could be further strengthened if the relative underdevelopment of the financial sector prevents consumers from borrowing against their anticipated future incomes.

Greater saving does not automatically mean a larger current account surplus or a smaller deficit, because investment could increase more than commensurately. But suppose that poor countries also suffer from capacity constraints in ramping up investment, even in the face of positive productivity shocks, especially if resources have to be invested at arm's length. This could occur because the financial system does not intermediate saving well.[40] Problems will be particularly acute in the investment of foreign private capital, which by definition is invested at arm's length (apart from FDI). It could also result from weak protection of property rights in poor countries, which militates against the long-gestation, investment-intensive, low-initial-profitability projects that are the most dependent on financing. Again, to the extent that foreign capital does not enjoy the domestic power relationships that substitute for institutional infrastructure such as property rights protection, it may be at a particular disadvantage in financing such projects.[41]

There are some important differences between our explanation and that of Ricardo Caballero, Emmanuel Farhi, and Gourinchas,[42] who argue that weak financial development and the consequent inadequate supply of reliable financial assets can explain the phenomenon of poorer countries running larger current account surpluses. In these authors' view, for example, developing country households prefer holding foreign bonds to holding domestic financial assets, and this portfolio decision drives local interest rates up and limits domestic investment. In our view domestic households do accumulate domestic financial assets, especially those intermediated through banks, and thus do finance domestic investment. Corporations can also do so through their own saving. Instead it is difficulties in funneling foreign capital into domestic corporate investment that limits the absorption of foreign capital.[43]

---

40. Wurgler (2000) provides evidence that underdeveloped financial sectors are unable to reallocate resources to their highest-productivity uses, leading to a mismatch between productivity increases and investment.

41. See Rajan and Zingales (1998).

42. Caballero, Farhi, and Gourinchas (2006).

43. In truth, many developing country households (for example, in China) have been accumulating domestic financial assets in the form of bank deposits. The final holder of foreign assets is often the government, not households. One could argue that households are willing to hold bank deposits only because banks hold central bank paper, which is eventually a claim on foreign bonds, but this seems a tenuous line of reasoning.

In other words, the real difficulty in these countries is not with domestic firms investing internally generated funds or even raising funds from domestic sources such as domestic banks, but with domestic firms raising funds at arm's length, especially from foreigners. Indeed, in growth episodes the firms with the best opportunities are likely to be new, typically private sector, firms that usually are not connected through old ties to the banking system or the government. Because these firms lack the contacts needed to borrow from banks, and because they have difficulty raising money at arm's length from domestic or foreign sources in an underdeveloped financial system, investment is likely to be constrained.

This line of argument can also explain the negative correlation between current accounts and growth for rich countries. Their greater financial and institutional development allows investment to be more responsive to productivity increases.[44] It also allows citizens to borrow against anticipated future wealth in order to consume. So for industrial (and transition) countries, investment may be significantly more responsive to productivity increases (the primary source of growth in these countries), but saving may be less responsive, than in nonindustrial countries, leading to larger current account deficits.

In this view, foreign capital inflows do not hurt growth in poor countries, but they do not help either. These countries are typically constrained not by resources, but by the investment opportunities that they can profitably exploit using arm's-length finance. Foreign capital is not directly harmful; it simply cannot be used well, especially in investment-intensive, low-initial-cash-flow, long-gestation projects.

This line of argument is plausible, but its empirical relevance remains open to question. For instance, Gourinchas and Jeanne argue that although frictions in financial markets (for example, underdeveloped financial systems) can result in the current account deficit being less responsive to growth in countries with less developed financial systems, plausible model parameterizations do not lead to the reversal in the sign on the correlation that we find.[45] Indeed, Aart Kraay and Jaume Ventura construct a plausibly parameterized model which implies that the impact of productivity shocks on

---

44. Glick and Rogoff (1995) showed that country-specific productivity shocks tend to generate investment booms and larger current account deficits (or smaller surpluses) in what were then the Group of Seven leading industrial countries.

45. Gourinchas and Jeanne (2006a).

a country's current account balance should be related to its initial net liability position. In countries with a net foreign liability position, such as most of the nonindustrial countries in our sample, productivity growth will typically lead to an *increase* in the current account deficit, not a reduction as we find.[46]

A LESS BENIGN VIEW. The fact that conventional theoretical models, or even recent models that depart from conventional theory (for instance, by positing habit formation in consumption), cannot fully explain our findings suggests the need to explore alternative explanations. The way forward may be to take a less benign view of the effects of foreign capital. Recall the textbook model (figure 7) with which we started the last section. Suppose now that foreign financing can have some deleterious effects, over and above its inability to be allocated properly in a country with a weak financial system. In particular, large inflows could lead to an increase in real wages, an appreciation of the currency in real terms, and a fall in the marginal product of investment. Equivalently, the higher domestic consumption that necessitates a greater reliance on foreign finance could fall substantially on nontraded goods, pushing up their price and leading to currency overvaluation. The greater the capacity of a country to expand nontraded goods, the less the overvaluation. Thus, where domestic saving is insufficient, the use of foreign capital to finance investment may further depress the profitability of investment by causing an overvaluation of the currency—a form of what is commonly known as Dutch disease. Countries that rely excessively on foreign capital to fund their investment may find themselves becoming increasingly uncompetitive on the trade front.

The textbook model will then have to be modified, and figure 10 suggests heuristically how this can be done. Suppose foreign capital inflows strengthen the real exchange rate, making potential exports less profitable. This will shift the investment schedule inward, reducing total investment at any interest rate. The size of the shift will depend on the magnitude of the inflows, the responsiveness of the exchange rate to those inflows, and the responsiveness of investment to the change in the exchange rate. One way of

---

46. Kraay and Ventura (2000). Their argument is based on the intuition that the marginal portfolio allocation decision (how to invest the extra saving generated by income shocks) will resemble the average decision (reflected in the existing net liability stock) unless investment risk is low and domestic investment is highly subject to diminishing returns.

Figure 10. Saving and Investment in an Economy Distorted by Foreign Capital Inflows

Interest rate

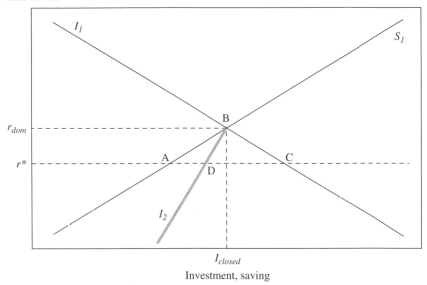

Source: Authors' model described in the text.

depicting the shift in investment is to illustrate what capital inflows would be at alternative levels of the elastic world supply of foreign capital (r^*). Above r_{dom} there will be no foreign capital inflow, and so the investment schedule will be unaffected. Below r_{dom} one can trace a new investment schedule at each level of r^*. This schedule will lie to the left of segment I_1 because of the negative relationship between inflows and investment that arises from the exchange rate effect. And it will lie further to the left, the lower is r^*, because inflows increase as r^* declines. If the exchange rate response to inflows and the investment response to exchange rate changes are sufficiently strong, the new investment schedule will rotate leftward around point B and be represented by the segment I_2. In this case, when the country opens up, the new equilibrium at point D is to the left of the old equilibrium B. There will be more capital inflows relative to B, but lower investment, lower domestic saving, and slower growth, generating the correlation we find in the data. Thus the introduction of distortions to the exchange rate and investment caused by capital inflows can further help account for our findings.

Figure 11. Impact of an Exogenous Increase in Domestic Saving in an Economy Distorted by Foreign Capital Inflows

Interest rate

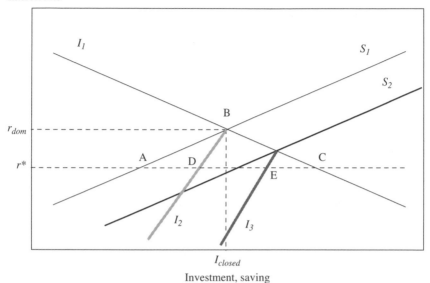

Investment, saving

Source: Authors' model described in the text.

Finally, an expansionary shift in domestic saving in such an economy (from S_1 to S_2 in figure 11) can lead to an expansion of investment and growth. A shift in domestic saving, by reducing foreign inflows at each level of the interest rate, will have a positive effect on investment by reducing the extent of overvaluation. Not only will the saving curve shift right, but there will be an associated rightward shift of the investment curve from I_2 to I_3 (because at each level of r^* there will be smaller inflows, and hence less overvaluation and greater investment). Note that, in this case, an exogenous shift in domestic saving will increase investment and growth even in a country with a fully open capital account, which would not have happened in a world in which inflows do not distort the exchange rate.

Does Foreign Finance Matter? Evidence from Industry-Level Data

Let us now see if we can provide any evidence for the details of these explanations. One explanation we have offered is that foreign capital is not a good method of financing investment in countries with underdeveloped financial systems. One way to verify this is to see whether industries that need a lot of finance are relatively better or worse off if the country where they are located gets a lot of foreign capital, and to see how this varies with the country's level of financial development. In a sense this allows us to determine whether foreign capital has a comparative advantage or disadvantage in financing.

The use of industry-level data has another big benefit: it allows us to get around the endogeneity and reverse causality problems that are rampant (and difficult to control for) in country-level data. For instance, even if rapid growth tends to pull in more capital inflows (rather than inflows causing growth), or if growth and inflows are jointly determined by other factors, there is no reason why the effect of inflows on industry-level growth through the financing channel should be different across industries within the same country. Similarly, it is unlikely that growth in a particular industry at this level of disaggregation can be a significant determinant of aggregate capital flows, and so aggregate capital flows can be considered exogenous to an industry's growth. Thus, by exploiting cross-industry variation and controlling for country- and industry-specific factors, we can make some progress toward tackling concerns about endogeneity. (As noted earlier, the potential endogeneity used as an illustration here should lead to a *positive* correlation between net foreign capital inflows and growth, whereas our cross-country results show the opposite correlation.)

RELATIVE INDUSTRY GROWTH. Using the methodology of Rajan and Luigi Zingales,[47] we first ask whether, correcting for industry-specific and country-specific factors, manufacturing industries that are dependent on outside finance (rather than internally generated cash flows) for funding investment grow faster in countries that get more foreign capital (or are more open to foreign capital). The estimation strategy is to run regressions of the form

$$(1) \qquad G_{ij} = \psi + \zeta_1'C_j + \zeta_2'I_i + \zeta_3 man_{ij} + \alpha\left(open_j \times dep_i\right) + \varepsilon_{ij},$$

where G_{ij} is the annual average rate of growth of value added in industry i in country j over ten-year periods (1980–90, 1990–2000), obtained by normalizing the growth in nominal value added by the GDP deflator; C_j is a vector of indicator variables for each country; I_i is a vector of indicator variables for

47. Rajan and Zingales (1998).

each industry; man_{ij} is the initial-period share of industry i in manufacturing in country j (which controls for convergence-type effects); $open_j$ is "openness to capital flows of country j," which is some de facto or de jure measure of the capital account openness of country j; dep_i is "dependence of industry i on finance," which is the fraction of investment in that industry that the typical firm could not fund from internally generated cash flows; and ε_{ij} is the error term.[48] Dependence is typically high in industries where investment is large and positive cash flows follow only after a lengthy gestation period.

The coefficient of interest for us is α. The textbook model would predict that countries that are more open to capital should see financially dependent industries grow relatively faster, and so we would expect the coefficient α to be positive (for tables 4 and 5 we use the current account deficit rather than the current account balance, so that the predicted coefficient is the same as for other measures of capital inflows).

The chief advantage of this strategy is that, by controlling for country and industry fixed effects, the problem of omitted-variables bias or incorrect model specification, which afflicts cross-country regressions, is diminished. Essentially, we are making predictions about within-country differences between industries based on an interaction between a country and an industry characteristic. Moreover, as discussed above, because we analyze differences *between* manufacturing industries, we can rule out factors that would affect manufacturing in a country as a whole as explanations of our results— these factors should not affect differences between manufacturing industries.

THE BASIC REGRESSION. Rajan and Zingales interact the country's level of domestic financial development with the industry's finance dependence.[49] Before we ask about the role of foreign capital, an immediate question is whether their methodology "works" for this group of countries. We estimate their basic regression including an interaction between the country's domestic credit–GDP ratio, our primary proxy for a country's domestic financial development, and the industry's finance dependence. The coeffi-

---

48. Rajan and Zingales (1998) describe how they calculate the number for the period 1980–89. We calculate a similar number using U.S. corporate data between 1990 and 1998 (after 1998, normal financing behavior would be contaminated by the equity bubble). In computing each industry's dependence on finance for 1990–98, we first compute the dependence on finance of each firm in the industry over the period, truncate outlier firms at the 10th and 90th percentiles, and then average across all firms. We then take the average of the industry's dependence for the 1980s and the 1990s to get our final measure.

49. Rajan and Zingales (1998).

cient on the interaction is positive and statistically significant for both the 1980s and the 1990s, suggesting that it is a reasonable exercise to use this methodology to investigate the role of foreign capital in finance.

We focus on six measures of capital account openness: five de facto measures and one de jure measure. The de facto measures are the ratio of the stock of inward FDI to GDP, the ratio of the stock of inward FDI and portfolio investment to GDP, the net flow counterparts of these two ratios, and the average current account deficit over the period. The de jure measure is taken from Menzie Chinn and Hiro Ito.[50]

We first ran these regressions without controlling for the level of domestic financial development, to get a sense of the unconditional effect of foreign finance (estimates available from the authors). The estimated interaction coefficients are neither uniformly significant nor of the sign expected in the textbook model. Indeed, the results for the 1980s are more mixed, with the coefficient on the current account deficit being negative and significant in the "wrong" direction. The coefficients for the 1990s sample are of the expected sign (with a positive coefficient on the current account deficit interaction) but are significant in only two of the six cases.[51]

THE IMPORTANCE OF DOMESTIC FINANCIAL DEVELOPMENT. It may well be that our specification is not complete. Countries that are more open also have better developed financial markets.[52] Financial integration may proxy for financial development. We should therefore include an interaction between our proxies for the country's domestic financial development and an industry's dependence on finance, to check whether the effects of foreign capital persist even after we control for domestic financial development. Our primary proxy for financial development is the ratio of domestic credit to GDP. A second proxy is the country index of the quality of corporate governance (which is available for fewer countries and does not vary across time).[53]

Also, we should check for threshold effects: the benefits of foreign capital may kick in only after a country's domestic financial development

50. Chinn and Ito (2006).
51. To reduce the effect of data errors, all variables are "winsorized" at the 99 percent and the 1 percent level. Standard errors are robust, and we report the estimates when we cluster by country. Results are qualitatively similar when we cluster by industry. These results are available from the authors upon request.
52. Kose and others (2006).
53. The index was constructed by De Nicoló, Laeven, and Ueda (2006).

exceeds a certain level.[54] So we include a separate interaction between our measure of foreign capital penetration and an industry's dependence on finance *if the country is below the median level of financial development* (as measured by the ratio of domestic credit to GDP) in our sample of countries. Since this is a triple interaction, we also have to include all the relevant double interactions. So the final specification is

(2)
$$G_{ij} = \psi + \zeta_1' C_j + \zeta_2' I_i + \zeta_3 man_{ij} + \alpha_1 \left(open_j \times dep_i \right)$$
$$+ \alpha_2 \left(open_j \times dep_i \times bmed_j \right) + \alpha_3 \left(cred_j \times dep_i \right)$$
$$+ \alpha_4 \left(cred_j \times dep_i \times bmed_j \right) + \alpha_5 \left(gov_j \times dep_i \right)$$
$$+ \alpha_6 \left(dep_i \times bmed_j \right) + \varepsilon_{ij},$$

where $cred_j$ is the ratio of domestic credit to GDP of country j; gov_j is the value of the corporate governance index for country j; and $bmed_j$ is an indicator variable equal to 1 if country j is below the median ratio of domestic credit to GDP. The other variables are identical to those in equation 1.

If there are threshold effects, so that countries with underdeveloped financial systems cannot utilize foreign capital well to finance investment, we should find α_1 to be positive and α_2 negative. Table 4 reports the results from this augmented specification for the 1980s and 1990s cross sections.

The results from this specification are much more stable and offer a consistent picture. Twenty-one of twenty-four coefficients have the expected sign (that is, expected in the model with threshold effects where we postulate different effects of foreign capital in less financially developed countries), and twelve are significant at conventional levels. The average effect we obtained from estimating equation 1 seems to conceal very different implications for financially developed and financially underdeveloped countries, effects that are visible only by estimating equation 2. In particular, for countries that have above-median levels of financial development, foreign capital aids the relative growth of those industries dependent on finance. In regression 4-7 the coefficient of the interaction term for countries that are above the median level of financial development is about 50 percent higher than the "average" coefficient for the specification in equation 1 (estimates available from the authors upon request).

But for countries below the median for financial development, the effect of foreign capital inflows is diametrically opposite. The sum of the

54. See Chinn and Ito (2006) and Alfaro and Hammel (2007).

Table 4. Cross-Sectional OLS Regressions of Growth in Value Added by Industry on Measures of FDI and Financial Dependence

Regression (dependent variable is average annual rate of growth of value added in industry i of country j)[a]

Independent variable[b]	1980s data						1990s data					
	4-1	4-2[c]	4-3[d]	4-4[e]	4-5[f]	4-6	4-7	4-8	4-9	4-10	4-11	4-12
Interaction of country j FDI stock ×												
Sector i dependence on external finance	0.126 (0.055)**						0.115 (0.030)***					
Above × dummy = 1 for below-median financial development	-0.198 (0.141)						-0.665 (0.237)***					
Interaction of country j FDI stock plus portfolio investment ×												
Sector i dependence on external finance		0.108 (0.053)**						0.069 (0.028)**				
Above × dummy = 1 for below-median financial development		-0.122 (0.101)						-0.591 (0.221)***				
Interaction of country j net FDI flows ×												
Sector i dependence on external finance			0.516 (0.351)						0.810 (0.251)***			
Above × dummy = 1 for below-median financial development			-2.246 (1.047)**						-3.984 (1.776)**			
Interaction of country j FDI and portfolio flows ×												
Sector i dependence on external finance				0.485 (0.334)						0.539 (0.225)**		
Above × dummy = 1 for below-median financial development				-2.004 (0.952)**						-0.743 (1.543)		

(continued)

Table 4. Cross-Sectional OLS Regressions of Growth in Value Added by Industry on Measures of FDI and Financial Dependence (*Continued*)

Regression (dependent variable is average annual rate of growth of value added in industry i of country j)[a]

Independent variable[a]	1980s data[b]							1990s data[c]				
	4-1	4-2	4-3	4-4	4-5	4-6	4-7	4-8	4-9	4-10	4-11	4-12
Interaction of country j Chinn–Ito capital account openness measure ×												
Sector i dependence on external finance					0.003						-0.004	
					(0.003)						(0.006)	
Above × dummy = 1 for below-median financial development					-0.005						-0.024	
					(0.007)						(0.015)	
Interaction of country j current account deficit-GDP ratio ×												
Sector i dependence on external finance						0.128						-0.113
						(0.183)						(0.214)
Above × dummy = 1 for below-median financial development						-0.994						1.399
						(0.336)***						(1.208)
No. of observations	929	929	918	918	929	929	1,114	1,114	1,095	1,095	1,114	1,114
R^2	0.47	0.47	0.47	0.47	0.47	0.47	0.28	0.28	0.28	0.28	0.28	0.28

Source: Authors' regressions using data from the United Nations Industrial Development Organization.

a. Data are period averages for individual industries. All estimations include country and industry fixed effects, the initial share of a sector's value added in total value added for that country, and two measures of domestic financial development: the country's ratio of domestic credit to GDP and its index of corporate governance (De Nicolo and others, 2006). The data differ from those in Rajan and Zingales (1998) for the 1980s and those of Laeven and others (2006) for the 1990s in that Nigeria was dropped because of data errors, and the index of corporate governance was available only for a subset of countries.

b. Includes thirty-four industrial and nonindustrial countries in the UNIDO database.

c. Includes thirty-seven industrial and nonindustrial countries in the UNIDO database.

d. FDI, portfolio investment, and current account balance are measured as ratios to GDP.

reported interaction coefficients in each specification reflects the marginal effect of foreign capital on the relative growth of dependent industries in countries that have below-median financial development. In eleven out of twelve specifications, the sign on the sum of coefficients suggests that industries dependent on finance grow relatively more slowly as a financially underdeveloped country draws in more foreign capital. Foreign capital seems to hurt rather than help the relative growth of industries dependent on finance in those countries.

Before we turn to interpretation, we present in table 5 our estimates from panel versions of equation 2; the estimates include industry-country dummies in addition to separate country and industry dummies. We use the within-country, within-industry, across-time variation to identify effects.[55] All the specifications clearly indicate that foreign capital detracts from the relative growth rate of financially dependent industries in countries that are below the median with respect to financial development. By contrast, all the specifications uniformly indicate that domestic financial development is good for the relative growth rate of industries dependent on finance, and especially so in countries that are below the median level of financial development.[56]

DISCUSSION. Foreign capital may need a developed domestic financial system to be effective, because it may lack access to the informal sources of information and power that allow domestic finance to operate even in an underdeveloped system. For instance, if property rights are not well protected (an element of a sound financial system), foreign capital may shy away from industries that require high long-term investment. Instead, incremental foreign capital may flow into industries that typically do not require high up-front investment and that have high cash flows in the short run, or into nonindustrial sectors that have clearly demarcated, collateralizable

55. Relative to the earlier specification, we drop the industry's initial share of manufacturing and the interaction of industry dependence on finance with the country's corporate governance index. The initial share of manufacturing should be absorbed in the industry × country indicator, and the interaction is not meaningful since neither the corporate governance index nor dependence on finance varies across time. Note that in this panel specification the openness to capital flows varies across time and countries, whereas dependence on external finance varies across industries, which, in the presence of industry-country fixed effects, allows identification within country, within industry, and across time.

56. The coefficient on the interaction in the panel is negative also for countries with above-median levels of financial development, unlike in the cross-sectional results. One interpretation of this is that the benefits of foreign capital accrue even to financially well-developed countries only in the medium run.

Table 5. Panel OLS Regressions of Growth in Value Added by Industry on Measures of FDI and Financial Dependence

Independent variable[b]	Regression (dependent variable is average annual rate of growth of value added in sector i of country j)[a]					
	5-1	5-2	5-3	5-4	5-5	5-6
Interaction of country j FDI stock × Sector i dependence on external finance	−0.122 (0.051)**					
Above × dummy = 1 for below-median financial development	−0.320 (0.057)***					
Interaction of country j FDI stock plus portfolio investment × Sector i dependence on external finance		−0.065 (0.024)**				
Above × dummy = 1 for below-median financial development		−0.269 (0.058)***				
Interaction of country j net FDI flows × Sector i dependence on external finance			−0.903 (0.209)***			
Above × dummy = 1 for below-median financial development			−2.838 (0.338)***			
Interaction of country j FDI and portfolio flows × Sector i dependence on external finance				−0.569 (0.120)***		

	(1)	(2)	(3)	(4)	(5)	(6)	(7)
Above × dummy = 1 for below-median financial development					-2.166 (0.378)***		
Interaction of country j Chinn-Ito capital account openness measure × Sector *i* dependence on external finance						0.011 (0.004)***	
Above × dummy = 1 for below-median financial development						-0.020 (0.007)***	
Interaction of country j current account deficit–GDP ratio × Sector *i* dependence on external finance							-0.240 (0.085)***
Above × dummy = 1 for below-median financial development							-0.380 (0.286)
No. of observations	2922	2922	2882	2882	2922	2914	2922
R^2	0.74	0.74	0.74	0.74	0.74	0.74	0.74

Source: Authors' regressions using same source data as for table 4.

a. Data are period averages for individual industries. All estimations include country and industry fixed effects and country-industry fixed effects. Data are from the UNIDO database and cover fifty-two industrial and nonindustrial countries. The data differ from those in Rajan and Zingales (1998) for the 1980s and Laeven and others (2006) for the 1990s only in that Nigeria was dropped because of data errors. Numbers in parentheses are robust standard errors; asterisks indicate statistical significance at the ***1, **5, and *10 percent level. GDP data are adjusted for international differences in purchasing power of the dollar.

b. FDI, portfolio investment, and current account balance are measured as ratios to GDP.

assets (such as real estate). This could explain why finance-intensive industries do relatively poorly or, equivalently, why industries that generate high and immediate cash flows with low up-front investment do relatively well, as additional foreign capital flows into countries with underdeveloped financial sectors. In other words, in such countries foreign capital does not come in as a source of financing, but to exploit domestic opportunities that require little financing, or to provide know-how.

Of course, our findings are also consistent with the possibility that foreign capital may actually hamper access to finance. Foreign capital may have to be channeled through domestic intermediaries when the financial sector is underdeveloped, and it may facilitate rather than hinder the formation of domestic financial monopolies, as the strongest domestic intermediaries are further strengthened by access to foreign capital. Foreign capital may also choose (and be able) to cherry-pick the few good opportunities in an underdeveloped country, leaving less incentive for domestic financial institutions to enter or participate.[57]

Note that, in these financially underdeveloped countries, although an increase in foreign capital does not help industries that are dependent on finance, an increase in domestic capital (which is largely what the ratio of domestic credit to GDP represents) is indeed helpful. Perhaps domestic credit institutions can better navigate the pitfalls of an underdeveloped system. Perhaps also, more domestic credit reflects, and leads to, a better financial system that can support more credit to financially dependent industries, and eventually from foreign sources.

Finally, one could ask whether domestic financial development is a proxy for development more generally, or for the broader institutions that accompany development. We reestimated the regressions in tables 4 and 5, replacing a country's measure of financial development with the logarithm of its GDP per capita (with additional interactions, where necessary, based on whether a country is below the median on this measure). The coefficient estimates of the triple interaction (available from the authors) were

---

57. Detragiache, Tressel, and Gupta (2006) show that, in poor countries, a stronger foreign bank presence is robustly associated with less credit to the private sector in both cross-sectional and panel tests. In addition, in countries with more foreign bank penetration, credit growth is slower and there is less access to credit. By contrast, they find no adverse effects of foreign bank presence in more advanced countries. Tressel and Verdier (2007) show that, in countries with weak institutions, financial integration leads to greater investment by politically connected firms, with a loss of efficiency. Our findings are not inconsistent with these results.

often insignificant and sometimes the opposite of what one might expect. It is not primarily underdevelopment (or the factors accompanying or causing it) that causes foreign capital to be ineffective in nonindustrial countries; instead what matter seem to be factors related to a specific form of underdevelopment, namely, financial underdevelopment.

In sum, the industry evidence can explain why foreign capital may not be an effective source of finance for nonindustrial countries. Although the evidence thus far cannot rule out a benign interpretation of the role of foreign capital, it strongly suggests that if poor countries are seeking to improve financing for industry, instead of just hankering after additional financing in the form of foreign capital, they can reap substantial benefits from focusing on domestic financial development.[58]

Overvaluation, Trade, and Growth

Let us now turn to the less benign explanation: that capital inflows may lead to an appreciation of the national currency in real terms, which in turn may reduce the profitability of exports and thus reduce investment. The consequences of capital inflows for international competitiveness may then be an important contributing factor to the patterns we observe.

OVERVALUATION AND CAPITAL FLOWS. Simon Johnson, Jonathan Ostry, and Subramanian construct a measure of a country's exchange rate competitiveness, accounting for the Balassa-Samuelson effect.[59] Essentially, the idea is to measure the deviation of a country's exchange rate from

---

58. This argument does not, of course, detract from the possibility that foreign capital has large indirect benefits, including on financial development itself. Some authors point to the beneficial effects of equity market liberalization on growth (for example, Bekaert, Harvey, and Lundblad, 2005, and Henry, 2006). In addition to the problem of timing that the literature notes—such liberalization is typically part of broader macroeconomic reforms that affect outcomes—the countries that liberalize might be the same ones that are typically able to reap the benefits from foreign finance, in part because they have stronger financial sectors. For this reason, our findings need not be inconsistent with the more positive tone of the equity market liberalization literature.

59. Johnson, Ostry, and Subramanian (2007). On the Balassa-Samuelson effect, see Meese and Rogoff (1983). We estimate the following cross-sectional equation for every year since 1960 for the full sample of countries: $\log p^i = \alpha + \beta \log y^i + \varepsilon^i$, where p is the log of the price level for country i relative to that in the United States, and y is GDP at purchasing power parity. Our measure of overvaluation is then $overval_i = \log p^i - (\hat{\alpha} + \hat{\beta} \log y^i)$. We average this measure for each country over the relevant period. This measure is also used by Rajan and Subramanian (2005).

purchasing power parity, after accounting for differences in incomes. This deviation we term overvaluation.

The immediate question is whether there is a relationship between overvaluation and capital inflows. In table 6 the dependent variable is our measure of the extent of overvaluation. We include as explanatory variables the ratio of the working-age population to the total population (since a larger working-age population should increase the supply response of an economy to any incipient overvaluation and help contain it) and, to capture financial openness, different measures of capital inflows or the Chinn-Ito de jure measure of openness. Regardless of the type of inflows included, the coefficient is always positive and nearly always significant: the larger the inflows, the less competitive the recipient economy at the current real exchange rate. For the Chinn-Ito de jure measure of openness, however, the coefficient is not significant (regression 6-6), suggesting that only actual flows lead to pressures for real appreciation.[60]

Figure 12 plots the relationship, conditional on the share of the working-age population, between overvaluation and one of the capital flow measures, total net private capital inflows. The figure shows a strong positive relationship and that no outliers are driving the relationship,

If overvaluation in nonindustrial countries as a result of capital inflows is to account for the observed positive relationship between current account balances and growth there, it must be that capital inflows do not cause overvaluation in industrial countries. So in the last two specifications of table 6 we include in the regression an interaction between the industrial country dummy and the relevant flows variable. The results are striking. For example, when we use net private inflows as the relevant capital flow variable, the coefficient on the interaction is negative and significant (regression 6-8), whereas the direct effect is positive; so, for nonindustrial countries, more inflows lead to more overvaluation. The total marginal effect of inflows on overvaluation ($-1,038 + 826 = -212$) is statistically insignificantly different from zero for industrial countries. The same result holds when we use net FDI inflows as the relevant measure of capital flows

---

60. We could run the same regression in a panel context, but there is more reason to expect the real exchange rate to be decoupled from capital flows in the short run; countries can use sterilized intervention, fiscal policy, and other measures to retain influence over the real exchange rate. Unless we can control for these short-run policies, it would be difficult to identify the effect of flows on overvaluation.

Table 6. Cross-Sectional OLS Regressions of Overvaluation on Capital Stock and Flow Measures

Independent variable	Regression (dependent variable is the degree of real overvaluation of the national currency)[a]							
	6-1	6-2[b]	6-3	6-4	6-5	6-6	6-7[c]	6-8
Working-age share of total population	-1.66	-1.66	-2.30	-3.02	-2.53	-2.11	-2.47	-2.88
	(0.88)*	(1.05)	(0.91)**	(0.98)***	(0.96)**	(0.86)**	(0.93)***	(0.94)***
Net liabilities–GDP ratio[d]	19.46	10.79						
	(11.20)*	(14.74)						
Net FDI liabilities–GDP ratio			30.90					
			(23.48)					
Net private inflows–GDP ratio[e]				843.69				825.88
				(327.58)**				(326.25)**
Net FDI flows–GDP ratio					675.57		670.13	
					(355.73)*		(354.93)*	
Chinn–Ito capital account openness measure						-1.92		
						(3.85)		
Industrial country dummy × net FDI flows–GDP ratio							-1,091.39	
							(444.68)**	
Industrial country dummy × net private flows–GDP ratio								-1,038.02
								(349.32)***
No. of observations	55	48	55	56	56	55	78	78
R^2	0.15	0.09	0.14	0.24	0.18	0.12	0.46	0.49

Source: Authors' regressions using same source data as tables 1 and 4 and authors' calculations based on Johnson, Ostry, and Subramanian (2007).
a. The dependent variable is overvaluation, measured as described in the text. Except as noted below, data are period annual averages for each of the fifty-six nonindustrial countries listed in appendix table A-1, from 1970 to 2004. Numbers in parentheses are robust standard errors; asterisks indicate statistical significance at the ***1, **5, and *10 percent level.
b. Sample omits countries receiving foreign aid averaging more than 10 percent of their GDP.
c. This regression and regression 6-8 include a dummy variable for industrial countries (coefficients not shown), and the sample includes the twenty-two industrial countries listed in appendix table A-1.
d. Net liabilities are gross liabilities minus assets; Sierra Leone is excluded from the sample because data are unavailable.
e. Net private inflows are gross private inflows (FDI plus portfolio equity flows plus portfolio debt flows) minus outflows.

Figure 12. Currency Overvaluation and Capital Flows, 1970–2004[a]

Unexplained overvaluation[b]

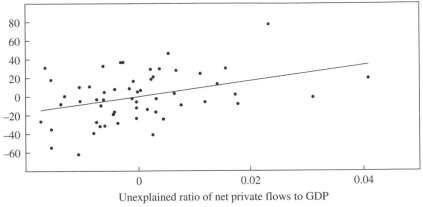

Unexplained ratio of net private flows to GDP

Source: World Bank, World Development Indicators; Lane and Milesi-Ferretti (2006); Johnson, Ostry, and Subramanian (2007); and authors' calculations.
a. The line plots the correlation between unexplained overvaluation and the unexplained ratio of net private inflows to GDP, defined below; this is the same as the conditional correlation obtained from regression 6-4 in table 6. Its slope is the coefficient on the ratio of net private flows to GDP (portfolio, equity, debt, and FDI) term in that regression. Data are for the fifty-six countries in the core sample.
b. Residuals from a regression of overvaluation on a constant and the working-age population. The unexplained component of the ratio of net private flows to GDP is defined analogously.

(regression 6-7). What this suggests is that overvaluation, and thus the distortion of investment returns caused by the use of foreign saving, may matter far less for industrial countries, which may help explain the positive correlation between their use of foreign saving and growth.

Having established that there is a positive correlation in nonindustrial countries between capital inflows and average overvaluation, let us now ask if such overvaluation has an effect on competitiveness and growth.[61]

61. One qualification to this result is that, when we use the current account–GDP ratio in place of private capital inflows, we do not find a statistically significant relationship with our measure of overvaluation, either in the cross section or in the panel. There is a huge endogeneity problem in such regressions, of course, which could explain this in the context of nonindustrial countries. Systematic undervaluation could stimulate speculative inflows through unofficial channels when there are selective capital controls in place; similarly, overvaluation may lead to capital flight. (Both these unofficial inflows and outflows would be reflected in the errors and omissions category of the balance of payments.) This is why measures of private capital inflows may be more relevant for understanding the effects of net flows on exchange rates. There is an endogeneity problem in this case as well, but it should drive the correlations that we report in table 6 negative (more overvaluation reduces inflows of private inflows through official channels). Hence the positive correlations that we find are still interesting.

If it does, it could explain the negative correlation between capital inflows and growth that we have already documented.

OVERVALUATION AND GROWTH. Table 7 introduces our measure of overvaluation into the core specification of tables 1 and 3, in both the cross section and the panel. In the cross section (regressions 7-1 and 7-2) the coefficient on overvaluation has the expected negative sign and is significant at the 10 percent level.[62] The coefficient is less negative when we exclude countries receiving high levels of aid. The addition of the share of the working-age population (regression 7-4) also reduces the impact of both the current account and overvaluation. As argued earlier, this may reflect the possibility that exogenous shifts in saving (due to demographic factors) lead to faster growth by way of reduced overvaluation.

In the panel version (in which the sample period is split into five-year subperiods), the coefficient on overvaluation is negative and significant at the 5 percent level for the large sample, both when the share of the working-age population is included (regression 7-8) and when it is not (regression 7-5), but it falls just short of significance ($p \approx 0.12$) when the sample is reduced and the working-age population share is omitted (regressions 7-6 and 7-7).[63] The magnitude of the coefficient in regression 7-6 suggests that, in the short run, a 1-percentage-point increase in the degree of overvaluation decreases annual growth by about 0.4 percentage point.[64]

Figure 13 conveys some of the flavor of the panel relationship. The figure plots growth and overvaluation over time for countries that experienced growth spurts,[65] differentiating their performance before and during the growth spurt. On average, overvaluation is substantially less during the growth spurt than before. It is noteworthy that the turnaround in overvaluation is more stark when we exclude, in the bottom panel, the three industrial countries (Ireland, Portugal, and Spain) from the group of sustained growers. This is also consistent with our findings on the differing experiences of industrial and developing countries.

It is also useful to ask whether countries can get as much of a competitive advantage from undervaluation as they will suffer a competitive disadvantage from overvaluation. We estimate separate slopes for countries with

62. Although this particular specification is sensitive to the inclusion of Mauritius, in others, where the Africa dummy is dropped, the result is more robust.

63. Alternative lag structures yield a significant coefficient on the overvaluation term.

64. Since the overvaluation term is instrumented in the panel, reverse causation should be less of a concern. See also Razin and Collins (1999).

65. Again, as identified by Hausmann, Pritchett, and Rodrik (2005).

Table 7. Cross-Sectional and Panel OLS Regressions of GDP Growth Rates on Real Overvaluation

Independent variable	Regression (dependent variable is average annual rate of GDP growth)[a]								
	Cross-sectional[b]				Panel[c]				
	7-1	7-2[d]	7-3[e]	7-4	7-5	7-6	7-7	7-8	7-9
Current account balance–GDP ratio	0.091 (0.040)**	0.086 (0.058)	0.185 (0.066)***	0.061 (0.055)	0.035 (0.086)	-0.004 (0.159)	0.181 (0.148)	-0.049 (0.132)	0.011 (0.106)
Working-age share of total population				0.181 (0.072)**				0.143 (0.156)	
Degree of overvaluation[f]	-0.010 (0.005)*	-0.011 (0.006)*	-0.006 (0.004)	-0.005 (0.004)	-0.039 (0.017)**	-0.037 (0.024)	-0.022 (0.014)	-0.038 (0.015)***	
Degree of overvaluation × dummy for overvaluation > 0									-0.044 (0.025)*
Degree of overvaluation × dummy for overvaluation < 0									-0.021 (0.026)
No. of observations	59	56	48	56	336	320	267	320	320
R^2	0.73	0.71	0.82	0.78					
Hansen test for overidentifying restrictions (p-value)					0.741	0.802	0.757	0.975	0.912
Arellano-Bond AR(2) test (p-value)					0.602	0.537	0.652	0.509	0.529

Source: Authors' regressions using same source data as for table 6.
a. Data are period averages of annual data for each of the fifty-nine nonindustrial countries listed in appendix table A-1, from 1970 to 2004. Numbers in parentheses are robust standard errors; asterisks indicate statistical significance at the ***1, **5, and *10 percent level. GDP data are adjusted for international differences in purchasing power of the dollar. Covariates are as in tables 1, 2, and 3 and are omitted for presentational simplicity.
b. All regressions include dummy variables for oil exporters and for sub-Saharan Africa.
c. The sample period is split into five-year subperiods. All right-hand-side variables are treated as endogenous, and the third and fourth lags are used for instrumentation.
d. In this regression and in regressions 7-4, 7-6, 7-8, and 7-9, sample omits Mozambique, Nicaragua, and Singapore.
e. In this regression and regression 7-7, sample omits countries receiving aid averaging more than 10 percent of their GDP.
f. Measured as described in the text.

Figure 13. Exchange Rate Overvaluation and Real Growth in GDP per Capita before and after Growth Spurts[a]

Percent a year

Sample of eleven countries

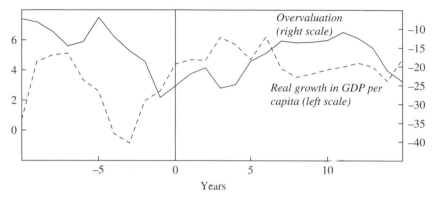

Sample of eight nonindustrial countries

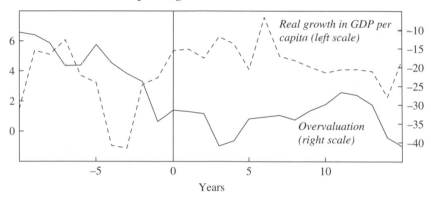

Source: Penn World Tables; Johnson, Ostry, and Subramanian (2007); and authors' calculations.
a. Simple averages of overvaluation and growth of GDP per capita. Countries and initial year (year 0) of their growth spurts are as in figure 8; bottom panel omits Ireland, Portugal, and Spain.

overvaluation and for countries with undervaluation (regression 7-9). The negative effect is twice as large, and statistically significant, in the former. It is also negative for the latter (suggesting that these countries secure a mild competitive advantage), but the coefficient in this case is not significantly different from zero. The true test, though, of whether exchange rate mis-alignment plays a symmetric role both when positive and when negative is whether the coefficients are different from each other. Here we cannot reject the possibility that they are the same. More work is clearly needed.

EXPORTS AND EXCHANGE RATES: WITHIN-COUNTRY, BETWEEN-INDUSTRY VARIATION. The reduced-form relationship between overvaluation and growth should be mediated through exports and, in particular, manufacturing exports. We now present evidence, based on industry-level data, that suggests that this is indeed the case. As in the previous section, we exploit the within-country, across-industry variation, which allows us to address issues of endogeneity and reverse causality that cannot easily be dealt with even using panel macroeconomic data. The intuition on which these regressions are based is that, in countries with more competitive exchange rates, industries that are "exportable" (that is, whose products have greater inherent export potential) should see faster growth than industries that are less exportable. This intuition is formalized in the following specification:

$$(3) \qquad G_{ij} = \psi + \zeta_1' C_j + \zeta_2' I_i + \zeta_3 man_{ij} + \alpha \left(overval_j \times xport_i \right) + \varepsilon_{ij},$$

where C_j is a vector of country indicator variables; I_i is a vector of industry indicator variables; man_{ij} is industry i's initial-period share of manufacturing in country j; $overval_j$ is real overvaluation in country j; and $xport_i$ is the exportability of industry i.

The coefficient of interest for us is α. It captures an interaction between a country-specific overvaluation variable and an industry's exportability. We posit that countries with greater overvaluation should see a more negative impact in industries that are more exportable, and so we would expect α to be negative.

Before running this regression, we need to measure the inherent exportability of an industry. Since this is clearly a function of a country's endowment and level of income, we are on safer ground in restricting our sample to developing countries, which are likely to be more similar in their potential export trading patterns. However, even within our sample, countries are at varying levels of development. We therefore define exportability in two ways. First, we divide the sample of developing countries into two groups, based on whether their income lies above or below the median. For each group we calculate the ratio of exports to value added for each industry i, averaged across all countries in the group. Industries that have ratios above the median within the group we call exportable. Finally, we create an exportable indicator that is equal to 1 for these above-the-median industries; for the other industries the indicator variable takes on a value of zero.

Our second measure of exportability is simpler. We know from the postwar history of world trade that developing countries typically have comparative advantage in the textiles and clothing industry and the leather and footwear industry. So we code the four industries in the U.N. Industrial Development Organization database that fall into these categories as exportable, and we create an indicator variable that takes a value of 1 for these industries and zero otherwise. The difference between this indicator variable and the first is that our textiles and leather indicator is common to all developing countries in the sample, whereas our first indicator can vary across the two groups of developing countries—richer and poorer—in our sample.

Table 8 presents results using the first indicator variable for the 1980s (regression 8-1), the 1990s (regression 8-4), and the pooled data (regression 8-7).[66] The coefficient on the interaction between the overvaluation variable and the exportability indicator is negative and significant for both the 1980s and the 1990s. One way to interpret the coefficient is to say that, in a country whose currency is overvalued in real terms by 1 standard deviation (about 24 percentage points) more than that of another country, exportable industries grow 1.4 percentage points (0.0006 × 24) a year more slowly than other industries in the first country relative to the second. This is substantial when compared with the annual growth rate of the average sector in the sample of about 3.5 percent.

Regressions 8-2, 8-5, and 8-8 are for the same specification but with the textiles, clothing, leather, and footwear industries as the exportable industries. Again the coefficient on the interaction term is negative and significant. It is also greater for these industries than for those in the previous sample, which is reassuring because it suggests that, even within exportable industries, the most obviously exportable ones suffer more in the presence of overvaluation. Finally, we repeat the exercise in regressions 8-3, 8-6, and 8-9, this time restricting the definition of exportable industries to just textiles and clothing, and again we find that the coefficients are significant and increase in magnitude for these clearly exportable sectors.

---

66. It is less easy to run these regressions in a panel context because the exportability index exhibits virtually no time variation, and the overvaluation variable is also quite persistent across the two decades. So there is very little time variation to enable identification.

Table 8. OLS Regressions of Industry Growth in Value Added on Real Overvaluation Interacted with Sector Exportability

Regression (dependent variable is annual average rate of growth of value added in sector i of country j)[a]

Independent variable	1980s			1990s			Pooled		
	8-1	8-2	8-3	8-4	8-5	8-6	8-7	8-8	8-9
Country j degree of overvaluation × sector i exportability measure 1[b]	-0.0006 (0.0003)**			-0.0006 (0.0003)**			-0.0002* (0.0001)		
Country j degree of overvaluation × sector i exportability measure 2[c]		-0.0012 (0.0006)**			-0.0006 (0.0003)*			-0.0008 (0.0003)**	
Country j degree of overvaluation × sector i exportability measure 3[d]			-0.0013 (0.0010)			-0.0009 (0.0005)*			-0.0010 (0.0005)*
No. of observations	619	619	619	751	751	751	1,370	1,370	1,370
R^2	0.37	0.37	0.37	0.25	0.24	0.24	0.20	0.21	0.21

Source: Authors' regressions using calculations based on Johnson, Ostry, and Subramanian (2007) and United Nations Industrial Development Organization (UNIDO).

a. Data are period averages for each of the thirty nonindustrial countries listed in appendix table A-1 for which data are available from UNIDO. All regressions include country and industry fixed effects and the initial industry share of value added in economy-wide value added. Numbers in parentheses are robust standard errors; asterisks indicate statistical significance at the ***1, **5, and *10 percent level.

b. Exportable industries are those for which the ratio of exports to value added, averaged across all countries in the group, is above the median.

c. Exportable industries are defined as the textiles, clothing, leather, and footwear industries only.

d. Exportable industries are defined as the textiles and clothing industries only.

To summarize, we have presented evidence that capital inflows can result in overvaluation in nonindustrial countries and that overvaluation can hamper overall growth. To bolster this claim, we have shown that overvaluation particularly impinges on the growth of exportable industries. Although the industry-level results go some way toward addressing concerns about endogeneity, the issue remains whether they scale up to the economy as a whole. Again, although these results are not conclusive, since they are, after all, based on reduced-form estimations, the fact that the macroeconomic evidence and the industry-level evidence tell a consistent story provides some comfort that our interpretation is reasonable. The results presented in this section in some ways also generalize the point made by Rajan and Subramanian about the deleterious effects of aid inflows on poor countries' exchange rate competitiveness.[67]

Conclusion

Our analysis makes clear that nonindustrial countries that have relied on foreign capital have not grown faster than those that have not. Indeed, taken at face value, there is a growth premium associated with these countries *not* relying on foreign finance. Equally clearly, though, the reliance of these countries on domestic rather than foreign saving to finance investment comes at a cost: investment and consumption are less than they would be if these countries could draw in foreign capital on the same terms as industrial countries, or on the same terms as they can use their own domestic capital.

It does not seem to us that these nonindustrial countries are building up foreign assets just to serve as collateral, which can then draw in beneficial forms of foreign financing such as FDI.[68] Rather, it seems to us that even successful developing countries have limited absorptive capacity for foreign resources, whether because their financial markets are underdeveloped, or because their economies are prone to overvaluation caused by rapid capital inflows or overly rapid consumption growth, or some combination of these factors.

As countries develop, absorptive capacity grows. The recent strong growth of the emerging economies of Europe, accompanied by rising

67. Rajan and Subramanian (2005).
68. See, for example, Dooley, Folkerts-Landau, and Garber (2004a, 2004b). Why, for example, would Korea or Taiwan be comforted, when making direct investments in China, by the fact that China holds enormous amounts of U.S. government securities?

current account deficits, probably has a lot to do with the strengthening of their financial sectors, in part through the entry of foreign banks. Only time will tell what effects there are on the exchange rate and on competitiveness, as well as whether this phenomenon is sustainable, and so all conclusions from this episode have to be tentative.[69]

In sum, our results suggest that insofar as the need to avoid overvaluation is important and the domestic financial sector is underdeveloped, greater caution toward certain forms of foreign capital inflows might be warranted. At the same time, however, financial openness may be needed to spur domestic financial development.[70] This suggests that even though reformers in developing countries might want to wait to achieve a certain level of financial development before pushing for financial integration, the prospect of financial integration and ensuing competition may be needed to spur domestic financial development. One approach worth considering might be a firm commitment to integrate financial markets at a definite future date; this would allow time for the domestic financial system to develop without possible adverse effects from capital inflows, even while giving participants the incentive to press for it by suspending the sword of future foreign competition over their heads.[71]

A bleak read of the message in this paper is that because development itself may be the antidote to the deleterious effects of foreign capital and may be necessary for countries to absorb more capital, only some forms of foreign capital may play a direct role in the development process. Certainly, the role of foreign capital in expanding a country's resource constraints may be limited. A more optimistic read would see a research and, eventually, policy agenda in determining how to increase the capacity of poor countries to absorb foreign capital.

---

69. Of course, if development helps countries absorb foreign capital better, why is the correlation between current account balances and growth for nonindustrial countries getting stronger over time, as figure 5 suggests? This is an important question for future research.

70. See, for example, Rajan and Zingales (2003), Mishkin (2006), and Kose and others (2006).

71. The Chinese approach of trying to spur banking reform by committing to open up the country's banking sector to foreign competition in early 2007, as part of their World Trade Organization accession commitments, can be seen in this light. Prasad and Rajan (2005) suggest an alternative strategy for dealing with the potential adverse effects of inflows through controlled liberalization of outflows (essentially by securitizing inflows), which would allow countries experiencing large capital inflows to develop their domestic financial markets and simultaneously mitigate appreciation pressures associated with those inflows.

Over time, and especially in the aftermath of the East Asian crisis of the late 1990s, certitudes about financial integration have gradually yielded to greater circumspection—a trend that this paper suggests was perhaps warranted. But what does all this mean for policies toward capital account openness? Certainly, the answer is not to go backward, but instead toward more country and context specificity in assessing the merits of capital account openness, and more flexibility and creativity in managing it.[72] Even in his avatar that was skeptical of financial integration, Keynes said, "Yet, at the same time, those who seek to disembarrass a country of its entanglements should be very slow and wary. It should not be a matter of tearing up roots but of slowly training a plant to grow in a different direction."

72. For instance, capital account openness means more than just opening up to inward flows; it also means allowing outward flows. Outward flows could well relieve incipient appreciation pressures on the national currency, but they could also be a source of fragility, especially if the financial sector is underdeveloped. The fragility associated with the exit of capital could be attenuated if an economy is more open to trade (see Calvo, Izquierdo, and Mejia, 2004, and Frankel and Cavallo, 2004); trade openness could also mitigate the adverse effects of crises.

APPENDIX A

Country Samples and Supplementary Regressions

Table A-1. Country Samples

Industrial	Transition	Nonindustrial, nontransition	
Australia	Albania	Algeria	Mali
Austria	Armenia	Argentina	Mauritius
Belgium	Belarus	Bolivia	Mexico
Canada	Bosnia & Herzegovina	Brazil	Morocco
Denmark	Bulgaria	Cameroon	Mozambique
Finland	Croatia	Chile	Nicaragua
France	Czech Rep.	China	Nigeria
Germany	Estonia	Colombia	Pakistan
Greece	Georgia	Costa Rica	Panama
Iceland	Hungary	Côte d'Ivoire	Paraguay
Ireland	Kazakhstan	Cyprus	Peru
Italy	Kyrgyz Rep.	Dominican Rep.	Philippines
Japan	Latvia	Ecuador	Rwanda
Netherlands	Lithuania	Egypt	Senegal
New Zealand	Moldova	El Salvador	Sierra Leone
Norway	Poland	Ethiopia	Singapore
Portugal	Romania	Ghana	South Africa
Spain	Russia	Guatemala	Sri Lanka
Sweden	Slovak Rep.	Haiti	Tanzania
Switzerland	Slovenia	Honduras	Thailand
United Kingdom	Ukraine	India	Trinidad & Tobago
United States		Indonesia	Tunisia
		Iran	Turkey
		Israel	Uganda
		Jamaica	Uruguay
		Jordan	Venezuela
		Kenya	Zambia
		Korea, Rep. of	Zimbabwe
		Madagascar	
		Malawi	
		Malaysia	

Table A-2. Growth and Alternative Measures of Financial Integration[a]

Independent variable	Regression			
	A-2-1	A-2-2	A-2-3	A-2-4
Log of initial GDP per capita	−1.712	−1.746	−1.780	−1.665
	(0.328)***	(0.284)***	(0.295)***	(0.340)***
Initial life expectancy	0.052	0.069	0.063	0.067
	(0.032)	(0.029)**	(0.032)*	(0.030)**
Initial trade policy[b]	1.127	0.994	0.965	1.160
	(0.808)	(0.824)	(0.826)	(0.969)
Ratio of fiscal balance to GDP	0.057	0.068	0.066	0.058
	(0.047)	(0.045)	(0.045)	(0.044)
Institutional quality[c]	6.375	6.269	6.220	5.675
	(1.692)***	(1.729)***	(1.648)***	(2.144)**
FDI liabilities–GDP ratio	1.524			
	(0.924)			
Net FDI flows–GDP ratio		10.374		
		(12.223)		
Ratio of gross private inflows (FDI + portfolio + debt) to GDP			12.688	
			(10.007)	
Capital account policy openness[d]				−0.098
				(0.203)
No. of observations	55	56	56	55
R^2	0.66	0.67	0.68	0.65

Source: Authors' regressions using same source data as for tables 1, 2, and 4.
a. The dependent variable is annual average growth in GDP per capita, 1970–2004.
b. Measure of trade openness from Sachs and Warner (1995).
c. Measure of institutional quality from Hall and Jones (1999).
d. Measure of capital account policy openness from Chinn and Ito (2006).

Comments and Discussion

Susan M. Collins: In this paper Eswar Prasad, Raghuram Rajan, and Arvind Subramanian update and extend their previous work on net foreign capital flows and economic growth. Their starting point is the well-known Lucas puzzle, that capital tends to flow uphill from relatively poor to relatively rich countries. Recent analyses have also highlighted the so-called allocation puzzle, that even among poor countries capital does not go primarily to those countries that are growing most rapidly, as some theories would predict. The story here focuses on a related observation: that among nonindustrial countries net capital outflows (as measured by the current account) are *positively* correlated with growth. The opposite appears to be true for industrial countries, for which faster growth is associated with net capital inflows (current account deficits). The authors first convincingly document this finding in a variety of ways. They then offer some very plausible explanations, together with some empirical evidence, and pull together some lessons for successful development strategies. Along the way they touch on a wide range of interesting issues, only a few of which I will attempt to discuss here.

In my view a strength of the paper is the extensive evidence the authors amass in support of their main finding. They consider time-series as well as cross-sectional and panel data. They present simple charts as well as results of regressions, some estimated by ordinary least squares and others by the generalized method of moments. They explore omitting outliers and altering the sample time period. Their finding does indeed seem to be quite robust and convincing. Thus they have added to the list of stylized facts that, among developing countries, faster growth tends to be associated with current account surpluses (net aggregate capital outflows), not current account deficits (net capital inflows). An important caveat, however, is that this finding does not hold across all types of capital. In particular, faster growth tends to be associated with net inflows of foreign direct investment (FDI).

It was less obvious to me that the authors' main finding should be characterized as a puzzle. Certainly some textbook models associate borrowing with faster growth for poor, finance-constrained economies. But even simple models can also generate a variety of realistic scenarios in which faster growth goes hand in hand with current account improvement (that is, a rising balance), not deterioration. And although I find the authors' two main explanations of their finding quite plausible, I can think of other plausible explanations as well. As discussed below, the additional empirics they provide do not really help in teasing out whether or not their conjectures are correct. Thus I would caution the authors against attempting to jump from their interesting correlations among jointly determined variables to drawing broad-brush conclusions about effective development strategy.

The first of the authors' two suggested explanations is an institutional underdevelopment story, which conjectures that faster income growth (for example, due to productivity shocks) results in increased saving but a limited increase in investment (possibly because of a weak financial system, or inadequate protection of private property, or both). In this scenario growth would be associated with current account improvement in developing but not in industrial economies. I certainly agree that weak financial systems and other differences in institutional development likely play a role in explaining the positive correlation between growth and the current account in poor but not in rich countries.

To support this conjecture, the authors present some interesting results using industry-level panel data. I think there is often much to learn from combining micro with macro evidence and that this is a potentially interesting direction for research. As expected, they find that, in countries with developed financial markets, increased capital inflows tend to spur growth in industries that rely on outside financing. Interestingly, the opposite is true for countries with less developed financial markets. One concern is that the dummy variable they use in their regressions to identify countries below the median in financial development is picking up a variety of other country characteristics as well, since various measures of development tend to be highly correlated. The insignificant results obtained by replacing that variable with GDP per capita, however, suggest that it really is financial development that matters.

212   *Brookings Papers on Economic Activity, 1:2007*

This is a provocative finding that suggests that domestic financial development has an important influence on industry-level finance and growth. However, it does not really allow one to conclude that, because of this underdevelopment, positive shocks to growth raise saving more than investment. Two concerns warrant more discussion. One is whether U.S. industries are reliably comparable, in terms of their financing characteristics, to industries in developing countries, as the authors' method assumes. A second is that the results are similar for the current account measure of foreign capital and for FDI, but FDI inflows are positively correlated with growth.

The authors offer a second conjecture that might explain the positive correlation between current account surpluses and growth. Capital inflows may cause real appreciation of the domestic currency and thus, through Dutch disease, reduced competitiveness, reduced investment, and slower growth. The authors present some convincing evidence relating foreign capital to appreciation, but only when they use private capital, not their preferred current account indicator, as the measure of capital inflows. They also report interesting evidence relating overvaluation to slower growth, especially among industries they identify as export oriented. Consistent with some work I did some years ago and with more recent work by Dani Rodrik,[1] they also find undervaluation to be associated with faster growth. Although reduced-form regressions like these are not conclusive, I agree with the authors that they are quite suggestive.

Thus both conjectures are plausible. But other stories are plausible as well. In earlier versions of this paper, the authors gave more attention to the possible influence of demographic shocks. A significant decline in birthrates has been associated with increased saving and faster growth. It seems quite likely that different combinations of these (as well as other) scenarios are relevant for different countries at different times. An aggregate analysis with pooled data and (necessarily) blunt indicators of the relevant country characteristics can only go so far toward untangling the myriad interrelationships. More-extensive theoretical analysis, as well as some careful case studies, could go a long way to deepening our understanding.

1. Rodrik (2007a, 2007b).

In the remainder of this comment I will address three issues. First, the authors find it puzzling that investment is much less important in their growth regressions than saving. In places, their interpretation seems to be that growth must be due more to increases in total factor productivity (TFP) than to increases in the contribution from capital deepening. Indeed, the paper highlights positive productivity shocks as a potential driving force behind the developments they see in the data. I do not think this interpretation is warranted, however, for two reasons. Similar regressions, discussed below, show a very strong and significant correlation between capital accumulation (properly measured) and growth. Furthermore, the strong correlation that the authors find between the saving-GDP ratio and growth is associated with the capital accumulation component of growth, *not* the TFP component.

A supply-side decomposition implies that capital accumulation should be one of the determinants of growth over the medium-to-long run. In the steady state, average investment is related one to one to growth in the capital stock. But this requires a constant capital-output ratio, an assumption that is not very plausible for developing countries at various stages of catch-up to the industrial world. My work with Barry Bosworth finds a surprisingly low correlation between investment-GDP ratios and growth in the capital stock in our sample of eighty-four countries since 1960, whether we use forty-year or twenty-year periods.[2] Intuitively, a country like Indonesia that is growing rapidly will exhibit much faster growth in its capital stock than a county like Guyana whose GDP performance has been stagnant—even though Guyana's average investment-GDP ratio actually exceeds Indonesia's using the authors' data (figure 1). Regressing growth in the capital stock on the investment share of GDP, using the Bosworth-Collins data on growth in the capital stock and the authors' data on investment, yields an adjusted R^2 of just 0.27. Thus the investment-GDP ratio is a poor measure of growth in a country's capital stock. (The issue is *not* measurement error, as the authors of this paper suggest.) Its performance in a growth regression says little about the relative importance of capital accumulation and productivity for growth. Our 2003 paper also reported that substituting a direct measure of growth in the capital stock for the investment-GDP ratio substantially increased the

2. Bosworth and Collins (2003).

Figure 1. Relationship between Changes in the Capital Stock and Average Investment, 1970–2004[a]

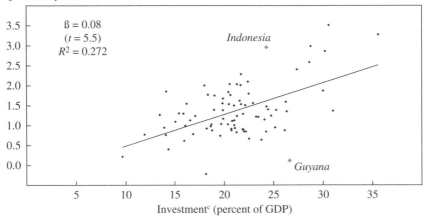

Change in capital stock[b]
(percent a year)

Source: Data from Prasad, Rajan, and Subramanian, this volume, and Bosworth and Collins (2003).
a. Data are for eighty-three countries in the Bosworth and Collins data set, excluding Taiwan.
b. Average annual change in the capital stock from 1970 to 2003, from the Bosworth and Collins data.
c. Average annual share of investment in GDP from 1970 to 2004, from the Prasad, Rajan, and Subramanian data.

explanatory power of a growth regression: the adjusted R^2 rose from 0.26 to 0.67.

The strong, robust, positive correlation between saving and growth has been the focus of an interesting literature, some of which the present paper discusses. The question I would like to pose here is whether the observed correlation is primarily associated with TFP or with capital accumulation. As Bosworth and I discussed in our 2003 paper, a growth accounting decomposition can be combined with growth regression analysis to explore the channels through which variables influence the growth in GDP. To explore this, the authors kindly ran a set of regressions for me combining their data with the Bosworth-Collins measures of growth per worker (instead of growth per capita) and its components: the contributions to growth from increases in capital per worker (K/L) and from increases in TFP. Each regression included the ratios of saving and investment to GDP (omitting the ratio of the current account balance to GDP) as well as the five additional right-hand-side variables used in the

Table 1. Regressions Relating Saving, Investment, and the Components of Economic Growth in Nonindustrial Countries, 1970–2004[a]

Independent variable	Dependent variable: growth in GDP per capita[b]	Dependent variable: growth in GDP per worker[c]	Contribution of Growth in capital per worker	Growth in TFP
Saving-GDP	0.097	0.056	0.049	0.006
ratio	(3.08)	(1.92)	(3.10)	(0.24)
Investment-GDP	−0.005	−0.001	0.006	−0.006
ratio	(−0.07)	(−0.02)	(0.17)	(−0.014)

Source: Author's regressions using the Prasad-Rajan-Subramanian (PRS) and Bosworth-Collins (BC; www.brookings.edu/es/research/projects/develop/develop.htm) datasets.

a. Regressions also include the other independent variables included in the regressions reported in columns 7 and 8 of table 1 of Prasad, Rajan, and Subramanian, this volume, excluding the current account balance (results not shown). Data are from the same fifty-six countries as in columns 2-1 and 2-4 of table 2 of that paper. Numbers in parentheses are *t*-statistics.

b. From the PRS data.

c. From the BC data. See Bosworth and Collins (2003) for details.

regressions reported in the authors' table 1. My table 1 shows only the coefficients of interest and their *t*-statistics.

The first column shows what happens if saving and investment (instead of saving and the current account balance, or investment and the current account balance) are included in a regression using the authors' data. As expected, saving enters with a high significance level whereas investment has an insignificant coefficient, very close to zero. Similar results are obtained in the second column, using the Bosworth-Collins measure of output growth, although the coefficient estimate for saving is notably smaller and less statistically significant.

The third and fourth columns use each of the growth components as dependent variables. Because these components sum to total growth (used in the second column) and the included right-hand-side variables are identical, each coefficient in the second column is equal to the sum of the corresponding coefficients in the third and fourth columns. Thus the method decomposes the channels of each variable's influence. The very clear implication is that the association between saving and growth comes primarily from the association between saving and capital deepening, with no significant association between saving and increases in TFP. Although these results are far from conclusive and reflect correlations among jointly determined variables, they do not point to productivity shocks as a key driver of the observed relationships. However, they do suggest that saving rates are better indicators of growth in the capital stock than investment rates.

The other two issues involve ways in which, in my view, the approach taken in the paper seems to make an already complex topic somewhat more difficult to untangle. The first is the primary focus on aggregate measures of cross-border capital flows. As the authors note, not all types of foreign capital are the same. Their own work finds that FDI exhibits very different correlations with growth than the composite indicators used in most of their paper. As Peter Henry stresses in his comment, non-FDI and FDI flows must therefore exhibit strikingly different behavior. I agree with him that there is a lot to be learned from analyses that recognize this heterogeneity.

Second, the paper uses various terms interchangeably that I see as quite distinct. In particular, the title highlights the linkages between (net flows of) foreign capital and economic growth. Indeed, the main objective of the paper is to first document and then explore why nonindustrial countries that have received more aggregate net foreign financing (had larger current account deficits) have tended to grow relatively slowly. Yet much of the discussion throughout the paper replaces "reliance on foreign capital" with the phrase "financial integration." Conceptually, this is confusing terminology because countries can have similar current account deficits or surpluses (relative to GDP) but very different degrees of integration with global financial markets, and vice versa. The authors do recognize that composite net capital flows are one of a great many available indicators of a country's external finance. However, their brief discussion suggests that these are all intended to measure the same concept. It would be much clearer if they explicitly defined what they mean by "financial integration" and then provided a candid discussion of the advantages and disadvantages of the current account balance measure relative to that concept.

I find it helpful to distinguish among three types of indicators, as follows. First, de jure (on the books) policy indicators are intended as indicators of a country's official or stated policy regarding openness to capital flows. The available indicators of this type have many well-known shortcomings, and I agree that they probably do a poor job of capturing the many dimensions of the effectiveness of capital controls (see the authors' footnote 25). Second, de facto policy indicators are intended to reflect the extent to which a country's policies, as actually implemented, are friendly to cross-border capital flows. However, such indicators are very difficult to construct, and I am unaware of any attempts to do so for a large sample of countries. The third category consists of outcome indicators, which measure actual capital movements. Unfortunately, these are usually also called "de facto" indicators—a terminology that is quite confusing to those coming from other literatures. Both stock and flow outcome indicators are now readily available for large samples over long periods.

It is also well known that different indicators can show very different things. Country A may have few barriers to cross-border capital flows (that is, it is de jure open) but very little actual capital flows. Country B may have extensive controls (de jure closed) but large actual cross-border flows or large accumulated stocks. Some authors have emphasized policy status when analyzing financial integration, thus treating country A as more financially integrated than country B. A growing number of studies, including this one, focus on outcome measures. As Prasad and his co-authors explain in another paper, "In the end, what matters most is the actual degree of openness."[3]

In sum, the authors have written an interesting and provocative paper about the fact that developing countries that run current account surpluses (are net capital exporters) tend to grow faster than those that run deficits. Despite my reservations about some aspects of the paper, I find the authors' two main interpretations of this finding very sensible. Poorly developed financial markets surely do limit the extent to which capital inflows can enhance growth. And large capital inflows can generate a real appreciation, reducing export competitiveness. These are crucial issues for developing countries as they become increasingly open, and I look forward to the next installments in this research agenda.

Peter Blair Henry: Eswar Prasad, Raghuram Rajan, and Arvind Subramanian deserve a lot of credit for tackling the important question of whether foreign capital helps or hinders economic growth. The topic is timely, and the authors are eminently qualified to write about the impact of global financial integration on the allocation of real resources. My discussion will focus on the results they obtain for developing countries, that is, the nonindustrial, nontransition countries in their sample, because the ongoing debate over the relative merits of free capital flows really centers on this group, not on the industrialized world.

The authors argue that foreign capital is of marginal importance to economic growth in developing countries, because a lack of saving is not the

3. Prasad and others (2006, p. 461).

primary obstacle to growth in these countries. The more important challenge, the authors assert, is the limited capacity of financial systems in developing countries to absorb saving and allocate it efficiently. Given this limited absorptive capacity, the authors warn that countries seeking to attract foreign capital inflows run the risk of a real appreciation of their currencies that undermines export competitiveness, and of a lending boom in the nontradables sector that ultimately ends in tears.

I agree that foreign capital is probably not the most important contributor to economic growth in developing countries. More mundane aspects of economic policy such as fiscal discipline, free trade, and flexible labor markets are much more important. I also agree that domestic financial markets in developing countries need strengthening so that they allocate capital more efficiently, more widely, and in some countries, more to consumption and less to investment. For instance, a growing consensus suggests that part of the long-run solution to the twin problem of excess saving and the buildup of international reserves in China and elsewhere is the development of a domestic banking system that does a better job of allowing households and individuals to increase their lifetime utility by borrowing against the present value of their expected future earnings.

Although the authors' conclusions seem reasonable, I am not sure that their analysis provides the basis from which to draw the principal lessons they would like us to take away from the paper. It may well be that foreign capital does not make a substantial contribution to economic growth in developing countries, but the tests in this paper do not speak to the issue as directly as one would like.

Consider the logical flow of the paper. Prasad, Rajan, and Subramanian base their conclusion that foreign capital does not matter for economic growth on a number of intermediate empirical exercises. Each aims to buttress the following observation: Countries that, on average, relied on foreign finance from 1970 to 2004 did not grow more swiftly than those that did not. The authors make this point in three different ways. First, they note that capital over this period flowed uphill, from poor to rich countries instead of the other way around as predicted by the neoclassical model. This observation is prima facie evidence that foreign capital does not make a significant contribution to growth in the developing world. Second, the authors cite the so-called capital allocation puzzle: High-growth developing countries attract less capital than low- and medium-growth developing countries. Third, when the authors run cross-country regressions of economic growth on current account deficits, they find that growth is positively correlated with current account surpluses. According to their interpretation of neoclassical theory, we should instead see high-growth countries running current account deficits. I now consider the merits of each of these three arguments in turn.

It is true that, on net, capital has been flowing from poor to rich countries, the opposite of what the neoclassical model predicts. Yet the data on aggregate net capital flows hide a lot of heterogeneity. Capital flows have three basic components: aid, equity, and debt. Aid flows can be ignored, because they are an almost negligible fraction of total flows and are not driven by market forces. Equity has two subcomponents: foreign direct investment (FDI) and portfolio equity. The authors note that net FDI flows to developing countries have been positive. Net flows of portfolio equity to developing countries have also been positive. Indeed, taken together, FDI and portfolio equity account for roughly 45 percent of total capital inflows to developing countries.[1] It follows that net debt flows to developing countries must be overwhelmingly negative. Hence it would seem that the puzzle may not be much about FDI or portfolio equity, because there is no Lucas paradox within those two categories.

Rather, the puzzle may be why such a large fraction of the saving that flows to developing countries ends up being held as debt, and why those debt-denominated savings end up being parked abroad. If all capital is fully mobile across sectors within the domestic economy and therefore fully fungible, the authors are right that the aggregate net outflow of capital from poor to rich countries is a puzzle. But the data may be trying to tell us that the neoclassical model, which treats all capital as one homogeneous lump, may not be the most useful way of trying to understand the debt puzzle. There may be distortions in the domestic financial system that allow the domestic economy to derive growth benefits from one type of capital flow but not from others. The paper (and this literature more broadly) would benefit from some harder thinking about how to interpret the heterogeneity in net capital flows.

The second step of Prasad, Rajan, and Subramanian's argument is to demonstrate the so-called capital allocation puzzle. The top panel of their figure 3 shows that net capital inflows to fast-growing countries have been smaller than net inflows to slow-growing countries. In the authors' view this observation runs contrary to a prediction of the neoclassical model. According to their interpretation of the model, rapid growth and high

---

1. Henry (2006, table 4).

returns go together. The rapid-growth countries, they argue, must have a higher marginal product of capital than the slow-growth countries, and therefore more capital should flow to those countries that are growing fastest. The observation that high returns and fast growth do not go together is a second strike against the neoclassical model, which to the authors' way of thinking implicitly undermines the idea that foreign capital contributes to economic growth.

The problem with this argument is that high rates of economic growth in the neoclassical model do not necessarily imply high rates of return. A simple example using the Solow growth model helps illustrate. Consider two emerging market countries, A and B, that are identical and therefore growing at the same rate. A standard result of the Solow model is that an increase in the saving rate of country A will temporarily raise its rate of growth. It is also a standard result that the same increase in the saving rate will reduce the rate of return to capital: The increase in saving drives up the country's rate of investment, making capital less scarce and reducing the marginal benefit of capital. When diminishing returns have run their course, country A settles down to a new steady state, with the same growth rate as country B but a higher GDP per capita and a lower rate of return to capital. In fact, in this example the rate of return to capital in country A throughout its transition to the new steady state will be lower than in country B.

The proposition that high rates of growth do not necessarily imply high rates of return is not a theoretical counterexample without empirical relevance. Consider the data on growth and returns in Asia, Latin America, and the United States. From 1985 to 2005 the average annual growth rate of GDP was slowest in Latin America, at 2.9 percent, and fastest in Asia, where it was 7.4 percent; the growth rate in the United States was in between, at 3 percent. Yet the rank ordering of stock market returns (a rough proxy for the rate of return to capital) in the three regions over the same period was exactly the reverse. Measured in real dollar terms, Latin America had the highest average annual (dividend-inclusive) stock market return, at 14.7 percent; the United States was second, at 9 percent, and Asia had the lowest average annual return, 7 percent.[2]

The third and most important body of data that the authors marshal to buttress their argument is the cross-country correlation between current account deficits and growth rates of GDP. The authors perform a series of regressions in which the left-hand-side variable is the average growth rate

2. Henry and Kannan (2007).

of GDP per capita and the right-hand-side variable is the average current account deficit. A priori, the authors expect to find a negative correlation: fast-growing countries, on average, should run larger current account deficits than slow-growing countries. They find exactly the opposite correlation in the data for developing countries and interpret it as a third strike against the neoclassical model.

I disagree with their interpretation. It is not inherently puzzling that developing countries running current account surpluses tend to have higher growth rates than those running deficits. Policies that tend to produce current account surpluses are also policies that tend to be good for growth. Some examples include maintaining low fiscal deficits, a competitive exchange rate, and institutions that promote saving. As in my earlier example about growth and returns, a country that introduces policies to increase its rate of saving may experience an increase in saving, an increase in investment, and an increase in growth. If the increase in saving outstrips the increase in investment, the country will also experience a current account surplus. The authors are aware of the importance of saving for high-growth countries, but I do not agree with the logic behind their attempt to link growth rates and current account deficits.

The neoclassical model does not predict that fast-growing countries will run current account deficits. What the neoclassical model does predict is the following. Start from an equilibrium where investment equals saving, and assume that a country with open capital markets experiences a positive (anticipated) shock to its future marginal product of capital. Investment demand will rise. (And because future income rises, consumption will also rise, reinforcing the impact of investment on the current account deficit.) At the given world interest rate, the quantity of desired investment will exceed the quantity of domestic saving, and the country will experience a current account deficit. In other words, a positive productivity shock means that the country will run a current account deficit. The converse, however, need not be true. A country running a current account deficit need not have experienced a positive shock to its growth opportunities. Thus it is not clear that one can make inferences about a country's growth opportunities—or the contribution of foreign capital in helping the country to realize those opportunities—by regressing growth rates on current account deficits.

The question the authors seek to answer—does foreign capital contribute to economic growth?—cries out for either an episodic analysis or some way of observing the response of countries to major shocks. It seems to me that if one wants to know whether foreign capital contributes to economic growth, it is more helpful to compare countries that experienced a positive shock to growth opportunities and had open capital markets with countries that experienced similar shocks but lacked access to foreign capital. Specifically, one would want to compare the time paths of investment, rates of return to capital, and economic growth in the two sets of countries. Another approach would be to look at shocks to countries' access to foreign capital. Does going from a closed to an open capital account regime have a significant impact on the relevant real variables?

Let me now turn briefly to the authors' results on the efficiency of domestic capital markets in allocating capital to industries that rely on external finance. Here I have one fundamental concern. As I understand it, the measure of dependence on external finance for each industry is taken from the corresponding industry in the United States. It is not obvious to me that a given industry in the capital-abundant United States should have the same dependence on external finance as the corresponding industry in a labor-abundant developing economy. This may be a valid assumption for industries, such as mining, that are extremely capital intensive without much latitude to substitute labor for capital. But in other industries where cheap labor can be substituted for expensive capital, I am not sure that the Rajan-Zingales approach is entirely valid.

The element of the paper with which I am most in agreement is the discussion of the potential dangers of capital inflows for overvaluation of the currency. As one of two economic advisers on loan from the Massachusetts Institute of Technology Ph.D. program to the Bank of Jamaica in the summer of 1995, I saw this potential danger of capital inflows firsthand.

In the early 1990s the Jamaican government decided to permit domestic residents to hold U.S. dollar-denominated bank accounts within the country. This change in policy precipitated a large inflow of U.S. dollars that had been held offshore. At the time of the policy change, the interest rate on U.S. dollar-denominated loans in Jamaica was several percentage points lower than rates on comparable loans denominated in Jamaican dollars, and this differential had persisted for some time. Jamaica's official exchange rate policy at the time of the liberalization was a float, but the nominal exchange rate had not moved much since the liberalization. The real exchange rate, on the other hand, had strengthened substantially.[3]

_____
3. Naranjo and Osambela (2004).

In the face of a stable nominal exchange rate and lower interest rates on U.S. dollar-denominated loans, the temptation to borrow in U.S. dollars proved too much to resist, in spite of the impending depreciation (as signaled by the interest rate differential and the real appreciation). By the time we arrived in June 1995, 40 percent of all loans outstanding in Jamaica were denominated in U.S. dollars.

When we pointed out the rapid increase in dollar-denominated loans to Bank of Jamaica officials and stressed the importance of assessing the extent to which these loans had been made to firms whose revenues were in U.S. dollars versus local currency, they informed us that there were no formal mechanisms in place to permit such an assessment. This lack of supervisory oversight proved critical. In fact, many of the U.S. dollar-denominated loans had been made to firms whose production and sales were in nontradable industries, and the liberalization had produced little or no real growth. When the inevitable devaluation occurred, a financial crisis ensued. Recapitalizing the banks cost 50 percent of GDP, drove government indebtedness to record levels, and forced drastic cuts in important public investment. Although other factors surely contributed to the crisis, the point is that financial liberalization—and the attendant capital inflows—in the absence of adequate prudential supervision played a substantial role.

The Jamaican example, along with numerous similar war stories from around the developing world, clearly suggests that permitting the free flow of foreign capital is not a panacea for economic growth. Nevertheless, when conducted in a measured way, capital account liberalization can be a helpful part of a broader financial policy that seeks first to shore up the efficiency of the domestic financial sector. Despite the questions I have raised about the analysis that underpins this message, I think it is a helpful one and that the authors strike just the right tone of caution. Other scholars doing research in this area should follow suit.

General discussion: Benjamin Friedman suggested that Franco Modigliani would have shared Susan Collins's concerns about the endogeneity of foreign capital inflows. According to the life-cycle model of consumption and saving behavior, in a country with a given, fixed investment rate, a positive shock to any other determinant of the growth rate, such as a productivity shock, would raise the saving rate. And at the fixed investment rate, foreign capital inflows will be smaller. In this case the observed negative correlation between foreign capital inflows and growth rates arises from the endogenous increase in the saving rate. Friedman also conjectured that the different results for industrialized than for emerging market economies might be explained by the much smaller range of growth rates across the industrial countries, which results in the Modigliani effect being swamped there.

Richard Cooper discussed the importance of recognizing the changing composition of capital inflows over time. He noted that although the authors do distinguish FDI and foreign aid in some of their regressions, they mainly treat the inflow of capital as homogeneous. In fact, from 1970 to the present, the period that the authors cover, capital flows to developing countries have gone through several very distinct and different phases. In the first five years these flows overwhelmingly consisted of aid, either from one government to another or from an international institution to a government. From the late 1970s through the 1980s, capital inflows were mostly bank loans, made mainly to governments. Only in the 1990s did private lending to corporations emerge on a significant scale, partly in the form of bank loans and partly in the form of corporate bonds, while investment in government bonds continued to be important. This period also saw mutual funds in the United States and the United Kingdom increasingly buying equities in some developing countries. FDI, which had been very limited in countries other than mineral and oil producers, grew very rapidly during this period as well.

There is no reason, Cooper continued, to consider these forms of capital inflows as equivalent, in part because the motivations behind each are quite different. For example, governments in developing countries are not known for their efficiency in using foreign aid. Indeed, there is a large literature on the ineffectiveness of aid in spurring growth. Furthermore, much of this aid was not given for what the national accounts consider investment, but was directed toward education and other activities that should have promoted growth. In short, capital flows are too heterogeneous to be treated in the same way in the regressions, and the lack of positive results should not be surprising. Raghuram Rajan replied that, when one looks at shorter periods, there is indeed a positive correlation between current account deficits and growth in the 1970s, even in the nonindustrial countries, but this pattern is reversed for the later decades.

Cooper also noted a further implication of the paper, namely, that contrary to the view of most of the economics profession, the major constraint on growth for developing countries is not a capacity constraint arising from limited labor and capital, but an effective demand constraint. If a country experiences an increase in domestic demand, its balance of payments will deteriorate because of the resulting increase in imports and appreciation of the currency. This foreign exchange constraint on growth has often been more binding than the capacity constraint, because most developing countries do not have a capital goods industry, apart from construction, and instead have to import their capital goods. This two-gap model of development is no longer used, Cooper continued, because in the last decade export promotion and undervalued currencies, as well as capital inflows, have significantly relaxed this foreign exchange constraint. A growing literature documents the importance of effective demand, in particular export demand, for growth. Although today this constraint is no longer binding for most countries, it was relevant in previous periods and should not be ignored in interpreting the authors' results.

Cooper also cautioned against using purchasing power parity indexes to draw conclusions about currency overvaluation; studies have repeatedly found that such indexes contain very little information about future exchange rates. Finally, Cooper reminded the panel that the phenomenon of capital flowing "uphill" from poor to rich countries has been observed before. The United States, despite being the richest country in the world for the two decades before 1914, was a net capital importer at the time.

Joshua Aizenman argued that the main obstacle to growth in many developing economies is not scarcity of saving, but scarcity of proper governance. For example, Africa has received potentially useful inflows of financial capital, but these have often been diverted to the offshore accounts of the ruling elites. It would be informative, he concluded, to include in the regressions some variables that could capture a host of such political economy and social issues.

Olivier Jeanne noted that the authors were justifiably cautious in suggesting policy implications regarding the consequences of capital mobility and the possible usefulness of current account restrictions. In their model, controls on inflows would be optimal in order to limit overappreciation of the currency. However, in their regressions, measures of current account openness do not have a statistically significant impact on growth rates, making it hard to draw conclusions about this issue, which is of great importance to policymakers.

References

Abiad, Abdul, Daniel Leigh, and Ashoka Mody. 2007. "International Finance and Income Convergence: Europe is Different." Working Paper 07/64. Washington: International Monetary Fund (March).

Aghion, Philippe, Diego Comin, and Peter Howitt. 2006. "When Does Domestic Saving Matter for Economic Growth?" Working Paper 12275. Cambridge, Mass.: National Bureau of Economic Research (June).

Aizenman, Joshua, Brian Pinto, and Artur Radziwill. 2004. "Sources for Financing Domestic Capital—Is Foreign Saving a Viable Option for Developing Countries?" Working Paper 10624. Cambridge, Mass.: National Bureau of Economic Research (July).

Alfaro, Laura, and Eliza Hammel. 2007. "Capital Flows and Capital Goods." *Journal of International Economics* 72, no. 1: 128–50.

Alfaro, Laura, Sebnem Kalemli-Ozcan, and Vadym Volosovych. 2005. "Why Doesn't Capital Flow from Rich to Poor Countries? An Empirical Investigation." Working Paper 11901. Cambridge, Mass.: National Bureau of Economic Research (December).

Arellano, Manuel, and Stephen Bond. 1991. "Some Tests of Specification for Panel Data: Monte Carlo Evidence and an Application to Employment Equations." *Review of Economic Studies* 58, no. 2: 277–97.

Bekaert, Geert, Campbell R. Harvey, and Christian Lundblad. 2005. "Does Financial Liberalization Spur Growth?" *Journal of Financial Economics* 77, no. 1: 3–55.

Bernanke, Ben S. 2005. "The Global Saving Glut and the U.S. Current Account Deficit." Remarks at the Sandridge Lecture, Virginia Association of Economics, Richmond, Va., March 10 (www.federalreserve.gov/boarddocs/speeches/2005/200503102/default.htm).

_____. 2006. "Global Economic Integration: What's New and What's Not?" Remarks at the Federal Reserve Bank of Kansas City's Thirtieth Annual Economic Symposium, Jackson Hole, Wyo., August 25 (www.federalreserve.gov/boarddocs/speeches/2006/20060825/default.htm).

Bernanke, Ben S., and Refet S. Gürkaynak. 2002. "Is Growth Exogenous? Taking Mankiw, Romer, and Weil Seriously." *NBER Macroeconomics Annual 2001*, edited by Ben S. Bernanke and Kenneth S. Rogoff. MIT Press.

Blundell, Richard, and Stephen Bond. 1998. "Initial Conditions and Moment Restrictions in Dynamic Panel Data Models." *Journal of Econometrics* 87, no. 1: 115–43.

Borensztein, Eduardo, José De Gregorio, and Jong-Wha Lee. 1998. "How Does Foreign Direct Investment Affect Economic Growth?" *Journal of International Economics* 45, no. 1: 115–35.

Bosworth, Barry P., and Susan M. Collins. 1999. "Capital Flows to Developing Countries: Implications for Saving and Investment." *BPEA*, no. 1: 143–69.

_____. 2003. "The Empirics of Growth: An Update." *BPEA*, no. 2: 113–79.

Caballero, Ricardo J., Emmanuel Farhi, and Pierre-Olivier Gourinchas. 2006. "An Equilibrium Model of 'Global Imbalances' and Low Interest Rates." Working Paper 11996. Cambridge, Mass.: National Bureau of Economic Research (February).

Calvo, Guillermo, Alejandro Izquierdo, and Luis-Fernando Mejía. 2004. "On the Empirics of Sudden Stops: The Relevance of Balance-Sheet Effects." Paper presented at a Federal Reserve Bank of San Francisco Conference on Emerging Markets and Macroeconomic Volatility: Lessons from a Decade of Financial Debacles, San Francisco, June 4.

Carroll, Christopher D., and David N. Weil. 1994. "Saving and Growth: A Reinterpretation." *Carnegie-Rochester Conference Series on Public Policy* 40: 133–92.

Caselli, Francesco, and James Feyrer. 2007. "The Marginal Product of Capital." *Quarterly Journal of Economics* 122, no. 2: 535–68.

Chinn, Menzie D., and Hiro Ito. 2006. "What Matters for Financial Development? Capital Controls, Institutions, and Interactions." *Journal of Development Economics* 81, no. 1: 163–92.

Chinn, Menzie D., and Eswar S. Prasad. 2003. "Medium-Term Determinants of Current Accounts in Industrial and Developing Countries: An Empirical Exploration." *Journal of International Economics* 59, no. 1: 47–76.

De Nicolò, Gianni, Luc Laeven, and Kenichi Ueda. 2006. "Corporate Governance Quality in Asia: Comparative Trends and Impact." International Monetary Fund.

Detragiache, Enrica, Thierry Tressel, and Poonam Gupta. 2006. "Foreign Banks in Poor Countries: Theory and Evidence." IMF Working Paper 06/18. Washington: International Monetary Fund (January).

Dooley, Michael P., David Folkerts-Landau, and Peter M. Garber. 2004a. "The Revived Bretton Woods System: The Effects of Periphery Intervention and Reserve Management on Interest Rates and Exchange Rates in Center Countries." Working Paper 10332. Cambridge, Mass.: National Bureau of Economic Research (March).

_____. 2004b. "The U.S. Current Account Deficit and Economic Development: Collateral for a Total Return Swap." Working Paper 10727. Cambridge, Mass.: National Bureau of Economic Research (September).

Edwards, Sebastian. 2005. "Capital Controls, Sudden Stops, and Current Account Reversals." Working Paper 11170. Cambridge, Mass.: National Bureau of Economic Research (March).

Frankel, Jeffrey A., and Eduardo A. Cavallo. 2004. "Does Openness to Trade Make Countries More Vulnerable to Sudden Stops, or Less? Using Gravity to Establish Causality." Working Paper 10957. Cambridge, Mass.: National Bureau of Economic Research (December).

Gertler, Mark, and Kenneth S. Rogoff. 1990. "North-South Lending and Endogenous Domestic Capital Market Inefficiencies." *Journal of Monetary Economics* 26, no. 2: 245–66.

Glick, Reuven, and Kenneth S. Rogoff. 1995. "Global Versus Country-Specific Productivity Shocks and the Current Account." *Journal of Monetary Economics* 35, no. 1: 159–92.

Glick, Reuven, Xueyan Guo, and Michael Hutchison. 2006. "Currency Crises, Capital Account Liberalization, and Selection Bias." *Review of Economics and Statistics* 88, no 4: 698–714.

Gourinchas, Pierre-Olivier, and Olivier Jeanne. 2006a. "Capital Flows to Developing Countries: The Allocation Puzzle." University of California, Berkeley, and International Monetary Fund.

_____. 2006b. "The Elusive Gains from International Financial Integration." *Review of Economic Studies* 73, no. 3: 715–41.

Hall, Robert E., and Charles I. Jones. 1999. "Why Do Some Countries Produce So Much More Output per Worker Than Others?" *Quarterly Journal of Economics* 114, no. 1: 83–116.

Hausmann, Ricardo, Lant Pritchett, and Dani Rodrik. 2005. "Growth Accelerations." *Journal of Economic Growth* 10, no. 4: 303–29.

Henry, Peter Blair. 2006. "Capital Account Liberalization: Theory, Evidence, and Speculation." Working Paper 12698. Cambridge, Mass.: National Bureau of Economic Research (November).

Henry, Peter Blair, and Prakash Kannan. 2007. "Growth and Returns in Emerging Markets." In *International Financial Issues in the Pacific Rim: Global Imbalances, Financial Liberalization, and Exchange Rate Policy*. East Asia Seminar on Economics, vol. 17. University of Chicago Press.

Houthakker, Hendrik S. 1961. "An International Comparison of Personal Savings." *Bulletin of the International Statistical Institute* 38: 55–69.

Hsieh, Chang-Tai, and Peter J. Klenow. 2003. "Relative Prices and Relative Prosperity." Working Paper 9701. Cambridge, Mass.: National Bureau of Economic Research (May).

Jappelli, Tullio, and Marco Pagano. 1994. "Saving, Growth, and Liquidity Constraints." *Quarterly Journal of Economics* 109, no. 1: 83–109.

Johnson, Simon, Jonathan D. Ostry, and Arvind Subramanian. 2007. "The Prospects for Sustained Growth in Africa: Benchmarking the Constraints." Working Paper 07/52. Washington: International Monetary Fund (March).

Jones, Benjamin F., and Benjamin A. Olken. 2005. "The Anatomy of Start-Stop Growth." Working Paper 11528. Cambridge, Mass.: National Bureau of Economic Research (August).

Keynes, John Maynard. 1920. *The Economic Consequences of the Peace.* New York: Harcourt, Brace, and Howe.

_____. 1933. "National Self-Sufficiency." *Yale Review* 22, no. 4: 755–69.

Kose, M. Ayhan, Eswar S. Prasad, and Marco E. Terrones. 2006. "How Do Trade and Financial Integration Affect the Relationship between Growth and Volatility?" *Journal of International Economics* 69, no. 1: 176–202.

Kose, M. Ayhan, and others. 2006. "Financial Globalization: A Reappraisal." Working Paper 06/189. Washington: International Monetary Fund (August).

Kraay, Aart, and Jaume Ventura. 2000. "Current Accounts in Debtor and Creditor Countries." *Quarterly Journal of Economics* 115, no. 4: 1137–66.

Lane, Philip R., and Gian Maria Milesi-Ferretti. 2002. "Long-Term Capital Movements." *NBER Macroeconomics Annual 2001,* edited by Ben S. Bernanke and Kenneth S. Rogoff. MIT Press.

_____. 2006. "The External Wealth of Nations Mark II: Revised and Extended Estimates of Foreign Assets and Liabilities, 1970–2004." Working Paper 06/69. Washington: International Monetary Fund (March).

Lucas, Robert E., Jr. 1990. "Why Doesn't Capital Flow from Rich to Poor Countries?" *American Economic Review* 80, no. 2: 92–96.

Meese, Richard A., and Kenneth Rogoff. 1983. "Empirical Exchange Rate Models of the Seventies: Do They Fit Out of Sample?" *Journal of International Economics* 14, nos. 1–2: 3–24.

Mishkin, Frederic S. 2006. *The Next Great Globalization: How Disadvantaged Nations Can Harness Their Financial Systems to Get Rich.* Princeton University Press.

Modigliani, Franco. 1970. "The Life Cycle Hypothesis of Saving and Inter-Country Differences in the Saving Ratio." In *Induction, Growth and Trade: Essays in Honor of Sir Roy Harrod,* edited by Walter A. Eltis, Maurice FitzGerald Scott, and James N. Wolfe. Clarendon Press.

Naranjo, Martin, and Emilio Osambela. 2004. "From Financial Crisis to Correction." In *Revitalizing the Jamaican Economy: Policies for Sustained Growth,* edited by Desmond Thomas. Washington: Inter-American Development Bank.

Obstfeld, Maurice, and Alan M. Taylor. 2004. *Global Capital Markets: Integration, Crisis, and Growth.* Cambridge University Press.

Prasad, Eswar S., and Raghuram G. Rajan. 2005. "Controlled Capital Account Liberalization: A Proposal." Policy Discussion Paper 05/7. Washington: International Monetary Fund (October).

Prasad, Eswar, and others. 2006. "Financial Globalization, Growth, and Volatility in Developing Countries." In *Globalization and Poverty,* edited by Ann Harrison. University of Chicago Press.

Rajan, Raghuram G., and Arvind Subramanian. 2005. "What Undermines Aid's Impact on Growth?" Working Paper 11657. Cambridge, Mass.: National Bureau of Economic Research (October).

Rajan, Raghuram G., and Luigi Zingales. 1998. "Financial Dependence and Growth." *American Economic Review* 88, no. 3: 559–86.

_____. 2003. "The Great Reversals: The Politics of Financial Development in the 20th Century." *Journal of Financial Economics* 69, no. 1: 5–50.

Razin, Ofair, and Susan Collins. 1999. "Real-Exchange-Rate Misalignments and Growth." In *The Economics of Globalization: Policy Perspectives from Public Economics,* edited by Assaf Razin and Efraim Sadka. Cambridge University Press.

Reinhart, Carmen M., and Kenneth S. Rogoff. 2004. "Serial Default and the 'Paradox' of Rich-to-Poor Capital Flows." *American Economic Review* 94, no. 2: 53–58.

Rodrik, Dani. 2006. "Capital Account Liberalization and Growth: Making Sense of the Stylized Facts." Remarks at the IMF Center Economic Forum: How Does Capital Account Liberalization Affect Economic Growth? Washington, November 10 (www.imf.org/external/np/tr/2006/tr061110.htm#rod).

_____. 2007a. "Why Does the Real Exchange Rate Matter to Growth?" Razin Lecture, Georgetown University, March 21.

_____. 2007b. "The Real Exchange Rate and Economic Growth: Theory and Evidence." Harvard University (July) (ksghome.harvard.edu/~drodrik/RER %20and%20growth.pdf).

Sachs, Jeffrey D., and Andrew Warner. 1995. "Economic Reform and the Process of Global Integration." *BPEA,* no. 1: 1–95.

Tressel, Thierry, and Thierry Verdier. 2007. "Financial Globalization and the Governance of Domestic Financial Intermediaries." Working Paper 07/47. Washington: International Monetary Fund (March).

Wurgler, Jeffrey. 2000. "Financial Markets and the Allocation of Capital." *Journal of Financial Economics* 58, no. 1–2: 187–214.

MALCOLM BAKER
Harvard University

STEFAN NAGEL
Stanford University

JEFFREY WURGLER
New York University

The Effect of Dividends on Consumption

MICROSOFT'S $32 BILLION CASH dividend of December 2004 was the largest corporate payout ever. Classical models of finance and consumption-saving decisions predict that this dividend will have little effect on the consumption of Microsoft investors. Under the assumptions of Merton Miller and Franco Modigliani, for example, investors can always reinvest unwanted dividends, or sell shares to create homemade dividends, and thereby insulate their preferred consumption stream from corporate dividend policies.[1] Thus, in traditional models, the division of stock returns into dividends and capital gains is a financial decision of the firm that has no "real" consequence for investor consumption patterns.

Yet there are a number of reasons to think that dividend policy, and dividends more generally, may indeed affect consumption. Most obviously, the popular advice to "consume income, not principal" suggests a potentially widespread mental accounting practice in which investors do not view dividends and capital gains as fungible, as in the homemade dividends story and traditional theories of consumption, but rather place them into

We thank Yakov Amihud, John Campbell, Alok Kumar, Erik Hurst, Martin Lettau, James Poterba, Enrichetta Ravina, Hersh Shefrin, Joel Slemrod, Nicholas Souleles, and seminar participants at the American Finance Association 2007 Meetings in Chicago and at Babson College, the University of British Columbia, the Brookings Institution, the University of Colorado, HEC, INSEAD, Imperial College (University of London), the National Bureau of Economic Research Working Group on Behavioral Finance, the New York University Stern School of Business, the Stanford Graduate School of Business, and the University of Southern California for helpful comments. We thank Terrance Odean for providing data. Malcolm Baker gratefully acknowledges financial support from the Division of Research of the Harvard Business School.
    1. Miller and Modigliani (1961).

different mental accounts from which they have different propensities to consume.[2] This behavior is also consistent with a belief that dividends, unlike capital gains, represent permanent income. Less exotic but equally realistic frictions, such as transaction costs (of making homemade dividends) and taxes, can also lead an investor to favor consuming dividends before capital appreciation.

Although the dividends-consumption link is a potentially fundamental one between corporate finance and the real economy, little empirical research has pursued the issue. The reason is probably that the most easily available data on consumption and dividends are aggregate time-series data, which have several limitations. Among other challenges, such data require one to identify the effect of a smooth aggregate dividend series using a small number of data points; they combine investors and noninvestors; and they face an essentially prohibitive endogeneity problem: omitted variables such as business conditions will jointly affect consumption, dividends, and capital appreciation, making it difficult to establish the causality behind any observed correlations.

This paper studies the effect of dividends on investor consumption using two micro data sets that reveal and exploit powerful *cross-sectional* variation in dividend receipts and capital gains. The first is the Consumer Expenditure Survey (CEX), which is a repeated cross section with data on expenditure measures and self-reported dividend income and capital gains (or losses). Our CEX sample includes several hundred households per year between 1988 and 2001. The second data set includes the trading records of tens of thousands of households with accounts at a large discount brokerage from 1991 through 1996.[3] Although these portfolio data do not contain an explicit expenditure measure, they complement the CEX by allowing us to accurately measure net withdrawals from the portfolio, a novel dependent variable in its own right and a precursor to expenditure. The data set also allows us to measure the withdrawal rates of different types of dividend income, including ordinary, special, and mutual fund dividends, which allows for finer comparisons.

We start with an analysis of the CEX data. Our most basic approach is to regress consumption on realized dividend income, *controlling* for

---

2. Mental accounting behavior of this sort is discussed in detail in Thaler and Shefrin (1981), Shefrin and Statman (1984), and Shefrin and Thaler (1988).
3. This data set was introduced by Barber and Odean (2000).

total returns including dividends. The coefficient on dividend income thus captures differences between the consumption responses to dividends and to capital gains. We find that the coefficient on realized dividend income for total consumption expenditure is large, positive, and significant. This basic result is robust to a variety of control variables and estimation techniques, including specifications in first differences. It suggests that, contrary to classical models, the form of returns does matter for consumption.

We then use the brokerage account data in an effort to test the mechanism behind this effect; that is, we test whether dividends are indeed withdrawn from the household portfolio at a higher rate than capital gains. The data strongly confirm this. On average, investors do not reinvest ordinary dividends: the propensity to withdraw modest levels of ordinary dividends is unity. A fraction of mutual fund and special dividends is also withdrawn. On the other hand, very large dividends of any type are not fully withdrawn. As in the CEX data, the effect of capital appreciation on net withdrawals is uniformly smaller than the effect of dividends.

We conduct a variety of subsample splits and robustness tests on each data set. The results suggest that the apparent differential effect of dividend income on net withdrawals and consumption is at least partly causal; that is, it does not arise only because investors who plan to consume dividends in the future buy dividend-paying stocks. In particular, we find that investors tend to withdraw from both predictable and unpredictable components of dividends. For instance, investors often withdraw special dividend income, which is unpredictable by definition.

In sum, although the CEX and the portfolio data involve completely different households and somewhat different data concepts, they lead to qualitatively similar results, namely, that investor consumption is affected by the form of returns, not just the level. What drives this effect? We first evaluate explanations based on well-understood frictions such as transaction costs, taxes, and borrowing constraints. Upon inspection, however, none of these explanations is fully satisfactory. Borrowing constraints are irrelevant in this setting, because the substitution of dividends for capital gains has no overall wealth effect, and homemade dividends can be created by selling shares. Tax stories are varied, but none seems consistent with key aspects of the data. Transaction costs cannot account for, for example, the fact that households with low rates of portfolio turnover withdraw dividends at rates similar to those of high-turnover households.

Although our findings are surely driven by a combination of factors, mental accounting seems among the most compelling. The notion that many investors do not view dividends and capital gains as fungible seems especially plausible in light of the popular adage to "consume income, not principal." Mental accounting offers a natural explanation for both our main findings and certain finer results. For example, ordinary dividends are more likely to be mentally accounted for as current income than are large special dividends. Hence, the mental accounting framework predicts a higher propensity to consume from ordinary dividends than from large special dividends. This is what we find in net withdrawals (where we can measure different types of dividends). Tax and transaction cost explanations, on the other hand, do not predict this pattern.

This paper builds on earlier work that uses aggregate data.[4] Some papers have viewed the equality of the propensity to consume from dividends and corporate retained earnings, not capital appreciation, as the null hypothesis of interest and found weak evidence that corporate saving affects consumption. Other papers find little evidence that capital gains and losses have an effect on aggregate consumption.[5]

Our results also relate to evidence, consistent with the existing literature on the consumption response to windfalls, that consumers have a relatively high propensity to consume moderately sized cash windfalls.[6] It appears that ordinary dividends are treated like moderate-size windfalls. However, our analysis differs from the existing literature in that we focus on the *relative* propensity to consume two forms of income, dividends and capital gains,

---

4. See Feldstein (1973), Feldstein and Fane (1973), Peek (1983), Summers and Carroll (1987), Poterba (1987), and Poterba (2000).

5. To our knowledge, the only paper to use micro data in this context is a contemporaneous paper by Rantapuska (2005). He analyzes Finnish investor registry data and finds that there is little reinvestment within two weeks after receipts of dividends or tender offer proceeds. His results are broadly consistent with and complementary to ours, but there are some important differences. In particular, the CEX data allow us to look at actual consumption, not just reinvestment. Moreover, reinvestment may occur over horizons much longer than two weeks, an issue that our brokerage account data allow us to investigate. Finally, automatic reinvestment plans are absent in Finland but common in the United States, so the effect of dividends on consumption and reinvestment could be quite different in any case.

6. For instance, Souleles (1999) finds that consumption responds to federal income tax refunds whether or not the household faces borrowing constraints, and Souleles (2002) documents that consumption responds to preannounced tax cuts. Related studies in this vein include Bodkin (1959), Kreinin (1961), Wilcox (1989), Parker (1999a), Stephens (2003), and Johnson, Parker, and Souleles (2006).

holding their sum, total return, constant. More broadly, this study falls into a growing literature on "household finance."[7]

At the end of the paper, we briefly consider what our estimates imply for the response of aggregate consumption to the May 2003 dividend tax cuts. Alternative scenarios suggest a consumption stimulus in the range of $8.3 billion to $49.9 billion, which is not insubstantial in relation to a standard deviation of total personal consumption expenditure of $66 billion over the preceding five years.

Evidence from the Consumer Expenditure Survey

Our first data set is drawn from the Consumer Expenditure Survey, obtained from the Inter-University Consortium for Political and Social Research at the University of Michigan. The strength of the CEX is its detailed data on household consumption and demographics. Its comparative weakness, for our purpose, is that dividends and portfolio returns are self-reported and thus likely to be noisy. After introducing the data and definitions, we describe our empirical methodology and then present regression estimates of the effects of dividends on consumption.

Data and Definitions

The CEX has been conducted annually by the Bureau of Labor Statistics since 1980.[8] It is a short panel based on a stratified random sample of the U.S. population. Selected households are interviewed quarterly for five quarters and are then replaced by new households. As we discuss more fully below, the information on financial asset holdings and changes in these holdings over the preceding twelve months is collected in the fifth interview; data on dividends, interest received, other income variables, and demographics are collected in the second and fifth interviews and cover the twelve months before the interview date. We extract most of the variables from the CEX family files, but the data on housing and credit are from the detailed expenditure files.

7. See Campbell (2006).
8. We use the average estimates in the interview survey of the CEX, not the more detailed records from the diary survey.

Basic variables are as follows. We consider both expenditure on non-durable goods and total expenditure (which includes durables) as measures of consumption. A priori it is not clear which of the two consumption measures is likely to be affected more strongly by dividends. On one hand, nondurables expenditure is less lumpy and could be adjusted more smoothly in response to changing dividend income than durables expenditure. On the other hand, durables consumption is more discretionary than non-durables consumption, and so the household might have more flexibility to adjust durables consumption when dividend income changes. We define nondurables consumption, C, as the sum of food, alcohol, apparel, transportation, entertainment, personal care, and reading expenditure.[9] We use the total expenditure variable as provided in the CEX. In both cases we sum consumption over the four quarters from the second to the fifth interview. Dividends, D, are defined as (in the words of the survey question) "the amount of regular income from dividends, royalties, estates, or trusts" over the past twelve months. We also collect interest, I, received by the household. We use reported income after taxes, Y, as a proxy for total income.

Total wealth, W, is the sum of home equity (property values less outstanding mortgage balances) and financial wealth. Financial wealth is the sum of balances in checking accounts, savings accounts, savings bonds, money owed to the household, and "stocks" (which includes not only holdings of stocks and mutual funds, but also corporate bonds and government bonds that are not savings bonds), minus other debt.[10] Before 1988, information on the level of mortgage balances is lacking from the CEX, so we use the 1988 to 2001 data only. Also, whereas for financial assets we can measure changes over the twelve months preceding the fifth interview, for other wealth components (home equity and "other debt") we can compute only the change over the nine months between the second and the fifth interviews.

In their fifth interview survey participants are asked about the amount of securities purchased and sold over the preceding twelve months. This information allows us to decompose the change in the value of stock holdings into an active investment or disinvestment component and a capital

---

9. This definition follows Parker (2001).

10. The surveys do not ask respondents to include retirement assets, but they also do not ask explicitly to exclude them, so it is unclear whether some respondents include them.

gains or losses component. To compute the latter, *G,* we need to make an assumption regarding the timing of investment. We assume that half the reported investment was made at the beginning of the period and half at the end.

We employ a few filters to screen out unusual observations. We require that there be only one consumer unit (family) in the household and that the marital status of the respondent and the size of the family remain the same from the second to the fifth interview. We delete observations where any wealth component or income is topcoded.[11] We require that lagged financial wealth be positive and that a nonzero fraction of this wealth be invested in stocks or mutual funds. This last screen is the most significant: most (roughly 80 percent) of the households in the sample do not participate in the stock market. We use the consumer price index (CPI) to deflate all variables to December 2001 dollars.

Summary Statistics

Table 1 presents summary statistics for the CEX data. After applying the filters, we have 3,106 household-year observations. In this sample, mean nondurables consumption, reported in the top panel, is $15,042, and the median is slightly lower. Total expenditure, including durables, is three to four times as large. The next two panels report wealth and income measures. Financial wealth is typically around a third of total wealth. Total income, which includes dividends but not capital gains, has a mean of $56,566 and again a slightly lower median. Comparing the first and third panels, one sees that, on average, total income is slightly higher than total expenditure. For the households in our sample that hold some stock, average interest income is $1,264 and average dividends total $935.

As one would expect, the mean capital gain of $363 is relatively small compared with total income, and its average share in total income is roughly the same as the average share of interest income. Capital gains, however, do show significant variation across households. Note that the extreme values

---

11. To preserve the anonymity of respondents, the CEX administrators reset observations above certain thresholds on wealth, income, and some other variables to a cutoff threshold value. Before 1995 the topcoding level was $100,000 for many items in the survey. However, since the topcoding threshold applies to single items, the total value of variables such as income after tax, for example, which is calculated as the sum of many single items, can be much larger than $100,000. After 1995, the topcoding thresholds were raised.

Table 1. Annual Summary Statistics for the Sample Drawn from the Consumer Expenditure Survey, 1988–2001[a]

Dollars except where stated otherwise

Variable	No. of observations	Mean	Percentile 50th	Percentile 5th	Percentile 95th	Minimum	Maximum
Consumption							
Nondurables[b]	3,106	15,042	13,698	4,463	30,003	1,347	78,548
Total	3,106	48,076	44,582	15,549	91,892	4,955	201,559
Wealth[c]							
Financial	3,106	67,700	38,701	2,928	222,207	14	984,165
Total[d]	3,106	161,822	127,276	10,943	428,919	190	1,199,269
Income							
Total (Y_t)[c]	3,106	56,566	52,316	12,282	115,505	49	303,793
Interest (I_t)	2,869	1,264	145	0	6,383	0	86,391
Dividends (D_t)	3,106	935	0	0	4,751	0	144,658
Other	2,869	54,128	50,526	10,192	112,245	-13,823	302,238
Capital gains (G_t)[f]	3,106	363	0	-16,014	18,988	-301,407	181,503

Income components as percent of total income

Interest	2,869	4.2	0.2	0.0	19.1	–137.1	2,086.4
Dividends	3,106	2.1	0.0	0.0	12.0	–36.4	236.7
Other	2,869	89.3	97.5	45.3	122.2	–13,249.2	3,996.0
Capital gains	3,106	4.4	0.0	–27.3	38.2	–5,216.1	13,397.0
Controls							
Share of financial wealth invested in stock (percent)	3,106	56.19	60.26	3.76	97.94	0.05	100.00
Age of household head (years)	3,106	52	49	30	80	21	93
Family size	3,106	2	2	1	5	1	11

Source: Consumer Expenditure Survey and authors' calculations.

a. Sample is limited to households with the following characteristics: household has nonzero financial wealth invested in stocks; data on income and consumption are not missing; household consists of only one consumer unit (family); marital status of the respondent and family size remain unchanged from the second to the fifth interview; none of the wealth components are topcoded. All variables are converted to December 2001 dollars using the consumer price index as the deflator. All means, percentiles, and minimum and maximum values refer to the distribution of households with respect to the indicated variable.

b. Sum of food, alcohol, apparel, transportation, entertainment, personal care, and reading expenditure over the four quarters from a household's second to fifth interview.

c. Both wealth variables are lagged one period.

d. Sum of home equity and financial wealth, which is the sum of checking and savings accounts balances, holdings of savings bonds, money owed to the household, and stock holdings (stocks plus mutual funds plus small positions in corporate and government bonds other than savings bonds) minus other debts.

e. After-tax income over the preceding four quarters, as reported by households in their fifth interview. It includes income from dividends (defined as dividends, royalties, and income from estates or trusts) and interest income, but not capital gains.

f. Difference between the change in reported stock holdings over four quarters and the reported net investment in stocks during the same period.

are from wealthy households with a large amount of financial wealth. What the table does not show is that capital gains also vary widely across time: virtually all of the largest negative observations, including the minimum of −$301,407, originate from 2001, where the measurement period includes the crash in technology stock prices during 2000 and 2001.

The fourth panel shows that, on average, interest and dividends account for 4 percent and 2 percent of total income, respectively. The distribution is skewed, with a median household dividend income of zero. It is likely that some of the zero-dividend observations in the CEX result from underreporting of dividends by the interviewees. To ensure that our results are not driven by the zero-dividend observations, we include a zero-dividend dummy variable in our regressions.

Empirical Methodology

The null hypothesis of interest is that capital gains and dividends are fungible, which means that households should react similarly to a change in wealth whether it comes in the form of a capital gain or in the form of a dividend. In other words, only the total return should matter, not the split of that return into dividends and capital gains or losses.

To test this hypothesis, we run ordinary least squares regressions with specifications alternatively in levels, first differences, and log differences. We describe and motivate these in turn. Our basic levels specification is as follows:

$$(1) \qquad C_{it} = a_0 + a_1'\mathbf{Z}_{it} + a_2'\mathbf{F}_{it} + gR_{it} + dD_{it} + u_{it},$$

where C_{it} is household i's consumption in period t (in this specification, consumption is summed over the four quarters preceding the fifth interview); $\mathbf{Z}_{it}$ is a vector of household characteristics; $\mathbf{F}_{it}$ is a vector of financial variables that includes income, lagged wealth, and interactions with $\mathbf{Z}_{it}$; R_{it} is the total dollar return on stocks including dividends; and D_{it} is total dollar dividend income. In equation 1 the total stock return is already accounted for with R_{it}, and therefore $d = 0$ under the null. However, if for some reason a household has a higher propensity to consume from dividends than from capital gains, we expect $d > 0$.

The levels specification can be interpreted as an approximation to the consumption rule used by households. Different consumption models map income, wealth, and other household characteristics onto consumption in different ways.[12] We are agnostic as to which consumption model is most accurate. Our goal is simply to distinguish between models in which capital gains and dividends are fungible and those in which the effect of dividends diverges from that of capital gains. We approximate the consumption rule with a range of variables that may be relevant for consumption decisions, allowing them to enter linearly, quadratically, and through interactions to approximate the nonlinear consumption function.[13] In the end the levels specification boils down to asking whether two consumers in the same financial situation, with similar income, similar household characteristics, and similar total return on financial assets, but different *compositions* of total returns across dividends and capital gains, have different consumption.

Household characteristics in Z_{it} include the education of the household head (dummies for high school and college graduation), the age of the household head, age of household head squared, family size, family size squared, and a set of year-month fixed effects to absorb seasonal variation in consumption as well as variation in macroeconomic factors.[14] Financial variables in F_{it} include variables that proxy for future income and for current cash on hand, including income after tax (excluding dividends),[15] lagged total wealth, lagged financial wealth, the percentage of financial wealth invested in stocks, and the squares of all these variables. We also allow for interactions of age and family size with income, lagged wealth, and lagged financial wealth.

In interpreting an estimate that $d > 0$, the key question is whether this set of controls is sufficient or whether some omitted variable could be positively correlated with dividends, thus biasing upward the estimate of d. Although all of these controls should do a reasonable job of approximating households' consumption rule, it is difficult to fully rule out the possibility

12. Under the basic form of the permanent income hypothesis, permanent income determines consumption, and so the right-hand-side variables in equation 1 matter to the extent that they are correlated with permanent income. In models of buffer-stock saving with impatience, such as those of Deaton (1991) and Carroll (1997), consumption depends on cash on hand (liquid wealth plus current income) relative to its target level.

13. This approach follows Hayashi (1985), Carroll (1994), and Parker (1999b).

14. The quarterly interviews are conducted for overlapping ends of quarters, and so we need year-month fixed effects, not simply year-quarter fixed effects.

15. The income variable does not include capital gains (realized or unrealized), so we only need to subtract dividends. In specifications where dividends plus interest is the explanatory variable, we subtract dividends and interest.

of some remaining unobserved difference between households that hold dividend-paying stocks and those that hold nonpaying stocks. Moreover, wealth and capital gains in the CEX survey are inevitably measured with error, and this sort of measurement error problem causes an upward bias in our dividend coefficient, to the extent that dividends proxy for mismeasured wealth changes. To address this omitted variables problem we also run regressions in first differences, which removes any household fixed effects that could be correlated with dividend income.

Differencing is also useful for addressing an important endogeneity concern, namely, that any relationship between dividends and consumption is not causal but rather reflects the fact that households that expect to consume might decide ex ante to hold securities that pay the preferred consumption stream in the form of dividends.[16] While such an "ex ante effect" would also mean that fungibility does not hold, in the sense that some consumers anticipate their unwillingness to consume from principal and adjust their portfolio accordingly, it would not imply that the composition of returns has an effect on consumption. However, to the extent that any such ex ante effect is largely a household fixed effect, with only slow time variation, differencing should help to eliminate it.

Our basic differences specification is as follows:[17]

$$(2) \qquad \Delta C_{it} = b_0 + b_1' \mathbf{Z}_{it} + b_2' \Delta \left(Y_{it} - D_{it} \right) + g R_{it} + d \Delta D_{it} + e_{it}.$$

Since the CEX offers at most four quarterly consumption observations per household, we define ΔC_{it} as the difference in consumption between the

16. See Graham and Kumar (2006) and references therein for clear evidence of dividend clienteles. Graham and Kumar show that the allocation to and trades of dividend-paying stocks depend on investor characteristics.

17. This is not an exact difference of the specification in equation 1. We have only a single observation per household of lagged wealth, lagged financial wealth, and capital gains, and so we are not able to compute first differences. The most notable issue is that we do not first-difference returns. Including R_t instead of ΔR_t in the regression means that we are leaving a $-R_{t-1}$ term in the residual as an omitted variable. Fortunately, this should have little effect on our test, as the change in dividends from $t-1$ to t is not likely to be highly correlated with R_{t-1}. To the extent that there is some correlation, high R_{t-1} should forecast higher dividend changes from $t-1$ to t as firms' dividend policy responds with a lag to unexpected increases in profits. As a result, the $-R_{t-1}$ term in the residual is negatively correlated with dividend changes, and hence this should lead to a downward bias on the dividend change coefficient. This effect would bias the test against our hypothesis.

fifth and the second interview. As mentioned above, dividends and income in the CEX are measured over overlapping twelve-month periods leading up to the second and fifth interviews. We define ΔD_{it} and $\Delta(Y_{it} - D_{it})$ as the difference in the reported values. Because of the imperfect matching of measurement periods between ΔC_{it} and ΔD_{it}, the d estimate is likely to be biased toward zero. (The same is true for b_2.) Inferences about the magnitude of d will thus be difficult, but a significant positive coefficient will still be meaningful, as the null is still $d = 0$. As before, Z_{it} is a vector of household characteristics and time dummies. In some specifications we also include the level of second-quarter consumption as an explanatory variable, because it may pick up some noise that is introduced through the measurement-period mismatch between ΔC_{it} and the income variables.

Finally, to check whether the results are robust to functional form, we also try a third set of specifications with the change in the logarithm of consumption as the dependent variable. There we use an indicator variable for the *sign* of dividend growth as our key explanatory variable, because we lack a clear prediction about how consumption growth would be affected quantitatively by dividend growth. For example, a 10 percent increase in dividends would presumably have a different effect on the percentage growth in consumption when dividends are a small proportion of total income than when they are a large proportion. By using an indicator variable, we simply estimate the average difference in consumption growth between households with dividend increases and those with dividend decreases.[18]

Effects of Dividends on Household Consumption

Table 2 reports estimates of equation 1. Specifications in the first four columns use nondurables consumption as the dependent variable, and the rest use total expenditure. Independent variables in the first specification include total returns, dividends, and a dummy for zero dividends, plus a large number of controls. We find little economic impact of total returns on consumption, and no statistically significant relationship. But dividends are positively related to the level of consumption, and the effect is statistically significant. A one-dollar difference between households in

---

18. See Johnson, Parker, and Souleles (2006) for a similar dummy variable approach to analyze the effect of tax rebates on log consumption.

Table 2. Regressions of Consumption on Dividends, Total Returns, and Other Sources of Income Using Consumer Expenditure Survey Data in Levels[a]

	Dependent variable							
	Nondurables expenditure[b]				Total expenditure			
Independent variable	2-1	2-2	2-3	2-4	2-5	2-6	2-7	2-8
Total return on stocks ($R_t = G_t + D_t$)	-0.01 (0.01)	-0.01 (0.01)			-0.01 (0.02)	-0.01 (0.02)		
Dividends (D_t)	0.16 (0.04)	0.16 (0.05)			0.75 (0.14)	0.72 (0.14)		
Dividends lagged one period (D_{t-1})		0.01 (0.04)				0.14 (0.11)		
Dummy variable equaling 1 if $D_t = D_{t-1} = 0$	-694 (249)	-688 (253)			-915 (639)	-772 (641)		
Total return ($R_t = G_t + D_t + I_t$)			-0.01 (0.01)	-0.01 (0.01)			-0.02 (0.02)	-0.02 (0.02)
Dividends and interest ($D_t + I_t$)			0.13 (0.04)	0.12 (0.04)			0.58 (0.13)	0.56 (0.13)
Dividends and interest lagged one period ($D_{t-1} + I_{t-1}$)				0.03 (0.03)				0.06 (0.09)
Dummy variable equaling 1 if $D_t + I_t = D_{t-1} + I_{t-1} = 0$			-595 (267)	-566 (268)			-980 (684)	-922 (687)
No. of observations	2,796	2,796	2,410	2,410	2,796	2,796	2,410	2,410
R^2	0.52	0.52	0.52	0.52	0.63	0.63	0.64	0.64

Source: Authors' regressions using Consumer Expenditure Survey data.

a. Consumption, total returns, dividends, and interest income are for the four quarters from the household's second to its fifth interview. Lagged variables cover the four quarters ending with the second interview. All regressions include year-month fixed effects, household controls (family size, high school education of respondent, college education of respondent), income and wealth controls (income, lagged income, financial wealth, total wealth, and percent of financial wealth in stocks, with all wealth variables for the period ending four quarters before the fifth interview), and variables interacting household controls with other household controls (high school education × age, college education × age, family size × age, age squared, family size squared) and with income and wealth variables (financial wealth × age, income × family size, total wealth × family size, income squared, total wealth squared, financial wealth squared, and percentage of financial wealth in stocks squared). Numbers in parentheses are heteroskedasticity-robust standard errors. All variables in dollars are deflated by the consumer price index.

b. Defined as in table 1.

dividends received is associated with a 16-cent difference in nondurables consumption.[19]

The second specification reported in table 2 includes the first lagged value of dividends, as a first step toward distinguishing between the "ex ante" (endogenous dividend-consumption clientele) and "ex post" (causal) effects that d could capture. (As mentioned previously, our main approach to dealing with this issue is differencing, results of which follow below.) Specifically, if ex ante matching of anticipated dividends and consumption were the full story, then lagged and contemporaneous dividends should have about the same correlation with current consumption. As it turns out, however, the effect of current dividends is far stronger than that of lagged dividends, consistent with a causal effect of dividends on consumption that goes beyond ex ante matching.

The third and fourth specifications look at the sum of dividends and interest income, $D_t + I_t$. It seems possible that mental accounting consumers, for example, would treat interest income and dividend income similarly; likewise, spending from interest income allows households to skirt the transaction costs of selling bonds in the same way that spending from dividends avoids the costs of selling stock. The results provide some support for these analogies, as the effect of $D_t + I_t$ on consumption is similar to that of D_t.

---

19. Dividends in our data are measured before tax. Our regressions therefore show the relationship between before-tax dividends and consumption. If one were to use after-tax dividends, the fraction that goes into consumption would exceed 16 cents of every dollar. At the same time, however, it is also not clear how households treat taxes on dividends in a mental accounting framework. Since taxes on dividends are not withheld, the before-tax dividend cash flow and the tax payment occur at different points in time. To what extent households "integrate" the before-tax dividend cash flow with the subsequent tax payment, and to what extent it is more appropriate to view them instead as separate income streams with possibly different effects on consumption, are interesting questions. Unfortunately, we cannot answer them with the data at hand. Our focus instead is on documenting that dividends have an independent effect on consumption, and showing that before-tax dividends affect consumption is sufficient for that purpose. The 0.16 unit consumption effect of 1 unit of dividends could in principle be compared with the coefficient on labor income. However, in our specifications we see income and wealth variables merely as controls for all the potential determinants of households' consumption rule that could be *correlated* with dividends. We would prefer not to claim that we have a complete and correct model that would deliver the marginal propensity to consume out of income. Nonetheless, for the interested reader, the total effect of current and lagged income is 0.18 in regressions 2-1 and 2-2, 0.71 in regression 2-5, and 0.70 in regression 2-6. So the effect of after-tax labor income is in the same range as that of before-tax dividends.

The last four specifications in table 2 use total expenditure as the dependent variable. The estimated coefficients on D_t and $D_t + I_t$ are roughly four to five times those in the regressions with nondurables consumption on the left-hand side. As total expenditure is proportionally higher than nondurables consumption, on average these results suggest that dividend income is not used exclusively for nondurables consumption but rather boosts expenditure of all types. In all other respects, the results in these specifications are similar to those for nondurables.

It is interesting that no evidence emerges of a significant effect of capital gains; indeed, all the point estimates on total returns are negative. Of course, a low (but positive) propensity to consume capital gains would not have been surprising. Under the permanent income hypothesis, for instance, forward-looking consumers spread the consumption from an unexpected increase in wealth over their lifetime, so that the coefficient on total returns is predicted to be on the order of the real interest rate. From this perspective, what is striking about the results in table 2 is the far higher consumption from the return component that we label "dividends." The very large effects of dividends on total expenditure, in particular, strongly suggest that individuals consume dividends disproportionately in the period in which they are received.

Table 3 reports estimates of equation 2. The first specification includes total returns, the change in dividends, and other controls, including a dummy for zero dividends over the preceding and current twelve-month periods and, in some specifications, lagged consumption. Since we are regressing the change in *quarterly* consumption (from the second to the fifth interview) on changes in dividends measured over *twelve-month* periods (preceding the second and fifth interviews), one would expect the coefficient estimates on ΔD_t to be about one quarter of those on D_t in the levels specifications.

The results indicate that multiplying the coefficient estimates on ΔD_t by four does yield numbers that are at least of the same order of magnitude as the estimates in table 2, although somewhat lower, in particular for the nondurables specifications. The moderate decrease is consistent with some ex ante effect in the levels estimates, but it could also reflect the noise introduced through the imperfect matching of dividends and consumption measurement periods. Consistent with the latter possibility, controlling for lagged consumption, which should absorb some of the noise, raises the magnitude of the coefficient on dividend changes. But

Table 3. Regressions of Consumption on Dividends, Total Returns, and Other Sources of Income Using Consumer Expenditure Survey Data in First Differences[a]

Independent variable	Dependent variable[b]							
	Change in nondurables expenditure[b]				Change in total expenditure			
	3-1	3-2	3-3	3-4	3-5	3-6	3-7	3-8
Total return on stocks ($R_t = G_t + D_t$)[c]	-0.003	-0.002			0.006	0.004		
	(0.003)	(0.003)			(0.008)	(0.008)		
Change in dividends (ΔD_t)[d]	0.017	0.005			0.093	0.057		
	(0.009)	(0.010)			(0.029)	(0.028)		
Dummy variable = 1 when $D_t = D_{t-1} = 0$	-279	-127			-850	-833		
	(92)	(110)			(256)	(255)		
Change in income less dividends ($\Delta[Y_t - D_t]$)[d]	-0.001	0.000			0.025	0.034		
	(0.003)	(0.004)			(0.007)	(0.008)		
Total return ($R_t = G_t + D_t + I_t$)			-0.004	-0.004			0.003	0.002
			(0.003)	(0.004)			(0.009)	(0.009)
Change in dividends plus change in interest ($\Delta D_t + \Delta I_t$)[d]			0.009	0.007			0.056	0.056
			(0.008)	(0.008)			(0.028)	(0.028)
Dummy variable = 1 when $D_t + I_t = D_{t-1} + I_{t-1} = 0$			-268	-78			0	-732
			(105)	(127)			(0)	(277)
Change in income less dividends and interest ($\Delta[Y_t - D_t - I_t]$)[d]			-0.002	0.000			0.028	0.039
			(0.004)	(0.004)			(0.008)	(0.010)
Consumption lagged one period (C_{t-1})	-0.678		-0.703		-0.621		-0.627	
	(0.047)		(0.049)		(0.041)		(0.045)	
No. of observations	2,796	2,796	2,410	2,410	2,796	2,796	2,410	2,410
R^2	0.38	0.06	0.39	0.06	0.37	0.07	0.39	0.08

Source: Authors' regressions using Consumer Expenditure Survey data.

a. The dependent (consumption) variables are defined as the difference between quarterly consumption in the fifth (and last) interview and that in the second interview three quarters earlier. All regressions include year-month fixed effects and household controls (family size and high school education, college education, and age of respondent) and the following interactions: high school education × age, college education × age, family size × age, age squared, and family size squared. Numbers in parentheses are heteroskedasticity-robust standard errors. All variables in dollars are deflated by the consumer price index.

b. Consumer nondurables expenditure is defined as in table 1.

c. Total returns are measured over the four quarters before a household's fifth interview.

d. Difference between annual income items reported at the fifth interview and the second interview three quarters earlier. This variable is only an approximation of the first difference because income is measured after tax whereas dividends are measured before tax.

for the nondurables specifications overall, standard errors are large, and the coefficient estimates are at best marginally significant. For total expenditure, on the other hand, all coefficient estimates for ΔD_t and $\Delta D_t + \Delta I_t$ are statistically significant.

Table 4 presents results of the regressions specified in log differences. As mentioned above, the analysis here focuses on a dummy variable for an increase in dividends. Its coefficient measures the average difference in consumption growth between households with dividend increases and those without. In all specifications the coefficient estimates on the $\Delta D_t > 0$ dummy is positive, and it is significantly different from zero in all but the first two nondurables specifications. But even there the point estimate is economically large: the average household that experiences an increase in dividend income increases its consumption by 2 percent relative to the average household that does not.

We also experimented with splitting the sample by age. Dividends account for a bigger fraction of income in households headed by older individuals and are larger in absolute terms: the mean dividend income for households with a household head below age 65 is \$614, versus \$1,818 for households with a household head of age 65 or older. On one hand, the consumption effects of dividends could be stronger for older households, because those households might be more aware of their dividend income, and that income is more likely to be retirement income. On the other hand, older households could be less prone to consume from dividends according to a simple mental accounting rule, because dividends make up a substantial part of their income and the household might therefore think more carefully about spending them.

The results are as ambiguous as the theoretical predictions. For example, rerunning the base case total expenditure regression (regression 2-5) from table 2, with dividends interacted with a dummy variable for age greater than 65, yields a negative coefficient on the interaction term (−0.43) that is on the borderline of statistical significance (standard error of 0.23). Interacting age with dividends produces similarly insignificant results. This seems consistent with the argument that older households' consumption is less sensitive to dividend income. However, even taking the point estimates at face value, dividend income has a quantitatively more important effect on dollar consumption for older households than for younger ones, because the variation in dividends across older households is so much larger.

Table 4. Regressions of Consumption on Dividends, Total Returns, and Other Sources of Income Using Consumer Expenditure Survey Data in Log Differences[a]

	Dependent variable							
	Change in nondurables expenditure[b]				*Change in total expenditure*			
Independent variable	4-1	4-2	4-3	4-4	4-5	4-6	4-7	4-8
Log $(1 + [G_t + D_t]/FW_{t-1})$[c]	-0.034	-0.013			0.011	-0.002		
	(0.025)	(0.029)			(0.030)	(0.034)		
Dummy variable = 1 when $\Delta D_t > 0$	0.026	0.020			0.074	0.083		
	(0.026)	(0.029)			(0.024)	(0.028)		
Dummy variable = 1 when $D_t = D_{t-1} = 0$	-0.035	0.002			-0.017	0.017		
	(0.022)	(0.025)			(0.021)	(0.025)		
Change in log of income less dividends ($\Delta \log[Y_t - D_t]$)[d]	0.010	0.020			0.035	0.047		
	(0.012)	(0.014)			(0.012)	(0.014)		
Log $(1 + [G_t + D_t + I_t]/FW_{t-1})$			-0.031	-0.003			0.010	0.003
			(0.027)	(0.032)			(0.033)	(0.038)
Dummy variable = 1 when $\Delta D_t + \Delta I_t > 0$			0.036	0.042			0.029	0.047
			(0.018)	(0.021)			(0.017)	(0.019)
Dummy variable = 1 when $D_t + I_t = D_{t-1} + I_{t-1} = 0$			-0.036	0.007			-0.040	-0.003
			(0.020)	(0.022)			(0.018)	(0.020)
Change in log of income less dividends and interest ($\Delta \log[Y_t - D_t - I_t]$)[d]			0.009	0.022			0.035	0.049
			(0.013)	(0.015)			(0.014)	(0.016)
Log of consumption lagged one period (C_{t-1})	-0.441		-0.451		-0.456		-0.440	
	(0.021)		(0.023)		(0.021)		(0.023)	
No. of observations	2,764	2,764	2,369	2,369	2,764	2,764	2,369	2,369
R^2	0.26	0.06	0.27	0.08	0.29	0.07	0.28	0.08

Source: Authors' regressions using Consumer Expenditure Survey data.

a. The dependent (consumption) variables are defined as the difference between the logarithm of quarterly consumption in the fifth (and last) interview and that in the second interview three quarters earlier. All regressions include year-month fixed effects, household controls (family size and high school education, college education, and age of respondent), and the following interactions: high school education × age, college education × age, family size × age, age squared, and family size × age squared, and family size squared. Numbers in parentheses are heteroskedasticity-robust standard errors. All variables are deflated by the consumer price index.

b. Consumer nondurables expenditure is defined as in table 1.

c. Total returns ($G + D$) are measured over the four quarters prior to a household's fifth interview. FW is financial wealth, defined as in table 1, note d.

d. Difference between annual income items reported at the fifth interview and the second interview three quarters earlier.

As an additional robustness check, we have also removed capital gains outliers from the regression. In a survey like the CEX, which is based on self-reported information, the capital gains data are likely to have substantial measurement error. We want to ensure that the absence of a capital gains effect on consumption is not caused by a few large and potentially erroneous outliers. Winsorizing capital gains at their 5th and 95th percentiles, however, results in quantitatively similar estimates.[20] Perhaps more important, winsorizing the capital gains data leaves the coefficients on dividends virtually unaffected. Overall, it seems that the results are not unduly influenced by outliers.

In summary, the best available U.S. micro data on consumption suggest that *controlling for total returns,* dividends have a significant effect on consumption. The relationship is generally robust across specifications in levels, simple differences, and log differences.

Evidence from Household Portfolios

As already mentioned, a concern with the self-reported CEX data is that dividends and capital gains are likely to be measured with substantial error. It is not clear to what extent measurement error influences the foregoing results. Furthermore, the results would be made even more persuasive if we could verify the intermediate, mechanical step between receipt of dividends and consumption expenditure—that dividends are in fact withdrawn from brokerage accounts, and at a higher rate than capital gains. Our second micro data set, based on household portfolios, achieves these objectives and thus complements the CEX data. Furthermore, it allows us to study net withdrawals from investment portfolios, an interesting and novel dependent variable in its own right.[21] Finally, the larger sample size and detail of the portfolio data allow for certain robustness tests and sample splits that are not possible in the CEX data.

20. Winsorizing replaces all observations in the tails of the distribution (in this case the top and bottom 5 percent) with the observed values at the 5th and the 95th percentiles, respectively. In the base case nondurables regression (regression 2-1) in table 2, the coefficient on the total return drops to −0.02 with a standard error of 0.02. In the base case total expenditure regression (regression 2-5) in table 2, the coefficient rises to 0.01 with a standard error of 0.04.

21. In a paper that is similar in spirit, Choi and others (2006) use shifts in savings into 401(k) plans to identify changes in consumption.

Data and Definitions

Our household portfolio data set contains monthly position statements and trading activity for a sample of 78,000 households with accounts at a large discount brokerage firm.[22] To enter the sample, households were required to have an open account during 1991. For the sampled households, position statements and accounts data were gathered for January 1991 through December 1996. The full data set covers all accounts, including margin and retirement accounts, opened by each sampled household at this brokerage. For our sample we exclude margin accounts, Individual Retirement Accounts (IRAs), Keogh accounts, and accounts that are not joint tenancy or individual accounts. Securities followed include common stocks, mutual and closed-end funds, American depository receipts, and warrants and options held in these accounts. We focus on common stocks and mutual funds, which represent all, or nearly all, of most households' portfolios.

We use household-month level observations on net withdrawals, portfolio value, capital gains, and total dividends. Net withdrawals C (we use C in analogy to our earlier definitions, although, to be precise, we are not studying consumption but rather net withdrawals in this data set) are inferred as the starting value of portfolio assets A, plus capital gains G, plus dividends D, minus the ending value of the portfolio. That is, for household i,

$$(3) \qquad C_{it} = A_{it-1} + G_{it} + D_{it} - A_{it},$$

where the components that can be directly estimated include total portfolio value, defined as the product of price P and quantity Q held in investment j and summed across investments,

$$(4) \qquad A_{it} = \sum_j Q_{jt} P_{jt};$$

capital gains,

$$(5) \qquad G_{it} = \sum_j Q_{jt-1} \left(P_{jt} - P_{jt-1} \right),$$

where prices are adjusted for stock splits; and total dividend income,

$$(6) \qquad D_{it} = \sum_j Q_{jt-1} D_{jt},$$

where D_{jt} is dividends paid per share of investment j.

22. See Barber and Odean (2000) for more details about the data set.

For simplicity, we suppress the household i subscript on per-share quantities, prices, and dividends.

To estimate these quantities from the brokerage data, we pool each household's accounts to obtain positions and trades by household-month. The brokerage data do not directly identify dividend income; we match portfolio holdings to the stock file of the Center for Research in Securities Prices (CRSP) database to measure dividends on common stocks, and to the CRSP mutual fund file to measure dividends on mutual funds. For each stock and mutual fund in a household's portfolio at the beginning of the month, we use the monthly CRSP data on dividend distributions to calculate the dollar amount of dividends received during that month. We assume that each household holds until the end of the month the securities in its portfolio at the beginning of the month. For common stock dividends, we use CRSP distribution codes 1232, 1212, 1218, 1222, and 1245 to identify ordinary dividends, and 1262 and 1272 to identify special dividends.[23] We then total the dollar amounts of stock and mutual fund dividends across all stocks and funds in the portfolio to get a monthly measure of dividends.

The data contain outliers due to account openings and closings that do not reflect actual consumption and saving decisions. We exclude household-month observations where we cannot identify a CRSP mutual fund or common stock match for at least 75 percent of the account value at month $t - 1$, and we exclude households where the account value falls below $10,000, or dividends are missing in any of the months t to $t - 11$. This leaves 93,312 household-months of data on lagged account value, dividends, capital gains, and net withdrawals. These data still contain some outliers; for instance, the minimum value for net withdrawals as a percentage of lagged account value is $-2,807.7$, indicating a very large net inflow of funds in that portfolio. To prevent a few such data points from driving results, we exclude household-months in which net withdrawals exceed 50 percent in absolute value. This screen excludes about 0.96 percent of the sample.[24] The final sample includes 92,412 household-months.

---

23. This method follows DeAngelo, DeAngelo, and Skinner (2000).

24. The results below are robust to choosing different cutoffs. For example, they are quantitatively similar when 5 percent or 0.5 percent of the most extreme observations are eliminated. But some deletion of outliers is necessary: the most extreme *single* observation would otherwise account for about *one-third* of the sum of squared net withdrawals (even though there are close to 100,000 observations in total), making any regression analysis practically meaningless.

The household portfolio data have fairly clear advantages over the CEX data, but also some limitations of their own. One is that we usually do not know how large the accounts we observe figure in the household's total wealth, although for a fraction of the sample we do have self-reported data on household net worth.[25] In any case it is not clear that this should lead to bias as opposed to just adding noise. Another limitation is that we observe net withdrawals, not consumption. Although, as mentioned above, this means that the portfolio data are a useful complement to the CEX, a concern is that dividends and realized capital gains may be deposited into a cash account that we cannot observe. If so, and if a portion of these funds is eventually reinvested and ultimately reappears in the portfolio, we should not be counting that portion as potential consumption. Therefore an important part of the analysis below is to examine the extent to which contemporaneous withdrawals are offset by delayed reinvestment; for consumption, we care only about long-run withdrawals.

Summary Statistics

The size and composition of the portfolios in the sample are described in the top panel of table 5. The mean account value is $54,410 and the median is $28,430. On average, common stocks make up 82.7 percent of the total portfolio value, and mutual funds another 13.5 percent.

Changes in portfolio value are reported in the second panel. To make cross-household comparisons, we scale net withdrawals, capital gains, and dividend estimates by portfolio value at the end of month $t - 1$. The mean rate of net withdrawals by household-month in our sample is low, at less than 0.1 percent, and the median rate is zero. The average total monthly return is positive, at 1.1 percent. The average dividend income per month, 0.2 percent of beginning-of-month portfolio value, is a significant fraction of the average month's total return, but much less volatile.

The final two panels of table 5 break dividend income down by type of dividend. Dividend income is positive in just under half of all household-months. For these observations (bottom panel), an average of 77.9 percent of dividend income is due to ordinary dividends, with mutual funds account-

---

25. Data from the Survey of Consumer Finances for 1992 and 1995 show that 87 percent and 89 percent, respectively, of U.S. households with a brokerage account have only one brokerage account. This suggests that our brokerage account data often capture at least the entire wealth these investors have invested in brokerage accounts.

Table 5. Summary Statistics for the Sample Drawn from the Brokerage Portfolio Data, 1991–96[a]

Percent of assets in previous period except where stated otherwise

Variable	No. of observations	Mean	Percentile			Minimum	Maximum
			50th	10th	90th		
Portfolio composition							
Assets in previous period (thousands of dollars)	92,412	54.41	28.43	13.85	99.78	10.00	5,018.89
Common stocks	92,412	82.69	0.00	0.00	100.00	0.00	100.00
Mutual funds	92,412	13.49	0.00	0.00	0.00	0.00	100.00
Other assets	92,412	3.82	0.00	0.00	15.48	0.00	25.00
Withdrawals, dividends, and total returns							
Withdrawals (C)[b]	92,412	0.06	0.00	−0.70	0.99	−50.00	50.00
Dividends (D)[c]	92,412	0.20	0.00	0.00	0.55	0.00	102.39
Returns (R)[d]	92,412	1.11	1.06	−6.13	8.28	−73.96	153.47
Dividends by type, all households[e]							
Ordinary	92,412	0.12	0.00	0.00	0.43	0.00	2.96
Mutual fund	92,412	0.07	0.00	0.00	0.07	0.00	29.91
Special	92,412	0.01	0.00	0.00	0.00	0.00	102.39
Dividends by type as percent of total current-period dividends[f]							
Ordinary	44,509	77.92	100.00	0.00	100.00	0.00	100.00
Mutual fund	44,509	21.79	0.00	0.00	100.00	0.00	100.00
Special	44,509	0.30	0.00	0.00	0.00	0.00	100.00

Source: Barber and Odean (2000) and authors' calculations.

a. Observations are excluded when a CRSP mutual fund or common stock match cannot be identified for more than 75 percent of household account value in the period preceding the returns calculations; when the account value falls below $10,000, or dividends are missing in any of the months t to $t − 11$; for margin accounts; for accounts that are not joint tenancy or individual accounts; and when the absolute value of consumption exceeds 50 percent of assets. All means, percentiles, and minimum and maximum values refer to the distribution of households with respect to the indicated variable.

b. Monthly withdrawals are estimated as the household's account value in the previous period (aggregating across all eligible accounts held by the household) less the account value in the current period plus dividends and capital gains earned on the previous-month account holdings.

c. Dividends are calculated from CRSP and the CRSP mutual fund database on common stock and mutual fund account holdings at the end of the previous month.

d. Dividends plus capital gains, the latter defined as capital appreciation as taken from CRSP and the CRSP mutual fund database on previous-month common stock and mutual fund account holdings.

e. Ordinary and special dividends are identified from CRSP (distribution codes 1232, 1212, 1218, 1222, and 1245 for ordinary, and 1262 and 1272 for special dividends). Mutual fund dividends are identified from the CSRP mutual fund database.

f. Distribution includes only those households receiving dividends.

Figure 1. Net Withdrawals versus Dividends Received by Individual Household Account[a]

Net withdrawals (percent of total assets)[b]

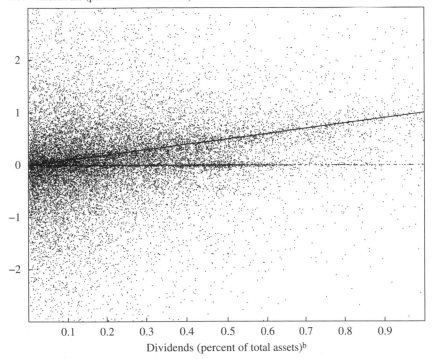

Dividends (percent of total assets)[b]

Source: Authors' calculations using data from Barber and Odean (2000).

a. Each observation represents activity (net withdrawals and contemporaneous dividends) in the brokerage account of a single household in a single month. Only household-month observations with positive dividends are included.

b. In period $t - 1$.

ing for almost all of the remainder. Special dividends are rare but can be very large when they do occur.

Effects of Dividends and Capital Gains on Net Withdrawals

Figure 1 is a scatterplot of household-month observations of net withdrawals against contemporaneous total dividends. The figure clearly shows two modal behaviors with respect to dividend income. The clustering of points along a line indicating a one-for-one increasing relationship between net withdrawals and dividends suggests that many investors follow a "zero (contemporaneous) reinvestment" policy; the clustering of points along a second line indicating a flat relationship suggests that many other

Figure 2. Net Withdrawals of Dividends versus Dividends Received and Total Returns, by Decile[a]

Percent of total assets[b]

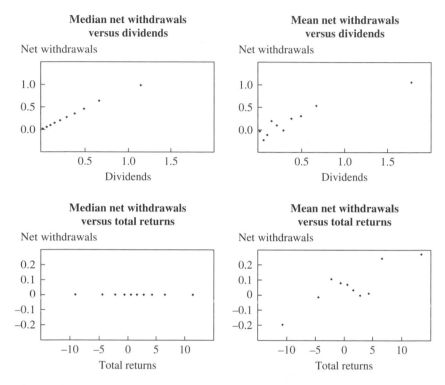

Source: Authors' calculations using data from Barber and Odean (2000).

a. Data for household-months with positive dividends are sorted into deciles according to the value of monthly dividends (top two panels) or total returns (bottom two panels); for the top two panels, an eleventh group consists of household-months with no dividends; median or mean net withdrawals is then computed for each group.

b. All data are expressed as a percent of household total assets in period $t-1$.

investors have an "automatic reinvestment" policy. The many thousands of observations that lie on neither line suggest a weakly positive relationship more generally. An analogous scatterplot of net withdrawals as a function of capital gains (not shown) reveals no visible patterns.

Figure 2 plots median and mean responses to dividend payouts. In the top left panel, dividend income is broken down into eleven groups, one for household-months with no dividend income and ten deciles for those with positive dividends. Within each group we plot median net withdrawals against median total dividends. The results suggest that the median household does not immediately reinvest moderate-size dividends: net withdrawals increase one for one with dividend income over the bottom several deciles; that is, in this range the first of the two modal behaviors noted in figure 1 is also the median behavior.

The top right panel of figure 2 depicts the mean responses to dividend payouts. We show mean net withdrawals for the zero-dividend group and for the mean level of dividends within each of the ten positive-dividend deciles. The figure again shows a positive relationship between dividends and net withdrawals. Note that the mean behavior is to contemporaneously withdraw most, but not all, of a relatively large dividend. (This could be consistent with a mental accounting practice in which the large dividends that result from cash acquisitions, for example, are treated not like ordinary dividends but rather as principal to be reinvested.)

The bottom two panels provide an initial look at the effect of total returns, again at the median and at the mean. The contrast with the picture for dividends confirms the CEX results: the effect of total returns appears to be much smaller. The bottom left panel shows that regardless of the level of total returns, the median contemporaneous net withdrawal is zero. The bottom right panel shows that, at the mean, very large total returns engender net withdrawals, and very low total returns net inflows. There is no clear effect in the intermediate range.

Table 6 reports regression estimates of the effects of contemporaneous dividends and total returns on the rate of withdrawals. The first three specifications include linear effects only; we then confirm the additional structure suggested in the figures using a piecewise linear specification. Specifically, we allow for a differential effect when dividends are in the top decile and a differential effect when total returns (primarily capital gains) are smaller than 2.5 percent in absolute value. Again suppressing the household i subscripts,

$$(7) \qquad \frac{C_t}{A_{t-1}} = a + d_1 \frac{D_t}{A_{t-1}} + d_2 \frac{D_t}{A_{t-1}} \left\{ \frac{D_t}{A_{t-1}} > 90\%ile \right\}$$
$$+ r_1 \frac{R_t}{A_{t-1}} + r_2 \frac{R_t}{A_{t-1}} \left\{ \left| \frac{R_t}{A_{t-1}} \right| < 0.025 \right\} + v_t.$$

It may be helpful to interpret the coefficients explicitly. Regression 6-1 indicates that, on average, investors have a propensity to contemporaneously withdraw dividends of about 0.35. Regression 6-2 shows an average

Table 6. Simple Regressions of Net Brokerage Withdrawals on Dividends and Total Returns[a]

	Dependent variable is net withdrawals as share of previous-period assets and regressions are					
	Linear			*Piecewise linear*		
Independent variable	*6-1*	*6-2*	*6-3*	*6-4*	*6-5*	*6-6*
Intercept	−0.01	0.04	−0.03	−0.06	0.04	−0.07
	(0.00)	(0.00)	(0.00)	(0.00)	(0.00)	(0.00)
Dividends as share	0.35		0.35	0.77		0.77
of previous-period	(0.09)		(0.09)	(0.09)		(0.09)
assets (D_t/A_{t-1})						
$D_t/A_{t-1} \times$ dummy = 1 if				−0.44		−0.44
$D_t/A_{t-1} >$ 90th percentile				(0.11)		(0.11)
Total returns as share		0.02	0.02		0.02	0.02
of previous-period		(0.00)	(0.00)		(0.00)	(0.00)
assets (R_t/A_{t-1})						
$R_t/A_{t-1} \times$ dummy = 1 if					−0.03	−0.05
$|R_t/A_{t-1}| < 0.025$					(0.02)	(0.02)
R^2	0.0025	0.0005	0.0029	0.0027	0.0005	0.0032

Source: Authors' regressions using data from Barber and Odean (2000).

a. All data are in percent. All regressions include an intercept (not reported). Heteroskedasticity-robust standard errors are in parentheses. The sample in each regression consists of 92,412 observations.

propensity to contemporaneously withdraw total returns of 0.02. Regression 6-3 shows that, for a given contemporaneous total return, investors have a 0.35 *higher* propensity to withdraw from the dividends component than from the capital gains component. Because the propensity to withdraw from contemporaneous total returns is almost zero, this also means that the total propensity to withdraw from dividends is around 0.35, as in the first regression. Although direct comparisons are not appropriate, it is interesting that these coefficients are of the same order of magnitude as the effects of dividends and capital gains on total consumption that we estimated in the CEX data (tables 2 and 3). And again, what is most striking is not that the coefficient on capital gains is so small, but that the coefficient on dividends is so large.

As an aside, it may seem that the relatively small coefficient on returns implies that the effect of capital gains on consumption is negligible, but this is not obvious. In fact, because the range between the 10th and the 90th percentile is about thirty times bigger for returns (from −6.13 to 8.28 percent of total assets) than for dividends (from 0.0 to 0.55; see table 5), the point estimates in table 6 suggest that the variation in withdrawals caused by dividends and capital gains may be of roughly similar magnitude. (Of course, we found at best weak effects of total returns in the CEX, and so, unlike in the case of dividends, we are unable to find any strong evidence that capital gains lead to withdrawal-financed consumption.) In any case, given our particular hypotheses, the appropriate focus is on the relative magnitude of the dividend and capital gains effects for a given change in wealth, not on the proportion of withdrawal variance explained by each effect.

Of the last three regressions in table 6, which estimate piecewise linear effects, the first indicates a propensity to withdraw contemporaneous dividends of 0.77 for typical levels of dividend income and of 0.33 (0.77 – 0.44) for unusually high levels. Regression 6-6 shows that, for small total returns, investors have a propensity to withdraw from contemporaneous capital gains of –0.03 (0.02 – 0.05; that is, they do not withdraw at all), whereas the differential propensity to withdraw contemporaneous dividends stays the same. All of these results are consistent with figure 2.

Delayed Reinvestment

Although the analysis so far suggests large differences in the withdrawal behavior of dividends versus capital gains, and hence that dividends may indeed affect consumption, several questions remain. One is whether a portion of dividends (and perhaps capital gains), rather than being withdrawn for consumption, may just have been temporarily moved to a cash account and later reinvested. To the extent that is the case, estimates based on contemporaneous effects will overstate the true potential impact on consumption.

To investigate this effect, we augment our previous model to allow for up to one year of delays in reinvestment. The resulting model is unsightly but easy to interpret:

$$
(8) \qquad \frac{C_t}{A_{t-1}} = a + d_1 \frac{D_t}{A_{t-1}} + d_2 \frac{D_t}{A_{t-1}} \left\{ \frac{D_t}{A_{t-1}} > 90\%ile \right\}
$$

$$
+ d_3 \frac{1}{11} \sum_{s=1}^{11} \frac{D_{t-s}}{A_{t-1}} + d_4 \frac{1}{11} \sum_{s=1}^{11} \frac{D_{t-s}}{A_{t-1}} \left\{ \frac{D_{t-s}}{A_{t-1}} > 90\%ile \right\}
$$

$$
+ r_1 \frac{R_t}{A_{t-1}} + r_2 \frac{R_t}{A_{t-1}} \left\{ \left| \frac{R_t}{A_{t-1}} \right| < 0.025 \right\}
$$

$$
+ r_3 \frac{1}{11} \sum_{s=1}^{11} \frac{R_{t-s}}{A_{t-1}} + r_4 \frac{1}{11} \sum_{s=1}^{11} \frac{R_{t-s}}{A_{t-1}} \left\{ \left| \frac{R_{t-s}}{A_{t-1}} \right| < 0.025 \right\} + v_t.
$$

In this specification, when the monthly total return is greater than 2.5 percent in absolute value, the long-run propensity to withdraw capital gains is $(r_1 + r_3)$. When smaller, the long-run propensity is $(r_1 + r_2 + r_3 + r_4)$. Likewise, the *differential* or "extra" long-run propensity to withdraw a small or medium-size dividend income realization is $(d_1 + d_3)$, and the differential long-run propensity to withdraw a top-decile dividend realization is $(d_1 + d_2 + d_3 + d_4)$. Note that in this setup any effect of delayed reinvestment shows up empirically as a *negative* estimate for d_3 and d_4 for dividends (r_3 and r_4 for capital gains), because dividends or capital gains that are reinvested will be detected as reduced net withdrawals as a function of the lagged variable.[26]

Table 7 shows that allowing for the possibility of a full year of delayed reinvestment does not alter earlier inferences about the effects of dividends. In the simple linear regressions (7-1 through 7-3), the contemporaneous coefficients are as before, and the effects of lagged dividends are nil. The full piecewise linear model (regression 7-6) shows that the long-run propensity to withdraw small or medium-size dividends is 0.73 (0.80 − 0.07) greater than that of total returns, statistically indistinguishable from the 0.77 gap in the short-run propensities to withdraw that we found in table 6, and thus indicating little or no reinvestment. On the other hand, the differential long-run propensity to withdraw very large dividends is still positive, but considerably smaller, at 0.33 (0.80 − 0.47 − 0.07 + 0.07), which is also the same as the estimate we obtained without allowing for delayed reinvestment. Finally, there is little evidence that capital gains engender reinvestment.

Thus accounting for delays in reinvestment does not change the conclusion that there is a large difference in the propensities to withdraw dividends and capital gains. Unless households in this sample are out of steady state, systematically accumulating cash balances (and doing so out of dividends, not capital gains), the results are consistent with the notion that a substantial portion of dividend income is permanently withdrawn to finance consumption.

---

26. In principle, one could also include individual lags of D_t and R_t instead of the summation terms, and then sum the estimated coefficients on the individual lags to calculate the total effect of delayed reinvestment. The approaches are equivalent when D_t and R_t and their lags, respectively, are uncorrelated. In our data these correlations are low, so both approaches lead to similar results. For simplicity, we report results from the summed lags approach.

Table 7. Regressions of Net Brokerage Withdrawals on Dividends and Total Returns Controlling for Effect of Delayed Reinvestment[a]

| | Dependent variable is net withdrawals as share of previous-period assets and regressions are | | | | | |
| | *Linear* | | | *Piecewise linear* | | |
Independent variable	*7-1*	*7-2*	*7-3*	*7-4*	*7-5*	*7-6*
Dividends as share of previous-period assets (D_t/A_{t-1})	0.35 (0.09)		0.35 (0.09)	0.81 (0.10)		0.80 (0.10)
$D_t/A_{t-1} \times$ dummy $= 1$ if $D_t/A_{t-1} >$ 90th percentile				−0.48 (0.12)		−0.47 (0.12)
Average of 11 monthly lags of dividends/assets $(\frac{1}{11}\,\Sigma_{s=1 \text{ to } 11}\,D_{t-s}/A_{t-1})$	0.01 (0.10)		0.01 (0.10)	−0.16 (0.17)		−0.07 (0.18)
$\frac{1}{11}\,\Sigma_{s=1 \text{ to } 11}\,D_{t-s}/A_{t-1} \times$ dummy $= 1$ if $D_{t-s}/A_{t-1} >$ 90th percentile				0.14 (0.18)		0.07 (0.18)
Total returns as share of previous-period assets (R_t/A_{t-1})		0.02 (0.00)	0.02 (0.00)		0.02 (0.00)	0.02 (0.00)
$R_t/A_{t-1} \times$ dummy $= 1$ if $\lvert R_t/A_{t-1}\rvert < 0.025$					−0.03 (0.02)	−0.04 (0.02)
$\frac{1}{11}\,\Sigma_{s=1 \text{ to } 11}\,R_{t-s}/A_{t-1}$		0.00 (0.01)	0.00 (0.01)		0.00 (0.01)	0.00 (0.01)
$\frac{1}{11}\,\Sigma_{s=1 \text{ to } 11}\,R_{t-s}/A_{t-1} \times$ dummy $= 1$ if $\lvert R_{t-s}/A_{t-1}\rvert < 0.025$					0.03 (0.06)	−0.06 (0.06)
R^2	0.0025	0.0005	0.0029	0.0027	0.0005	0.0032

Source: Authors' regressions using data from Barber and Odean (2000).

a. All data are in percent. All regressions include an intercept (not reported). Heteroskedasticity-robust standard errors are in parentheses. Data on household net worth and tax rate are self-reported and were supplied to the brokerage firm at the time the account was opened. The sample in each regression consists of 92,412 observations.

Household Characteristics

To check the robustness of our results, we split the sample across several household and portfolio characteristics (table 8). First, we split by portfolio size. These accounts are believed to typically represent a rather small fraction of the household's net worth, but for about a fifth of the sample we have self-reported data on net worth and tax rates supplied to the brokerage firm when the account was opened, so we can test whether the results extend to households for which the portfolio represents at least half of reported net worth. Second, we split by net worth itself. Third, we split by marginal income tax rate, which is obviously also a proxy for income. Fourth, we split the sample by portfolio turnover.

Table 8. Split-Sample Regressions of Net Brokerage Withdrawals on Dividends and Total Returns[a]

| | Dependent variable is net withdrawals as share of previous-period assets and sample is split according to | | | | | | | | |
| | Household portfolio value | | | Household net worth | | Household tax rate | | Household portfolio turnover | |
Independent variable	<Median	>Median	>Half of net worth	<Median	>Median	<Median	>Median	<Median	>Median
Dividends as share of previous-period assets (D_t/A_{t-1})	0.77 (0.12)	0.80 (0.13)	0.84 (0.43)	0.67 (0.32)	0.81 (0.36)	0.44 (0.29)	1.00 (0.40)	0.75 (0.07)	0.89 (0.19)
D_t/A_{t-1} × dummy = 1 if D_t/A_{t-1} > 90th percentile	-0.43 (0.15)	-0.48 (0.16)	-0.54 (0.44)	-0.16 (0.32)	-0.72 (0.36)	-0.32 (0.30)	-0.57 (0.41)	-0.45 (0.11)	-0.52 (0.21)
Total returns as share of previous-period assets (R_t/A_{t-1})	0.02 (0.00)	0.02 (0.00)	0.01 (0.01)	0.02 (0.01)	0.02 (0.01)	0.04 (0.01)	0.00 (0.01)	0.01 (0.00)	0.03 (0.01)
R_t/A_{t-1} × dummy = 1 if $|R_t/A_{t-1}|$ < 0.025	0.00 (0.03)	-0.08 (0.03)	-0.02 (0.08)	-0.07 (0.06)	-0.01 (0.07)	-0.07 (0.06)	-0.01 (0.08)	-0.02 (0.02)	-0.07 (0.04)
No. of observations	45,092	47,320	6,240	11,947	7,973	11,768	8,152	48,353	44,059
R^2	0.0042	0.0026	0.0012	0.0035	0.0010	0.0021	0.0026	0.0062	0.0029

Source: Authors' regressions using data from Barber and Odean (2000).
a. All data are in percent. All regressions include an intercept (not reported). Heteroskedasticity-robust standard errors are in parentheses.

The results suggest that the higher propensity to withdraw dividend income is broadly robust across the available household characteristics. Wealthier households appear more likely to reinvest very large dividends, but again standard errors are too large to allow any confident conclusions.

Composition of Dividends

Intuition and mental accounting theories suggest that it may be inappropriate to treat all types of dividends as equivalent. The nonlinear effects documented in figure 2 and table 6 may be due to differences in the treatment of special dividends and ordinary dividends, for example, and the reinvestment of dividends could also vary by type.

Figure 3 shows scatterplots of contemporaneous net withdrawals as a function of dividends of each type. An immediate result is that the "automatic reinvestment" mode is apparent only in mutual fund dividends (middle panel), likely reflecting formal elections to automatically reinvest. In addition, both mutual fund dividend recipients and many ordinary dividend recipients (top panel) engage in the "zero reinvestment" mode. Perhaps because large special dividends are so rare, there is little visually apparent pattern in how they are withdrawn or reinvested (bottom panel).

Figure 4 depicts median and mean net withdrawals by dividend type. The median behavior (top left panel) is to withdraw ordinary dividends dollar for dollar. For mutual fund dividends, the median behavior (middle left panel) is to withdraw nothing. For special dividends, on the other hand, the median behavior is to withdraw (bottom left panel). In means (the three right-hand panels), the patterns are rougher, as expected, and affected by the fact that the average household is a net saver into its portfolio over this period. Even in means, however, there are generally monotonic relationships for dividends of each type, although very high values of mutual fund dividends do not increase mean net withdrawals one for one.

These impressions are confirmed formally in table 9. Households' propensity to contemporaneously withdraw ordinary dividends (near unity) is 0.80 higher than their propensity to withdraw capital gains (near zero). Also, reflecting the automatic reinvestment policy that many mutual fund investors pursue, mutual fund dividends are withdrawn at a lower rate. The standard errors are too large to allow finer observations about reinvestment and how behavior changes for unusually large dividends. Small special dividends are withdrawn at roughly the same rate as ordinary dividends,

Figure 3. Net Withdrawals versus Dividends Received by Individual Household Account, by Type of Dividend[a]

Ordinary dividends

Net withdrawals (percent of total assets)[b]

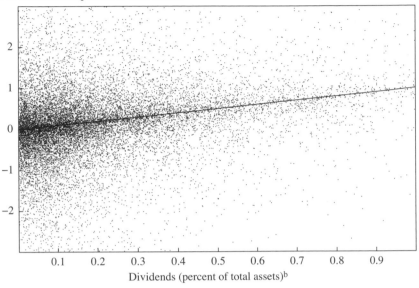

Dividends (percent of total assets)[b]

Mutual fund dividends

Net withdrawals (percent of total assets)[b]

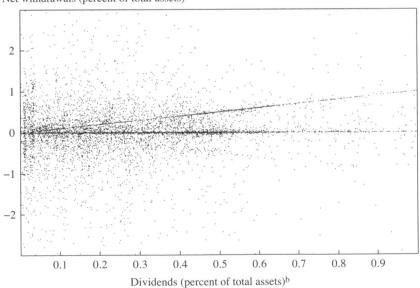

Dividends (percent of total assets)[b]

Figure 3. Net Withdrawals versus Dividends Received by Individual Household Account, by Type of Dividend[a] (*Continued*)

Special dividends

Net withdrawals (percent of total assets)[b]

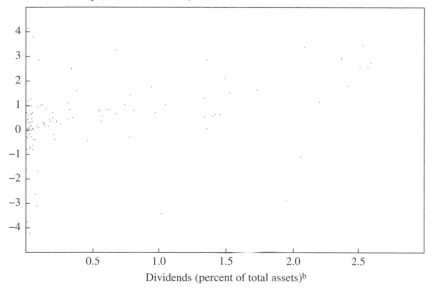

Dividends (percent of total assets)[b]

Source: Authors' calculations using data from Barber and Odean (2000).
a. Each observation represents activity (net withdrawals and contemporaneous dividends) in the brokerage account of a single household in a single month. Only household-month observations with positive dividends are included.
b. In period $t - 1$.

whereas the point estimates suggest that large special dividends are mostly reinvested.

Reverse Causality

Like the CEX results, the above results may be affected by an endogeneity problem. Some households may have chosen their ordinary-dividend-paying stocks and, to a lesser extent, their mutual funds ex ante in anticipation of consuming the dividends. If so, the evidence presented so far is insufficient to demonstrate that dividends, particularly ordinary dividends, have a causal effect.

For the ex ante effect to dominate, there would have to be a large predictable component in dividends such that it is feasible for households to match desired future consumption with anticipated dividend streams. Unlike

Figure 4. Net Withdrawals versus Dividends Received, by Type of Dividend and Decile[a]

Percent of total assets[b]

Median net withdrawals versus ordinary dividends

Net withdrawals

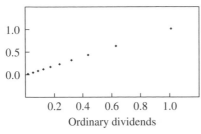

Ordinary dividends

Mean net withdrawals versus ordinary dividends

Net withdrawals

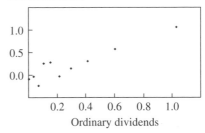

Ordinary dividends

Median net withdrawals versus mutual fund dividends

Net withdrawals

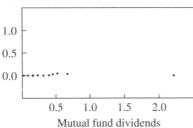

Mutual fund dividends

Mean net withdrawals versus mutual fund dividends

Net withdrawals

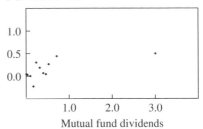

Mutual fund dividends

Median net withdrawals versus special dividends[c]

Net withdrawals

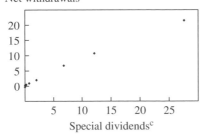

Special dividends[c]

Mean net withdrawals versus special dividends

Net withdrawals

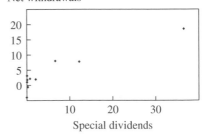

Special dividends

Source: Authors' calculations using data from Barber and Odean (2000).

a. Data for household-months with positive dividends are sorted into deciles according to the value of monthly dividends of various types; an eleventh group consists of household-months with no dividends; median or mean net withdrawals is then computed for each group.

b. All data are expressed as a percent of household total assets in period $t - 1$.

c. All dividends other than ordinary or mutual fund dividends; includes special dividends, liquidating dividends, and cash acquisitions.

Table 9. Regressions of Net Brokerage Withdrawals on Dividends of Different Types and Total Returns[a]

	Dependent variable is net withdrawals as share of previous-period assets and dividends are					
	Ordinary		Mutual fund		Special and other	
Independent variable	9-1	9-2	9-3	9-4	9-5	9-6
Dividends as share	0.82	0.71	0.40	0.35	0.75	0.75
of previous-period	(0.11)	(0.13)	(0.12)	(0.14)	(0.13)	(0.13)
assets (D_t/A_{t-1})						
$D_t/A_{t-1} \times$ dummy $= 1$ if	0.16	0.16	-0.26	-0.23	-0.46	-0.46
$D_t/A_{t-1} > $ 90th percentile	(0.12)	(0.12)	(0.13)	(0.13)	(0.19)	(0.19)
Total returns as share	0.02	0.02	0.02	0.02	0.02	0.02
of previous-period	(0.00)	(0.00)	(0.00)	(0.00)	(0.00)	(0.00)
assets (R_t/A_{t-1})						
$R_t/A_{t-1} \times$ dummy $= 1$ if	-0.02	-0.02	-0.04	-0.04	-0.03	-0.03
$\left| R_t/A_{t-1} \right| < 0.025$	(0.02)	(0.02)	(0.02)	(0.02)	(0.02)	(0.02)
Ratio of 12-month lag		0.13		0.05		-0.08
of dividends to total		(0.09)		(0.06)		(0.04)
assets (D_{t-12}/A_{t-1})						
R^2	0.0023	0.0023	0.0007	0.0007	0.0021	0.0022

Source: Authors' regressions using data from Barber and Odean (2000).

a. All data are in percent. All regressions include an intercept (not reported). Heteroskedasticity-robust standard errors are in parentheses. The sample in each regression consists of 92,412 observations.

in our CEX analysis, dividends here are scaled by portfolio value, which already reduces a potential source of cross-sectional predictability. As it turns out, scaled dividends *in total* (the sum of ordinary, mutual fund, and special dividends) are unpredictable from lagged dividends (that is, almost all variation is "unexpected"): twelve months of lagged dividends explains only 4 percent of the variation in scaled dividends in the current month. Hence reverse causality is empirically not a major concern in the total-dividends results that we reported above, unless we are to believe that investors are rapidly rebalancing their portfolios in anticipation of changing consumption needs.

Ordinary dividends on their own (scaled by beginning-of-period portfolio value), however, are highly predictable, with the one-year-lagged value explaining 57 percent of the variation in ordinary dividends, and the one-year- and three-month-lagged values together explaining 81 percent. Mutual fund dividends are less predictable, with the one-year-lagged value explaining 43 percent and the three-month-lagged value (as expected) adding little. Special dividends are, of course, unpredictable by definition. Therefore, like our results for total dividends, our results for special dividends are not subject to reverse causality concerns.

The question in terms of understanding causality is whether this predictable component in ordinary and mutual fund dividends alone explains consumption, or whether the unpredictable component also plays a role. To examine this, our second specification in table 9 includes the twelve-month lag of dividends as an additional control for the potential ex ante effect of expected consumption on holdings of dividend-paying assets. If the ex ante effect is the full story, and it is largely a household fixed effect with slow time variation, then the twelve-month lag of dividends and contemporaneous dividends should have about the same correlation with withdrawals. And if the ex ante effect is not a complete explanation, then the coefficient on the contemporaneous dividend should be larger than that on the twelve-month lag, since it captures effects on withdrawals related to the dividend component that is not predictable by D_{t-12}.

Consistent with a modest ex ante effect, the coefficient estimate on D_{t-12} is greater than zero for both ordinary and mutual fund dividends, although the effects are statistically insignificant. But the coefficients for the contemporaneous dividend terms remain highly significant and far larger than the coefficients on the twelve-month lag. We find similar results for mutual fund dividends.

These results suggest that reverse causality in the form of ex ante matching of withdrawals and dividends most likely plays a fairly modest role in the case of ordinary and mutual fund dividends. It plays even less of a role for our other results, including special dividends and total dividends. Although one cannot establish causality with complete confidence, all of the results are consistent with an important element of causality running from dividends to withdrawals—and, based on our analysis of the CEX data, to consumption.

Explanations

Our results from two quite different micro data sets suggest that investors have a higher propensity to consume from dividends than from capital gains. So far we have focused solely on documenting the basic facts and their robustness. Now we move on to potential explanations.

Borrowing Constraints

A standard explanation for the high sensitivity of consumption to current income is borrowing constraints.[27] However, borrowing constraints by themselves do not predict a different propensity to consume from dividends than from capital appreciation. The substitution of dividends for capital gains has no overall wealth effects, and homemade dividends can always be created by buying and selling shares. Hence, borrowing constraints are not an important factor.

Transaction Costs

The transaction costs of making homemade dividends are a more relevant factor a priori. Perhaps households recognize that reinvesting dividends, especially in the modest amounts that accrue in the smaller accounts in our sample, would require the purchase of an odd lot of shares, which carries relatively high transaction costs. To the extent such costs are substantial, rational households should prefer to consume from recent dividends rather than from selling shares.

The CEX data allow us to examine a transaction cost explanation in which the trading costs (and perhaps taxes) of creating extra homemade dividends constrain consumption. For households where income exceeds total expenditure, this constraint does not bind: these households could create homemade dividends at no cost by simply saving less. In unreported results, we find coefficients of a similar magnitude and generally lower standard errors (a coefficient of 0.90 with a standard error of 0.12 in a variation on regression 2-5 in table 2) among households that save income, casting doubt on this effect as a complete explanation.

The brokerage data results in table 8 also contain results that cast doubt on transaction costs as a complete explanation. First, if households view odd-lot transactions costs as an important consideration, one might expect a higher propensity to withdraw dividends in smaller accounts, which face the odd-lot costs more often. But the propensity to withdraw dividends appears not to depend on the size of the portfolio. Second, the propensity to withdraw dividends is similar, if not even higher, for high-turnover households. These households would be able, if they wished, to reinvest

---

27. A closely related, but behavioral, explanation for the high propensity to consume current income is hyperbolic discounting as in Angeletos and others (2001).

unwanted dividends at little, if any, marginal cost; in other words, again, the transaction costs are not binding.[28]

Taxes

Perhaps investors fail to fully reinvest dividends (that is, have a higher propensity to withdraw them) because they regularly withhold a portion for federal and state taxes. Of course, taxes can be paid from any source, and so this story is already founded on mental accounting. Table 8 shows that high-tax households are more likely than low-tax households to withdraw dividend income. In fact, the difference between the two groups is much too large (although standard errors are also large) to attribute to differential taxation: higher-tax households withdraw 100 percent of their small and medium-size dividends, far more than they would need to cover taxes.

Another tax consideration is the higher tax rate on dividend income than on capital gains that prevailed in our sample period. Perhaps households made mistakes ex ante in buying the highly taxed dividend-paying assets, or purchased them at a discount, and ex post, given their holdings, it makes sense to finance consumption through dividends rather than capital gains. But, to develop this same idea further, many households in our sample have individual stocks with accumulated capital losses at any given time, and so from an ex post tax perspective these households should consume from realized losses even before dividends. Yet empirically the evidence indicates that investors are more likely to sell winners than losers in every month except December.[29]

Different "Permanence" of Dividends and Capital Gains

The results might yet be reconciled with fully optimizing, forward-looking behavior if stock returns have permanent and transitory components. In our regressions we control for total returns, and so dividends do not add any additional information about the size of wealth shocks. But if changes in dividends are more strongly correlated with the permanent component of stock returns than with the transitory component, changes in dividends

28. See Odean (1999) and Barber and Odean (2000) for more general arguments that investors trade too much and fail to properly consider transaction costs.
29. See Odean (1998).

could provide some information about the permanence of wealth shocks.[30] In this case one would expect dividends to be correlated with consumption even after controlling for total returns.

At the level of the aggregate market, such an explanation could have relevance, although it would be difficult to distinguish it from other explanations such as mental accounting. A large proportion of the variation in market-level returns appears to be transitory, driven by temporary movements in discount rates.[31] There is also empirical support for the idea that aggregate consumption responds more to permanent than to transitory changes in asset values.[32]

However, our results are driven by *cross-sectional*, not aggregate variation in returns and dividends. This is an important difference, because movements in discount rates are systematic, driven by macroeconomic variables. As a result, the variation in returns induced by changes in discount rates is, to a large extent, a common component across stocks.[33] The time fixed effects in our regressions absorb aggregate movements in asset values, leaving the market-adjusted and largely permanent component of returns. Thus differences in the permanence of dividends and capital gains also cannot explain our results.

Mental Accounting

Finally, a higher propensity to consume from dividends than from capital gains is predicted by typical mental accounting theories. Indeed, Hersh Shefrin and Richard Thaler explicitly describe such a higher propensity as an important (but as yet untested) prediction of their mental accounting framework.[34]

---

30. Note that the issue of permanence of wealth shocks correlated with dividends is unrelated to the issue of whether companies set dividends equal to the permanent component of earnings. It is perfectly possible for a company's earnings to have a strongly transitory component while its stock returns are entirely permanent, and vice versa. The relevant issue here is the permanence of stock returns, not of earnings.

31. See Poterba and Summers (1988), Fama and French (1988), and Campbell and Shiller (1988).

32. See Lettau and Ludvigson (2004).

33. Vuolteenaho (2002) and Cohen, Polk, and Vuolteenaho (2006) find that only a small fraction of individual variation in stock returns around the market return is transitory.

34. See Shefrin and Thaler (1988).

In the Shefrin and Thaler model, households place wealth into one of three mental accounts: current income, current assets, and future wealth.[35] Shefrin and Thaler argue that the propensity to consume wealth categorized as current income, such as dividends, is greater than the propensity to consume wealth categorized as assets, such as capital and its appreciation. Household behavior in their model is thus consistent with the popular advice to "spend from income, not from principal."

Our main results fit well with these predictions. The propensity to withdraw and consume dividends is indeed far higher for dividends than for capital gains. Moreover, in the CEX data, the propensity to consume dividends is similar to the propensity to consume labor income, consistent with the notion that both are placed in the "current income" mental account.

In addition, mental accounting seems to offer more natural explanations for some finer aspects of our results than do the other theories. For example, it is natural that ordinary dividends and small special dividends would be categorized as current income to a greater extent than large special dividends, which, in turn, would be seen as still more income-like than capital appreciation. Under mental accounting, one would thus expect a higher propensity to consume ordinary than large special dividends, and a higher propensity to consume the latter than capital gains. Table 9 shows precisely this pattern.

The underlying psychology behind this sort of mental accounting is an important open question. Self-control and prospect theory are potential psychological roots.[36] Another, anecdotally plausible possibility is that although firm-level stock returns and cross-sectional variation in portfolio performance are largely permanent, individuals do not view them as such. A quasi-rational rule of thumb for a passive investor facing perceived stock market mispricing may then be to consume dividends but not capital gains.

Mental accounting of any type suggests bounded rationality, and so a natural way to close this discussion is to comment on the welfare consequences of deviating from fully optimizing behavior in this setting. We suspect that these consequences are relatively small for two reasons: dividends make up a small fraction of total portfolio returns, and more important, they have a much lower standard deviation. Corporations smooth dividends,

---

35. See also Shefrin and Statman (1984).
36. See Shefrin and Statman (1984).

adjusting only partially and only to the permanent component of earnings, as captured by the Lintner dividend model. This behavior on the corporate side limits the welfare consequences of an investor rule of thumb to consume from dividends.

The May 2003 Dividend Tax Cut

The Jobs and Growth and Taxpayer Relief Reconciliation Act of 2003 reduced the maximum federal tax rate on dividend income from over 38 percent to 15 percent. After taking into account state income taxes and their deductibility from federal income tax, the average household marginal tax rate on dividends fell from 32.1 percent in 2002 to 18.5 percent in 2003.[37]

The tax cuts were designed to stimulate economic growth. Reducing the double taxation of corporate profits was expected to lower the cost of capital and thereby spur capital formation and growth, although there is a debate in the economics literature over whether this view is true. An alternative view is that retained earnings are the marginal source of finance for new investment projects. In that case taxes on dividends would have no effect on real investment.[38]

Our results suggest that the dividend tax cut of 2003 may have had another, more direct impact on growth through its impact on household consumption, just as the Microsoft dividend might have had a measurable impact on consumer spending. An interesting exercise then is to use our estimates from (pre-2003) micro data to assess how much the increase in after-tax dividend income may have increased aggregate consumption.

An important preliminary note is that taxes are not withheld when dividends are paid, and so the May 2003 tax cut did not have a direct effect on the cash flows occurring on the date when the dividends are paid. Our estimates are based on how individuals' consumption reacts at that point. So, for our estimates to be valid measures of the propensity to consume from *after-tax* dividend income, we need to assume that individuals' monthly withdrawal behavior fully reflects the relevant taxes that are to be paid when the tax year ends. For this exercise, we will assume that our estimated

37. These numbers are from Poterba (2004).
38. See Auerbach and Hassett (2006) for a discussion of the two views on the investment effect of dividend taxes and of the evidence in the context of the 2003 tax cuts.

marginal propensities to consume before-tax dividends in tables 2 and 6 come from a *constant* marginal propensity to consume (MPC) after-tax dividends, or

$$(9) \qquad MPC_{pre-tax,t} = MPC_{after-tax} \times (1 - \tau_t),$$

where τ is the tax rate.

A second caveat is that our estimates come from a representative sample of U.S. households. Dividends are paid disproportionately to the highest-income households, which are perhaps more sophisticated in their financial planning and less likely to use mental accounting rules of thumb. In this regard it is a useful feature of our CEX analysis that the variables are defined in dollars, which implies that the regressions put more weight on households with higher income and higher dividends. Moreover, the sample is restricted to stockholders. This ensures that our results are driven by households with substantial income. Nevertheless, it is possible that we still are not capturing the behavior of the richest households. For now we will assume that our estimates apply, but we interpret them as upper-bound impacts.

We first consider a scenario in which the dividend tax cut has no effect on the supply of dividends by corporations. In this case the impact on consumption is simply the change in the before-tax MPC times dividends D. Rearranging equation 9 yields

$$(10) \quad \left(MPC_{pre-tax,2003} - MPC_{pre-tax,2002} \right) \times D = \left(\frac{1 - \tau_{2003}}{1 - \tau_{2002}} - 1 \right) \times MPC_{pre-tax,2002} \times D.$$

According to the IRS *Statistics of Income,* individuals reported dividend income of \$103 billion in 2002. With a fall in the dividend income tax rate from 32.1 percent to 18.5 percent and an initial before-tax MPC of 0.4—a number that appears to be around the middle of our baseline estimates—we obtain \$8.3 billion as the estimated effect on aggregate consumption. Table 3 points to a before-tax MPC somewhat lower than 0.4, whereas table 2 suggests a value above 0.7. At this high end, where the after-tax MPC is essentially 1.0, the estimated effect for 2003 is \$14.0 billion.

A second scenario is that the dividend tax cut, by reducing the relative tax disadvantage on dividend income, may have increased the supply of dividends. Raj Chetty and Emmanuel Saez suggest that the tax cut caused an increase in dividend payouts.[39] In fact, they find that a sample of firms with limited tax incentives—the largest shareholder is not taxable—did not increase the rate at which they initiated dividends, for example, and thus they attribute the entire change to tax effects. On the other hand, Alon Brav and coauthors surveyed hundreds of financial executives in the wake of the tax cut and found that they only occasionally cite the tax cut as a motivator of payout decisions.[40] Stock market sentiment may also have affected dividend behavior during this period, as some firms initiated or increased dividends in an attempt to distance themselves from the non-dividend-paying "new economy" firms that had crashed in 2000 and 2001.[41] In any case, suppose for the sake of argument that the entirety of the observed change in dividends from 2002 to 2003, from $103 billion to $115 billion, was due to the tax cut. Recall that the before-tax MPC rises as the tax rate falls, from 0.4 to 0.48:

$$(11) \qquad MPC_{pre-tax,2003} = MPC_{pre-tax,2002} \times \frac{1 - \tau_{2003}}{1 - \tau_{2002}}.$$

Applying this estimate to the before-tax increase in dividends, the supply channel adds another $5.8 billion to the effect on consumption, for a total effect of $14.1 billion. At the higher MPC estimate, the total effect is $23.8 billion.

Dividends in the *Statistics of Income* continued to increase in 2004, to $147 billion, including the large Microsoft payout; hence this calculation might still underestimate the effect for subsequent years. Let us suppose the tax cut took two years to have its full effect, and therefore take the rise from the 2002 to the 2004 value as the supply increase. Then the estimates of total consumption effects in the previous paragraph rise to $29.4 billion and $49.9 billion, respectively.

To gain some perspective on these estimated changes in consumption, which range from $8.3 billion to $49.9 billion, consider that total personal consumption expenditure in 2003 was $7.7 trillion, and that the average increase in total personal consumption over the previous five years was

---

39. See Chetty and Saez (2005) and Poterba (2004).
40. See Brav and others (2007).
41. Baker and Wurgler (2004a, 2004b) study how investor sentiment affects dividend payment.

$365 billion, with a standard deviation of $66 billion. Against this standard deviation, effects on the order of those estimated above do not seem trivial.

Conclusion

How investors consume from dividends versus capital gains is important to a range of questions in corporate finance, macroeconomics, behavioral economics, and tax policy. Classical theories suggest that investor consumption patterns are independent of how returns are split into dividends and capital gains, whereas mental accounting and various economic frictions motivate an alternative hypothesis that investors are relatively more likely to consume dividends. The contribution of this study is to exploit the cross-sectional variation in two household-level data sets in order to document the effect of dividends on consumption.

The main finding is that consumption indeed responds much more strongly to returns in the form of dividends than to returns in the form of capital gains. Data from the Consumer Expenditure Survey show a strong relationship between household consumption and dividends, after controlling for total returns (which include dividends). A sample of household portfolio data also shows that dividends are much more likely than capital gains to generate withdrawals from investment accounts, thus illustrating the mechanical process of translating dividend income into consumption. We stress that the interesting result is not that the propensity to consume capital gains is rather low—indeed, it should be low for forward-looking consumers acting according to the permanent income hypothesis—but that the propensity to consume dividends is so high. A review of alternative explanations suggests that the results may in part reflect mental accounting processes of the sort summed up in the adage, "consume income, not principal."

Comments and Discussion

James Poterba: This paper by Malcolm Baker, Stefan Nagel, and Jeffrey Wurgler asks whether the division of corporate earnings between retentions and payouts affects consumer spending. The authors bring novel insight and a creative empirical strategy to bear on a question that has a long pedigree in empirical macroeconomics. Early attempts to model aggregate consumption related consumer spending to disposable income and household wealth. Estimates of the marginal propensity to consume out of income were typically an order of magnitude greater than estimates of the marginal propensity to consume out of wealth. Taken at face value, such estimates implied that if a firm reduced its retained earnings by a dollar, thereby reducing its share price, and paid a dollar of dividends, consumer spending would rise by the difference between the marginal propensity to consume out of disposable income and the marginal propensity to consume out of wealth. Some researchers argued that, to avoid this stark result, consumption should depend on corporate retained earnings as well as disposable income. This suggestion led to an empirical debate about whether consumers "pierce the corporate veil" and recognize the firm's underlying earnings, or fail to do this and instead consume at different rates out of different components of corporate earnings.

In contemporary textbook models of consumer behavior, current household spending depends on the present discounted value of current and future labor earnings and on current financial assets. In the absence of taxes and other institutional rigidities, a dividend payment, as opposed to a capital gain, should not change a household's net financial assets and therefore should not affect consumer spending. Yet the possibility remains that different ways of transmitting earnings to shareholders have different effects on consumption. Various models in behavioral economics can

277

justify such an outcome. This paper offers intriguing evidence in support of these models.

In linking this paper and its findings to the debate concerning the corporate veil, it is important to recognize that even if one does not reject the null hypothesis that consumers have equal propensities to consume from dividends and other components of equity returns, the corporate payout decision may still affect consumption. To illustrate this possibility, assume that a project generates a dollar of after-tax corporate profits for an equity-financed firm. The firm could distribute the dollar as a dividend payment, or it could retain the dollar. In the latter case the firm's share price would be higher, by dV, than if the earnings were distributed to the shareholders. The change in consumption spending from the dividend payout would be MPC_{div}, and the change in the retained earnings case would be $MPC_{cg}dV$. Even if $MPC_{div} = MPC_{cg}$, which is the proposition that the authors study, it is still possible that distributing earnings could affect consumption if dV is not equal to unity. Tax considerations could break this equality, for example if retained earnings may be distributed in the future by repurchasing shares and therefore face a lower tax burden than dividend payments. Corporate governance factors may also come into play. If a dollar of retained earnings may be reinvested by the management team at a rate of return below that demanded by the marketplace, but not low enough to warrant shareholders incurring the costs of removing the managers, then dV may be less than 1.

Previous researchers have found it difficult to distinguish the consumption impact of dividends from that of accruing capital gains, because there are few exogenous shocks to corporate distribution policy that cannot be plausibly linked in other ways to consumer spending. This paper presents two ingenious tests of whether households consume at different rates from dividend income and from accruing capital gains. By presenting empirical findings suggesting that dividends increase consumption more than do accrued capital gains of equal value, this paper suggests that policies that encourage firms to distribute earnings may increase aggregate consumer spending.

The identification problem confronting earlier studies is easily summarized. In time-series data, most of the variation in the mix between dividends and retained earnings is due to shocks to corporate earnings. Such shocks may affect consumer spending through their informational effect on future earnings prospects, as well as through coincident changes in dividends or retentions. One strategy for avoiding this endogeneity, which I exploited in a previous study of the corporate veil,[1] is to use changes in the relative tax treatment of dividend income and of capital gains as an instrumental variable for corporate payout.

This paper takes a different tack. It exploits cross-sectional differences in the dividend payments received by different households. The authors control for the total return earned by different investors and study how the *composition* of this return between dividends and capital gains affects consumer spending. This approach avoids time-series endogeneity, but it brings with it a new set of concerns about the factors that determine cross-sectional differences in portfolio dividend yields. The authors recognize the potential for omitted variables to contaminate their cross-sectional inferences, and they control for many household-specific attributes that may lead to differences in both consumption behavior and dividend receipts. The identification hinges on whether one believes that even after controlling for many household attributes, there may still be some omitted variables that affect *both* the choice of portfolio dividend yield and consumption outlays. To completely explain the results, such an omitted variable would need to move in tandem with both dividends and consumer spending, since the paper's key empirical findings emerge when the household data are differenced. An example illustrates the potential problem. Household-level empirical work on portfolio structure has shown that a household's marginal tax rate is correlated with the dividend yield of its stock portfolio. If the marginal tax rate is also correlated with a household's consumption spending, the possibility of a spurious relationship arises. If household tax rates change over time, thereby inducing changes in both portfolio dividend yield and consumer spending, then even differencing may not solve the problem.

The paper begins with an analysis of Consumer Expenditure Survey (CEX) data. A key limitation of these data is the topcoding of income components, including dividends. The topcoding limits information on the behavior of the high-income, high-net-worth investors who hold most of the corporate stock outside of retirement accounts and pension plans. The authors omit from their sample all survey respondents who have a topcoded entry. This restriction to lower-income households may limit the extent to which the empirical findings can be used to describe the impact of changing

---

1. Poterba (1987).

Table 1. Distribution of Taxable Dividends by Household Income, 2004

	Taxpayers reporting dividends		Dividends reported	
Adjusted gross income (thousands of dollars)	Millions	Percent of all taxpayers reporting dividends	Billions of dollars	Percent of all dividends reported
< 10	3.55	11.6	5.8	3.9
10–50	9.91	32.3	19.0	13.0
50–100	9.41	30.7	22.6	15.4
100–200	5.41	17.6	23.8	16.2
200–500	1.80	5.9	20.3	13.8
500–1,000	0.38	1.2	11.3	7.7
> 1,000	0.22	0.7	44.1	30.0
All households	30.69	100.0	146.8	100.0

Source: U.S. Treasury Department, *Statistics of Income: Individual Income Tax Returns,* table 1.4.

payout patterns. My table 1 presents information on the concentration of dividend income on individual income tax returns filed in 2004. Just over half of all dividends are received by taxpayers with adjusted gross income of more than $200,000—a group that includes fewer than 8 percent of all taxpayers with dividend income, and about 2 percent of all taxpayers. Data from the Survey of Consumer Finances suggest that households in the top decile of the wealth distribution receive roughly 90 percent of all dividends. In contrast, the highest-income respondent in the CEX has an annual income of just over $300,000, and the mean annual consumption expenditure is approximately $60,000. This underscores the absence of households in the top strata of income and wealth.

The reason topcoding and the absence of high-income households are concerns is that the behavior of these households may differ from that of lower-income households. Their consumption decisions, in particular, may be less sensitive to cash flow considerations. This possibility suggests the need for caution in using the coefficient estimates in the current study to estimate how broad changes in corporate dividend payouts may affect consumer spending.

Another concern with the CEX is that the measure of accrued capital gains is very noisy. There are two sources of measurement error in the equity capital gains data. The first is that financial asset values are self-reported. If households do not know the current value of their stock portfolios at the time of the survey, this will translate into noisy data. The second problem, which may be even more important, is that when households sell stock between two survey dates, there is no record of the timing of the sale. This requires assuming an arbitrary time pattern for such sales, inducing further measurement error. If capital gains are measured with substantial error, while cash dividend income is measured precisely, standard errors-in-variables arguments will lead to an estimate of the marginal propensity to consume from capital gains that is biased toward zero. Such a bias could explain the paper's empirical results in both the level and difference specifications.

The second part of the paper focuses on withdrawals from brokerage accounts. This component of the paper is particularly innovative, and evidence on whether investors withdraw dividends from their accounts or reinvest them is of independent interest. The authors note that withdrawals are not the same as consumption, and that message bears emphasis. The CEX-based project uses a measure of consumption as the dependent variable. The brokerage account-based project implicitly assumes that withdrawals are consumed—an assumption that may not be valid for all households. The findings on withdrawal patterns are nevertheless intriguing. The data suggest that relatively few investors reinvest dividend payments. This is particularly true for ordinary dividends; large special dividends do appear to be reinvested.

A key limitation of this study, and of other studies that have used information provided by financial institutions, is the restriction to information from a single brokerage firm. If investors hold assets at multiple firms, cross-firm reinvestment decisions will look like withdrawal or consumption decisions from the vantage point of a single firm. This is a concern but it may not be a serious empirical limitation. In the 2004 Survey of Consumer Finances, 87 percent of households with a brokerage account have only one. Investors with multiple brokerage accounts are likely to account for a disproportionate share of total dividend income and total stock ownership, but, at least for middle-income households, using data from a single brokerage firm is likely to provide valuable insights.

A more subtle concern involves the *timing* of reinvestment decisions, even decisions with respect to the same brokerage account. An investor who receives a dividend check, deposits it in a money market account or checking account that is not visible to the brokerage firm, and then decides after some time to purchase additional shares of stock will appear to have consumed the dividend if the reinvestment does not happen within the same month as the dividend payment. If dividends are uniformly distributed throughout each month, that leaves on average only two weeks for the investor to make the reinvestment decision before the end-of-month cutoff. The authors recognize this potential problem and note that they can reduce it by widening the time interval over which they measure dividend income and withdrawals. They painstakingly track net account inflows and withdrawals as a function of lagged dividend payments; this offers another way of attacking the measurement interval problem.

One concern about the brokerage account data used in this study is whether they are representative of the broader population of U.S. households. Different broker types may attract different types of clients. A discount broker, for example, is likely to attract investors who are more inclined to trade than the population at large, whereas a full-service broker may attract clients who view themselves as needing disproportionate levels of advice and assistance in making financial decisions. It is not clear how best to control for any differences between these groups, or between them and investors more generally.

The paper concludes with an interesting analysis of how changes in the relative tax burden on dividends and capital gains in 2003 may have affected consumer spending. Three potential effects of the Jobs and Growth Tax Relief Reconciliation Act of 2003 (JGTRRA) warrant consideration. First, the tax reform reduced the average tax burden on dividends paid to U.S. investors, thereby increasing the disposable income of these taxpayers. This might increase consumer spending. Second, JGTRRA reduced the tax penalty for paying dividends relative to retained earnings, thereby increasing the incentive for firms to pay dividends. Several studies suggest that this led to an increase in dividend payments.[2] If the marginal propensity to consume from dividends is greater than that from retention-induced capital gains, this effect would also support higher consumption. In light of the empirical evidence in this study, higher dividend payouts might increase consumer spending. Finally, the tax change *may* have provided new incentives for investment in the corporate sector. The caution here arises from the temporary nature of the dividend tax cut. A permanent cut in the dividend tax would reduce the burden on payouts from new corporate sector investments, making it more attractive for firms to

2. See, in particular, Chetty and Saez (2005).

issue new shares and use the proceeds to undertake new investments. The temporary nature of the tax cut undermines this incentive, since relatively few projects would be expected to generate returns before the expiration of the dividend tax relief. The magnitude of the investment incentives associated with the dividend tax change is unclear, as is the corresponding countervailing force that might dampen the other pro-consumption effects of JGTRRA. If investors expected the dividend tax relief to be permanent— and much of the rhetoric at the time of JGTRRA's passage suggested that this might be the case—then the investment effects associated with the tax change could weaken or reverse the pro-consumption effects described above.

Let me close with two observations about the research opportunities, and needs, associated with the 2003 change in tax rates. First, on the opportunities, this paper does not exploit JGTRRA as a source of variation that could be used to study the extent to which consumer spending responds to dividend income. Consider the impact of the Microsoft special dividend of December 2004, which the authors cite. This was a $32 billion extraordinary payout that occurred after JGTRRA reduced marginal dividend tax rates. This dividend provides an ideal experiment—or would if only one could isolate and study the behavior of Microsoft shareholders. It represented a transfer of $32 billion in cash from the firm to its shareholders, and if it were possible to compare Microsoft shareholders, who received dividend income and a concomitant reduction in the value of their equity portfolio, with other shareholders who did not have Microsoft stock in their portfolios, it might be possible to test the authors' hypothesis in a particularly powerful fashion.

Second, this paper's central theme highlights an important problem in studying how taxes affect portfolio behavior, and it suggests a need for further post-JGTRRA research. If changes in tax policy, or in other components of the economic environment, lead firms to distribute a greater fraction of their earnings as dividends, this may lead to changes in investors' portfolio choices. The set of investors who hold dividend-paying stocks may differ before and after a substantial tax reform. This adds a new complication to analyzing the consumption effects of a tax change like JGTRRA. If the tax change induces a shift in the investor clienteles who hold different types of stock, then evidence on how dividend income affected the investors who held dividend-paying stocks before the reform may not carry over to the postreform environment. The extent to which portfolio clienteles shift in response to tax changes is likely to depend on the magnitude of the tax reform and on the distribution of households by marginal tax rate and wealth. Only by studying the consumption behavior of stockholders after the reform can one determine whether the prereform patterns continue to hold.

Joel Slemrod: This paper by Malcolm Baker, Stefan Nagel, and Jeffrey Wurgler is an ambitious and thought-provoking take on a fascinating question—in short, it is a discussant's dream. It challenges the Modigliani-Miller view that, taxes aside, because dividend payments "just" move money from one pocket of shareholders to another, they do not affect consumption. The authors offer an alternative hypothesis based on mental accounts, in which dividends move money from one mental account to another, namely, the shareholder's pocket, from which the shareholder is more likely to spend. The plausibility of this story depends on the context. For example, it is less plausible if the business transferring funds to its owners is a ma-and-pa grocery store, a small partnership, or even a closely held corporation; it is more plausible—and certainly plausible enough to take seriously—with respect to public corporations.

To investigate this hypothesis empirically, the authors examine two kinds of data. The first consists of data from a discount brokerage, which the authors use to examine whether dividend payments trigger withdrawals from individual (actual, not mental) accounts. This is an interesting question, but, as the authors admit, withdrawals from a discount brokerage account are not acts of consumption. Yet neither are they, as the authors assert, "precursors" to consumption. Withdrawals are neither necessary nor sufficient indicators of consumption unless an individual maintains no other brokerage account and indeed no other financial account—no checking account, no credit card account, no mortgage, and so on. The authors claim that this disjunction between account withdrawals and consumption adds noise but not bias to their estimates. I would say it threatens the interpretation of the estimated coefficients as informing us about consumption.

What factors, including dividends, affect withdrawals from such a brokerage account is an interesting question for household finance in and of itself. The answer presumably depends on such questions as who invests in discount brokerages and what other accounts they have. Answering these questions would contribute to the theory and evidence for account choices and account shifting. In the same way that the connection between portfolio choice and consumption has been worked out, the connection between account choice and consumption needs to be clarified.

The authors' second data source is the Consumer Expenditure Survey (CEX). The CEX data are not perfect, but unlike the brokerage account data, they do purport to measure consumer expenditure directly, and the issues of measurement error in these data have been widely recognized and studied. Some of these issues are particularly relevant to the question at hand. One is the topcoding of the data, and a second is that the CEX data do not oversample high-income people, who hold a disproportionate amount of stock held outside of institutions. For these reasons one might worry that any behavioral response of the usable CEX sample is not representative of aggregate dollar-weighted stock ownership. That the stockholders in the sample are not high rollers becomes clear when one notes that the median value of dividends and accrued gains in the sample is zero and that the mean annual capital gain is $363 (with a huge dispersion). This will be a problem if, for example, Bill Gates does not keep the same kind of mental accounts as the average stockholder, a plausible notion if there are fixed costs to constructing "better" mental accounts.

Perhaps the most troublesome issue in this analysis is the fact that capital gains are probably subject to much greater measurement error than dividend receipts. This will bias the outcome toward finding that dividends matter for consumption and capital gains do not matter, not only for consumption but for anything. Perhaps the Survey of Consumer Finances (or other sources with better capital gains measures) can give a sense of the size of the measurement error problem as well as the induced bias.

To be sure of the causal relationships, it would be helpful to have panel data that span a longer period. In their absence one wonders to what extent the authors' results are driven by heterogeneity—do those people who choose high-dividend stocks also behave differently in managing their accounts? For example, do they also move money in and out of their brokerage accounts more frequently? However, if the observed correlations were due to (persistent) heterogeneity of this type, one would expect that lagged dividends would explain such behavior as well as current dividends, but the authors show that they do not, and that is reassuring, as is the fact that the results survive first-differencing.

The tax system is one source of exogenous cross-sectional variation, in part because the federal income tax has graduated rates. If dividends are taxed more heavily than capital gains at the individual level, the income tax system should induce a clientele effect so that, other things equal, highly taxed individuals do not hold high-dividend-paying stocks. One might be initially optimistic that the variation in the marginal tax rate across people provides an instrument with which to examine the effect of dividends on consumption. But, alas, the marginal tax rate is highly correlated with income, and so it would be difficult to separate the effect of receiving dividends from the effect of income itself. Note, however, that although highly taxed individuals normally would be unhappy about higher dividends, they also would benefit most from a temporary cut in the dividend tax, which may be part of what the 2003 tax change, discussed below, was perceived by many to be.

The authors want to make assertions about the aggregate consumption impact of dividend changes. To make such statements with the data they have, one would need to know *why* dividends, or after-tax dividends, change over time for different shareholders. It could be that higher dividends are a signal of improved company prospects, in which case there would be both a dividend effect and a wealth effect. If instead changes in dividends reflect a changed payout policy, then higher dividends would imply lower expected capital gains, with no first-order wealth effect.

What if a change in dividends results from a tax policy change, one that either changes the incentive to pay out a given amount of after-tax earnings, or changes the amount of after-tax earnings itself, or both? The tax issues are tricky and are controversial among public finance economists, with the varying theories loosely classified as either "new view" or "old view." What is distinctive about the new view is that it implies that a permanent dividend tax cut will not change the payout behavior of mature firms (those whose earnings exceed good investment opportunities). In this case the dividend tax cut represents a windfall gain to shareholders (and, presumably, a windfall loss to other taxpayers). In general, the fact that a dividend tax cut should have different effects on different companies may help to identify the effect of a tax change, the payout responses to it, and shareholders' responses to both. To the extent that a dividend tax cut is perceived as temporary, this is a good time to get money out of a corporation.

The paper gives little attention to the authors' preferred explanation of their findings, namely, mental accounts. The behavior the authors identify does seem to follow the maxim about consuming income but not principal. But is it a rule of thumb that economizes on cognitive capital and transaction costs, one that works well in most situations but may work poorly in unusual circumstances? Is the goal also to smooth saving, rather than consumption, so that unexpected income can be spent but spending can be cut back in bad times?

Individuals' reliance on mental accounting is certainly heterogeneous. Who, then, is likely to use it—does it relate to one's sophistication in dealing with financial issues? Does it relate to wealth, as seems plausible if there are fixed costs to be saved by using simple rules of thumb? What might cause users of mental accounting to abandon their rule of thumb? One possibility is special dividends. Another is windows of time created by temporary, or possibly temporary, tax changes. Prominent news stories about corporations reacting to a tax change might be noticed by some tax- payers, who react by altering their usual mental accounting.

Once we are in the realm of behavioral economics, how far do we need to expand it? One might, for example, also consider the cognitive process of corporate officers. Surveys suggest they do not act as if they solve either the new view or the old view problem, but themselves use rules of thumb as well.[1] How shareholders react to dividends induced by tax changes also overlaps with the nascent field of behavioral public finance.[2] Note that the response of cognitively constrained individual shareholders to corporate behavior is in some ways similar to the response to government behavior: both corporate and government policies may move taxpayer "money" from one pocket, or mental account, to another. This raises a large set of inter- esting questions, including whether people have particular cognitive issues with respect to tax cuts. Do taxpayers have the cognitive sophistication to be Ricardian, or is this a particularly difficult cognitive problem whose so- lution involves rules of thumb and mental accounts? These issues arise in trying to understand taxpayer responses to anticipated tax refunds or occa- sional tax "rebates."

The paper ends by relating the authors' research program to the U.S. experience in 2003, when the tax on dividends was cut substantially. I would like to see the authors clarify the prediction of mental accounting with respect to exogenous changes in payouts. Do their findings imply that a permanently increased dividend payout ratio would induce share- holders to consume more forever? This seems implausible and would

1. Brav and others (2007).
2. See McCaffery and Slemrod (2006).

indeed be impossible in a life-cycle model (unless bequests decline), because lifetime income has not risen. Or would it increase consumption only until shareholders figure out that their mental accounting is not performing well in this scenario and they readjust their rule of thumb?

As my remarks suggest, although I found this paper ambitious and thought-provoking, I am not persuaded that the empirical analyses—especially the analysis of the brokerage accounts—shed much light on the determinants of consumption, at either the individual or the aggregate level. But I am quite sure that this research has enriched the conversation about this and other important questions of macroeconomics and public economics.

General discussion: William Gale drew parallels between the current paper and a 1987 paper by Yves Balcer and Kenneth Judd in the *Journal of Finance,* which examined the life-cycle accrual of capital gains, deriving formally that the marginal propensity to consume out of capital gains should, for tax reasons, be different from the marginal propensity to consume out of dividends. The taxation of realized capital gains provides an incentive to defer these gains for as long as possible in order to lower the effective tax rate on them. William Brainard agreed, commenting that the current tax treatment and the fact that increases in dividends are more permanent than capital gains are both nonbehavioral explanations of the authors' results.

Richard Cooper noted that trust funds are often an important source of income to shareholders and that, at least under New York State law, trust funds may pay out only dividends and not capital gains. Therefore the authors' results may reflect not mental accounting, but rather a legal doctrine that draws a sharp distinction between dividends and gains and treats only the former as income.

Benjamin Friedman noted that although only a fraction of gains are realized in any given year, and when they occur they usually reflect a decision on the part of the shareholder, shareholders occasionally realize gains inadvertently because shares are taken over by some other entity. He would find it informative to know how stockholders respond to the receipt of proceeds from such takeovers and whether their behavior is in line with the authors' estimate of the response to ordinary dividends.

References

Angeletos, George-Marios, and others. 2001. "The Hyperbolic Consumption Model: Calibration, Simulation, and Empirical Evaluation." *Journal of Economic Perspectives* 15, no. 3: 47–68.

Auerbach, Alan J., and Kevin A. Hassett. 2006. "Dividend Taxes and Firm Valuation: New Evidence." *American Economic Review* 96, no. 2: 119–23.

Baker, Malcolm, and Jeffrey Wurgler. 2004a. "A Catering Theory of Dividends." *Journal of Finance* 59, no. 3: 1125 65.

_____. 2004b. "Appearing and Disappearing Dividends: The Link to Catering Incentives." *Journal of Financial Economics* 73, no. 2: 271–88.

Barber, Brad M., and Terrance Odean. 2000. "Trading Is Hazardous to Your Wealth: The Common Stock Investment Performance of Individual Investors." *Journal of Finance* 55, no. 2: 773–806.

Bodkin, Ronald G. 1959. "Windfall Income and Consumption." *American Economic Review* 49, no. 4: 602–14.

Brav, Alon, and others. 2007. "Managerial Response to the May 2003 Dividend Tax Cut." Duke University.

Campbell, John Y. 2006. "Household Finance." *Journal of Finance* 61, no. 4: 1553–1604.

Campbell, John Y., and Robert J. Shiller. 1988. "The Dividend-Price Ratio and Expectations of Future Dividends and Discount Factors." *Review of Financial Studies* 1, no. 3: 195–228.

Carroll, Christopher D. 1994. "How Does Future Income Affect Current Consumption?" *Quarterly Journal of Economics* 109, no. 1: 111–47.

_____. 1997. "Buffer-Stock Saving and the Life-Cycle/Permanent Income Hypothesis." *Quarterly Journal of Economics* 112, no. 1: 1–55.

Case, Karl E., John M. Quigley, and Robert J. Shiller. 2005. "Comparing Wealth Effects: The Stock Market versus the Housing Market." *Advances in Macroeconomics* 5, no. 1: 1–32.

Chetty, Raj, and Emmanuel Saez. 2005. "Dividend Taxes and Corporate Behavior: Evidence from the 2003 Dividend Tax Cut." *Quarterly Journal of Economics* 120, no. 3: 791–833.

Choi, James L., and others. 2006. "Consumption-Wealth Comovement of the Wrong Sign." Yale University, Harvard University, and University of Pennsylvania.

Cohen, Randolph B., Christopher K. Polk, and Tuomo Vuolteenaho. 2006. "The Price is (Almost) Right." Harvard University.

DeAngelo, Harry, Linda DeAngelo, and Douglas J. Skinner. 2000. "Special Dividends and the Evolution of Dividend Signaling." *Journal of Financial Economics* 57, no. 3: 309–54.

Deaton, Angus. 1991. "Saving and Liquidity Constraints." *Econometrica* 59, no. 5: 1221–48.

Fama, Eugene F., and Kenneth R. French. 1988. "Permanent and Temporary Components of Stock Prices." *Journal of Political Economy* 96, no. 2: 246–73.

Feldstein, Martin S. 1973. "Tax Incentives, Corporate Saving, and Capital Accumulation in the United States." *Journal of Public Economics* 2, no. 2: 159–71.

Feldstein, Martin S., and George Fane. 1973. "Taxes, Corporate Dividend Policy and Personal Savings: The British Postwar Experience." *Review of Economics and Statistics* 55, no. 4: 399–411.

Graham, John R., and Alok Kumar. 2006. "Do Dividend Clienteles Exist? Evidence on Dividend Preferences of Retail Investors." *Journal of Finance* 61, no. 3: 1305–36.

Hayashi, Fumio. 1985. "The Effect of Liquidity Constraints on Consumption: A Cross-Sectional Analysis." *Quarterly Journal of Economics* 100, no. 1: 183–206.

Johnson, David S., Jonathan A. Parker, and Nicholas S. Souleles. 2006. "Household Expenditure and the Income Tax Rebates of 2001." *American Economic Review* 96, no. 5: 1589–1610.

Kreinin, Mordechai E. 1961. "Windfall Income and Consumption: Additional Evidence." *American Economic Review* 51, no. 3: 388–90.

Lettau, Martin, and Sydney Ludvigson. 2004. "Understanding Trend and Cycle in Asset Values: Reevaluating the Wealth Effect on Consumption." *American Economic Review* 94, no. 1: 279–99.

McCaffery, Edward J., and Joel Slemrod, eds. 2006. *Behavioral Public Finance.* New York: Russell Sage Foundation.

Miller, Merton H., and Franco Modigliani. 1961. "Dividend Policy, Growth, and the Valuation of Shares." *Journal of Business* 34, no. 4: 411–33.

Newey, Whitney K., and Kenneth D. West. 1987. "A Simple, Positive Semi-Definite, Heteroskedasticity and Autocorrelation Consistent Covariance Matrix." *Econometrica* 55, no. 3: 703–08.

Odean, Terrance. 1998. "Are Investors Reluctant to Realize their Losses?" *Journal of Finance* 53, no. 5: 1775–98.

_____. 1999. "Do Investors Trade Too Much?" *American Economic Review* 89, no. 5: 1279–98.

Parker, Jonathan A. 1999a. "The Reaction of Household Consumption to Predictable Changes in Social Security Taxes." *American Economic Review* 89, no. 4: 959–73.

_____. 1999b. "The Consumption Function Re-Estimated." Princeton University.

_____. 2001. "The Consumption Risk of the Stock Market." *BPEA*, no. 2: 279–333.

Peek, Joe. 1983. "Capital Gains and Personal Saving Behavior." *Journal of Money, Credit, and Banking* 15, no. 1: 1–23.

Poterba, James M. 1987. "Tax Policy and Corporate Saving." *BPEA*, no. 2: 455–503.

_____. 2000. "Stock Market Wealth and Consumption." *Journal of Economic Perspectives* 14, no. 2: 99–118.

_____. 2004. "Taxation and Corporate Payout Policy." *American Economic Review* 94, no. 2: 171–75.

Poterba, James M., and Lawrence H. Summers. 1988. "Mean Reversion in Stock Prices: Evidence and Implications." *Journal of Financial Economics* 22, no. 1: 27–59.

Rantapuska, Elias H. 2005. "Do Investors Reinvest Dividends and Tender Offer Proceeds?" Helsinki School of Economics.

Shefrin, Hersh M., and Meir Statman. 1984. "Explaining Investor Preference for Cash Dividends." *Journal of Financial Economics* 13, no. 2: 253–82.

Shefrin, Hersh M., and Richard H. Thaler. 1988. "The Behavioral Life-Cycle Hypothesis." *Economic Inquiry* 26, no. 4: 609–43.

Souleles, Nicholas S. 1999. "The Response of Household Consumption to Income Tax Refunds." *American Economic Review* 89, no. 4; 947–58.

_____. 2002. "Consumer Response to the Reagan Tax Cuts." *Journal of Public Economics* 85, no. 1: 99–120.

Stephens, Melvin, Jr. 2003. " '3rd of tha Month': Do Social Security Recipients Smooth Consumption between Checks?" *American Economic Review* 93, no. 1: 406–22.

Summers, Lawrence, and Chris Carroll. 1987. "Why Is U.S. National Saving so Low?" *BPEA*, no. 2: 607–35.

Thaler, Richard H., and Hersh M. Shefrin. 1981. "An Economic Theory of Self-Control." *Journal of Political Economy* 89, no. 2: 392–406.

Vuolteenaho, Tuomo. 2002. "What Drives Firm-Level Stock Returns?" *Journal of Finance* 57, no. 1: 233–64.

Wilcox, David W. 1989. "Social Security Benefits, Consumption Expenditures, and the Life Cycle Hypothesis." *Journal of Political Economy* 97, no. 2: 288–304.

D A V I D   K .   B A C K U S
New York University

J O N A T H A N   H .   W R I G H T
Board of Governors of the Federal Reserve System

Cracking the Conundrum

BETWEEN JUNE 29, 2004, and February 2, 2005, the Federal Open Market Committee increased the target federal funds rate by 150 basis points (bp), or 1.50 percentage points. Over the same period, the long end of the yield curve fell, with the ten-year yield declining by 70 bp and the ten-year (instantaneous) forward rate by more than 100 bp. This pronounced rotation in the yield and forward rate curves caught many by surprise. Then–Federal Reserve chairman Alan Greenspan was one. In his February 2005 testimony to Congress, he noted:[1]

> This development contrasts with most experience, which suggests that . . . increasing short-term interest rates are normally accompanied by a rise in longer-term yields. Historically, even . . . distant forward rates have tended to rise in association with monetary policy tightening. . . . For the moment, the broadly unanticipated behavior of world bond markets remains a conundrum.

Bill Gross was another. PIMCO's legendary bond investor advised clients in February 2004 to reduce the duration of their bond holdings, only to see

This paper was written while Jonathan Wright was on leave at the University of Pennsylvania. It began as two separate discussions of a paper by John Cochrane and Monika Piazzesi (2006). We thank them for their insights. We also thank Frank Diebold, Don Kim, Richard Sylla, and Stanley Zin for comments and advice. The views expressed are the sole responsibility of the authors and should not be interpreted as reflecting the views of the Board of Governors of the Federal Reserve System or of any other employees of the Federal Reserve System.

1. Greenspan (2005).

long-term bonds rally. Thirteen months later he confessed confusion over what had occurred:[2]

> Who would have thought that the bond market could have [done so well]? Not yours truly, nor Alan Greenspan. . . . How then to explain it? . . . I must tell you that we at PIMCO have been talking about this topic for months. We, too, have been befuddled.

The Federal Reserve continued raising the federal funds target thereafter, but the ten-year forward rate continued to fall. In all, the ten-year forward rate fell 170 bp between June 2004 and June 2005 and has rebounded only about 50 bp since then.

If the word "conundrum" from a respected central banker covered red faces in the investment community, other observers had no shortage of explanations for what had happened: some linked the decline in long-term yields to a decline in expectations of long-run economic growth or inflation, others to an increase in the global supply of savings, or to an improvement in the ability of global capital markets to allocate risk efficiently, or to massive purchases of U.S. Treasury securities by Asian central banks and petroleum exporters, or to increased demand for long-term bonds on the part of pension funds, or to reduced supply of long-maturity instruments following the Treasury's 2001 decision (later rescinded) to discontinue auctions of the thirty-year bond, or to a global decline in macroeconomic and financial market uncertainty, perhaps the result of improved procedures for monetary policy or the state of the business cycle.

In this paper we look at several of these proposed explanations, holding each up to a broad array of evidence. The paper's first section is devoted to establishing the facts. Among those we consider key are the following: over the conundrum period, real interest rates fell along with nominal rates; long-term survey expectations of inflation, growth, and interest rates were roughly flat; volatilities and risk spreads fell across a wide range of assets; and distant-horizon forward rates on British and German government bonds fell. The next section considers various interpretations of the facts based on affine bond-pricing models, which allow us to decompose forward rates into term premiums and expected future short-term rates, and then to further parse each into real and inflation components. The models suggest that term premiums declined considerably over the period of interest. The final section considers changes in the macroeconomic environ-

2. Gross (2005).

Figure 1. Daily Federal Funds Target Rates and Ten-Year U.S. Treasury Yields and Forward Rates, 1985–2006

Percent a year

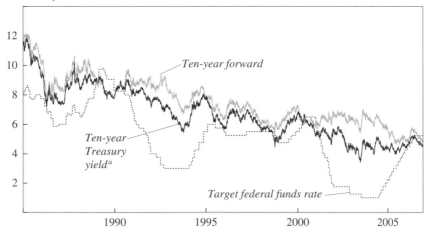

Sources: Federal Reserve Board and Gürkaynak, Sack, and Wright (2006).
a. Continuously compounded yield on zero-coupon nominal (non-inflation-protected) securities, approximated using the Nelson-Spiegel-Svensson method as described by Gürkaynak, Sack, and Wright (2006).

ment that might help explain such changes in term premiums, including a discussion of the explanations mentioned above.

Facts

Here we collect a number of related facts to provide a context for the later discussion. We organize them around a series of topics.

Cyclical Behavior of Interest Rates

The essence of the conundrum is evident in figure 1. During the three preceding episodes of monetary policy tightening, starting in 1986, 1994, and 1999, the ten-year yield on U.S. Treasurys increased sharply along with the federal funds target. However, as figure 2 shows more clearly, during the first year of the most recent period of tightening, ten-year yields declined. The ten-year forward rate, as already noted, fell 170 bp from June 2004 to June 2005, reaching its lowest point in thirty years in the summer of 2005. The more modest decline in the ten-year yield is

Figure 2. Daily Federal Funds Target Rates and U.S. Treasury Yields and Forward Rates, 2004–05ᵃ

Percent a year

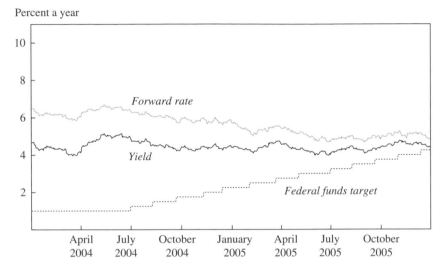

Sources: Federal Reserve Board and Gürkaynak, Sack, and Wright (2006).
a. Ten-year yields and instantaneous forward rates, calculated as described by Gürkaynak, Sack, and Wright (2006).

essentially an average of the sharp decline in long-term forward rates and the concurrent increase in short-term rates. We focus much of our analysis on forward rates, since they capture the behavior of interest rates in a particularly clean way. Here and below, yields and forward rates are derived from prices of Treasury securities by the Nelson-Siegel-Svensson method.[3] Data sources and descriptions are given in appendix A.

The recent behavior of forward rates is clearly different from that in the three preceding tightening episodes (figure 1), but what can one say about the cyclical behavior of forward rates more generally? Figure 3 is a scatterplot of monthly ten-year forward rates against the monthly unemployment rate, a convenient indicator of the state of the business cycle.[4] There is a clear positive association between the two variables (the correlation coefficient is 0.64), indicating that long-term forward rates have been countercyclical. The slope of the relationship in the recent past (the gray diamonds) is not very different from what it was before, but the level appears 1½ to 2 percentage points lower.

3. As described in Gürkaynak, Sack, and Wright (2006).
4. Lehman Brothers (2007) includes a similar figure (figure 6).

Figure 3. Monthly Unemployment Rate and Ten-Year U.S. Treasury Forward Rate, January 1985–February 2007[a]

Ten-year forward rate
(percent a year)

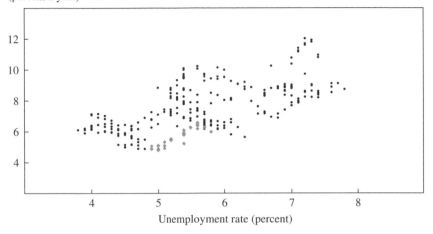

Unemployment rate (percent)

Sources: Bureau of Labor Statistics and Gürkaynak, Sack, and Wright (2006).
a. Gray diamonds represent observations from 2004-05.

Real and Nominal Interest Rates

Figure 4 compares the change in the nominal forward rate curve between the end of June 2004 and the end of June 2005, in the top panel, with the analogous change in the real forward rate curve, as measured by rates on Treasury inflation-protected securities (TIPS), in the bottom panel. Evidently the two curves experienced similar shifts, although the nominal curve shifted by a larger amount. Measured at the ten-year horizon, the nominal curve dropped by 172 bp and the real curve by a little more than half that (96 bp). The difference between the two curves reflects compensation for inflation. It is often used as a measure of inflation expectations, but it actually includes both an inflation risk premium and a TIPS liquidity premium. We will return to this later.

Expectations of Inflation and Growth

Figure 5 shows that there was no apparent change in forecasts of inflation, GDP growth, or short-term interest rates in 2004–05 that might account for the drop in long-term forward rates. The data summarized in

Figure 4. Nominal and Real U.S. Treasury Forward Rate Curves, June 2004 and June 2005[a]

Percent a year

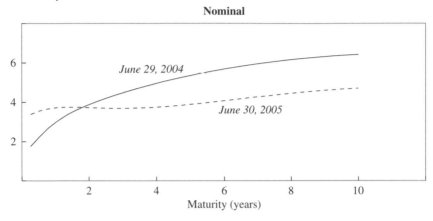

Nominal

June 29, 2004

June 30, 2005

Maturity (years)

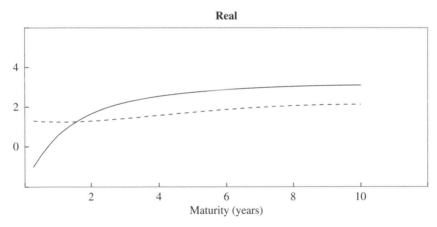

Real

Maturity (years)

Sources: Federal Reserve Board and Gürkaynak, Sack, and Wright (2006).
a. Instantaneous ten-year forward rates on non-inflation-protected Treasury securities (nominal) and TIPS (real).

the figure are "long-range" (five- to ten-year) forecasts produced by Blue Chip Economic Indicators and consist of averages over a large number of professional forecasters. The steady drop in the forecast of long-term expected inflation over the 1990s coincided with a similar drop in the ten-year yield (compare with figure 1), but there was little or no movement in expected inflation or in expected GDP growth during 2004–05.

Figure 5. Semiannual Blue Chip Long-Range Forecasts of Inflation, GDP Growth, and Treasury Bill Rates, 1987–2006

Percent a year

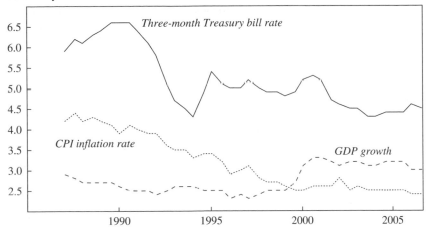

Source: Authors calc ulations using data from Blue Chip Economic Indicators.
a. Data are averages of estimates by about fifty professional forecasters for periods five to ten years after the indicated survey date.

The inflation forecast in the figure is for the consumer price index; the analogous series for the GDP deflator (not shown) is lower throughout but moves similarly through time. The long-range GDP growth forecast increased dramatically in 2000; one might have expected such a rise to be associated with an increase in long-term forward rates, but that did not happen. Similarly, the long-range forecast of the three-month Treasury bill rate has been flat over the last three years. Given this evidence, it is hard to argue convincingly that the recent decline in long-term yields reflects expectations of lower inflation, slower growth, or lower short-term interest rates.

Credit Spreads and Volatility

One striking feature of the recent past has been the unusually narrow spreads on risky instruments. The spread between yields on Baa- and Aaa-rated corporate debt, for example, is an indication of how much the market discounts lower-rated bonds. It reflects a combination of the risk inherent in these bonds and the price applied to such risk. The top panel of figure 6 shows that the Baa-Aaa spread declined sharply between 2004 and early 2005. The middle panel depicts a measure of interest rate risk: the implied volatility of one-year interest rate caps, which is a market-based measure of short-term volatility of a short-term interest rate (the six-month London interbank offer rate). It, too, fell sharply over the period of interest. More-over, realized volatility—in this case, the standard deviation of daily changes in forward rates—also fell, as Richard Berner and David Miles have noted.[5] The annual standard deviation of one-day changes in the ten-year instantaneous forward rate dropped from 6.8 bp in 2003 to 4.1 bp in 2006. Over the conundrum period, not only did investors expect less interest rate volatility; there *was* less volatility. The bottom panel of fig-ure 6 shows that the Chicago Board of Exchange's volatility index, whose price is tied to the short-term (thirty-day) volatility of S&P 500 stock index options, also declined between 2002 and 2005. Together this evidence indicates that financial market risk and risk premiums across a range of assets were substantially lower in 2005 than they had been two or three years earlier.

Macroeconomic Uncertainty

The underlying source of the decline in asset market volatility remains unclear. Federal Reserve communications have, in the last few years, given markets more forward-looking guidance on the path of monetary policy, making it more predictable. This might account for a fall in near-term interest rate uncertainty, but its broader impact on asset market volatility is less evident. Macroeconomic uncertainty, particularly at long horizons, is inherently difficult to measure, but the dispersion of long-horizon survey predictions serves as a crude proxy.

The Blue Chip surveys report a simple dispersion measure for their long-horizon survey questions: the difference between the averages of the ten highest and ten lowest responses. Figure 7 shows a time series of this measure for five- to ten-year expectations of consumer price inflation, real GDP growth, and three-month Treasury bill yields. Although somewhat noisy, all three measures have been trending noticeably lower. Note, too, that this period of reduced macroeconomic volatility came well after the start of the so-called Great Moderation, the decline in macroeconomic

---

5. Berner and Miles (2006).

Figure 6. Daily Credit Spreads and Interest Rate and Stock Market Volatility, 1985–2007

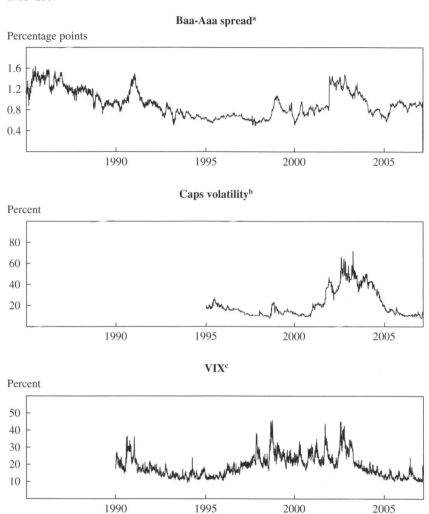

Baa-Aaa spread[a]

Percentage points

Caps volatility[b]

Percent

VIX[c]

Percent

Source: Datastream.

a. Difference in average yields on Baa- and Aaa-rated bonds.

b. Implied volatility of one-year interest rate caps (options on short-term interest rates), measured as the standard deviation of the logarithm of the six-month London Interbank Offered Rate.

c. Chicago Board Options Exchange Volatility Index, an indicator of the implied volatility of the S&P 500 stock index, measured as the standard deviation of the logarithm of this index.

Figure 7. Dispersion of Semiannual Blue Chip Long-Range Forecasts of Inflation, GDP Growth, and Treasury Bill Rates, 1987–2006[a]

Percentage points

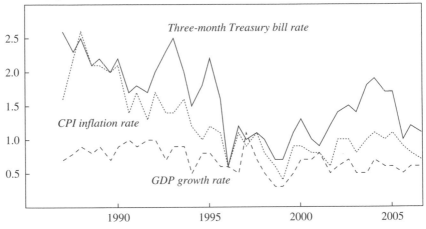

Source: Authors' calculations using data from Blue Chip Economic Indicators.
a. The dispersion for each indicator is the difference between the average of the ten highest of about fifty forecasts and the average of the ten lowest.

volatility that researchers typically date to the early 1980s. Most of the decline in the dispersion of interest rate and inflation expectations occurred in the early 1990s. They then rose again in the last recession before moving back down over the conundrum period. Perhaps investors believe that macroeconomic uncertainty has declined further, or perhaps they only lately became convinced of the Great Moderation.

Forward Rates in Germany and the United Kingdom

The fall in forward rates since mid-2004 is not unique to the United States. Figure 8 plots ten-year forward rates for the United States, Germany, and the United Kingdom. The conundrum is evident in all three, even though they are at different stages of the business cycle. Indeed, forward rates in these countries have been unusually highly correlated over the last two or three years. Randall Kroszner observes that long-term rates have declined even in such middle-income countries as Brazil, Chile, Colombia, Indonesia, Mexico, Russia, and Thailand.[6] Several of these countries now

6. Kroszner (2006).

Figure 8. Daily Ten-Year Forward Rates on U.S., U.K., and German Government Bonds, 1995–2007

Percent a year

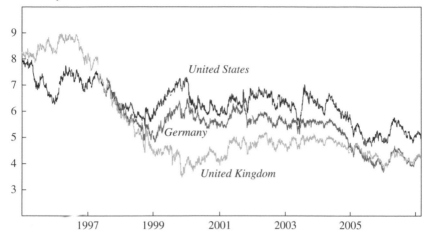

Sources: Bank of England, Deutsche Bundesbank, and Gürkaynak, Sack, and Wright (2006).

issue local-currency debt at modest yields at maturities at which they did not even issue debt a decade ago.

Affine Interpretations of Forward Rates

The recent decline in long-term forward rates, the similar decline in many measures of volatility, and the apparent absence of any change in expectations of inflation and Treasury bill rates suggest to us that smaller term premiums play a role in explaining the conundrum. We would call the evidence suggestive, however, rather than definitive. A complementary source of information is estimates of affine bond pricing models. There are many examples in the literature, not all of them the same, but a collection of models estimated by researchers at the Federal Reserve illustrates their potential to shed light on the behavior of long-term forward rates.

In the context of any bond pricing model, the starting point is a common decomposition of long-term forward rates into expected future short-term rates and term premiums:

$$(1) \qquad f_t^{(n)} = E_t\left(r_{t+n}\right) + tp_t^{(n)}.$$

Here $f_t^{(n)}$ is the *n*-periods-ahead forward rate at date *t*, $r_{t+n} \equiv f_{t+n}^{(0)}$ is the short-term rate *n* periods in the future, and $tp_t^{(n)}$ is a term premium. Equation 1 is essentially a definition of the term premium; it has content only if we have a way to identify the components.

We face two hurdles in turning equation 1 into a usable decomposition. The first is the time-series variability of long-term forward rates. Stationary ergodic models imply that the variance of forward rates converges to zero as the maturity increases. Robert Shiller made this point in a setting with constant term premiums, but it applies more generally.[7] It applies, for example, to most affine models. One way or another, a realistic model must incorporate a high degree of persistence somewhere, so that convergence works slowly enough that forward rates with maturities of (say) ten years still have significant volatility. A related issue is the impact of news on long-maturity forward rates. It is not uncommon for a single macroeconomic news announcement to cause large changes in forward rates for maturities of ten years or more.[8] Whether this reflects changes in expectations of distant future short-term rates or term premiums remains to be seen, but it is clear that persistence is needed in one or the other.

The second hurdle is identifying the two components of equation 1. An older line of research used the expectations hypothesis, which in this context amounts to the assumption that term premiums are constant: they can vary with *n* but not with *t*. In this case all of the movement in long-term forward rates is associated with changes in expected short-term rates. This not only assumes the answer to the decomposition in equation 1, but it conflicts with an enormous body of work documenting the empirical weaknesses of the expectations hypothesis.[9] One issue is the predictability of long-term yields. Under the expectations hypothesis, a steep yield curve implies that short-term interest rates are expected to increase, and so long-term yields should rise. In U.S. data, however, we find the opposite, as Frederick Macaulay noted years ago:[10]

> The yields on [long-maturity] bonds should *fall* during a period in which short-term rates are higher than the yields of the bonds and *rise* during a

7. Shiller (1979).
8. See, for example, Beechey (2007), Gürkaynak, Sack, and Swanson (2005), and Lu and Wu (2006).
9. See, among many others, the survey and synthesis in Dai and Singleton (2002).
10. Macaulay (1938).

period in which short-term rates are lower. Now experience is more nearly the opposite.

Similarly, excess returns on long-term bonds can be predicted from the term structure of interest rates, which also contradicts the expectations hypothesis. All of this evidence implies that term premiums vary with time, and therefore that the expectations hypothesis is a poor guide to interest rate dynamics.

Financial models use this predictability to estimate term premiums from observed bond yields and perhaps other data. They have the potential to distinguish between changes in term premiums and changes in expected short-term rates, and they therefore point to the source of the conundrum. The most popular of these models are affine: they generate yields and forward rates that are linear functions of a vector of state variables, which in turn follows a linear autoregressive process. We describe below some of the properties of estimated versions of Gregory Duffee's "essentially affine" model, an example of the more general class of affine models characterized by Darrell Duffie and Rui Kan.[11] We describe a one-factor version in appendix B.

The Kim-Orphanides Model

Most estimated essentially affine models identify the two components of forward rates from the predictability of yields or returns alone, as described in the previous paragraph. Don Kim and Athanasios Orphanides add direct information about the dynamics of interest rates to such a three-factor model.[12] They use professional forecasts of Treasury bill rates to help identify the expected future short-term rate component of the forward rate, which allows relatively precise estimation of the term premium through equation 1. The estimated model is stationary but very persistent: the half-life of the most persistent factor is thirteen years, which allows it to generate substantial movement in long-maturity forward rates.

The results are apparent in figure 9, which plots the components of the ten-year forward rate implied by the model. This decomposition suggests that the decline in ten-year-ahead forward rates from June 2004 to June

11. Duffee (2002); Duffie and Kan (1996).
12. Kim and Orphanides (2005).

Figure 9. Components of Monthly Ten-Year U.S. Treasury Forward Rates: Kim-Orphanides Model, 1980–2007

Percentage points

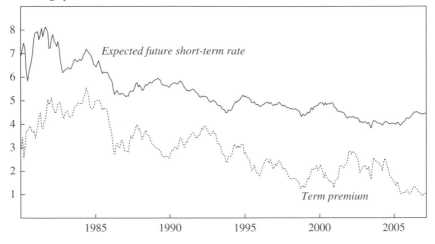

Source: Federal Reserve staff calculations updating the estimates of Kim and Orphanides (2005).

2005 is nearly fully explained by a declining term premium. Expected future short-term rates edged lower over this period, but the forward term premium declined from 2½ percentage points to 1 percentage point. Since June 2005, forward rates have risen a little, but the term premium has remained at around 1 percentage point. One can likewise decompose long-term yields into components. The term premium component of the ten-year yield is estimated to have fallen from 1¼ percentage points in June 2004 to a scant 30 bp in June 2005.

Real and Nominal Term Premiums

We can look further into the role of inflation in these developments by incorporating inflation and TIPS rates into the analysis. If one adds the dynamics of inflation to the model, it becomes possible also to price synthetic real bonds and to decompose real forward rates into a real term premium and the expected future real short-term interest rate. Such an exercise does not require TIPS: it is a real term structure model constructed from inflation and nominal interest rate data alone. Don Kim and Andrew

Ang, Geert Bekaert, and Min Wei provide two such models.[13] Both allow for a four-way decomposition of nominal forward rates into the expected future real short-term interest rate, expected future inflation, the real term premium, and the inflation risk premium. The expected nominal rate is the sum of the expected future real short-term interest rate and expected future inflation; the nominal term premium is the sum of the real term premium and the inflation risk premium.

It seems a pity, however, to completely ignore the information in TIPS. TIPS have only been trading since 1997, and evidently they were subject to large liquidity premiums in the early years of trading, whereas the synthetic real bond that we would wish to price would have liquidity comparable to that of a nominal Treasury bond. But the liquidity of TIPS has improved, and the inflation compensation implied by TIPS is now a widely used barometer of inflation expectations, even though inflation compensation is not the same thing as expected inflation.

Motivated by these considerations, Stefania D'Amico, Kim, and Wei augment a real term structure model with TIPS.[14] The model is estimated over the period since 1990. TIPS are treated as missing data before 1999, which is straightforward to handle via the Kalman filter. Also, the yields on TIPS are assumed to equal the sum of yields on the synthetic liquid real bonds and a TIPS liquidity premium. The properties of their specification are illustrated in figure 10, which plots the four components of the ten-year forward rate. The estimates suggest that the real term premium has fallen sharply since June 2004, and the inflation risk premium by a lesser amount. On the other hand, expected future real short-term interest rates have been flat, and expected future inflation has actually risen modestly.

Accounting

All in all, given the time variation in term premiums, the facts about risk spreads and volatilities (figure 6), survey expectations (figure 5), and the Kim-Orphanides estimates of the affine model (figure 9), we think that a decline in term premiums is likely to be the principal explanation for the decline in long-horizon forward rates from June 2004 to June 2005. But we

---

13. Kim (2004); Ang, Bekaert and Wei (2007).
14. D'Amico, Kim, and Wei (2007). We refer the reader to that paper for more details on the specification.

Figure 10. Components of Monthly Ten-Year U.S. Treasury Forward Rates: D'Amico-Kim-Wei Model, 1990–2007[a]

Percentage points

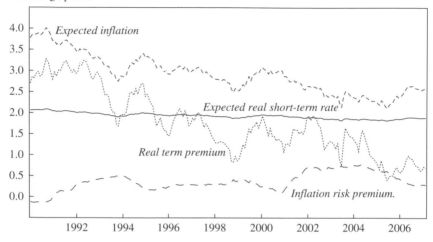

Source: Federal Reserve staff calculations updating the estimates of D'Amico, Kim, and Wei (2007).
a. Estimated using the model of D'Amico, Kim, and Wei (2007).

cannot be sure. What we *can* be sure of is the arithmetic identity that forward rates are the sum of expected future rates and term premiums. If term premiums did not decline, then the long-run expectation of the federal funds rate must have fallen by about 1.7 percentage points. Indeed, there are economic forces that may have pushed expected equilibrium real interest rates down. For example, an increase in the global supply of savings could represent a permanent leftward shift in the IS curve, resulting in lower expected future real short-term interest rates. Or investors may have scaled back their expectations about productivity growth amid weak business investment. Still, during the period in question, economic growth was robust, inflation was drifting upward, and a 1.7-percentage-point decline in expected future short-term interest rates would seem surprising. But arithmetically this is the only alternative explanation to a fall in the term premium. In a similar calculation, on average over the last twenty years, the spread between ten-year forward rates and the federal funds rate has been 2 percentage points, which is an estimate of the average term premium over that period. The ten-year forward rate now stands around 5 percent. This means that either the federal funds rate ten years hence is expected to be close to 3 percent, or the term premium is below its average over the past twenty years.

Integrating Macroeconomics and Finance

Affine models suggest that term premiums have fallen in the recent past, but the absence of macroeconomic structure in these models makes it difficult to say why. Did Federal Reserve policy change? Did macroeconomic risk fall? Are any of the ideas mentioned in the introduction persuasive? We fill the gap with a combination of speculation and casual empiricism.

The first issue is the cyclical behavior of the term premium. A wide range of evidence on asset returns suggests that risk premiums in general are countercyclical, smaller in booms than in recessions.[15] Since the recent period has been an expansion, one would indeed expect term premiums to have declined. And this helps explain the otherwise puzzling correlation between unemployment and the distant-horizon forward rate shown in figure 3.

A secular decline in asset price volatility could also account for lower risk premiums in general, and lower term premiums in particular.[16] That in turn raises the question of why asset price volatility fell. But as figure 7 showed, judging from surveys, the dispersion of agents' long-run macroeconomic expectations, and especially their long-run inflation expectations, has fallen, which is at least suggestive of a decline in uncertainty about long-run inflation rates. This could in turn owe to more credible and transparent monetary policy, in which future interest rate moves are indicated well in advance. The last decade has seen a global trend toward central banks becoming more independent of political influences, providing more explicit information to the public about their decisions (including publishing forecasts), and adopting some form of inflation targeting. Also, greater integration of financial markets may reduce the potential short-term gain from any one country adopting more inflationary policies, which in turn would make a commitment to a low and stable level of inflation

---

15. Cochrane and Piazzesi (2005, 2006) and Ludvigson and Ng (2006) are good examples for bond returns.

16. As discussed by Rudebusch, Swanson, and Wu (2006).

more credible. All this might help account for a global decline in inflation uncertainty and hence in inflation risk premiums.

Some evidence for this interpretation is the especially sharp decline in forward rates in the United Kingdom around 1997, when the Bank of England was granted operational independence, as can be seen in figure 8. Arguably, in the last few years investors in the United States and abroad have become persuaded that inflation has been conquered forever—or at least for the relevant time horizon—and so no longer demand large inflation risk premiums. In the United States the Volcker disinflation took place a long time ago, and it is indeed a little hard to see why only in the last three years investors should suddenly have become confident that inflation would remain contained indefinitely. Still, reduced inflation uncertainty amid changes in central bank policy seems to be high on the list of plausible explanations for the global decline in distant-horizon forward rates. Uncertainty about economic growth might also have declined, for a variety of reasons: monetary policy, financial innovation, or inventory management.

Some analysts have suggested that a fall in term premiums may owe to increased demand for longer-duration securities stemming from the prospect that corporate pension reform might encourage pension funds to better match the durations of their assets and liabilities. This seems a plausible story in the United Kingdom, where pension funds must satisfy strict duration-matching requirements. The real yield on fifty-year inflation-indexed government bonds in the United Kingdom fell below 50 basis points in January 2006, which is consistent with special demand from pension funds for this unusually long duration security. Still, the explanation does not make as much sense in the United States, where corporate pension reform has proceeded more slowly.

Another possible explanation is that Asian central banks are buying up Treasury securities, driving the term premium down.[17] This does not seem satisfying as a complete explanation for the conundrum because, as shown earlier, forward rates in Germany and the United Kingdom exhibited swings similar to those in the United States. But U.S. Treasurys and the bonds of other industrial-country governments may be close substitutes, so that purchases of Treasurys may drive foreign term premiums down. One recent natural experiment strongly suggests that Asian central bank

17. See Bernanke, Reinhart, and Sack (2004); Warnock and Warnock (2006).

purchases are part of the story. On July 21, 2005, the Peoples' Bank of China announced that it was modestly revaluing the renminbi and adopting a new exchange rate regime. The announcement came at 7 a.m. Eastern time and was immediately understood by market participants as implying that China would not need to buy as many Treasurys to hold the value of the renminbi down as had previously been thought. At the time of the announcement, the yield of the on-the-run ten-year Treasury note jumped up about 7 bp. To be sure, 7 bp represents a tiny share of the conundrum, but the revaluation of the renminbi was not large, and so the episode suggests that foreign central bank purchases of Treasury securities have at least played some role. Capital flows from petroleum-exporting countries could have a similar effect.

Some analysts have pointed to demographics as a possible explanation for falling term premiums, as substantial cohorts of the populations of industrialized economies approach retirement. In this explanation, aging populations in industrialized countries are expected to shift their holdings away from risky assets such as equities and toward bonds and other assets perceived to be relatively safe, and these shifts may place some downward pressure on term premiums (and upward pressure on equity risk premiums). However, demographics are slow-moving and predictable, and it can hardly be claimed that there has been a substantial or unexpected shift in demographics since June 2004.

Finally, changes in term premiums need not have any fundamental explanation but could instead be a consequence of irrational behavior on the part of investors. Arguably, the choppy behavior of ten-year forward rates is hard to make sense of in terms of either expected short-term interest rates or risk compensation from any rational equilibrium asset pricing model.

A Regression Model

The affine term structure models introduced in the previous section use a set of latent factors as the state vector. This has the advantage of fitting the data well but the disadvantage of lacking a direct economic interpretation. To get some sense of the ability of some of the economic explanations discussed above to account for the conundrum, we regressed the ten-year forward nominal term premiums as estimated by the model of Kim and

Figure 11. Actual and Fitted Monthly Term Premiums in the Ten-Year U.S. Treasury Yield, 1987–2006

Percentage points

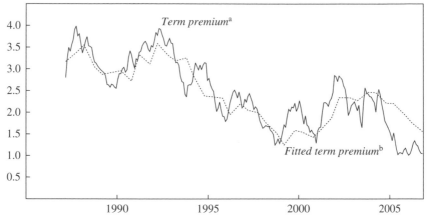

Sources: Figure 9 and authors' regressions.
a. Term premium on the instantaneous forward nominal ten-year Treasury yield, from figure 9.
b. Fitted values of the same term premium obtained from a regression of the term premium on the unemployment rate and the dispersion of long-range Blue Chip inflation expectations.

Orphanides on the unemployment rate (to capture the cyclical patterns in term premiums) and the dispersion of Blue Chip long-horizon survey measures of inflation (to proxy the impact of inflation uncertainty on term premiums). The regression was run at the same frequency as the Blue Chip long-horizon survey. The results are as follows:[18]

Constant	−0.83
Coefficient on unemployment	0.42
Coefficient on Blue Chip long-term inflation dispersion measure	0.78.

Greater dispersion of inflation expectations and higher unemployment are both associated with larger term premiums, and both coefficients are statistically significant. The actual and fitted term premiums from this regression are plotted in figure 11. The model is able to explain a good bit of the decline in term premiums since 1990, and even some of the fall in the last

18. The survey is published twice a year, for a total of forty observations from March 1987 to October 2006. Both estimated slope coefficients are statistically significant at the 1 percent level, using Newey-West standard errors.

three years, as the dispersion of inflation expectations has fallen even as the economy has been expanding. Only some of the decline in term premiums since June 2004 can be explained by this model, but it suggests that these factors may be at least part of the explanation.

Conclusion

We think the evidence points to a declining term premium as the primary source of the recent fall in long-term forward rates. This interpretation is broadly consistent with observed changes in risk spreads, interest rate and stock market volatility, the dispersion in long-range forecasts, and estimates of (some) affine bond-pricing models. In contrast, long-range forecasts of inflation, growth, and short-term interest rates provide little reason to believe that they might account for the same decline in long-term forward rates. In this sense we follow a long line of work in suggesting that the expectations hypothesis intuition, based on constant term premiums, is likely to be misleading not only in this case but more generally.

The next step, in our view, should be to develop models in which macroeconomic policy and behavior can be tied more directly to the properties of interest rates. One might want to know, for example, whether changes in the volatility of output or in the nature or communication of monetary policy had an impact on the behavior of long-term rates in the recent past. Neither hypothesis can be tested with existing models. Ang and Monika Piazzesi show how macroeconomic variables influence the behavior of bond yields, but this and related work has little in the way of macroeconomic structure.[19] Bekaert, Seonghoon Cho, and Antonio Moreno, as well as Michael Gallmeyer, Burton Hollifield, and Stanley Zin, have made progress on setting up affine term structure models in which the short-term interest rate is related to inflation and output growth by a monetary policy rule, while inflation and output growth are in turn determined within a structural New Keynesian model. Perhaps this will lead to further advances that allow the next attack on this issue to bring the macroeconomic contributions in line with the financial contributions—to the benefit of both.[20]

19. Ang and Piazzesi (2003).
20. Bekaert, Cho, and Moreno (2005) and Gallmeyer, Hollifield, and Zin (2005).

APPENDIX A

Data Sources and Definitions

U.S. INTEREST RATES in this paper are estimated from quoted prices of Treasury securities. Estimates of nominal yields and forward rates are constructed from a smooth Nelson-Siegel-Svensson curve as described by Gürkaynak, Sack, and Wright (2006). The data are available on the Federal Reserve website. A similar curve (estimated by Federal Reserve staff) is used to estimate yields and forward rates from TIPS. Throughout, yields are understood to be continuously compounded rates on zero-coupon bonds. Forward rates are instantaneous.

U.K. and German forward rate data were provided by the Bank of England and the Deutsche Bundesbank, respectively, and are available on their public websites. In the case of the German data, forward rates are constructed from Nelson-Siegel-Svensson parameters provided by the Bundesbank. Other macroeconomic and financial data are taken from Datastream.

Term premium estimates were calculated by Federal Reserve staff using the models of Kim and Orphanides (2005) and D'Amico, Kim, and Wei (2007). Those using the Kim and Orphanides model are updated quarterly, and daily estimates from 1990 on are available to the public at federalreserve. gov/pubs/feds/2005/200533/feds200533.xls.

APPENDIX B

Affine Models

Modern asset pricing theory works as follows: in an arbitrage-free setting, there exists a pricing kernel m_{t+1} that relates the market price v_t at date t of a claim with value c_{t+1} at date $t + 1$:

(B.1) $$v_t = E_t\left(m_{t+1}c_{t+1}\right).$$

Bond pricing is a particularly elegant application. If $b_t^{(n)}$ is the price at date t of one unit (a dollar, say) paid at $t + n$, bond prices can be computed recursively from

(B.2) $$b_t^{(n+1)} = E_t\left(m_{t+1}b_{t+1}^{(n)}\right),$$

starting with $b_t^{(0)} = 1$.

Affine models put enough structure on the pricing kernel that prices are log-linear functions of a state vector z:

$$(B.3) \qquad -\log b_t^{(n)} = A_n + B_n^T z_t,$$

for some parameters $\{A_n, B_n\}$. In essentially affine models, the link between forward rates and the dynamics of z is particularly transparent. Consider a one-dimensional example:

$$(B.4) \qquad -\log m_{t+1} = [\lambda(z_t)]^2/2 + z_t + \lambda(z_t)\varepsilon_{t+1},$$

where

$$\lambda(z_t) = \lambda_0 + \lambda_1 z_t$$

and

$$z_{t+1} = (1-\varphi)\theta + \varphi z_t + \sigma\varepsilon_{t+1}.$$

Here z is a (scalar) state variable, ε is an i.i.d. normal random variable with zero mean and unit variance $\sigma > 0$, and $0 < \varphi < 1$. The last equation describes the dynamic behavior of the state variable: it follows a linear process with the autoregressive parameter φ. The "price of risk" $\lambda(z)$ governs risk premiums; in particular, λ_1 controls the sensitivity of the term premium to movements in z.

The key to the solution is that the model is linear in the right places. Equation B.2 and our guess (equation B.3) imply that the coefficients satisfy

$$(B.5) \qquad A_{n+1} = A_n + B_n(1-\varphi)\theta + B_n\sigma\lambda_0 - (B_n\sigma)^2/2$$
$$B_{n+1} = 1 + (\varphi + \sigma\lambda_1)B_n$$

starting with $A_0 = B_0 = 0$. If we set $\varphi^* \equiv \varphi + \sigma\lambda_1$, the second can be solved directly:

$$(B.6) \qquad B_n = [1 - (\varphi^*)^n]/(1 - \varphi^*).$$

The first we compute recursively.

The beauty of this solution lies in the difference between φ and φ^*. The former represents the dynamics of the state variable, the latter the "risk-neutral" (or risk-adjusted) dynamics that are built into long-term forward rates and term premiums. If $\lambda_1 = 0$, the two are the same and we are back in the world of the expectations hypothesis: term premiums are constant and all the variation in forward rates comes from expected future short-term rates. In general, however, they are different, and their difference is what generates time-varying term premiums. To be specific, let us define one-period (as opposed to instantaneous) forward rates by

(B.7) $$\log\left(b_t^{(n)}/b_t^{(n+1)}\right) = f_t^{(n)}.$$

Then

$$f_t^{(n)} = \left(A_{n+1} - A_n\right) + \left(B_{n+1} - B_n\right)z_t = \left(A_{n+1} - A_n\right) + \left(\varphi^*\right)^n z_t,$$

and $r_t \equiv f_t^{(0)} = z_t$ (the short-term rate is z).

In words: the sensitivity of forward rates comes from the risk-neutral dynamics. The expected future short-term rate, in contrast, follows from the true dynamics, represented here by φ:

(B.8) $$E_t\left(r_{t+n}\right) = \left(1 - \varphi^n\right)\theta + \varphi^n z_t.$$

The term premium is therefore

(B.9) $$tp_t^{(n)} = constant + \left[\left(\varphi^*\right)^n - \varphi^n\right]z_t,$$

which evidently depends on the difference between the two kinds of dynamics. The term premium component is more sensitive to movements in z (hence more variable) if

(B.10) $$\left[\left(\varphi^*\right)^n - \varphi^n\right] > \varphi^n.$$

This holds for large n if $\varphi^* > \varphi$.

Comment and Discussion

Glenn D. Rudebusch: This paper by David Backus and Jonathan Wright examines a timely topic of interest to macroeconomists, financial economists, and the general public of long-term savers and investors. They investigate the recent episode of continuing low long-term interest rates—a behavior that appears to some to be a "conundrum" given that short-term rates worldwide have been rising. For example, in the United States, while the Federal Reserve raised the federal funds rate from 1 percent in June 2004 to 5¼ percent in December 2006, the rate on ten year U.S. Treasury notes actually edged down, on balance, from 4.7 percent to 4.6 percent. This directional divergence between short- and long-term rates is at odds with historical precedent and appears even more unusual given other economic developments at the time, such as a solid economic expansion, a falling unemployment rate, rising energy prices, and a deteriorating federal fiscal situation, all of which have been associated in the past with higher long-term interest rates rather than lower.

Of course, determining whether recent long-term interest rate movements truly represent a puzzle requires a theoretical framework that takes into account the various factors that affect long-term rates. The paper takes a joint macro-finance perspective on this problem, which, as much recent research suggests,[1] is a promising strategy that can capture two broad sets of determinants of long-term rates. In particular, from a macroeconomic perspective, the short-term interest rate is a policy instrument under the direct control of the central bank, which adjusts that rate to achieve its macroeconomic stabilization goals. Therefore financial market participants' understanding of central bank behavior, along with their views of

---

1. See, for example, Diebold, Piazzesi, and Rudebusch (2005).

the future direction of the economy, will be an important element in forming their expectations of future short-term rates, which, in turn, will be key in pricing longer-term bonds. For example, the widespread view over the past few years that the Federal Reserve had inflation pretty well in hand has undoubtedly helped hold down long-term bond rates. In addition, a finance perspective, which stresses the importance for bond pricing of investor perceptions of risk, is also likely to be a crucial element in assessing whether there is any bond rate conundrum. Indeed, many have suggested that a reduction in the risk premium is responsible for recent low bond rates. Such a reduction may be attributable to changes in the amount of risk or to changes in the pricing of that risk, and numerous factors have been suggested that could have induced such changes.

The paper identifies a declining term premium, and in particular a declining inflation risk premium, as the proximate source of the recent fall in long-term interest rates. This seems reasonable, but in some sense one can interpret the authors' analysis as showing that there has been no conundrum. The estimated term structure models in the paper seem to fit the recent episode as well as the earlier sample (their figures 9 and 10); that is, the recent episode is not so puzzling that it requires a shift in model coefficients or produces unusually large residuals. The analysis in the paper has essentially defined the "conundrum" away. Of course, such a conclusion would require that the authors had the correct model of interest rates and the term premium, which is far from certain. It seems useful to examine other term structure representations in order to evaluate the robustness of the authors' conclusions; therefore my figure 1 plots five different measures, taken from the literature, of the term premium in the zero-coupon nominal ten-year U.S. Treasury yield:[2]

—*VAR measure:* This is obtained from a standard, three-variable, macroeconomic vector autoregression (VAR), comprising four lags each of the unemployment rate, quarterly inflation in the consumer price index, and the three-month Treasury bill rate. This VAR can be used in each quarter to forecast the short-term rate over the next ten years, which, after averaging, provides one estimate of the risk-neutral ten-year rate. The difference between the observed ten-year rate and that risk-neutral rate provides an estimate of the term premium.

---

2. These measures are described in detail in Rudebusch, Sack, and Swanson (2007).

Figure 1. Five Estimates of the Ten-Year Term Premium, 1984–2005

Percentage points

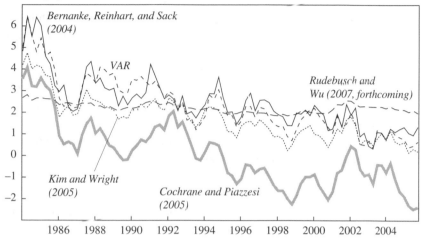

—*Bernanke-Reinhart-Sack measure:* A potential shortcoming of using a VAR to estimate the term premium is that it does not impose consistency between the yield curve at a given point in time and the VAR's projected time path of yields over time. Such pricing consistency is imposed in the model of Ben Bernanke, Vincent Reinhart, and Brian Sack (BRS),[3] which attaches a no-arbitrage model of the term structure to a VAR and provides an estimate of the term premium.

—*Rudebusch-Wu measure:* No-arbitrage restrictions can also be imposed on top of a New Keynesian macroeconomic model, as in the model of Rudebusch and Tao Wu (RW),[4] which provides another estimate of the term premium.

—*Kim-Wright measure:* Don Kim and Wright estimate the term premium using a standard, no-arbitrage, dynamic latent factor model from finance (with no macroeconomic structure underlying the factors).[5] In models of this kind, risk-neutral yields and the term premium are determined

---

3. Bernanke, Reinhart, and Sack (2004).
4. Rudebusch and Wu (2007, forthcoming).
5. Kim and Wright (2005).

by latent factors that are themselves linear functions of the observed bond yield data. This measure is the closest to the versions considered in the present paper.

—*Cochrane-Piazzesi measure:* John Cochrane and Monika Piazzesi analyze one-year-holding-period excess returns for a range of Treasury securities.[6] Their primary finding is that a single factor—a particular combination of current forward rates—predicts a considerable portion of these excess returns for Treasury securities. These, in turn, together with the one-year risk-free rate, imply an expected set of zero-coupon yields one year ahead (since the only way to generate expected returns on zero-coupon securities is through changes in yield). By iterating forward, one can compute the expected excess return for each of the next ten years, thereby yielding a measure of the term premium on the ten-year security.

All five of these measures of the term premium show declines over the past few years and are generally consistent with the conclusions of Backus and Wright. However, these various measures also illustrate the considerable uncertainty that should be attached to any measure of the term premium. This caveat is worthy of elaboration; therefore I next consider in detail the implications of the results of the BRS and RW models for the recent behavior of long-term rates.[7]

My figure 2 shows the ten-year zero-coupon U.S. Treasury yield from 1984 through 2006 together with the BRS model decomposition of that yield. The risk-neutral rate implied by the BRS model is the model's estimated yield on a riskless ten-year zero-coupon bond, the implied ten-year Treasury yield is the model's estimated yield on the same bond after accounting for risk, and the implied term premium is the difference between the two. The BRS model does not match the data perfectly, and so the model's residuals—the difference between the model predictions taking into account risk and the data—are graphed in figure 3. Despite the model's excellent fit to the data overall, the recent period of low ten-year yields is one episode that the model notably fails to fit. From mid-2004 through the end of 2006, the model overestimates the ten-year Treasury yield by around 50 basis points on average. Figures 4 and 5 present the analogous pair of graphs for the ten-year bond yield decomposition implied by the RW model. Again the fit of the model to the data is excel-

6. Cochrane and Piazzesi (2005).
7. This discussion is based on the analysis of Rudebusch, Swanson, and Wu (2006).

Figure 2. Decomposition of the Ten-Year Treasury Yield, 1984–2006: Bernanke-Reinhart-Sack Model[a]

Percentage points

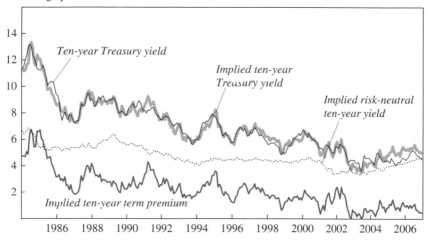

Source: Rudebusch, Swanson, and Wu (2006).
a. Bernanke, Reinhart, and Sack (2004).

Figure 3. Unexplained Portion of the Ten-Year Treasury Yield, 1984–2006: Bernanke-Reinhart-Sack Model

Basis points

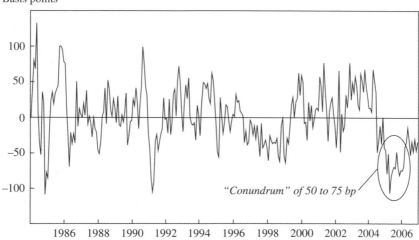

Source: Rudebusch, Swanson, and Wu (2006).

Figure 4. Decomposition of the Ten-Year Treasury Yield, 1988–2006: Rudebusch-Wu Model[a]

Percentage points

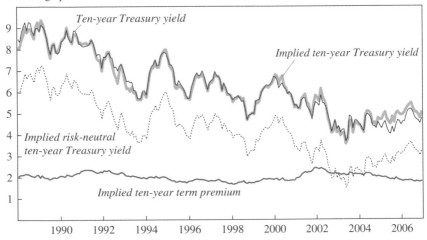

Source: Rudebusch, Swanson, and Wu (2006).
a. Rudebusch and Wu (2007, forthcoming).

Figure 5. Unexplained Portion of the Ten-Year Treasury Yield, 1988–2006: Rudebusch-Wu Model

Basis points

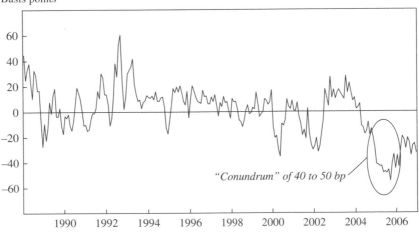

Source: Rudebusch, Swanson, and Wu (2006).

lent, which is all the more remarkable given that the RW model was not optimized to fit the ten-year yield at all (indeed, the five-year yield is the longest maturity used in the estimation, and the estimation sample ends in 2000).

The two models' implied decompositions into the expected short-term rate and the term premium are very different. In the RW model the term premium is relatively constant over 1988–2006, hovering around the 2 percent level, with little high-frequency variation but a notable cyclical movement. Furthermore, the RW model attributes most of the variation in the ten-year yield over time to changes in the expected future path of short-term rates. By contrast, the BRS model attributes most of the high-frequency variation in the ten-year yield to changes in the term premium component, with the risk-neutral component generally trending smoothly downward. The differences between the estimates of the ten-year term premium in these two models largely reflect different assumptions about the long-run persistence of movements in the nominal short-term rate. The BRS model is based on estimates of a macroeconomic VAR that is specified in levels. The smoothly downward-trending risk-neutral rate from the BRS model is essentially a VAR projection of the future path of the short-term rate that reverts to its sample mean fairly quickly. In the RW model the future path of short-term interest rates is instead affected greatly by highly persistent changes in the perceived value of the central bank's target for inflation, which allows significant variation in the risk-neutral ten-year yield. Obviously, then, estimates of the ten-year term premium are very sensitive to assumptions about the long-run properties of the short-term rate.[8] However, such long-run properties are difficult to determine,[9] and so, once such specification uncertainty is accounted for, the confidence intervals associated with any term premium estimate are quite substantial.

Still, despite their differences, the BRS and RW models are largely in agreement that there is, in fact, a conundrum. Specifically, the recent level of long-term bond yields is substantially lower, on the order of 30 to 80 basis points, than can be explained by either of these models. Of course, documenting the conundrum, especially as a sequence of large residuals of the same sign, is only one step toward explaining it. Rudebusch, Eric Swanson, and Wu examined several popular explanations for the conun-

---

8. Kozicki and Tinsley (2001).
9. Rudebusch (1993).

Figure 6. S&P 500 Volatility Index (VIX) and Ten-Year Term Premium, 2007

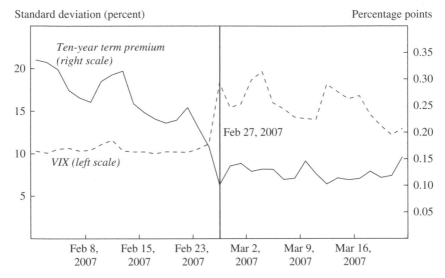

Source: Federal Reserve Board and Chicago Board Options Exchange.

drum by regressing the BRS and RW macro-finance models' residuals on various proxies for uncertainty or volatility, and they found that most of the conundrum remained unexplained.[10] Backus and Wright have to take a somewhat different strategy because their finance yield-curve representations are so flexible that the residuals in fitting yields are apparently minuscule. Therefore they employ a two-step strategy, regressing an estimate of the term premium on macroeconomic variables, and it is only in this final regression that a bond yield conundrum can be said to emerge. Specifically, the large recent residuals from their second-stage regression, which are apparent in their figure 11, suggest that *if* the authors have the correct term structure model, then the conundrum is an unusually low term premium relative to macroeconomic fundamentals.

It is important to stress that even if the explanatory power of these second-stage regressions had been higher, we are still some distance away from a model that integrates the various explanations of recent low long-term rates into an underlying asset pricing model. Only such a unified

---

10. Rudebusch, Swanson, and Wu (2006).

one-step formulation can provide a complete and compelling accounting of the recent episode. To give some sense of how much we do not understand, figure 6 plots daily data on the Kim-Wright term premium along with the VIX measure of implied volatility from options on the S&P 500 index as a measure of uncertainty in the stock market. Backus and Wright note that the decline in the VIX measure of financial market risk is broadly consistent with the fall in the term premium. Unfortunately, as the daily data show, this correlation does not always hold. On February 27 of this year, when financial markets were shaken by surprising news on durable goods orders and drops in Chinese equity prices, the implied volatility jumped, but the term premium fell. Of course, one could speculate that although financial risk had clearly risen, the price attached to that risk fell even more as funds flowed into the bond market in a "flight to quality." However, such speculation shows that much remains unknown about movements in the term premium and in bond rates more generally.

General discussion: Benjamin Friedman called attention to the decomposition, in the authors' figure 10, of the nominal forward rate into expected inflation and an inflation risk premium as well as the expected future real interest rate and a real term premium. He found it striking that the estimate of expected inflation had gone up rather than down with the advent of the present Federal Reserve chairman, noting that it was inconsistent with the common explanation of the long-term yield conundrum, namely, that market participants find credible the assurances that inflation is going to remain in check over the long term. The rise in expected long-run inflation should be particularly surprising to those economists who believe that an explicit inflation target should keep inflation expectations in check. To Friedman this evidence, which suggests that market participants are not convinced that inflation will remain low, made the current low level of nominal long-term rates even more puzzling.

Gregory Mankiw remarked that the paper did not so much crack the forward rate conundrum as recharacterize it as a term premium conundrum. He suggested that the next step is to explain the behavior of such premiums. He also suggested that if they are to be interpreted as risk premiums, they should be related to some measure of risk. He reminded the panel of a Brookings paper he had presented twenty-one years ago, in which he had tried but failed to find a relationship between term premiums and the risks captured in second moments.

Mankiw was also surprised by the authors' finding of an empirical relationship between forward rates and dispersion in expectations. He cautioned against interpreting this as evidence of a risk premium, noting that dispersion is a measure of disagreement, not a measure of uncertainty. For example, all would agree that the expected outcome of a roll of dice is seven even though the actual outcome is quite uncertain, ranging from two to twelve. Disagreement must have something to do with varying information sets or different interpretations of similar information. Unfortunately, economics lacks good models of disagreement.

Richard Cooper regarded the label "term premium" as misleading and drew parallels to the panel's discussion of the paper by Oliner, Sichel, and Stiroh in this volume, where some had criticized what they saw as the reification of the productivity residual. The label "term premium" simply denotes the unexplained residual from the estimation and should be referred to as such.

Eswar Prasad suggested looking at asset markets other than the market for U.S. Treasury securities to learn about the importance of Asian central banks' behavior in holding down long-term rates. He noted that the Chinese authorities are putting similar amounts of money into agency bonds, such as Ginnie Maes, as into Treasury bonds. Although there is no good measure of term premiums for agency bonds, Prasad believed it could be informative to compare the behavior of those markets with that of the Treasury market. He observed further that if one assumes U.S. and foreign industrial bonds to be close substitutes, any future announcement of a revaluation of China's currency should have had effects on those markets as well. An asymmetric response of term premiums on U.S. and foreign bond markets to the announcement that the Chinese central bank intends to diversify away from dollars into other currencies would provide further evidence of the importance of foreign bank behavior to U.S. interest rates.

References

Ang, Andrew, and Monika Piazzesi. 2003. "A No-Arbitrage Vector Autoregression of Term Structure Dynamics with Macroeconomic and Latent Variables." *Journal of Monetary Economics* 50, no. 4: 745–87.

Ang, Andrew, Geert Bekaert, and Min Wei. 2007 (forthcoming). "The Term Structure of Real Rates and Expected Inflation." *Journal of Finance.*

Beechey, Meredith. 2007. "A Closer Look at the Sensitivity Puzzle: The Sensitivity of Expected Future Short Rates and Term Premia to Macroeconomic News." Finance and Economics Discussion Paper 2007-06. Washington: Board of Governors of the Federal Reserve System.

Bekaert, Geert, Seonghoon Cho, and Antonio Moreno. 2005. "New-Keynesian Macroeconomics and the Term Structure." Working Paper 11340. Cambridge, Mass.: National Bureau of Economic Research (May).

Bernanke, Ben S., Vincent R. Reinhart, and Brian P. Sack. 2004. "Monetary Policy Alternatives at the Zero Bound: An Empirical Assessment." *BPEA*, no. 2: 1–78.

Berner, Richard, and David Miles. 2006. "The Term-Premium Case for Higher Yields." Morgan Stanley Global Economic Forum (January 20).

Cochrane, John H., and Monika Piazzesi. 2005. "Bond Risk Premia." *American Economic Review* 95, no. 1: 138–60.

————. 2006. "Decomposing the Yield Curve." Unpublished. Graduate School of Business, University of Chicago (November).

Dai, Qiang, and Kenneth J. Singleton. 2002. "Expectation Puzzles, Time-Varying Risk Premia, and Affine Models of the Term Structure." *Journal of Financial Economics* 63, no. 3: 415–41.

D'Amico, Stefania, Don H. Kim, and Min Wei. 2007. "TIPS from TIPS: The Information Content of Treasury Inflation-Protected Security Prices." Washington: Federal Reserve Board (March).

Diebold, Francis X., Monika Piazzesi, and Glenn D. Rudebusch. 2005. "Modeling Bond Yields in Finance and Macroeconomics." *American Economic Review* 95, no. 2: 415–20.

Duffee, Gregory R. 2002. "Term Premia and Interest Rate Forecasts in Affine Models." *Journal of Finance* 57, no. 1: 405–43.

Duffie, Darrell, and Rui Kan. 1996. "A Yield-Factor Model of Interest Rates." *Mathematical Finance* 6, no. 4: 379–406.

Gallmeyer, Michael F., Burton Hollifield, and Stanley E. Zin. 2005. "Taylor Rules, McCallum Rules and the Term Structure of Interest Rates." *Journal of Monetary Economics* 52, no. 5: 921–50.

Greenspan, Alan. 2005. "Testimony of Chairman Alan Greenspan: Federal Reserve Board's Semiannual Monetary Policy Report to the Congress." Washington: Board of Governors of the Federal Reserve (February 16).

Gross, Bill. 2005. "I've Got to Admit It's Getting Better, Getting Better all the Time." PIMCO *Investment Outlook* (March) (www.pimco.com/LeftNav/Featured+Market+Commentary/IO/2005/March_IO_2005.htm).

Gürkaynak, Refet S., Brian P. Sack, and Eric T. Swanson. 2005. "The Sensitivity of Long-Term Interest Rates to Economic News: Evidence and Implications for Macroeconomic Models." *American Economic Review* 95, no. 1: 425–36.

Gürkaynak, Refet, Brian P. Sack, and Jonathan H. Wright. 2006. "The US Treasury Yield Curve: 1961 to the Present." Finance and Economics Discussion Paper 2006-28. Washington: Board of Governors of the Federal Reserve System (June).

Kim, Don H. 2004. "Inflation and the Real Term Structure." Working paper. Washington: Board of Governors of the Federal Reserve.

Kim, Don H., and Athanasios Orphanides. 2005. "Term Structure Estimation with Survey Data on Interest Rate Forecasts." Finance and Economics Discussion Paper 2005-48. Washington: Board of Governors of the Federal Reserve System (October).

Kim, Don H., and Jonathan H. Wright. 2005. "An Arbitrage-Free Three-Factor Term Structure Model and the Recent Behavior of Long-Term Yields and Distant-Horizon Forward Rates." Finance and Economics Discussion Paper 2005-33. Washington: Board of Governors of the Federal Reserve System (August).

Kozicki, Sharon, and Peter A. Tinsley. 2001. "Shifting Endpoints in the Term Structure of Interest Rates." *Journal of Monetary Economics* 47, no. 3: 613–52.

Kroszner, Randall S. 2006. "Why Are Yield Curves So Flat and Long Rates So Low Globally?" Remarks presented at the meeting of the Institute of International Bankers, New York, June 16.

Lehman Brothers. 2007. "Outlook 2007: The Conundrum Runs Its Course." *Global Weekly Interest Rate Strategy* (December 21).

Lu, Biao, and Liuren Wu. 2006. "Systematic Movements in Macroeconomic Releases and the Term Structure of Interest Rates." Paper presented at the annual meeting of the European Finance Association, Zurich, August 23–26.

Ludvigson, Sydney C., and Serena Ng. 2006. "Macro Factors in Bond Risk Premiums." New York University (August).

Macaulay, Frederick R. 1938. *Some Theoretical Problems Suggested by the Movements of Interest Rates, Bond Yields and Stock Prices in the United States since 1856.* Cambridge, Mass.: National Bureau of Economic Research.

Rudebusch, Glenn D. 1993. "The Uncertain Unit Root in Real GNP." *American Economic Review* 83, no. 1: 264–72.

Rudebusch, Glenn D., Brian P. Sack, and Eric T. Swanson. 2007. "Macroeconomic Implications of Changes in the Term Premium." Federal Reserve Bank of St. Louis *Review* 89, no. 4: 241–69.

Rudebusch, Glenn D., Eric T. Swanson, and Tao Wu. 2006. "The Bond Yield 'Conundrum' from a Macro-Finance Perspective." *Monetary and Economic Studies* 24, no. S-1: 83–109.

Rudebusch, Glenn D., and Tao Wu. 2007. "Accounting for a Shift in Term Structure Behavior with No-Arbitrage and Macro-Finance Models." *Journal of Money, Credit, and Banking* 39, no. 2–3: 395–422.

_____. 2007 (forthcoming). "A Macro-Finance Model of the Term Structure, Monetary Policy, and the Economy." *Economic Journal.*

Shiller, Robert J. 1979. "The Volatility of Long-Term Interest Rates and Expectations Models of the Term Structure." *Journal of Political Economy* 87, no. 6: 1190–1219.

Warnock, Francis E., and Veronica Cacdac Warnock. 2006. "International Capital Flows and U.S. Interest Rates." Working Paper 12560. Cambridge, Mass.: National Bureau of Economic Research (October).